Thomas Gage's Travels in the New World

THE AMERICAN EXPLORATION AND TRAVEL SERIES

THOMAS GAGE'S

Travels
in the New World

Edited and with an Introduction

by J. Eric S. Thompson

UNIVERSITY OF OKLAHOMA PRESS : NORMAN

By J. Eric S. Thompson

Ethnology of the Mayas of Southern and Central British Honduras
(Chicago, 1930)
*Archaeological Investigations in the Southern Cayo District, British
Honduras* (Chicago, 1931)
Mexico before Cortez (New York, 1933)
Excavations at San José, British Honduras (Washington, 1939)
Maya Hieroglyphic Writing: An Introduction (Washington, 1950;
Norman, 1960)
The Rise and Fall of Maya Civilization (Norman, 1954, 1966)
Thomas Gage's Travels in the New World (ed.) (Norman, 1958)
A Catalog of Maya Hieroglyphs (Norman, 1962)
Maya Archaeologist (Norman, 1963)

STANDARD BOOK NUMBER: 8061–0881–9

LIBRARY OF CONGRESS CATALOG CARD NUMBER: 58–6856

New edition copyright 1958 by the University of Oklahoma Press, Publishing
Division of the University. Manufactured in the U.S.A. First printing, July, 1958.
Second printing, December, 1969.

Editor's Preface

IN PREPARING this present edition of Thomas Gage's classic—*The English-American . . .* or, *A New Survey of the West India's . . .* (London, 1648)—I have tried to compromise between keeping the original style and spelling of the 1648 edition and complete modernization. General spelling has been modernized, and spellings of all personal and place names have been corrected or brought up to date. Old constructions have been modified to make reading easier for the present-day reader, but a fair sprinkling of such obsolete forms as *hath, keepeth, unto,* and *conceiting* are retained so that they may give a seventeenth-century flavor. This is not so arbitrary as it sounds, for Gage himself occasionally uses *keeps* instead of *keepeth*.

Gage's paragraphs are often of inordinate length; in some cases a single paragraph occupies seven pages of print. His sentences, too, are often of great length and considerable confusion, and what would be separate sentences in modern usage are linked together with *which*'s, *whereof*'s, and *whereupon*'s. In the present edition these paragraphs and sentences are broken up. Such rearrangement has sometimes required minor changes in wording, but here again I have tried to show moderation and to steer a fair course between clarity and fidelity to the original.

In one short chapter (12) Gage's original style is retained throughout, and his appeal to the Mayor of Sandwich, which forms Appendix 1, is reproduced in its original form.

The 1648 edition consisted of twenty-two chapters and an appendix (although not labeled as such) on the Pokoman language. In the present edition the following chapters are omitted:

1. How Rome doth yearly visit the American and Asian kingdoms

2. Showing that the Indians' wealth, under a pretence of their conversion, hath corrupted the hearts of poor begging friars with strife, hatred, and ambition

3. Showing the manner of the missions of friars and Jesuits to the Indias

All three are short and deal largely with religious polemics of little interest to the modern reader.

Gage incorporated in his book large sections which he translated from the Spanish of López de Gómara, published a century earlier. As this material describing conditions at the time of the conquest of Mexico in the 1520's has no direct bearing on Gage's book, which deals with conditions in Mexico and Guatemala as they were in the 1620's, I have omitted it. As a result, Gage's original chapters 10 and 11 are here joined to form a single chapter 7. The exclusion of López de Gómara's material shortens chapters 8 and 9.

Of Gage's original material, apart from remarks which might offend Roman Catholic readers, I have omitted only some six pages, which relate conversations with a Creole of Ciudad Real, which were supposed to show the ignorance and stupidity of the Spaniard and Gage's nimble wit. They are pointless, and I suspect the Creole was not so stupid as Gage supposed him to be and, indeed, was quietly pulling Gage's leg all the time he was displaying his abject ignorance. The material on the Pokoman language is also omitted.

It is a pleasure to acknowledge so much friendly help in the preparation of this edition. Lord Gage, who, like his ancestor and Thomas Gage's great-grandfather, lives at Firle in Sussex, and his secretary, Mrs. Sugrue, have helped me to arrange the sixteenth-century Gages in order. Miss Winifred Keens, of Llanbedry, Cennin, has been of very great assistance in bringing to light new material on Gage's period as a "Preacher of the Word," and through her I would thank the Reverend Raymond O. Clark, rector of St. Leonard, Deal, for his help, Mr. A. E. Peacock for kindly permitting me to use his charming pen and ink sketches, and also Mr. Alfred Baker, of T. F. Pain and Sons, Ltd., Deal, for his kind loan of the blocks used in certain illustrations, and for permission to reproduce this most interesting material.

I must also express my thanks to the Reverend P. G. Harrison, rector of St. Martin Acrise, for his helpful co-operation and his permission to Miss Keens to examine the parish registers, and to Mr. Jack Williams, of Acrise, for his kindness in arranging for photographs of St. Martin Acrise.

I am indebted to my colleague in Maya archaeology of many years' standing, Mr. Frans Blom, for arranging for photographs of the retablo in the Cathedral of San Cristóbal de las Casas. Professor Geoffrey Bushnell, of Cambridge University, undertook the tedious task of abstracting for me the verbose *Survey of Sion and Babylon;* Mrs. Lyman, of Cambridge, Massachusetts, drew most of the delightful chapter decorations, but I must take responsibility for the apparel sewed on the amice, which almost certainly had ceased to be used by Gage's time. Through the intercession of Miss Sue Miles, graduate of the Department of Anthropology at Harvard University, Mr. A. V. Cooper, of Guatemala City, made a special trip to Mixco and Amatitlán to take the splendid photographs reproduced among the illustrations.

I am much indebted to the Reverend Father Basil FitzGibbon, S.J., for sound advice and for help with the published sources on the Roman Catholic underground in seventeenth-century England and, particularly, for directing me to the evidence that Gage was never at St. Alban College, Valladolid.

Lastly, I would express my deep appreciation of the Reverend Father Godfrey Anstruther, O.P., and Blackfriars Publications, who with rare generosity sent me, then a complete stranger, page proofs of his forthcoming *A Hundred Homeless Years*, with its completely new material on Gage's contacts with the Dominicans after his return to England. In a letter of January 27, 1958, Father Anstruther wrote the following paragraph, which I quote with his permission:

I have just returned from an historic occasion at the [Church of Santa María Sopra] Minerva, none other than the opening of the tomb and the recognition of the remains of Fra Angelico, as the first step to his solemn beatification. It was quite a private occasion, with three cardinals, the usual crowd of officials, and a grand gathering of his brethren. As we stood round the jumble of mouldering bones that is all that remains of such a genius, and said the *De Profundis*, I mentally included poor Tom Gage, who must have said almost his last Mass in that church, for it was then the headquarters of the Order, and also had a hostel for visiting Dominicans. Perhaps the happy artist will help the unhappy writer, if he hasn't done so a few centuries ago.

J. Eric S. Thompson

Harvard
Ashdon, Saffron Walden
Essex, England

Contents

Chapter numbers in parentheses are those of the first edition. For a note on omitted material and reasons for its omission see pp. vii and viii.

Illustrations

Maps

Editor's Introduction

THOMAS GAGE, the author of this book, was born in England, probably in 1603, and died in Jamaica in 1656. His book, which recounts his life and travels as a Dominican friar in Mexico and Guatemala between 1625 and 1637, was first published in London in 1648, when the Puritan cause was victorious in England. This book is decidedly influenced by political and religious considerations and carries the deep impress of Gage's character, which in his later years, at any rate, was not a pleasant one. This is not only a modern appraisal; it is amply supported by contemporary sources. His eldest brother, the gallant and beloved cavalier Sir Henry Gage, remarked that he strove entirely to eradicate all remembrance of Thomas and his misdeeds from his mind. Another brother, the Reverend George Gage, wrote of him as "my graceless brother," whose activities "our whole family doth blush to behold."

The Gages, a proud and ancient family, had cause to be ashamed of their black sheep. Thomas was no credit to the Dominican Order, to which he belonged for some sixteen years, nor to the Puritan divines, in whose ranks he was enlisted for the last fourteen years of his life. A man has every right to change his religion; he has not the right to vilify his former coreligionists and hold up their beliefs to contempt. Worse than that, Gage committed the foul infamy of bearing witness against former friends who were priests of the church to which he himself had so long been faithful, and his testimony was largely instrumental in sending at least three to their deaths.

One's first impression is that Gage was an avaricious and unmitigated scoundrel interested only in his own advancement. Yet, there is, I believe, beneath the surface a side to Gage's character which

xiii

is not sordid, and which reveals him as the bewildered victim of his own failure to reach a clear and lasting decision on his religious beliefs. In an age not remarkable for its tolerance, Gage seems to have been able to identify himself with both extremes of the Christian faith at one time or another, but the spirit of the age forced him to chose sides. It is not unreasonable to suppose that the doubts which gnawed him inwardly found outward expression in violent and sweeping statements against the church which he had left and in the despicable betrayals of his former comrades. He became a Protestant when it was to his advantage to do so, but one doubts that his complex character can be dismissed by merely identifying him as another Vicar of Bray determined to be on the right side.

It is perhaps somewhat unusual for the editor of a book to point out in the first paragraphs of his introduction that the author was a scoundrel, although there were, perhaps, mitigating factors. I have followed that course in order to forestall any unpleasant impressions a reader might receive. Gage wrote *The English-American, or A New Survey of the West India's* after he had thrown in his lot with the Puritans. As originally published, in the seventeenth century, the book contained many crude and offensive slanders of Roman Catholic priests and friars and their beliefs which no modern author would dream of writing. I have deleted the greater part of those unpleasantries, certainly those calculated to hurt most the feelings of Roman Catholics, but I have felt obliged to retain some in this present edition.

The complete removal of all remarks directed against Roman Catholicism would stultify Gage's two chief reasons for writing this book. Firstly, he wished to assure the Puritans, who were in complete control of England by the time his book first appeared in 1648, that he had completely foresworn his former Papist practices and beliefs; and, in the spirit of the age, the best way to demonstrate this whole-hearted conversion was to indulge in cheap abuse of his former coreligionists. Secondly, he was anxious to promote the theory that the Spanish possessions in much of America could easily be seized by an enterprising nation, such as England. He based this idea on the almost complete absence of defenses and military forces in many parts which he visited,[1] and he is careful to point out spe-

---

[1] Pages 65, 112, 115, 148, 194–95.

The English-American his Travail by Sea and Land:

OR,

A NEW SVRVEY
OF THE
WEST-INDIA'S,

CONTAINING

A Journall of Three thousand and Three hundred
Miles within the main Land of AMERICA.

Wherin is set forth his Voyage from *Spain* to *S*.*Iohn de Ulhua*;
and from thence to *Xalappa*, to *Tlaxcalla*, the City of *Angeles*, and
forward to *Mexico*; With the description of that great City,
as it was in former times, and also at this present.

Likewise his Journey from *Mexico* through the Provinces of *Guaxaca*,
Chiapa, *Guatemala*, *Vera Paz*, *Truxillo*, *Comayagua*; with his
abode Twelve years about *Guatemala*, and especially in the
Indian-towns of *Mixco*, *Pinola*, *Petapa*, *Amatitlan*.

As also his strange and wonderfull Conversion, and Calling from those
remote Parts to his Native C O U N T R E Y.

With his return through the Province of *Nicaragua*, and *Costa Rica*,
to *Nicoya*, *Panama*, *Portobelo*, *Cartagena*, and *Havana*, with divers
occurrents and dangers that did befal in the said Journey.

A L S O,

A New and exact Discovery of the Spanish Navigation to
those Parts; And of their Dominions, Government, Religion, Forts,
Castles, Ports, Havens, Commodities, fashions, behaviour of
Spaniards, Priests and Friers, Blackmores, Mulatto's, Mestiso's,
Indians; and of their Feasts and Solemnities.

With a Grammar, or some few Rudiments of the *Indian* Tongue,
called, *Poconchi*, or *Pocoman*

By the true and painfull endevours of T H O M A S G A G E , *now Preacher of*
the Word of God at Acris *in the County of* K E N T, Anno Dom. 1648.

London, Printed by *R Cotes*, and are to be sold by *Humphrey Blunden* at the
Castle in *Cornhill*, and *Thomas Williams* at the Bible in *Little Britain*, 1648.

Title page of the first English edition.

cific instances of this, maintaining that the Indians, Negroes, and mulattoes had been so exploited by the Roman Catholic church and by the land-owning descendants of the Spanish *conquistadores* that they would welcome with open arms the liberating forces of England. As we shall see, Gage had the ear of leading members of the Commonwealth, and even of Oliver Cromwell himself, and there is no doubt that Gage's writings played an important part in Cromwell's expedition to the Spanish Main. It is hard to believe that Gage himself had much confidence in a revolt by the Indians because of exploitation by the church, and his years of residence among the Pokoman Maya Indians of Guatemala must have led him to doubt that the Indians would take kindly to Puritanism. Nevertheless, it was essential that his book should contain many examples of exploitation and cruelty by priests and friars to support his argument.

Closely related to this last was another point which Gage wished to make, namely, that the Spaniards in the New World were such evil livers that it was the duty of the saintly English of Puritan England to eradicate such depravity, and, indeed, God would welcome such action. This argument is well brought out in the memorandum he submitted in 1654 to Oliver Cromwell detailing the arguments favoring Guatemala and Chiapas as targets of the English attack on Spanish American possessions then under consideration. Gage wrote:

Though God be long-suffering, yett he is not ever sufferring and ever bearing with a proud sinfull people; but no people more sinfull then the Spaniards in America, both greate and small, Viceroys, Judges, and poore pesants, who in general sinne, and hide not their sinne, as the prophet saieth, but sinne publikely, sinne like beasts uncontrowledly: therefore their sinnes will betray them and fight against them, if ever any nation shall oppose them.

This point could best be driven home by attributing all and sundry vices to Papists in general and their priests and friars in particular, for every good Puritan knew perfectly well that that was so; he had imbibed stories of the deviltries of priests, friars, and monks with his mother's milk. Gage gave his readers what they wanted to read, and made his point at the same time. Nevertheless, these strictures on the behavior of some of his companions in religious orders are not entirely false or hypocritical. With a quite high proportion of the population of Spain entering religious orders, there was certainly a minority of friars and priests who took their vows somewhat lightly, and such characters usually found their way to the New World, where discipline was laxer and standards of conduct lower than in Spain. Such indecorous behavior must have shocked young Gage, with his Anglo-Saxon upbringing, and in the end infected his own idealism. For instance, there is no reason to doubt that Gage was gravely perturbed by the gambling he witnessed in the Friary a few days after reaching Mexico,[2] but the liberal seasoning of Latin gusto may have conveyed to Gage an exaggerated impression of dissolute conduct which certainly lost nothing in the telling twenty years later.

Lastly, to delete all unkind remarks by Gage about his old friends would be to tamper with the self-portrait Gage gives us. For example, Gage was so avaricious and so unashamedly recounts examples of that failing in his writings that it is a matter of considerable psychological interest that he is continually accusing his fellow friars of the same offense. Such traits of character influenced the writing of the book, but they do not impair the value of the eye-witness account of life in Mexico and Guatemala which he has left us.

It is worth bearing in mind that Gage wrote his book at a time when the tide of sanctimonious bigotry was at full flood in England. Puritans who had banned the maypole, dancing, sports, and the theater in a wave of sad-faced conformity were not likely to look with a kindly eye on a friar who whiled away an hour with a game of cards or, in the free-speaking tradition of Spain, exchanged Latin jests with a broad-minded matron. It is possible that Gage, for all his years in America, never understood Latin temperament and culture to the point of realizing that such matters were essentially innocent, not examples of "publike sinne."

The importance of *The English-American* lies in the fact that it was the first book on conditions in Spanish America written by a non-Spaniard or one who was not a citizen of the Holy Roman Empire. Spanish America was reserved for Spaniards; citizens of northern Europe were forbidden to settle within its bounds. Indeed, it was only by trickery that Gage was able to sail with the Spanish fleet

[2] Page 44–45.

despite the fact that he had been recruited to make the journey by the Dominican Order. For nearly 150 years there had been a fence around Spanish America. Occasionally, men such as Drake broke through one part or another, but their interest was loot and a quick departure; even had they wished to do so, they could not have written sober accounts of everyday life behind that fence. People in western Europe were not completely ignorant of the ancient civilizations of Peru and Mexico, and the story of the Spanish conquest of the New World was available to them. Several of the most important books, notably López de Gómara's *History of the Conquest of Mexico*, Peter Martyr's *de orbe novo*, and Joseph Acosta's *Natural and moral history of the Indies* had been translated into English. In addition, translations of Bartolomé de las Casas' far from judicious pamphlets had been circulated widely, and had succeeded in confirming the average Englishman's very biased opinion of Spaniards and their doings in the New World. Yet, at bottom, those books were rated not quite trustworthy because they had been written by those Dons on whose word no right-minded Englishman would rely. On the other hand, one could have complete confidence in *The English-American* precisely because it had been written by an Englishman, and one, moreover, who had seen the errors of his Romish ways and—so it was said—had the ear of Cromwell.

Furthermore, Gage wrote an eye-witness account of life and everyday events in the New World which made livelier reading than the impersonal narrative of the historian. In various descriptive passages Gage brings to life events of three centuries ago with marked resplendence. The sailing of the fleet from Cádiz, the celebrations in mid-Atlantic in honor of St. Ignatius, the attack by the Caribs on Guadeloupe, the welcome for the runaway friars in Chiapas first by the Provincial in his retreat, and then by the Prior with trumpets and dancing, the discovery of the idol and its sudden disclosure in the pulpit, the flight from Petapa, and Portobello when the fleet was in are outstanding descriptive passages which bring those events of far away and three centuries ago very near to us—only the picture of the writer eludes us. I do not believe that any other writer gives us such a vivid picture of an Atlantic crossing in those days. There are little touches—Father Calvo slaughtering the carefully guarded fowls once land was sighted is a good example; the burial at sea is another—in which Gage rises above religious polemics to descriptive narrative of a high order. No wonder the book was in its day a best seller.

The first edition of 1648 was followed by a second in 1655, published to increase English interest in the expedition under the command of Venables, and with Gage himself as chaplain, just dispatched to capture Hispaniola. There was a third edition which appeared in 1677, when England was once more a monarchy with Charles II on the throne. The original dedication to Lord Fairfax, captain-general of the Parliamentarian army, was tactfully changed to read "To the Reader," and there was no mention of the author's former profession of "Preacher of the Word of God," for by then Gage was dead and militant Puritanism was in deep disfavor. A call to the Saints to redeem the New World from wickedness was likely to fall on deaf ears; with the Merry Monarch's court close at hand, there was little need to travel four thousand miles to wrestle with sin. Nevertheless, interest in the New World was not abated. A fourth edition appeared in 1699, a fifth in 1702, and a sixth in 1711. With British expansion of the eighteenth century, interest in Central America dwindled, and over two centuries passed before the book was again printed in England.

However, in 1758 an edition was printed and sold by James Parker of Woodbridge, New Jersey, under the title *The Traveller. Part 1. Containing a Journal of three thousand and three hundred miles within the main land of America by Mr. Thomas Gage, an Englishman and a missionary friar in New Spain, twelve years.* There is a note that this work is "to be published monthly in the *New American Magazine.*" Mr. Howard Cline, of the Library of Congress, informs me that Gage's work was published in the first seventeen numbers (with continuous pagination) of *The New American Magazine,* January, 1758–May, 1759. There is doubt whether the work first appeared complete or in its serial form; the same title page was used for the complete work as for Part I in the serial. A series of the magazine may be found in the Ridgway Library, Philadelphia.

In 1928 the eighth edition was published in "The Broadway Travellers Series" of George Routledge and Sons, copies being marketed in the United States under the imprint of Robert M. McBride and Company, New York. This edition was severely abridged, but carried a fine introduction by Professor A. P. Newton, of London University, which contained much biographical material on Gage. Professor Newton's citations of sources have been a great help to me in preparing this present introduction. There was a second printing of this edition in 1946 by Routledge and Kegan Paul, of which some copies with a different title page were supplied to El Patio, Guatemala. There have also been editions in French, Dutch, German, and Spanish. The only recent foreign edition was a Spanish version published in 1946 under the auspices of the Sociedad de Geografía e Historia de Guatemala, as volume eighteen of the *Biblioteca Goathemala*. The text is taken from the Spanish edition published in Paris in 1808; the introduction is largely a translation of Professor Newton's prefatory remarks in the 1928 edition. This present volume—one might term it the tercentenary edition, for Gage died in 1656—is the tenth edition in English and appears just two centuries after the first American edition was run off the press of James Parker.

The Gage family has been prominent in English history for some five centuries; the present Lord Gage lives at Firle Place, Sussex, which has been the family seat since the fifteenth century. General Gage, in command of the royalist garrison at Boston at the outbreak of the Revolution, was a member of the family, which was one of those that rose to importance in Tudor times to fill the vacuum left by the slaughter of the old English aristocracy in the Wars of the Roses. Thomas's great-grandfather, Sir John Gage (1479–1556), served Henry VIII faithfully for many years, but was in temporary eclipse during the reign of Edward VI. With the accession of Queen Mary (Bloody Mary) in 1553, he returned to his post of constable of the Tower of London and was also appointed court chamberlain. As constable of the Tower, he received the young Princess Elizabeth when she was sent a prisoner there on her half-sister's orders, and it was he who refused her permission to have her meals brought in. He seems to have treated the young princess somewhat severely. This, says the seventeenth-century historian Heylyn, was "more for love of the Pope than for hate of her person." Sir John was prominent in the suppression of the Wyatt rebellion, and became a very strong advocate of Mary's unpopular marriage to Philip of Spain.

On the death of Sir John in 1556, two years before Queen Elizabeth's accession, the family property at Firle, in Sussex, went to the eldest son, John; another property, Haling Park, near Croydon, now a suburb of London, was inherited by a younger son, Robert, who was Thomas's grandfather. In addition to his properties, Sir John bequeathed to his descendants a position in the national life which was to affect the lives of his descendants for a century to come, and was indirectly to lead to the writing of this book. Sir John had fervently stood by the old religion, and he had been strongly pro-Spanish, an attitude which was far from popular either then or in the subsequent reign of Queen Elizabeth. His family loyally stood by his convictions.

In the second half of Queen Elizabeth's reign, pro-Spanish Roman Catholics were open to serious suspicion of treason. The Pope, by declaring Elizabeth a usurper, excommunicating her, and absolving all her subjects of their oaths of allegiance to her, had presented English Roman Catholics with the unpleasant task of choosing between their spiritual and their temporal ruler. The more loyal a family was to the old faith, the more it was suspect in the eyes of the Protestant majority.

Robert Gage, Thomas's uncle, was one of the minority of Roman Catholics actively disloyal. He was involved in the famed Babington plot to murder Queen Elizabeth and place Mary, Queen of Scots, on the throne in her stead. Captured with Babington and other conspirators with faces stained with walnut juice and ignominiously hiding beneath straw in a barn at Harrow, Robert Gage suffered the unpleasant end accorded all traitors at that time (1586). This was two years before the Spanish armada, sailing with papal blessing to drive Elizabeth from the throne, was itself destroyed with the not inconsiderable help of English Roman Catholics, whose loyalty to Elizabeth never faltered.

The whole Gage family, which stood firmly by the old faith, remained under suspicion for the rest of Elizabeth's reign, and this suspicion was particularly directed against John Gage, brother of the traitor Robert and father of Thomas, who inherited Haling Park on the death of his father in 1587. He had been arrested, but later freed, when the Babington plot was uncovered, but soon he was again in trouble, for, in 1590, he and his wife Margaret, a daughter of Thomas Copley, a famed recusant, were arrested on a charge of sheltering a Jesuit priest. This, if proved, was a capital offense. John Gage was committed close prisoner to the Tower in January, 1591. In 1592 the two were tried and sentenced to death, but thanks to the intervention of Lord Howard of Effingham, who had commanded the English fleet which had defeated the Spanish armada four years before and who was distantly related to the Copleys, the sentence was revoked and the couple was released, but at the cost of losing Haling House. In that same persecution of Papists, Robert Southwell, Jesuit priest and poet, also perished. He was a second cousin of Thomas Gage. Indicative of the involvement of the Gage family is the report of an informer of about this date that there were always two or three priests hiding in the house of Mr. Edward Gage at Bentley in Sussex. In February, 1601, Mrs. John Gage was again arrested, together with a Mrs. Line, for being implicated in the sheltering of a Jesuit, Father Francis Page. Mrs. Line and Father Page paid with their lives, but Mrs. Gage was set free, again thanks to the intercession of the Howard family.

These events confirmed John Gage in his devotion to the old faith, and made him a fervent admirer of the Jesuits, but they impoverished him and led to his loyalty's being suspect. They also embittered him with consequences which affected the life of his son Thomas.

John Gage, who was twice married, had several children, five of whom entered the Roman Catholic church. George and John became secular priests; William and Francis, Jesuits; Thomas, who was destined to be a Jesuit, became a Dominican.

Henry, the eldest son, was born in 1597, and like many boys of recusant families, was sent at an early age to the Jesuit college for English boys at St. Omer, in French Flanders. From there he passed in 1615, at the age of eighteen, to the English College in Rome, which was also a Jesuit establishment. On completing his education, he turned to soldiering, and as there were no opportunities open in England, he spent most of his adult life with the English legion in the service of the Spanish monarchy, rising to the command of a regiment. In 1644, when the civil war was raging in England, he returned to his native country to offer his services to Charles I, supplying sorely needed military experience to the royalist cause.

In one of the most brilliant minor exploits of the war, he relieved Basing House, seat of the Marquis of Winchester, which after a long siege was on the point of surrender from starvation. For this and other services Henry was knighted and made governor of Oxford, Charles's headquarters. He was fatally wounded in a skirmish early in 1645, and died in the arms of Father Peter Wright, his Jesuit chaplain and old friend of Flanders days, after receiving from him the last rites of his church in the shelter of a carriage. Everyone is agreed that Sir Henry Gage was an upright and lovable man. Edward Hyde, Lord Clarendon, who had known him intimately at Oxford, wrote of him in his great *History of the Rebellion* that he was "a very good scholar in the polite parts of learning" and "among the very few soldiers who made himself to be universally loved and esteemed." This warm testimony by a man of the character of Lord Clarendon is of considerable importance in view of Thomas Gage's accusations against his brother at the trial of Father Peter Wright, S. J.

William Gage, born in 1599, was probably next brother to Sir Henry. After passing through St. Omer and the English College in Rome, he became a Jesuit, and lived until 1683. George may have been the next son. There is doubt about his age. He was ordained in 1626 by special licence, and as canonical age for ordination is not less than twenty-four years completed, it is likely that he was born in 1601 or 1602. Like his brothers, he studied at St. Omer. He became a secular priest, and was engaged in much diplomatic work for his church. He was arrested and died in prison in 1652. According to a bill against him for appearance before the courts, his own brother Thomas was an informer against him. Vile as were other actions of Thomas Gage, I hesitate to accept this terrible suggestion on such tenuous evidence, for we have no further information on the matter. Possibly Thomas was cited as an informer because of what he had written about George in this book.[3]

Thomas, perhaps a year younger than George, and Robert, still younger, complete the tally of sons by the first wife. John and Francis, brothers, by a second marriage, were born in 1618 and 1621. John became a secular priest; Francis was head of Douai College, another establishment beyond the seas for the training of young

[3] Page 345.

Englishmen for the Roman Catholic priesthood. There were also two or three sisters. A Gage on his mother's side was Father Edward Petrie, S. J., a favorite of James II, who because of his unwise counsel to the King is said to have been the commoner most responsible for the end of the Stuart dynasty.

Thomas Gage was born in 1602 or 1603, although no direct evidence of his birth has survived. In his sermon of recantation, preached in August, 1642, he spoke of having lived nearly thirty-eight years in the Roman Catholic faith (in typical Puritan phraseology he likened himself to one lying around the Pool of Bethesda "neare 38 years" waiting to be lowered into the waters at the right moment). He also says that he had "almost 40 years warred obstinately against my Lord and Maker." He decided to throw in his lot with Protestantism at the close of 1640, but did not take the final step until 1641. To complicate matters, Gage, as a consequence of his many years in Spanish lands, often calculated Spanish fashion, counting year of start and finish. In either case, as he was born into the old faith, the calculations give 1602 or 1603 as the year of his birth. In his evidence against Father Thomas Holland, S. J., referred to below, he said that they had been schoolmates at St. Omer for five years. As Father Holland was there from 1615 to 1621, Gage's years there are fairly well established. Boys left at eighteen, so Gage must have been that age in 1620 or 1621. Finally, Gage tells us that on his return to England late in December, 1637, he had been away twenty-four years.[4] As at that time he spoke and thought only in Spanish and probably wrote the remark in his diary, which he subsequently quoted, he almost certainly reckoned Spanish fashion. That would give an interval of twenty-three years English style. Subtracted from the close of 1637, that would indicate the very close of 1614 or early 1615 as the date of his departure for St. Omer.

The place of Gage's birth is not known. Part of his youth was perhaps spent in Clerkenwell, in the city of London. As we have seen, he was sent to St. Omer, in the footsteps of his brothers Henry and William, both of whom may have still been students there when Thomas arrived, and of his cousin, Thomas Plowden. George Gage was also a contemporary of Thomas's at St. Omer; they may have

[4] Page 341.

been admitted at the same time. The college at that time contained about 130 students, not all of whom were destined for the church, although most went on to take orders. The secrecy and adventure which surrounded the departure for school, for the English government did all it could to prevent the boys crossing to get their education under what were regarded as subversive conditions, must have bred in the boys a spirit of adventure and self-reliance, which certainly was very marked in Thomas's life. Obviously, with residence of at least five years, relatively small numbers, and the bond of belonging to a minority which was persecuted for its beliefs and drew together in self-defense, the boys—at least those of the same age group—must have been very close to one another. This is a matter of some importance in judging Gage's character or the forces that swayed him, for his testimony, freely given, sent to his death Thomas Holland, guilty of having said mass in England, although he had been ordained abroad and, as we have just seen, he and Gage had been schoolmates together for five years at St. Omer.

On leaving England for St. Omer as a boy of thirteen, Thomas probably took the name of Howard, as his brothers Henry and George had done, for boys usually enrolled under an assumed name because their schooling abroad was illegal; often a boy took his mother's maiden name or that of a relative. Thomas Plowden, for example, took the name of his relatives, Gage. The Howard family had been very helpful to John Gage and his wife, as we have seen, and the assumption of their name by Henry and George, and perhaps by Thomas, may have been a sort of compliment. Father FitzGibbon, S. J., suggests that it is more probable that the name of Howard was chosen because John and Margaret Gage suffered imprisonment for their faith at the same time as Philip and Anne Howard, Earl and Countess of Arundel.

The acts of the Privy Council for 1616–17 contain entries that a certain Thomas Gage had been arrested in 1617, had been held incommunicado as a dangerous man, and had been brought before the Privy Council, the most important body in England with the exception of King James. This "man," as he is termed in the report, can hardly be our Thomas, who at that time was a boy of fourteen or fifteen, and hardly could have merited the attention of such an august body. Moreover, boys at St. Omer did not normally return to England until their studies were completed. This may have been another Thomas Gage, or perhaps someone who had assumed the name of Gage, just as Gage was probably Howard.

Little is known of what happened to Thomas Gage in the years immediately following his presumed graduation at St. Omer (the records are lost). From his writings we learn that he studied in the college of San Gregorio, Valladolid, in northern Spain, where Las Casas spent the last years of his life. This was staffed by Dominicans from the adjacent friary of San Pablo, Valladolid. Like most students of San Gregorio, Gage passed on to the friary of San Pablo, where he made his vows, but he would have been too young to have been ordained at that time; probably he was ordained after he reached the New World. Before entering San Gregorio College, Gage was probably in one of the colleges in Spain or Portugal under Jesuit control. All one can say with certainty is that he was not at the English college of St. Alban, also in Valladolid, which was largely under Jesuit control and recruited from graduates of St. Omer; the full records of entries at St. Alban make that very clear.

Gage tells us that an angry letter from his father, received a short while before, was one of the factors in his decision to volunteer for the Dominican mission to the Philippines in 1625. In this letter, he said, his father wrathfully reproached him for having left the Jesuits for the Dominicans, expressed the opinion that he would rather see his son a scullion in the Society of Jesus than general of the Dominican Order, and announced his decision to disinherit him. This suggests that Gage had recently left the Jesuits, but one must remember that an exchange of letters in those days between England and Spain took months, and this may well have been the last of several letters.

Certainly John Gage would not have shown such anger merely because Thomas had refused to become a Jesuit, for other sons became priests without entering the Society of Jesus, and John Gage was not the sort of man who would wish to force his son into a religious order if he did not have an inclination for it. He also well knew that such an action was fraught with danger in those days of persecution of the recusants, for a priest not filled with righteous enthusiasm could easily be brought to betray his cause.

Gage was telling the truth, so far as the records at Somerset

House reveal, that late in 1625 his father did in fact draw up a will, and in that will there is no mention of Thomas. However, John Gage's anger was not for the reason Thomas emphasizes, but for a second reason he also gives, that Thomas had not only refused to become a Jesuit, "but had proved in my affections a deadly enemy to them." This suggests that Thomas's break with the Society of Jesus (he was too young to have entered the order) was accompanied by recriminations and perhaps sensational charges against the order which could be given added emphasis by enemies of the Papacy because they had been uttered by a member of one of the prominent families of England that had stood by the old faith and suffered for it. We shall never know the full story, but it would seem that Thomas left the Jesuits with a grievance, justified or irrational, and he had not kept it to himself. This animosity toward the Society, then engendered, remained with him all his life, and is apparent in his later actions and in all his writings. Nevertheless, the circumstances of Gage's departure from the Society cannot have left a serious blot on his character, for when he did return to England after his years in the New World, he was warmly welcomed by his relatives, and participated in all the efforts to keep the flame of the old faith alive. From his own writings and from his evidence at the trials of Father Holland and the Franciscan Friar Bell, it is obvious that he was privy to all underground religious activities. Indeed, he testified that Father Bell complained to him that it was often impossible to say mass before noon because Gage's relative, whose chaplain he was, was so slow in rising. Had his character or his devotion to the old faith been in doubt, he would not have been privy to such activities, which could lead to Tyburn gallows if notified to the authorities.

It is just as well Gage rejected or was rejected by the Society of Jesus early in his career. Englishmen who entered the Society were likely to be sent to England, and Gage was hardly the stuff of which martyrs are made.

Early in 1625 Gage, then a young friar of about twenty-two in the Dominican friary at Jerez, met Father Antonio Meléndez, an old friend and former fellow student of San Gregorio College, Valladolid. Young Antonio, full of enthusiasm for the missionary cause, persuaded him to volunteer for service in the Philippines, and thereby changed his whole life. It is at this point that the present book opens.

Gage, telling the story twenty years later for his Puritan readers, gives it an antipapist twist, but one gets the impression that at the time he was filled with genuine enthusiasm to serve as a missionary overseas, although his love of travel, a very important factor in his life, surely influenced his decision. Gage and Antonio Meléndez were to share the adventures which brought them a year later to Chiapas in southern Mexico. This seems to have been one of the few genuine friendships in Gage's life. When Gage continued to Guatemala, Antonio stayed behind in Chiapas and seems to have been assigned to work among the Tzeltal Mayas. He must have had good qualities, for in 1639 he was elected first prior of Ocosingo, a remote Tzeltal town on the edge of the lowland rain forest, and it was there he died in 1646, when Gage, then vicar of Acrise, in England, was busy writing his book.

Gage's life and adventures from the moment of meeting with Antonio Meléndez until his return to England and subsequent visit to Rome and renunciation of Roman Catholicism in 1642 form the material of this book. In brief, after reaching Mexico on his way to the Philippines, he, Antonio Meléndez, and two other young Dominicans in the mission were so discouraged by what they heard of conditions in the Philippines that they ran off, making their way to Chiapas, which then formed part of Guatemala both politically and spiritually, for it formed part of the Dominican province of San Vicente de Chiapa y Guatemala.

A kindly Dominican Provincial, Father Pedro Álvarez, welcomed them to Chiapas, apparently treating as a young man's prank the flight from Mexico and not wishing to send the men back to ignominy and punishment in Mexico. Gage's description of the warmhearted Provincial watching the young friars skylarking in the garden and pelting one another with oranges and lemons is very moving.[5] A shortage of friars to man the many missions in the extensive province of Chiapa and Guatemala and the fact that the accession of four recruits from Europe helped to maintain the ascendancy of the Spanish faction over those born and educated in the Americas undoubtedly weighed in the decision not to send the

[5] Pages 126–30.

young men back. However, an increase in the European group was not merely a political matter, as Gage would have one believe; there is little doubt that recruits from Spain were desirable because they had enjoyed better educational facilities than were available in Mexico or Guatemala, and often they were of tougher moral fiber than the Creole group.

After some months in Chiapas, during which time he claims to have been on very friendly terms with both the Bishop and the Dominican prior, Gage proceeded to the city of Guatemala, capital of the Captaincy General of Guatemala. For the three years (1627–29) following his stay in Chiapas, Gage resided in the Dominican friary in Guatemala City. This was not the present city of that name, but the former capital, now called Antigua, "the old," which was abandoned as the capital following the terrible destruction wrought there by a series of earthquakes culminating in one of outstanding violence in 1773. Old Guatemala lies about fifteen miles west of the present Guatemala City in a direct line, but by the winding mountainous road the distance is considerably greater. In all Central America there can be few more attractive towns than Antigua, with the massive ruins of baroque church, public building, convent, and friary, and towering above it the three extinct volcanoes of Agua, Fuego, and Acatenango. The Cakchiquel Indians who come in from the surrounding villages to hold market add a brave note of color. The hand-woven *huipils* (sacklike blouses) brocaded with birds and beasts and trees worn by the women of today are surely no brighter or finer made than those worn by the Indian women in Gage's time, but of such matters he says nothing in his book, perhaps because gay colors were unseemly in Puritan eyes. Although Gage says little of the Indians, he gives a full and entertaining description of the city and its Spanish inhabitants in his day. Gage spent his time in Guatemala studying, preaching, and apparently teaching in the seminary for novices attached to the Dominican friary.

One gets the impression that during those three years Gage was a happy man, deeply immersed in his studies. One does not doubt his truthfulness when he tells us that he did not wish to be licensed to preach lest that extra duty should interfere with his studies. He does not mention that the license to preach carried with it the privilege of spending much time outside the walls of the friary and, therefore, would have been ardently sought had he been unhappy or weary of his life of chapel, cloistered garth, and cell. Surely Gage at this time had no doubts about his faith, despite what he says to the contrary. I find it hard to banish from my mind a picture—perhaps entirely false—of Gage in later years, when he was "Preacher of the Word" at Deal, on the cold English Channel, longing with all his maimed soul for a view of Fuego from the cloisters of Antigua, or a morning cup of chocolate in the company of old friends such as Antonio Meléndez, Father Jacinto Cabañas, or fat Friar Juan Bautista, and yearning to hear instead of extemporaneous prayer "the blessed mutter of the Mass" with a small Indian server ready to move the missal from Epistle to Gospel side.

For some reason, perhaps restlessness, although he gives religious doubts, a reason likely to prove popular with his readers, Gage left his sheltered life in Guatemala to join his old friend Father Francisco Morán in one of his missionary trips to the Chol Mayas in the forest country of what is today the southeastern corner of the Petén District of Guatemala and adjacent southwestern British Honduras. Dominican missions had been working for many years, but with indifferent success, among the pagan Chols, who had an unpleasant habit of burning the mission towns and slipping off into the almost impenetrable rain forest whenever anything happened to frighten them. This mission, in the early months of 1630, was of short duration, but gave Gage new travel experience.

After a short visit to the north coast of Guatemala and adjacent Honduras, which in later years supplied material for the memorandum to Oliver Cromwell on the lack of defenses in that area, Gage took charge of the Dominican mission of Mixco and Pinola. Mixco, where he resided from the middle of 1630 until the beginning of 1635, is a pleasant little town, near the modern Guatemala City and only about twelve miles in a direct line, but a day's trip by mule from the old capital of Gage's day. Early in 1635 he was moved to Amatitlán, a town on the lake of the same name and now a favorite bathing place. Gage was by then agitating to be allowed to return to Europe, as he had almost completed the requisite ten years in the New World, and he appears to have been appointed to the pleasant vicariate of Amatitlán to keep him satisfied. Unfortunately, such towns as Mixco and Amatitlán, despite the pleasantness of their surroundings, seem to have had little appeal for Gage. With the exception of a very few Spanish-speaking persons, mulattoes or *mestizos* for the most part, the population was entirely Indian, of the Pokoman branch of the Mayas. Gage busied himself in learning the Pokoman language and seems to have become quite proficient in it, but he lived an isolated life without intellectual stimulus. The days when he could dispute with Jesuits in Guatemala City or discuss points of theology with fellow Dominicans or with Franciscans were passed. Early in his years of residence among the Pokoman he seems to have decided that he would have difficulty in getting back to Europe and that he might have to depend on his wits and on his purse. Perhaps in his loneliness he brooded on what he may have regarded as unfair treatment from his superiors, and from there it may have been a short step to see himself the disinherited victim of his father's stubborn attachment to the Jesuits. Whether his thoughts followed some such course or not, there seems no reason to disbelieve his own very candid revelations about the avaricious way in which he started to build a small private fortune at the expense of his Indian parishioners.

From Amatitlán he was transferred at his own request to Petapa, another Pokoman town lying roughly between Mixco and Amatitlán, but today less important than either. During the year he spent there he seems finally to have made up his mind to run away. This he did in January, 1637, leaving for the Provincial a letter in which he excused his action on the grounds that for two years he had held the license from Rome to return to Europe so as to work for the conversion of England. The journey overland to Panama was one any traveler might be proud of having made. There was extremely little traffic by land between Guatemala and Costa Rica. Gage makes light of the long, fatiguing, and sometimes perilous journey with its discouraging detours and back-tracking. Finally, after being relieved by Dutch pirates of much of his ill-gotten gains, Gage reached Panama, and passed thence to Portobello to await the arrival of the Spanish fleet.

Portobello! The very name is linked in our imagination with viceroys and their stately ladies, pieces of eight, buccaneers, and Davy Jones' locker—in short, the very epitome of the Spanish Main. No English pen, save Gage's, has ever described the little port when the fleet was in, and probably no other Englishman walked its sun-seared lanes in peace, watching the mules arrive with their loads of silver ingots. Unwittingly, in dwelling upon his anxieties about the outrageous prices charged for lodging when the fleet was in, he helps the reader to see the annual awakening of the somnolent little town to the clatter of the throngs free for a while of the straight confine-ment of shipboard, the scramble of merchants to exchange the lux-uries of Spain for the raw produce of the Indies, and the impatience of the admiral of the fleet to be gone.

Gage worked his passage to Spain as chaplain of the *San Sebastián*. His account of the Dutch privateers hovering on the edge of the convoy to cut off stragglers is strangely anticipatory of narratives of submarine warfare in our century. From Spain he took ship to England, landed at Dover, and reached London a day or two before Christmas, 1637 (new style). The journey from Guatemala had taken only a few days less than a whole year, and it was just short of twenty-three years since he had left England as a boy of about twelve to start his studies at St. Omer. As he tells us, he could hardly speak English.

For the next fifteen to eighteen months Gage lived in the house of his uncle, Mr. Copley, of Gatton in Surrey, from whom he re-ceived a stipend, almost certainly in return for his services as domes-tic chaplain, for the Copleys were ardent supporters of the old faith. Gage's father had died about four years earlier and had not men-tioned him in his will, as he had threatened when Gage left the Jesuits. Gage relates that he was often in London in the year fol-lowing his return, and attended services at St. Paul's and other churches to learn of the beliefs and liturgy of the Church of Eng-land, but he was in good standing with the English Catholics. From his testimony at Father Holland's trial we know he was still saying Mass and preaching. Once he was arrested as a Roman Catholic priest, but through the intervention of Sir Francis Windebanke, the secretary of state, the matter was not proceeded with.[6]

I have drawn heavily on the newly published *A Hundred Home-less Years* of Father Anstruther, O.P., for Gage's relations at that time with his fellow Dominicans, a small band of less than a dozen, under the leadership of Thomas Middleton, alias Dade, the Provin-

[6] Page 345.

cial. Anstruther quotes several letters of George Conn, the papal agent in England, and his successor, Carlo Rossetti. Since the first letter is written in October, 1638, it is evident that Gage had wasted little time in becoming active in the affairs of the group. The pertinent paragraph reads:

> Some young men of these missionaries of St. Dominic would like to remove the present provincial, who is a discreet man and of good government. . . . The names of the more factious are: Thomas de S. María, alias Gage, George of S. Dominic, alias Popham, Peter Martyr, alias Cresen [Craft].

In another letter of February, 1639, and in a third in March, he writes:

> Between some Dominicans and their provincial there is hatred and serious detraction. I have heard both parties and I find the provincial innocent, and the other two most culpable. . . .

> There being a schism between two Dominicans and their provincial, to the extent of injuring him atrociously by words and by threats of violence, I have endeavoured to restore harmony, and the two subjects have many times in my presence prostrated to kiss the feet of the provincial, who is a discreet man and a religious worthy of his office.

As Father Anstruther points out, the opposition was reduced to two because Craft seems to have gone to Flanders to become chaplain to Sir Henry Gage. One has difficulty in imagining Gage prostrate and kissing the feet of his superior, but one must remember that apparently those three in opposition comprised all the Dominicans in the London neighborhood, and, furthermore, Father Middleton was at loggerheads with other Roman Catholic groups in England, so perhaps Gage and his companions were not entirely to blame. Gage's active part in these quarrels hardly bears out his repeated statements that his opposition to Roman Catholicism dated from the time he was in Guatemala, for obviously he would not have taken the dangerous course of becoming an active member of that Dominican group had he really been so opposed at that time to what they stood for; he was in far less danger staying quietly at Gatton with his uncle.

What the trouble between Middleton and his subordinates was is not known, but an envoy was sent from Rome to inquire into the matter and was given faculties to appoint a new Provincial. He recommended the appointment of a new Provincial and apparently the removal of Thomas Gage to another area.

Gage says nothing of these matters, but having, as he tells us, obtained from the Master General of his order permission to visit Rome "to confer some points with him," in the early summer of 1639 he crossed to Flanders, where he was warmly welcomed by his brother Henry, who was then colonel of the English legion in the service of the Spanish monarchy, and was stationed near Ghent. Henry gave him more money (Mr. Copley had been very liberal to Gage when he set forth) and provided him with letters of introduction to various notables in Rome, among whom was Cardinal Barberini, the Pope's nephew. While with his brother he met Father Peter Wright, S. J., chaplain and close friend of the Colonel, in whose arms Sir Henry died six years later near Oxford. That meeting was to cost Father Wright his life. Gage made his way leisurely to Cologne and, down the Rhine, to Frankfurt, where, he would have us believe, he was tempted to become a Lutheran. Thence, after passing by Bavaria, the Tyrol, and Trentino, he made a grand tour of Verona, Milan, Genoa, Leghorn, Pisa, and Florence before finally going to Rome.

Gage's account of what he learned in Rome must be taken with a large grain of salt. He was probably misled by what he heard, but the story of intrigue lost nothing in the retelling. Apparently, he could not make up his mind what to do. In April, 1640, he obtained from the General of the Order an order of transfer to the Dominican friary in Orleans. He tells us that he planned to go there to learn French, but as soon as he had learned it, he proposed to join a French Protestant church and spend the rest of his life in France. He did not require such a transfer to enter France, nor would one choose a friary as the best place to pick up a foreign language other than Latin. It is more reasonable to suppose that Gage did not relish the prospect of returning as a Dominican to England, where, apart from the unpleasantness of his relations with his superior, he was in considerable danger. On the other hand, by spending some time in a Dominican friary in France, he could indulge his craving for travel and—this was an important point to Gage—at no cost to himself. There, out of harm's way, he could watch developments. The optimism of exiles in distant Rome anticipated a quick restoration of the old faith in England; the Scottish invasion of England and the rising tide of Puritanism seemed to preclude that possibility. It will never be known whether the plan to go to France was Gage's, or whether, as is more probable, it was the solution planned by the Master General to end the strife in England.

At any rate, Gage finally decided not to transfer to the French Dominicans, but, instead, to return to England, where, after an adventurous journey, he landed on Michaelmas Day (September 29), 1640. By then he seems to have made up his mind to join the Church of England when the opportunity arose. Perhaps his failure to obtain redress in Rome for imagined wrongs at the hands of his superior may have been the last straw, for Gage was hardly the type to turn the other cheek, let alone prostrate himself to kiss the feet of an enemy. Yet, there was more to it than that, for he had genuine religious doubts, particularly with regard to the doctrine of transubstantiation, which he had great difficulty in resolving.

He waited another eighteen months before making the plunge. By then the first session of the Long Parliament had tried and executed Stafford, had impeached Archbishop Laud and sent him to the Tower of London, and had showed that Parliament intended to rule the country. In his account of events in Rome, Gage speaks of the close contacts of Laud, then Archbishop of Canterbury, with Rome and would have his readers believe that Laud was plotting to lead the Church of England into submission to Rome. He relates the absurd story that Laud forwarded the Scottish Book of Common Prayer to Rome for advice before trying to force it on Scotland. Laud was a high churchman, but no Papist. Of such charges, Lord Clarendon, who had known him well, wrote: "They [the Puritans] accused him of a design to bring in Popery, and of having correspondence with the Pope, and such like particulars as the consciences of his greatest enemies absolved him from. No man a greater or abler enemy to Popery; no man a more resolute and devout son of the Church of England." Those charges against him are belied by his own words as he was taken to his execution, so basely plotted by his enemies: "This is no time to dissemble with God, least of all in matters of religion, and therefore I desire it to be remembered I have always lived in the Protestant religion established in England, and in that I come now to die."

Nevertheless, Gage may have believed the stories about Laud, and the imprisonment of the Archbishop and, later, the flight of the Queen, who had for so long protected the Roman Catholic priests, may have decided him that the time had come to take the final step. This was probably early in 1642, but may have been late in 1641. He approached Sir Samuel Owlfield, member of Parliament for Gatton and without doubt a friend of his from the time Gage was living with his uncle at Gatton. By him, he says, "I have been quietly brought into the church." He was introduced to Ralph Brownrigg, who had been elevated to the see of Exeter in May, 1642, and from an obscure sentence in his pamphlet *A full survey of Sion and Babylon,* one gets the impression that Brownrigg was already a bishop. Thence he was brought to the Bishop of London, and on August 28 he preached his sermon of public recantation in St. Paul's Cathedral. This was not Wren's building, but the great Gothic pile which was to perish twenty-four years later in the great fire of London. The sermon was soon republished as a tract under the title, *The Tyranny of Satan, Discovered by the teares of a Converted Sinner in a Sermon Preached in Paules Church on the 28 of August, 1642, by Thomas Gage, formerly a Romish Priest, for the Space of 38 yeares, and now truly reconciled to the Church of England.* In this (page 18) Gage speaks of the "true, ancient, and Apostolike Church of England," yet in our present book he gives us to understand that in 1638, when he began to inquire into Protestantism, he found the ritual and the Book of Common Prayer of the Church of England as full of error as the practices and missal of the Church of Rome. Howbeit, between the date of this sermon and the publication of the book in 1648, the victorious parliamentarians had suppressed Episcopacy and the Book of Common Prayer, had executed Archbishop Laud, the spiritual head of the Anglican church, and were on the point of executing King Charles, its temporal head. Gage, swimming with the tide, had cast aside Anglicanism to become a "Preacher of the Word" and a sectary with Presbyterian leanings.

Six days before Gage's recantation sermon was preached, the

Royal Standard was raised at Nottingham, the visible sign of the outbreak of civil war; and in October, 1642, the first battle of the war was fought at Edgehill. From the very start, London and the eastern counties were firmly in Parliamentarian hands. In the shadow of those events Gage married, to authenticate he tells us,[7] his complete break with Rome, but in October of that same year he corroborated his apostasy by an unforgivable act.

Father Thomas Holland, a schoolmate of Gage's at St. Omer for five years was brought to trial charged with being a Roman Catholic priest who had said mass in England, an offense still held as treasonable and punishable with death. The evidence against Father Holland was negligible until Gage came forward to testify that the two had been fellow students together for five years at St. Omer, that Father Holland had gone thence to St. Alban College, and another witness testified that Father Holland had been chosen to go to Madrid in 1622 to give an address of loyalty on behalf of the college to Prince Charles, who was there on a visit. Father Holland admitted the truth of the statements, but claimed they were irrelevant since many Englishmen were educated abroad without taking orders. Gage also testified that about five years prior to this time Father Holland had been in the chapel of the Spanish embassy in London on an occasion when Gage had preached there, and afterwards had come to congratulate him on his sermon. Furthermore, that on one occasion when Father Holland was indisposed, Gage had been asked to say mass for him in Holborn. In that last piece of testimony Gage sent his old schoolmate to the gallows. Father Holland was hanged, drawn, and quartered at Tyburn on December 12, 1642, praying that his death might bring to the faith his betrayer, Thomas Gage.

The Gage family, who had suffered so much for their religion, were filled with horror and shame, first at Gage's apostasy, with the crude gibes at the doctrine of transubstantiation in the sermon of recantation which had just been published, and now at this shameful betrayal of an old schoolmate. Colonel Gage, who seems to have been aware of his brother's besetting avarice, offered him one thousand pounds to leave England. His brother, the Reverend George Gage, wrote to Father Holland a day or two before his execution

[7] Page 357.

a letter from which I quoted a sentence in the opening lines of this introduction. Father George adds what every Roman Catholic in England must have felt in saying that, were it not for his ill health, "I would in person come and beg at once your blessing and your pardon, the first for myselfe, the second for my graceless brother who hathe now so basely apostatized from his birth and nature, as he had before from his faith and religious vowes."

In December, 1643, Gage testified that Father Arthur Bell, a Franciscan, had been chaplain in the home of an unspecified relative, probably his cousin, Lady Penelope Gage, and that he had frequently said mass there. On that testimony Father Bell was found guilty and executed.

Gage was rewarded for his activities by appointment as rector of Acrise, a small parish in Kent but with a living of eighty pounds a year. Humphrey Peake, the incumbent, was probably deprived of the living because of loyalty to Anglicanism. In the parish register of St. Martin Acrise, there is a final entry by the old rector on December 20, 1643, and a first entry by Gage two days later. An entry in Gage's writing records the baptism of his daughter Elizabeth in October, 1644. Parochial duties probably were not exacting, and allowed Gage time to write *The English-American*, parts of which certainly were composed in 1644 and 1645, and to spend much time in London in connection with its publication. It was probably at this time that Gage became friendly with Thomas Chaloner, a power in the Commonwealth, who sponsored the book and wrote some doggerel as a preface to it. In October, 1648, the writing in the Acrise register changes. This marks Gage's departure for the more important living of Deal. Late in that year he became rector of the parish church of St. Leonard, Deal, in Kent, an incumbency he held until his death over seven years later.

In the spring of 1651, Father Peter Wright, in whose arms Sir Henry Gage had died near Oxford, was brought to trial as a Jesuit priest. He had been caught in the house of the Marquis of Winchester in Covent Garden. This was the same Marquis to whose country house, Basing House, Sir Henry and he had ridden with the relief force in that daring exploit of seven years before. Father Dade, alias Middleton, the Provincial of the Dominicans in England and Gage's old adversary, was tried at the same time. Gage was summoned from Deal as witness for the prosecution, and on reaching London, immediately went to see Chief Justice Rolles and Bradshaw, the regicide and president of the Privy Council. In a pamphlet which Gage later wrote in defense of his conduct he rather suggests that he acted under pressure, for he wrote: "My coming out of the country hath been misconstrued by some, who will not know that high powers have commanded me up, and by those that know it, aspersions have been laid upon me that for delinquency and siding with some gentlemen in Kent, now prisoners in London, by warrant from high powers I was commanded to come and answer for some misdemeanour against the present government."

Father George Gage sought his brother before the trial and extracted from him a pledge that he would say nothing to harm either prisoner. Nevertheless, on being taken to Newgate prison the day before the trial, he identified Father Wright as priest and chaplain of his brother in Flanders and at Oxford, although he had no direct knowledge of events at Oxford. According to one close to the priest, the two had a private conversation in which Father Wright "sorely wounded the unhappy man's guilty conscience." At the trial Gage kept his word so far as Father Middleton was concerned, and by his argument that one could be a friar without being a priest, citing St. Francis as an example, he won his acquittal; toward Father Wright he acted very differently. In the words of a witness, he "declaimed against the Father for nearly half an hour in so violent and marked a manner that it was evident from the beginning that he was instigated by hatred and a thirst for blood," and "he raved against his brother," whom he accused of having plotted to kill him, claiming that Father Wright was equally guilty because, knowing of the plan through the confessional, he had done nothing to prevent it. Father Wright entirely denied any such plot, and the character of Sir Henry makes it certain that he was telling the truth. On Gage's testimony Father Wright was found guilty and was duly executed in the barbarous fashion reserved for traitors, on May 9, 1651, three days after his condemnation.

Gage's conduct had brought on him the indignation of many and the contempt of all but the most insensate sectaries. Subsequently, he defended his actions in a clumsy pamphlet, *A Duell between a Jesuite and a Dominican, begun at Paris, gallantly fought at Madrid, and victoriously ended at London upon Fryday 16 May 1651.* It is possible that Father Wright in that prison conversation did tax Gage in a way that turned him to implacable malevolence, but Gage had an obsessive hatred of the Jesuits.

The Reverend George Gage was arrested and died in prison in 1652. According to a bill against him for appearance before the courts, his own brother, Thomas, was an informer against him. We have no further information on this point, but vile as were other actions of Thomas Gage, one hesitates to accept this terrible suggestion on such tenuous evidence. Possibly, statements in his book led to the citing of Thomas as informer.

Of Gage's activities in Deal something is known, certainly much more than is known of the life of William Shakespeare a few decades earlier. An entry by Gage in the church register tells of the death of his daughter Mary in March, 1652. In the following month he made his appeal to the mayor of Sandwich for help in saving the church, which appears as Appendix 1 of this book. In August, 1653, he, the church wardens, and thirteen others signed and forwarded to the authorities in London a certificate in favor of Anne, widow of Thomas Trice, formerly a pilot of Deal, who had been pressed (i.e., forcibly enlisted) as a pilot and had apparently died in that service, leaving seven children in addition to his widow. In 1654, Gage was carrying on a long controversy with a certain Charles Nichols, who had set up a rival congregation and much annoyed Gage by calling him and his church "Babylonish," a title which in Gage's opinion should be reserved for the Church of Rome. Gage let loose at him an eighty-six-page broadside published in London that same year. More than parochial matters were to engage his attention that year.

In 1654, with peace at home, Cromwell's thoughts turned to expansion overseas. Gage's book, as had been intended, had been excellent propaganda for an English incursion into the Spanish Main. Perhaps on the recommendation of Chaloner, Gage was called upon to submit for Oliver Cromwell's consideration the memorandum, from which I have already quoted above, on the prospects for an attack against the Spanish possessions. This memorandum is preserved among the papers of John Thurloe, then secretary to the Council of State and the very able head of Intelligence.

Gage advocated the attack, employing arguments he had already advanced in *The English-American.* His chief points were: (1) The area was thinly populated; (2) "Within the maine land, in my time, in the greatest cities there was not one gun or field piece, or wall, castle, or any bulwarke"; (3) the Indians were unarmed and could not be counted on by the Spaniards; (4) the Spaniards were too lazy, untrained, and full of lust to defend their land successfully; (5) mulattoes and Negroes, if armed, might rise against their masters, and they, as well as the Indians, could be expected to support any nation proclaiming liberty for them; (6) the jealousy between Spaniard and Creole would help an invader; (7) resistance would be less because "it hath been these many yeares their owne common talke, from some predictions, or (as they call them) prophecies, vented out amongst them, that a strange people shall conquer them, and take all their riches from them"; and (8) God would aid the upright English against those sinners.

To an archaeologist the argument about the prophecies of a people coming from overseas to rule the land is of unusual interest, for this is surely a reference to the belief current among the Indians of Mexico and Central America that Quetzalcoatl, the feathered-serpent god, would return to rule his people. A century earlier, Cortés and his men were at first identified as Quetzalcoatl and his followers, a factor which contributed to the comparative ease with which the Spaniards conquered the land. Later, the Mayas seem to have identified with Quetzalcoatl certain Protestant buccaneers who had a lodging in Yucatán, and expected deliverance from the Spanish rule with their aid. Accordingly, Gage was not far-fetched in citing this possible aid, but Quetzalcoatl and Oliver Cromwell make strange bed fellows, and one hardly expects to find the influence of Quetzalcoatl weighed in a British intelligence report of the seventeenth century.

Other plans, notably that of Colonel Muddiford for a descent on the Orinoco, were considered, but Gage's alternative suggestion of an attack on Hispaniola was finally chosen. Bishop Gilbert Burnet, in his *History of His Own Times,* throws an interesting light on this matter:

Gage, who had been a priest, came over from the West Indias and gave Cromwell such an account of the feebleness, as well as the wealth, of the Spaniards in those parts as made him conclude, that it would be both a great and an easy conquest to seize on their dominions. By this he reckoned he would be supplied with such a treasure, that his government would be established before he should need to have any recourse to a parliament for money. . . . He equipped a fleet with a force sufficient, as he hoped, to have seized Hispaniola and Cuba. And Gage had assured him that success in that expedition would make all the rest fall into his hands.

He adds that a certain Stoupe saw Cromwell measuring distances on a map of the Bay of Mexico which Cromwell had had secretly prepared. Father Anstruther quotes a letter from the Venetian ambassador in London, in which the plans for the expedition are credited to "the information of a Dominican friar who has been in those parts and knows them well, who has had many secret conferences with the Protector on the subject." Wisely, Gage's plan for an attack on Guatemala had been rejected. Cromwell may have studied longingly that map of the Bay of Mexico, but his advisers must have warned him that a sea power should attack islands, not mainland.

In December, 1654, the expedition sailed with Gage as chaplain to General Venables, who shared with Penn, father of William Penn, the command of the expedition. In the Admiralty records there is a report that on the orders of Cromwell, the frigate *The Fagons* had sailed to Deal to pick up and carry Gage to Portsmouth, where the fleet was fitted out. It is not everyone who has a frigate sent to fetch him, and brand new, too (built 1654; 262 tons, 22 guns).

Despite the high hopes and Gage's assurances, the attack on Hispaniola was a complete failure and brought heavy casualties to the English force. One of the causes of the defeat was the nonappearance of Negro guides who were expected to lead the English forces to attack their fellow countrymen. Of this mishap Clarendon wrote, "The common opinion that the negroes, natives of those parts, are such enemies to the Spaniards that they are willing to betray them and do any mischief to them might possibly incline the English to give credit to those guides." It was, as we have seen, Gage who had repeatedly put forward that idea in his book as well as in his memorandum to Cromwell, so it may well be that Gage was largely responsible for the defeat at Hispaniola.

From Hispaniola the expedition sailed to Jamaica, which was

quickly captured and has remained under the British flag ever since, so if Gage is responsible for the failure at Hispaniola, he also deserves credit for the addition of Jamaica to the incipient British empire. Venables and Penn returned immediately to England, where they were promptly sent as prisoners to the Tower of London for their failure at Hispaniola; Gage stayed in Jamaica as chaplain to the occupying force. It was just a month or two short of thirty years since he had sailed as a young friar for the New World. The old traveler must have sniffed the familiar scents of the tropics, caught again the silhouette of coconut palms, and heard once more the lap of wave against mangrove root. Then the joy of drinking again a cup of chocolate, so missed in England, and of savoring maize *tortilla* dipped in chile would have recalled to him the two main strands of his old life, church and the Indians. Now he would have a congregation of the disputatious who thought they knew as much or more than he did about religion instead of the humble Indian with his simple offering quietly waiting until one had drunk chocolate.

Early in 1656, Gage died on Jamaica. His widow received a small pension from a not overgrateful government. In a list, dated January, 1671, of contributors in Deal to a brief, or fund, for the redemption of captives of the Barbary pirates held in Algiers is listed "Mrs. Gage, widow, and her daughters." In view of her late husband's interest in travel and his two encounters with pirates, Mrs. Gage's interest in the cause is understandable, and for those of us who have followed with some dismay Gage's career, it is nice to find that the last record of him or his family is one of being charitable.

I cannot leave Thomas Gage without a word in his favor. His character has long puzzled me, for I have felt that there was a good side to him, particularly in his early days, and that this can be perceived beneath the base cynicism with which he cloaks all his activities as he relates them in *The English-American*. Constantly in his writings and in his published sermons, he seems to be bent on revealing himself in the worst possible light, yet he was a man of marked intelligence[8] and obviously did not give himself away unwittingly. In that connection one or two points may better illuminate his character.

[8] Pages 135, 177–79, 257.

Gage's ability to inspire loyalty and affection in those who served him speaks in his favor. The mulatto Miguel Dalva and his Indian servant cheerfully accompanied him on his arduous hegira from Guatemala to Granada. Miguel, at least, must have had grave suspicions about the legality of Gage's journey, and could have profited by betraying him, but both stood loyally by him.

In all matters, except religious, which can be verified, I have found Gage truthful and reliable. It is abundantly clear that he made great use of the journals he kept on his travels, for without them he could not have remembered names of places and persons with such accuracy. Had he so wished, he could have lied with impunity, for there was no one in seventeenth-century England to disprove his statements. The fact that he wrote with such attention to accuracy is very much in his favor. Only in the incident of the crocodile[9] does Gage spin a traveler's yarn, and even there it is a matter of exaggeration rather than playing himself up as a hero. Indeed, nowhere does he glorify himself, although he certainly was no coward. He is a little too ready to accept hearsay as truth if thereby he can make his point. That is evident in gossip of improper conduct by priests or friars which he passes on as the truth. Unfortunately, he went beyond that, for he lied on such matters. A flagrant case concerns his old friend Father Francisco Morán, who, he says,[10] in urging him to go on the missionary trip to southeastern Petén, spoke of the great wealth to be had in that area which would compensate both of them for the dangers of the trip. Now Father Ximénez gives us a great deal of information about Francisco Morán, who was a devoted missionary, a great linguist, and a brave and enthusiastic man. It is inconceivable that a man of his caliber and missionary zeal could have had any interest in acquiring wealth. In any case, he well knew that the only wealth in that backward area lay in such bulky and not easily transported articles as cacao and copal. Gage must have lied deliberately in attributing avarice to his old friend. Similarly, he tells us that prospects of acquiring wealth was one of the motives that led his other friend, Antonio Meléndez, to go to the New World,[11] but from his own

[9] Page 312.
[10] Page 249.
[11] Page 8.

account of that evening it is clear that his young friend was motivated only by apostolic zeal. Over and over again Gage charges friars with avarice, although wealth so gathered was of no use to a friar in a convent.

Again, Gage speaks of the "base, lewd, light, and wanton" ways and conversations of the Dominican friars in London. Common sense tells us that men who were in constant peril of their lives because of their religion would be the last people to lead dissolute lives. Similarly, one can hardly take seriously the charge that his brother George hoped to be made a bishop, and then, he claimed, he would get a bishopric also for Thomas. Such talk was obviously chaff, and Thomas must have known it. At the time this book was first published, George was still alive and at liberty. Statements about his activities as a priest might have seriously endangered him. Indeed, these very sentences may have been the grounds for citing Thomas as an informer in the warrant for his arrest. Gage, as we have seen, almost certainly lied also about the supposed contacts of Archbishop Laud with Rome.

We have, then, this picture of Gage as a man scrupulously honest about his activities and travels in the New World, who did not attempt in any way to make himself out to be a hero—rather the contrary. Indeed, consciously or unconsciously he depicts himself as unusually rapacious, although he surely must have realized that such candid displays of his weakness must have put him in a bad light with his readers. Yet, when religion is a factor, he lies about his friends and distorts the words and motives of even his own brother. Outside his book, in real life, he gives testimony—and in those cases there was no need to lie—which sends former friends and coreligionists to the gallows, and their deaths bring no regrets on his part. Is there any logical explanation for such conflicting standards of conduct?

Gage in his last years and in his writings reveals himself, I think, as a man whose religious susceptibilities have been deeply wounded. The young English Roman Catholics who entered the seminaries on the continent of Europe were dedicated men who knew that their calling would bring them into constant danger of losing their lives, and for the most part they were drawn from the aristocracy.

To Gage, who had reached manhood in that atmosphere, the slackening of religious fervor and the mundane attitudes observable in a by no means negligible proportion of the friars and priests in Mexico and Guatemala came as a shock, and in the end was probably, as he notes, one of the factors in his desertion of his old faith. So that, although he was giving his Protestant readers the kind of exposé of Catholic misconduct they both expected and enjoyed, he was driven to disclose and execrate all such frailties, however improbable they may have been, because they had contributed to his religious insecurity.

Gage constantly speaks of the dangers at the hands of Papists which he had to face: That danger was one of his reasons for going to the New World;[12] in his sermon of recantation at St. Paul's, he claimed to be in dire danger for having apostatized; at the trial of Father Holland and of Father Wright he testified to the danger he ran, and there perhaps with greater cause. At the Wright trial he asked for the equivalent of police protection, and, according to his "Sion and Babylon" sermons, he was so protected while in London; in his confrontation with Father Wright, he charged that his brother, Sir Henry, plotted his death, and he dwells on that point in his book;[13] he also charged that Sir Henry had come over to England to do him mischief, whereas Sir Henry had come over to fight for King Charles, and wished only to forget the very existence of his brother. In any case, danger from the harried Papists was at all times negligible. Yet, Gage's life and travels—for example, the mission to the Chols for which he volunteered—indicate very clearly that he was not a timid man. One can only conclude that all this talk of danger from his Papist former comrades was to establish him as a good Protestant.

It is likewise of interest to examine some of Gage's references to money. He lost his inheritance because he would not be a good Jesuit, and in his "Sion and Babylon" sermons he complains that in his journeys to London to give evidence against Roman priests, he wasted much of his poor estate which ought to have been spent on his wife and children. He lost the huge sum of one thousand pounds offered him by his brother because he would not cease his

[12] Page 11.
[13] Page 11, 357.

attacks on Rome and its priests.[14] Here again his devotion to Protestantism is shown by the heavy financial losses that its support entailed.

Finally, it was to prove the sincerity of his conversion that he entered into "the state of marriage . . . which the Church of Rome disavows to all her priests."

Gage seems to have been overdoing it in recounting the many physical dangers, the pecuniary losses, and the discomforts of matrimony which he faced for the Protestant cause. Surely there was no need for such extremes to convince people of the validity of his conversion; all good Protestants were more than ready to welcome any brand snatched from the burning without too much questioning when, as in this case, the conversion was not the result of pressure.

Notwithstanding these gestures with the apparent purpose of emphasizing his irrevocable break with Rome, we find Gage displayed attitudes which might easily have excited the suspicions of ultra-Protestants. In his sermons "Sion and Babylon," preached in 1553 when he was rector of Deal, he was quite insistent that the Commonwealth Presbyterian organization had come down from the primitive church and that its orders were valid, as were its baptism and other ordinances, in spite of having been transmitted all through the Middle Ages by Rome. Furthermore, in his sermon at St. Paul's, eleven years earlier, he affirmed his belief in the validity of the Apostolic Succession of the Anglican church. Such views were hardly in keeping with the ferocity with which he attacked Rome.

It is, I think, highly significant that Gage cherished through all the vicissitudes of his religious and secular fortunes his license from the Dominican Provincial as a reader of arts and his license from the Bishop of Guatemala to preach, hear confessions, and give absolution throughout the diocese. These were extremely dangerous documents for a man to have in his possession in the England of 1637; they could easily have sent their possessor to Tyburn gallows. Gage was liable to search in entering and leaving England and at any moment as a suspect papist priest. Yet, although he would have us believe that he was a disillusioned Roman Catholic long before he left America, he kept these papers, as well as his order of transfer from the Dominican General in Rome and his far from innocuous

[14] Page 357.

journal. I think he did this, at considerable risk to his life, partly because they were keepsakes of a life that had been dear to him, and partly because he could not make up his mind to break with the church of his birth and upbringing, and these papers were in a sense his credentials as a Dominican in good standing. It is evident that Gage hesitated a very long time and suffered great mental intranquillity before he crossed—in reverse direction—his Rubicon.

Gage's pamphlet, *A Duell between a Jesuite and a Dominican, begun at Paris, gallantly fought at Madrid and victoriously ended at London upon Fryday 16 May 1651*, written in justification of his part in the trial of Father Wright, is an extraordinary document, for this duel between the two orders, which is fought in some very silly sermons, is carried to its victorious conclusion when the Dominican sends the Jesuit Father Wright to his death at Tyburn. The triumphant Dominican is Thomas Gage, who had ceased to be a member of that order nine years before. Gage, the Puritan Preacher of the Word, completely identifies himself with the Order of Preachers, to give the Dominicans their official name. "Preacher of the Word" was a common enough title in Puritan times, but I believe that Gage, who relished anything in the nature of a pun, especially if he could keep it to himself, used it because it was a symbol of his past life as well as of his present one. That identification of himself with his past is, I believe, the key to his enigmatic life after his sermon of recantation.

It is in my opinion probable that almost as soon as he embraced Protestantism, he began to doubt whether he had made the right decision. About the doctrine of transubstantiation I am sure he had very serious misgivings, but I don't believe that he was ever a wholehearted Puritan despite all his thunderings against Rome, and he had to convince not only others, but also himself, that he was. His marriage, I feel, was not so much to convince the people of his Protestantism as to be, for his peace of mind, the point of no return. His dangers and financial losses must be recorded and magnified to remind him that Rome was their cause; the kindliness and piety of nearly all his old comrades in the friaries of Spain and the New World must be blackened lest they lure him back to that old life. In his Sion and Babylon sermons, addressed to his parishioners in Deal, twelve years after he became a Protestant, there is a sentence which may be highly significant: "I am informed some have said my heart is still at Rome."

In the trials of Fathers Holland, Wright, and Bell he was not, I believe, fighting Roman Catholicism, but the attraction the old faith had for him. Against the first two he had the spur of his intense antipathy for Jesuits. Against Father Middleton, the Dominican Provincial, he could not bring himself to give evidence despite the bad feelings between them. Indeed, his testimony was so presented as to procure the father's release, surely because he was a Dominican, and as such symbolized for Gage his earlier years of peace and happiness in Guatemala. Perhaps Father Middleton reminded him of another Dominican Provincial who had treated kindly his young friend Antonio Meléndez and himself when they were in trouble.

Gage's tragedy I believe to have been the inner conflict and doubts as to which faith was right which, I think, rent him for the last fifteen years of his life. If this is the key to his despicable behavior, one must regard him not with contempt, but with some understanding and a compassion that is more than transient.[15]

[15] Long after the above was written, I read in Father Godfrey Anstruther's *A Hundred Homeless Years* part of a letter from Dr. Leyburn, president of Douai College to Cardinal Barberini, written on January 10, 1654: "I have heard moreover from England that Thomas Gage, religious of the order of St. Dominic, has returned to a better state of life, whose fall from the faith of Christ was the worst and most vile of all." Perhaps Gage expressed regret for having apostatised to some member of his former faith. Yet his memorandum to Cromwell, which is definitely anti-Roman Catholic, is of later date than this letter. Living in Deal, Gage could easily have slipped across to Roman Catholic France had he so desired. Probably he remained irresolute to the end.

Editor's Introduction to the
Second Printing

SINCE PUBLICATION of this book in 1958 a few more details concerning the author have come to light.

Gage's description of the route between Mexico and Oaxaca followed in the flight is confused (pp. 109–11). My colleague Leslie B. Simpson suggests that the Taxco Gage mentions is not the famed mining town in Guerrero, but Tlaxco, sometimes spelled Taxco, in Tlaxcala, and Zumpango is one of the Zumpangos in the state of Mexico. That interesting explanation produces as many fresh difficulties as it solves, for Tlaxco lies as far off a direct route in one direction as Taxco does in the other. Gates, writing over twenty years later, may not have had full notes to guide him. Simpson is surely right that Gage did not pass through Taxco, Guerrero.

In the *Boletín del Archivo General del Estado* [de Chiapas], No. 5, Tuxtla Gutiérrez, 1955, appears a contemporary account of the troubles in November, 1624, a year before Gage's arrival in Ciudad Real, which followed Bishop Salazar's excommunication of the Alcalde Mayor of Chiapas. In a memorable scene, Don Gabriel, the governor, and his supporters, drawing their swords, pointed them at the Bishop's breast. The Bishop, undaunted, refused to yield, and in the end the Governor had to sue for forgiveness and the lifting of the excommunication. This is again confirmation of the veracity of Gage's writings. His account (pp. 143–45) of the commotion caused by the Bishop's wholesale excommunication of the ladies who drank chocolate at mass and which seemingly led to his murder seemed far-fetched anti-papist propaganda; it is now apparent that it fits the Bishop's pattern of behavior.

France Scholes and Eleanor Adams, in their introduction (p. 12) to Martin A. Tovilla's *Relación histórica descriptiva de la Provincia*

1

de la Vera Paz y de la Manché del Reino de Guatemala (Guatemala, 1960), suggests that the fellow Dominican Fr. Francisco Morán mentions as a companion on the 1631 incursion into Manche territory and who, he hints, left him in the lurch, was Gage.

That interesting theory, I am happy to say, is not admissible. Gage's trip with Morán (pp. 249–54) was in 1630, as a study of this book makes abundantly clear. For instance, he mentions the terrible outbreak of *tabardillo* plague as occurring during his second year at Mixco, but we know that disaster occurred in 1631.

Moreover, as Gage recounts, he and Morán, after leaving Manche territory, visited Trujillo and then made their way overland to Guatemala. After resting some time in Guatemala and turning down Fr. Morán's request that he revisit the Manche Chol, Gage left for his new post at Petapa "two weeks before Midsummer day" (p. 256). The supposed Itza attack was on May 18, and Morán, who had stayed on at Toro de Acuña, wrote a letter from there dated June 28, 1631. Clearly, they could not have been under attack in Manche Chol territory and traveling around Honduras at the same time. Gage was with Morán in 1630; some other Dominican accompanied him in 1631 because of Gage's unwillingness to return to Chol missionary work. What a picture Gage would have left us had he been present at the pompous founding of Toro de Acuña and that, as I suspect, phony attack on the Spanish force!

Father Anstruther brought to light a license dated June 16, 1640, for Gage's return to England, just two months after his license to proceed to France had been issued (p. 354). One wonders what excuse Gage gave his superior for his swift change of plans.

Gage, as one might have supposed, acted as interpreter in the negotiations for the surrender of Jamaica to the Puritan force (p. xlv). There is an entry to that effect in the official Diary of the *Swiftsure*, Penn's flagship, quoted in Granville Penn, *Memorials of the professional life and times of Sir William Penn* (London, 1833; II, 103).

In 1968, Mr. Benjamin Dawson, of Berkeley, California, who had become interested in Gage from reading this book, commissioned a brass processional cross, which was made by Blunt and Wray, of Clerkenwell, London, and was sent as a gift to the Episcopal church of Mexico (La Iglesia Episcopal de México). The cross carries the inscription "Thomas Gage 1603–1656." Mr. Dawson asked me to inspect it before it was shipped.

It was strange that this cross, ordered by a man in California, over six thousand miles away, should have been made in the little parish of Clerkenwell, just outside London Wall, where Gage perhaps lived before he went to school at St. Omer's and the place to which he first returned when he reached England after his wanderings in the West Indies, for St. John's is St. John Clerkenwell (pp. xxvi, 341). The place takes its name from the Order of St. John of Jerusalem, which has had its headquarters in the parish since mediaeval times—the ancient buildings are less than a stone's throw from Blunt and Wray's. A police informer circa 1640 reported George Gage as being much at his sister's in Bloomsbury and "much at Sir John Gage's at Clerkenwell," and it was in Clerkenwell that a Jesuit college was uncovered in 1628.

As the cross was rewrapped for its long journey to Mexico in that little parish which had sheltered members of that embittered family, the story seemed at last to have come full circle: a cross, in Puritan times despised symbol of popish superstition, was going thence as a gift to that land which Tom so loved and later tried so hard to hate. What would he have made of it?

J. ERIC S. THOMPSON

Spring, 1969

Thomas Gage's Travels in the New World

To their many friends, of then and now,
in Mexico and Guatemala,
with deep affection

THOMAS GAGE – ERIC THOMPSON

Thomas Gage
The English American

To His Excellency
SIR THOMAS FAIRFAX, KNIGHT
LORD FAIRFAX OF CAMERON

CAPTAIN-GENERAL OF THE PARLIAMENT'S ARMY, AND
OF ALL THEIR FORCES IN ENGLAND, AND THE
DOMINION OF WALES

May it please your Excellency,
The Divine Providence hath hitherto so ordered my life, that for
the greatest part thereof I have lived (as it were) in exile from my
native country: which happened partly by reason of my education
in the Romish religion, and that in foreign universities; and partly
by my entrance into monastical orders. For twelve years' space of
which time I was wholly disposed of in that part of America called
New Spain, and the parts adjacent. My difficult going thither, being
not permitted to any but to those of the Spanish nation; my long
stay there; and lastly my returning home, not only to my country,
but to the true knowledge and free profession of the Gospel's purity,
gave me reason to conceive that these great mercies were not appointed me by the Heavenly Powers to the end I should bury my
talent in the earth, or hide my light under a bushel, but that I should
impart what I there saw and knew to the use and benefit of my
English countrymen. And which the rather I held myself obliged
unto, because in a manner nothing hath been written of these parts

3

for these hundred years last past, which is almost ever since the first Conquest thereof by the Spaniards, who are contented to lose the honor of that wealth and felicity they have there since purchased by their great endeavors, so they may enjoy the safety of retaining what they have formerly gotten in peace and security. In doing whereof, I shall offer no collections but such as shall arise from mine own observations, which will as much differ from what formerly hath been hereupon written as the picture of a person grown to man's estate from that which was taken of him when he was but a child; or the last hand of the painter to the first or rough draft of the picture. I am told by others that this may prove a most acceptable work; but I do tell myself that it will prove both lame and imperfect, and therefore had need to shelter myself under the shadow of some high protection, which I humbly pray your Excellency to afford me; nothing doubting, but as God hath lately made your Excellency the happy instrument not only of saving myself, but of many numbers of godly and well-affected people in this county of Kent (where now I reside by the favor of the Parliament) from the imminent ruin and destruction plotted against them by their most implacable enemies, so the same God who hath led your Excellency through so many difficulties towards the settlement of the peace of this kingdom, and reduction of Ireland, will, after the perfecting thereof (which God of his mercy hasten), direct your noble thoughts to employ the soldiery of this kingdom upon such just and honorable designs in those parts of America as their want of action at home may neither be a burden to themselves nor the kingdom. To your Excellency therefore I offer a New World, to be the subject of your future pains, valor, and piety, beseeching your acceptance of this plain but faithful relation of mine, wherein your Excellency, and by you the English nation, shall see what wealth and honor they have lost by one of their narrow-hearted princes, who, living in peace and abounding in riches did notwithstanding reject the offer of being first discoverer of America, and left it unto Ferdinand of Aragon, who at the same time was wholly taken up by the wars in gaining of the city and kingdom of Granada from the Moors; being so impoverished thereby that he was compelled to borrow with some difficulty a few crowns of a very mean man to set forth Columbus upon so glorious an expedition. And yet, if time were closely followed at the heels, we are not so far behind but we might yet take him by the fore-top. To which purpose our plantations of the Barbados, St. Christophers, Nevis, and the rest of the Caribbean Islands, have not only advanced our journey the better part of the way, but so inured our people to the clime of the Indies as they are the more enabled thereby to undertake any enterprise upon the firm land with greater facility. Neither is the difficulty of the attempt so great as some may imagine; for I dare be bold to affirm it knowingly that with the same pains and charge which they have been at in planting one of those petty islands they might have conquered so many great cities and large territories on the main continent as might very well merit the title of a kingdom. Our neighbors the Hollanders may be our example in this case; who whilst we have been driving a private trade from port to port, of which we are likely now to be deprived, have conquered so much land in the East and West Indies that it may be said of them, as of the Spaniards, *That the sun never sets upon their dominions.* And to meet with that objection by the way, *That the Spaniard being entitled to those countries, it were both unlawful and against all conscience to dispossess him thereof,* I answer that (the Pope's donation excepted) I know no title he hath but force, which by the same title and by a greater force may be repelled. And to bring in the title of first discovery, to me it seems as little reason that the sailing of a Spanish ship upon the coast of India should entitle the King of Spain to that country, as the sailing of an Indian or English ship upon the coast of Spain should entitle either the Indians or English unto the dominion thereof. No question but the just right or title to those countries appertains to the natives themselves, who, if they shall willingly and freely invite the English to their protection, what title soever they have in them no doubt but they may legally transfer it or communicate it to others. And to say that the inhuman butchery which the Indians did formerly commit in sacrificing of so many reasonable creatures to their wicked idols was a sufficient warrant for the Spaniards to divest them of their country, the same argument may by much better reason be enforced against the Spaniards themselves, who have sacrificed so many millions of Indians to the idol of their barbarous cruelty, that many populous islands and large territories upon the main continent are thereby at this day utterly uninhabited, as Bartholomeo de las Casas, the Spanish Bishop of Oaxaca[1] in New Spain, hath by his writings in print sufficiently testified. But to end all disputes of this nature; since that God hath given the earth to the sons of men to inhabit, and that there are many vast countries in those parts not yet inhabited either by Spaniard or Indian, why should my countrymen the English be debarred from making use of that which God from all beginning, no question, did ordain for the benefit of mankind?

But I will not molest your Excellency with any further argument hereupon, rather offering myself, and all my weak endeavors (such as they are), to be employed herein for the good of my country. I beseech Almighty God to prosper your Excellency, who am

> The most devoted and humblest of
> your Excellency's servants,
> THO. GAGE.

---

[1] A slip of the pen. Gage well knew he had been bishop of Chiapas.

1. *Of the mission sent by the Dominicans to the Philippines in the year 1625*

THE CHIEF STRENGTH of the Church of Rome in the Philippines is of missionaries brought from Spain, and they are more frequently conveyed thither than to any part of Spanish America. First they are sent in the ships that are bound for *Nueva España,* that is to say, Mexico. After they have rested two or three months in Mexico, they are sent to Acapulco on the *Mar del Sur* [the Pacific]. From there they are shipped in two great carracks [galleons] which yearly come and go, returning from Manila to Acapulco richly laden with wares from China, Japan, and all the East Indies to enrich Mexico with far greater riches than are sent by the *Mar del Norte* [the Atlantic] from Spain. The voyage from Acapulco thither is longer than from Spain to Mexico, and it is easy and pleasant, although the return journey is far longer and most dangerous.

In the year of our Lord 1625 there were four missions sent. One was of Franciscans to Yucatán, one of Mercenarians to Mexico; the other two, of Dominicans and Jesuits, were for the Philippines. At that time it was my fortune to reside among the Dominicans in Jerez, in Andalusia.

The Pope's Commissary for the Dominican mission was Friar Mateo de la Villa, who having a commission for thirty recruits and having gathered some twenty-four of them about Castile and Madrid, sent them by degrees well stored with money to Cádiz, to take up a convenient lodging for himself and the rest of his crew, till the time of the setting forth of the Indian fleet. This Commissary named one Friar Antonio Calvo to be his substitute, and to visit the cloisters of Andalusia lying in his way, namely, Cordova,

Seville, San Lucar, and Jerez, to try if out of them he could make up his complete number of thirty, which was after fully completed.

About the end of May came this worthy Calvo to Jerez, and in his company one Antonio Meléndez of the College of St. Gregory in Valladolid, with whom I had formerly near acquaintance. This Meléndez greatly rejoiced when he had found me; and being well stocked with Indian patacones, the first night of his coming invited me to his chamber to a stately supper.

The good Jerez sack, which was not spared, set my friend in such a heat of zeal of converting Japanese, that all his talk was of those parts never yet seen, and at least six thousand leagues distant. Bacchus metamorphosed him from a Divine into an orator, and made him a Cicero in parts of rhetorical eloquence. Nothing was omitted that might exhort me to join with him in that function, which he thought was apostolical. "No prophet is without honor save in his own country" was a great argument with him. Sometimes he propounded martyrdom for the Gospel sake, and spoke the glory after it. He would have his life and death printed, and poor Friar Anthony, a clothier's son of Segovia, would be styled St. Anthony by the Pope, and made collateral with the Apostles in heaven. Thus did Bacchus make him ambitious of honor upon the earth, and preferment in heaven.

When he thought this rhetoric had not prevailed, he began to act a Midas and Crœsus, fancying the Indies paved with tiles of gold and silver, the stones to be pearls, rubies, and diamonds, the trees to be hung with clusters of nutmegs bigger than the clusters of grapes of Canaan, and the fields to be planted with sugar-canes, which should so sweeten the chocolate that it should far exceed the milk and honey of the land of promise. The silks of China he conceited so common that the sails of the ships were nothing else, and finally he dreamed of Midas' happiness, that whatsoever he touched should be turned to gold.

Thus did Jerez nectar make my friend and mortified friar a covetous worldling. And yet from a rich covetous merchant did it shape him to a courtier in pleasures. He fancied the Philippines to be the Eden, where was all joy without tears, mirth without sadness, laughing without sorrow, comfort without grief, plenty without want, no not of Eves for Adams, excepted only that in it should be no forbidden fruit, but all lawful for the taste and sweetening of the palate. As Adam would have been as God, so Meléndez imagined himself a God in that Eden. Indian waits and trumpets should accompany him when he traveled, and nosegays should be presented to him when he entered any town; flowers and boughs should be strewed in his way; arches should be erected to ride under; bells for joy should be rung; and Indian knees for duty and homage, as to a God, should be bowed to the very ground.

From this inducing argument, and representation of a Paradise, he fell into a strong rhetorical point of curiosity, finding a tree of knowledge, and a philosophical maxim, "*Omnis homo naturaliter scire desiderat*," "man naturally inclines to know more and more." This knowledge he fancied could be nowhere more furnished with rare curiosities than in these parts. The gold and silver, which here are fingered, there should be known in their growth in the bowels of the earth; there should pepper be known in its season; the nutmeg and clove; the cinnamon as a rind or bark on a tree. There should we behold the fashioning of the sugar from a green growing cane into a loaf; the strange shaping the cochineal from a worm to a rich scarlet dye. The changing of the *tinta*, which is but grass with stalk and leaves, into an indigo black dye should be taught and learned. Thus should our ignorance be instructed without much labor with various and sundry curiosities of knowledge and understanding.

Finally, though Jerez liquor (grapes' bewitching tears) had put this bewitching eloquence into Antonio's brain, yet he did not doubt that he would like better his wine of the Philippines, growing on tall and high coconut palms, and he longed to drink in it a Spanish *brindis* in my company to all his friends remaining behind in Spain. Who would not be moved by these arguments to follow him, and his Calvo, or bald-pated Superior?

Thus supper being ended, my Meléndez desired to know how my heart stood affected to his journey, and breaking out into a "*Voto á Dios*" with his converting zeal, he swore he should not have a quiet night's rest until he were fully satisfied of my resolution to accompany him. And having learned the poet's expression, "*Quid non mortalia pectora cogis, Auri sacra fames?*" he offered unto me half-a-dozen of Spanish *pistoles*, assuring me that I should want nothing, and that the next morning Calvo should furnish me with whatsoever moneys I needed to buy things necessary for the comfort of that long and tedious journey.

I answered him that sudden resolutions might bring future grief and sorrow, and that I should that night lie down and take counsel with my pillow. I assured him that for his sake I would do much, and that if I resolved to go, my resolution should draw on another friend of mine, an Irish friar, named Tomás de León. Thus I took my leave of my Meléndez, and retired to my chamber and bed, which that night was no place of repose and rest to me as formerly it had been.

I must needs say that though most of Meléndez' arguments moved me not, yet the opportunity offered me to hide myself from all sight and knowledge of my dearest friends stirred up in me a serious thought of an angry and harsh letter, which not long before I had received out of England from mine own father. In this he had signified to me the displeasure of most of my friends and kindred, and his own grievous indignation against me, for that after he had spent so much money in training me up to learning, I had not only utterly refused to be of the Jesuits' Order (which was his only hopes) but had proved in my affections a deadly foe and enemy unto them. He had added that he would have thought his money better spent if I had been a scullion in a college of Jesuits than if I should prove a General of the Order of Dominicans; that I should never think to be welcome to my brothers nor kindred in England, nor to him. He had written that I should not expect ever more to hear from him, nor dare to see him if ever I returned to England, but expect that he would set upon me even Jesuits, whom I had deserted and opposed to chase me out of my country. He had also told me that though he had lost Haling House with much more means for his religion during his life, yet with the consent of my eldest brother (now governor of Oxford, and Mass-founder in that our famous University)[1] he would sell it away so that neither from the estate nor from money made of it, might I enjoy a child's part due unto me.

[1] Sir Henry Gage was made governor of Oxford, King Charles' headquarters, late in 1644, following his brilliant exploit of lifting the siege of Basing House. He died early in 1645. This aside of Gage's shows that he must have started writing his book about the beginning of 1645. It was first published in 1648.

These reasons stole that night's rest from my body, and sleep from my eyes, tears keeping them unclosed and open, lest Cynthia's black and mourning mantle should offer to cover, close, and shut them. To this letter's consideration was joined a strong opposition, which serious studies and ripeness of learning, with a careful discussion of some school-points and controversies, had bred in me against some of the chief Popish tenets.[2] Well could I have wished to come to England, there to satisfy and ease my troubled conscience. I well considered that if I stayed in Spain when my studies were completely finished, the Dominicans with a Pope's mandamus would send me home for a missionary to my country. But then I well considered the sight of a wrathful father and the power of a furious brother, a colonel, who (now, as I write, he is landed in England to search me out, and do me mischief) might violently assault me. I well considered the increased rabble of both Jesuits, who, with the influence of friends at court and with subtle plots and policies, would soon and easily hunt me out of England. Lastly, I well considered Meléndez' last inducing argument of the increase of knowledge natural by the insight of rich America and flourishing Asia, and of knowledge spiritual by a long contemplation of that new-planted Church, and of those Church planters' lives and conversations.

Wherefore, after a whole night's strife and inward debate, as the glorious planet began to banish night's dismal horror, rising with a bright and cheerful countenance, there rose in my mind a firm and settled resolution to visit America, and there to abide till death should surprise my angry father, that devoted Maecenas of Ignatius Loyola. I would remain there till I might there gain out of Potosí or Zacatecas treasure that might counterpoise that child's part, of which, for detesting the four-cornered cap and black coat of Jesuits, my father had deprived me.

So in recompense of the supper which my friend Anthony had bestowed upon me, I gave him a most pleasing breakfast by discovering to him my purpose and resolution to accompany him in his

[2] It is very difficult to believe that at this time Gage had any religious doubts. Such comments, which are frequent, were surely for the benefit of his Puritan readers. More than fifteen years after his encounter with Meléndez, Gage was still a priest in good standing in the Roman Catholic church. He had had ample opportunity to leave the church any time after his return to England in December, 1637.

long and naval journey. And at noon I feasted him with a dinner of one dish more than his breakfast, to wit, the company also of my Irish friend Tomás de León.

After dinner we both were presented to Calvo, the bald-pate Superior,[3] who immediately embraced us and promised us many courtesies in the way. He read to us a memorandum of what dainties he had provided for us, what varieties of fish and flesh, how many sheep, how many gammons of bacon, how many fat hens, how many hogs, how many barrels of white biscuit, how many jars of wine of Casalla, and what store of rice, figs, olives, capers, raisins, lemons, sweet and sour oranges, pomegranates, comfits, preserves, conserves,

and all sorts of Portugal sweetmeats. He flattered us that he would make us Masters of Arts and of Divinity in Manila. Then he opened his purse, and freely gave us to spend that day in Jerez, and to buy what most we had a mind to, and enough to carry us to Cádiz. Lastly, he opened his hands to bestow upon us the Holy Father's benediction, that no mischief might befall us in our way.

We were much frowned at by the Dominicans, our chief friends

[3] *"Calvo"* means "bald" in Spanish. Gage relishes the pun, which must have been meaningless to most of his readers, for he makes it three times in this chapter. Probably it was a standing joke among the young friars, and its use here may have recalled to Gage those happy and carefree days.

of Jerez, but the liberty which with Meléndez we enjoyed that day about the city of Jerez took from us all sad thoughts, which so sudden a departure from our friends might have caused in us. And Calvo with cunning policy persuaded us to depart from Jerez the next morning. This willingly we performed in company of Meléndez and another Spanish friar of that city, leaving our chests and books to Calvo to send after us, and that day we traveled like Spanish Dons upon our little *borricos,* or asses, towards Puerto de Santa María, taking in our way that stately Convent of Carthusians, and the river of Guadalethe, the former poets' river of oblivion, tasting of the fruits of those Elysian fields and gardens and drinking of Guadalethe's crystal streams, that so perpetual oblivion might blind and cover all those abstractive species which the intuitive knowledge of Spain's and Jerez' pleasant objects had deeply stamped in our thoughts and hearts.

At evening we came to that *puerto* so famous for harboring Spain's chief galleys, and at that time Don Federico de Toledo, hearing of the arrival of four Indian Apostles, would not lose that occasion of some soul-sanctification (which he thought might be his purchase) by entertaining us that night at supper. The town thought their streets blessed with our walking in them, and wished they might enjoy some reliques from us, whom they beheld as appointed to martyrdom for Christ and Anti-Christ's sake together; the galley slaves strived who should sound their waits and trumpets most joyfully. Don Federico spared no cost in fish and flesh that night, doubting that by receiving four prophets, he should receive a fourfold reward hereafter. Supper being ended, we were conveyed by Don Federico's gentlemen to the cloister of the Minims [Franciscan mendicants] appointed by Don Federico to lodge us that night. To show their brotherly love, they washed our feet, and so recommended us to quiet and peaceable rest.

The next morning, after a stately breakfast bestowed upon us by those poor mendicant friars, a boat was prepared for us and Don Federico's gentlemen waited on us to convey us to Cádiz, where we found out our fellow Apostles and the Pope's Commissary, Friar Mateo de la Villa, who welcomed us with Rome's indulgences, *a culpa & a pena,* and with a flourishing table stored with fish and flesh for dinner. There we continued in daily honor and estimation, enjoying the most pleasant sights which Cádiz both by sea and land could afford unto us, until the time of the fleet's departing. When it drew near, our Grand Apostle Friar Mateo de la Villa (whom we thought burned with zeal of martyrdom) took his leave of us, showing us the Pope's commission to nominate in his place whom he list, and naming bald Calvo for Superior. He himself returned to Madrid with more desire to enjoy a bishopric in Spain (as we understood) than to sacrifice his life in Japan.

His departure caused a mutiny among us, and cooled the spirit of two of our missionaries, who privily fled from us. The rest were pleased with honest Calvo, for he was a simple and ignorant old man (whom they could more jeer than any way respect), more scullion-like in daily greasing his white habit with handling his fat gammons of bacon than like a Pope's Commisary. The Pope's toe the proudest of our missioners then would willingly have kissed, yet Calvo's greasy fists the humblest would loath to have kissed. Thus under a sloven was that Apostolical Mission to be conveyed first to Mexico, three thousand Spanish leagues from Spain, and afterwards three thousand leagues further from thence to Manila, the Metropolitan and Court-City of the Philippine Islands.

2. Of the Indian Fleet that departed from Cádiz, Anno Dom. *1625, and of some remarkable passages in that voyage*

UPON THE FIRST of July in the afternoon, Don Carlos de Ybarra, admiral of the Galleons that then lay in the Bay of Cádiz, gave order that a warning piece should be shot off to warn all passengers, soldiers, and mariners to betake themselves the next morning to their ships. O, what was it to see some of our apostolical company who had enjoyed much liberty for a month in Cádiz now hang down their heads, and act with sad and demure looks, loath to depart, and cry out, *"Bonum est nos hic esse,"* "It is good for us to be here." Amongst them one Friar Juan de Pacheco made the warning piece to be a warning to him to hide himself and could no more be found amongst his fellow missioners, thinking it a part of hard cruelty to forsake a young Franciscan nun to whom he had engaged and wholly devoted his heart.

The second of July in the morning early, notice was given unto us that one Friar Pablo de Londres, an old crab-faced English friar living in San Lucar, had got the Duke of Medina's letter and sent it to the Governor of Cádiz charging him to search for me and to stay me, signifying the King of Spain's will and pleasure that no English should pass to the Indies, having a country of their own to convert. This that old friar did to stop my passage, having before wrote unto me many letters to the same purpose. Previously he had sent me a letter from that father master that was in England before, with the Count of Gondomar, alias Friar Diego de la Fuente, then Provincial of Castile, wherein that Superior offered me many kind offers of preferment if I would desist from my journey, and return

15

to him to Castile, but none of these letters could prevail with me. Nor did the Governor's searching stop me, for immediately I was conveyed alone to our ship, and there closely hid in a barrel that was emptied of biscuit to that purpose. When the Governor came a shipboard to enquire for an Englishman, Friar Calvo, having the father of liars in my stead about him, resolutely denied me, who would not be found, because not sought for in a barrel's belly. Thus found our Apostles sport and talk that first day.

Then the ships went out one by one, crying, "*A dios, A dios*," and the town replying, "*Buen viaje, buen viaje*"; when all were out and no hopes of enjoying more Cádiz' pleasures and liberty, then began my young friars to wish themselves again aland: some began presently to feed the fishes with their nuns' sweet dainties; others to wonder at the number of stately ships, which with eight galleons that went to convey us beyond the Canary Islands were forty-one in all, some for one port of the Indies, and some for another. To Porto Rico went that year two ships; to Santo Domingo three, to Jamaica two, to Margarita one, to Havana two, to Cartagena three, to Campeche two, to Honduras and Trujillo two, and to San Juan de Ulua, or Vera Cruz, sixteen; all laden with wines, figs, raisins, olives, oil, cloth, kerseys [coarse woolens], linen, iron, and quicksilver for the mines, to fetch out the pure silver of Zacatecas from the earthen dross from whence it is digged.

The persons of most note that went that year was first the Marqués de Serralvo with his lady, who went for viceroy of Mexico instead of the Count de Gélves, then retired to a cloister for fear of the common people, who the year before had mutinied against him. This Marqués went in the ship called San Andrés, and with him in the same ship went Don Martín de Carrillo, a priest and inquisitor of the Inquisition of Valladolid, who was sent for visitor-general to Mexico to examine the strife between the Conde de Gélves and the Archbishop, and the mutiny that for their sakes had happened, with full commission and authority to imprison, banish, hang, and execute all delinquents. In the ship called *Santa Gertrudis* went Don Juan Niño de Toledo, who was sent to be president of Manila in the Philippines, and in the same ship with him went the whole Mission of thirty Jesuits sent to the Philippines, who had already got the favor of the President, and politicly sought to be passengers in the same ship, that so they might the more ingratiate themselves to him, for this cunning generation studies purposely how to insinuate themselves with kings, princes, great men, rulers, and commanders. In the ship called *San Antonio* went my Dominican Mission of twenty-seven friars. In the *Nuestra Señora de Regla* went four and twenty Mercenarian friars bound for Mexico, part of those that afterwards drew their knives to slash and cut the Creoles of their profession.

Thus with the convoy of eight galleons for fear of Turks and Hollanders (whom the Spanish Dons shake and tremble at) our fleet set forward with a pleasant and prosperous gale, with a quiet and milken sea, until we came to the gulf called *Golfo de Yeguas*, or of Kicking Mares. There the waves and swelling surges did so kick our ships that we thought they would have kicked our St. Anthony's gilded image out of our ship, and bereaved my Antonio Meléndez of his gilt and painted idol, to whom he daily bowed and prayed against the merciless element. We feared that all our ship's galleries would have been torn from us with these spurnings and blows of that outrageous gulf. But at last, having overcome the danger of this gulf, the eight galleons took their leave of us, and left our merchant ships now to shift for themselves.

The departure of these galleons was most solemnly performed on each side, saluting each other with their ordnance, visiting each other with their cock-boats, the Admiral of the Fleet feasting with a stately dinner in his ship the Admiral of the Galleons; and the like performing most of the other ships to the several colonels and captains and other their allied friends that were of the Royal Fleet. Here it was worth noting to hear the sighs of many of our Indian Apostles, wishing they might return again in any of those galleons to Spain. Their zeal was now cold, and some endeavored many ways for Calvo's licence to return, but that could not be granted; others employed themselves most of that day in writing letters to their friends in Cádiz.

Thus dinner being ended, and the two Admirals solemnly taking their leaves, the warning piece being shot off for the galleons to join together, and turn their course to Spain, we bad mutual *adieu*, crying one to another, *"Buen viaje, Buen pasaje."* We kept our course towards America, sailing before the wind constantly till we came to America. A thing worth noting in that voyage from Spain to the

Indies is that after the Canary Islands are once left, there is one constant wind continuing to America still the same without any opposition or contrariety of other winds. This so prosperous and full on the sails, that did it blow constantly and were it not interrupted with many calms, doubtless the voyage might be ended in a month or less.

Such were the many calms we had that we got no sight of any land till the twentieth day of August, so that near six weeks we sailed as on a river of fresh water. We much delighted and sported ourselves in fishing many sorts of fishes, but especially one, which by the Spaniards is called *dorado*, the golden fish, for the skin and scales of it that glitter like gold. Of this sort we found such abundance that no sooner was the hook with any small bait cast into the sea, when presently the *dorado* was caught, so that we took them many times for pleasure and cast them again into the sea, being a fish fitter to be eaten fresh than salted. Many were the feasts and sports used in the ships, till we discovered the first land, or island, called Deseada.

The last day of July, which was, according to the Jesuits' Order, and Rome's appointment, the day of Ignatius their patron and founder of their religion, the gallant ship called *Sta Gertrudis*, wherein went thirty Jesuits, for their and their saint's sake made to all the rest of the fleet a most gallant show. She was trimmed round about with white linen, her flags and top-gallants representing some the Jesuits' arms, others the picture of Ignatius himself, and this from the evening before. They shot off that night at least fifty shot of ordnance, besides four or five hundred squibs (the weather being very calm), and all her masts and tacklings were hung with paper lanthorns having burning lights within them; the waits ceased not from sounding, nor the Spaniards from singing all night. The day's solemn sport was likewise great, the Jesuits increasing the Spaniards' joy with an open procession in the ship, singing their hymns and anthems to their saint, and all this seconded with roaring ordnance, no powder being spared for the completing of that day's joy and triumph.

The fourth of August following, being the day which Rome doth dedicate to Dominic, the first founder of the Dominicans or Preachers' Order, the ship wherein I was, the *San Antonio*, strove to exceed

Sta Gertrudis by the assistance of the twenty-seven Dominicans that were in her. All was performed both by night and day as formerly in *Sta Gertrudis* both with powder, squibs, lights, waits, and music. And further did the Dominicans' joy and triumph exceed the Jesuits', in that they invited all the Jesuits, with Don Juan Niño de Toledo, the president of Manila, and the Captain of the *Sta Gertrudis* to a stately dinner both of fish and flesh. This dinner being ended, they had prepared for the afternoon's sport a comedy out of famous Lope de Vega, to be acted by some soldiers, passengers, and some of the younger friars. This I confess was as stately acted and set forth both in shows and good apparel, in that narrow compass of our ship, as might have been upon the best stage in the Court of Madrid. The comedy being ended, and a banquet of sweetmeats prepared for the closing of that day's mirth, both ours and *Sta Gertrudis'* cock-boat carried back our invited friends, bidding each other *adieu* with our waits and chiefest ordnance. Thus went we on our sea voyage without any storm, with pleasant gales, many calms, daily sports and pastimes till we discovered the first land called Deseada upon the twentieth day of August.

3. Of our discovery of some islands, and what trouble befell us in one of them

THE ADMIRAL of our Fleet wondered much at our slow sailing, for from the second of July to the 19 of August we had neither seen nor discovered any land, save only the Canary Islands, and so the same day in the morning he called to council all the pilots of the ships, to know their opinions concerning our present situation and the nearness of land. The ships therefore drew near the Admiral one by one, that every pilot might deliver his opinion. Here was cause of laughter enough for the passengers to hear the wise pilots' skill; one saying we were three hundred miles, another two hundred, another one hundred, another fifty, another more, another less, all erring much from the truth (as afterward appeared) save only one old pilot of the smallest vessel of all. He affirmed resolutely that with that small gale wherewith we then sailed we should come to Guadeloupe the next morning. All the rest laughed at him, but he might well have laughed at them, for the next morning by sunrising we plainly discovered an island called Deseada by the Spaniards, or the Desired Land, for that at the first discovery of the Indies it was the first land the Spaniards found, they being then as desirous to find some land after many days' sailing as we were. After this island, presently we discovered another called Marie Galante, then another called Dominica, and lastly, another named Guadeloupe,[1] which was that we aimed at to refresh ourselves in, to

[1] Gage seems to be a little mixed. For unless the fleet was blown off its course, it would hardly have sighted Dominica. The other two islands are much closer to Guadeloupe. Occasional errata of this nature probably result from a misreading by Gage of a somewhat obscure entry in his diary, which he obviously kept. Indeed,

wash our foul clothes, and to take in fresh water, whereof we stood in great need. By two or three of the clock in the afternoon we came to a safe road lying before the island, where we cast our anchors, no ways fearful of the naked barbarians of that and the other islands, who with great joy do yearly expect the Spanish fleet's coming. By the moons they reckon the months, and thereby make their guess at their coming, and some prepare their sugar-canes, others plantains, others tortoise, some one provision, some another to barter with the Spaniards for their small haberdashery, or iron, knives, or such things which may help them in their wars, which commonly they make against some other islands. Before our anchors were cast, out came the Indians to meet us in their canoes, round like troughs, some whereof had been painted by our English, some by the Hollanders, some by the French, as might appear by their several arms, for it is a common road and harbor to all nations that sail to America.

Before we resolved to go to shore, we tasted of those Indian fruits, the plantain above all pleasing our taste and palate. We could not but much wonder at that sight never yet seen by us of people naked, with their hair hanging down to the middle of their backs, with their faces cut out in several fashions, or flowers, with thin plates hanging at their noses, like hog-rings. They fawned on us like children, some speaking in their unknown tongue, others using signs for such things as we imagined they desired. Their sign for some of our Spanish wine was easily perceived, and their request most willingly granted by our men, who with one reasonable cup of Spanish sack presently tumbled up their heels, and left them like swine tumbling on the deck of our ship.

After our people had sported a while with these rude and savage Indians, our two cock-boats were ready to carry to shore such as either had clothes to wash or a desire to bathe themselves in a river of fresh water which is within the island, or a mind to set their feet again upon unmovable lands after so many days of uncertain footing in a floating and reeling ship. But that day being far spent, our friars resolved to stay in the ship, and the next whole day to visit the island. Many of the mariners and passengers of all the

the original title speaks of the book as "containing a journall of three thousand and three hundred miles within the main land of America."

ships went that evening to shore, some returning at night, and some without fear continuing with the Indians all night on shore. The next morning I and most of our friars went, and, having hired some Spaniards to wash our clothes, we wandered sometimes all together sometimes two and two, and sometimes one alone about the island, meeting with many Indians, who did us no hurt, but rather like children fawned upon us, offering us of their fruits, and begging of us whatsoever toys of pins, points, or gloves they espied about us. We ventured to go to some of their houses which stood by a pleasant river, and were by them kindly entertained, eating of their fish and wild deer's flesh.

About noon we chanced to meet in the midst of the mountain with some of the Jesuits of the *Santa Gertrudis*, who were in very earnest talk with a mulatto, all naked like the rest of the Indians. This mulatto was a Christian, born in Seville in Spain, and had been slave there formerly to a rich merchant. His name was Luis; and he spoke the Spanish language very perfectly. Some twelve years before he had run away from his master by reason of hard and slavish usage, and having got to Cádiz, offering his service to a gentleman then bound for America, the gentleman fearing not that his true master should ever have more notice of him from a new world, took him a shipboard with him as his slave. The mulatto, remembering the many stripes which he had suffered from his first cruel master, feared that from America he might by some intelligence or other be sent back again to Spain, and he also feared that his second master (whose blows he had begun to suffer in the ship) would prove as cruel as his first. Accordingly, when the ships arrived at Guadeloupe, he resolved rather to die among the Indians (which he knew might be his hardest fortune) then evermore to live in slavery under Spaniards. So casting his life upon good or bad fortune, he hid himself among the trees in the mountain till the ships were departed. After being found by the Indians, and giving them some toys which he had got by stealth from his master, he was entertained by them, they liking him, and he them.

Thus this poor Christian slave continued among those barbarians from year to year, and he had care to hide himself at the coming of the Spanish fleet yearly. In twelve years that he had thus continued amongst them he had learned their language, and was married to an Indian, by whom he had three children living. The Jesuits by chance having met with him, and perceiving more by the wool upon his head that he was a mulatto than by his black and tawny skin (for those Indians paint themselves all over with a red color), they presently imagined the truth, that he could not come thither but with some Spaniard, so entering into discourse with him, and finding him to speak Spanish, they got the whole truth of him.

Then we, joining with the Jesuits, began to persuade the poor Christian to forsake that heathenish life, wherein his soul could never be saved, promising him if he would go along with us he should be free from slavery for ever. Poor soul, though he had lived twelve years without hearing a word of the true God, worshipping stocks and stones with the other heathens, yet when he heard again of Christ, of eternal damnation in hell's torments, and of everlasting salvation in Heaven's joys, he began to weep, assuring us that he would go with us, were it not for his wife and children, whom he tenderly loved and could not forsake. To this we replied that he might be a means of saving likewise their souls, if he would bring them with him; and further that we would assure him that care should be taken that neither he, his wife, nor children should ever want means competent for the maintenance of their lives. The mulatto hearkened well to all this, though a sudden fear surprised him, because certain Indians passed by and noted his long conference with us. The poor and timorous mulatto then told us that he was in danger for having been known by us, and that he feared the Indians would kill him, and suspect that we would steal him away. If they did that, and it were noised about the island, we should soon see their love changed into cruel rage and mutiny.

We persuaded him not to fear anything they could do to us, for we had soldiers, guns, and ordnance to secure ours and his life also. We wished him to resolve to bring his wife and children to the seaside, where our men were drying their clothes, and they would defend him, and a boat should be ready to convey him with his wife and children a shipboard. The mulatto promised to do as we had counselled him, and that he would entice his wife and children to the seaside to barter their wares for ours, desiring some of the Jesuits (whom he said he should know by their black coats) to be there ready for him with a cock-boat. Luis departed, and as he seemed resolute in what he had agreed, our joy likewise was great with the hope of bringing five souls out of the darkness of heathenish idolatry to the light of Christianity.

The Jesuits who had begun with this mulatto were desirous that the happy end and conclusion might be their glory. So taking their leaves of us, they hastened to the sea to inform the Admiral of what they had done, and to provide that the cock-boat of their ship might be in readiness to receive Luis and his family. We likewise returned to the shore to see if our shirts and clothes were dry. Most of us, myself included, finding our linen ready and our boat on shore, went aboard our ship, leaving two or three of our company with many from other ships on shore, especially the Jesuits waiting for their prey. When we came to our ship, most of our friars, with what love that they had found in the barbarians, were inflamed with a new zeal of staying in that island and converting those heathens to Christianity, apprehending it an easy business (they being a loving people) and no ways dangerous to us, by reason of the fleet that yearly passeth that way and might enquire after our usage. But by some it was objected that it was a rash and foolish zeal with great hazard of their lives, and many inconveniences were objected against so blind and simple an attempt. But those that were most zealous slighted all reasons, saying that the worst that could happen to them could be but to be butchered, sacrificed, and eaten up, and that for such a purpose they had come out of Spain to be crowned with the crown of martyrdom for confessing and preaching Jesus Christ.

While we were hot in this solemn consultation, behold an uproar on the shore. Our people were running to and fro to save their lives, leaving their clothes and hasting to the cock-boats, filling them so fast and so full that some sunk with all the people in them. Above all, most pitiful and lamentable were the cries of some of our women, many casting themselves to the sea, choosing rather to venture to be taken up by some boat, or at worst to be drowned, than to be taken and to be cruelly butchered by the Indians. We wondered at this sudden alteration, not knowing the cause of it, but at last perceived the arrows to come out thick from the wood from behind the trees, and thereby guessed at the truth that the barbarians were mutinied. The uproar lasted not half an hour, for presently our Admiral shot off two or three pieces of ordnance and sent a company of soldiers to shore to guard it and our people with their muskets. This was well and suddenly performed, and all the Indians soon dispersed. Our cock-boat brought to us three of our friars who had remained on the land, among them one Friar Juan de la Cueva, who was dangerously shot and wounded in one of his shoulders. This friar had been earnest with me to stay on shore with him, which I refused, and so escaped that cruel and fiery onset of the Indians. Besides those that were drowned and taken up at shore (which were fifteen persons), two Jesuits were found dead upon the sand, three more dangerously wounded, three passengers likewise slain, ten wounded, besides three more of the fleet who could never be found alive or dead, and were thought to have been found in the wood by the Indians, and to have been murdered by them.[2]

Our mulatto Luis came not according to his word, but in his stead a sudden army of treacherous Indians, which gave us motive enough to think that either Luis himself had discovered the Jesuits' plot to take him away with his wife and children, or that the Indians suspecting it by his talk with us, had made him confess it. And certainly this was the ground of their mutiny; for whereas Luis before had said that he would know the Jesuits by their black coats, it seems he had well described them above all the rest unto the Indians, for (as it was after well observed) most of their arrows were directed to the black marks, for five of them were slain and wounded in little above a quarter of an hour.

All that night our soldiers guarded the coast, often shooting off their muskets to affright the Indians, who appeared no more unto us. All that night we slept little, for we watched our ship, lest the Indians in their canoes should set upon us and take us asleep. Some lamented the dead and drowned, others pitied our wounded Friar Juan de la Cueva, who all that night lay in great torment and mis-

---

[2] Irving Rouse, of the Department of Anthropology, Yale University, and a leading authority on the Indians of the West Indies writes: "The sequence of events given by Gage is quite similar to other accounts I have seen; i.e., peaceful reception followed by attack. The use of poisoned arrows and the painting of the body red are also characteristic of the Carib. So far as I know, the first settlements in the area were not made until 1623, when the British and the French conquered St. Kitts. The settlement of Guadeloupe came shortly thereafter. Therefore, I would have expected to find the conditions on the island which he describes."

ery, others laughed and jeered at those zealous friars who would have stayed in that island to convert the barbarians, saying they had had their full desire of martyrdom, for had they been but that night with the Indians, doubtless they had been shred for their suppers. But we perceived their zeal was now cool, and they desired no more to stay with such a barbarous kind of people, but rather wished the Admiral would shoot off the warning piece for us all to take up our anchors and depart from so dangerous a place. In the morning all the ships made haste to take in such fresh water as was necessary for their voyage yet to America. A strong watch was kept along the coast, and a guard guarded our men to the river; and all the morning while this was doing, not one Indian could be found or seen, nor did our three men that were missing appear. Thus at noon with a pleasant and prosperous gale we hoisted up our sails, leaving the islands and harbor of Guadeloupe.

4. Of our further sailing to San Juan de Ulua, alias Vera Cruz, and of our landing there

UPON THE 22 day of August, we sailed so pleasantly that we soon left the sight of the islands. The Indians' uproar had weaved for us a thread of long discourse. It made some hate their calling to teach and convert Indians. But Calvo encouraged us, telling us many stories of the good and gentle nature of the Indians of the Philippines, to whom we were going, and that most of them were Christians already, esteeming their priests as gods upon the earth; and that those that were not as yet converted to Christianity were kept in awe by the power of the Spaniards. Our chief care the first two or three days was to look to our plantains which we got from the Indians. This fruit pleased us all exceedingly, judging it to be as good or better than any fruit in Spain. It is not gathered ripe from the tree; but being gathered green, it is hung up some days, and so ripens and grows yellow and mellow, and every bit as sweet as honey. Our sugar-canes were no less pleasing unto us, whilst chewing the pith, we refreshed and sweetened our mouths with the juice. We fed for the first week upon almost nothing but tortoise; which seemed to us, who had never before seen it, a sea monster, the shell being so hard as to bear any cart-wheel, and in some cases above two yards broad. When first they were opened, we were amazed to see the number of eggs that were in them, a thousand being the least that we judged to be in some of them. Our Spaniards made with them an excellent broth with all sorts of spices. The meat seemed rather flesh than sea fish, which, being corned with salt and hung up two or three days in the air, tasted like veal. Thus our hens, our sheep, our powdered beef, and gammons of bacon, which we brought

27

from Spain, were some days slighted, while with greedy stomachs we fell hard to our sea veal.

After four days' sail, our Friar Juan de la Cueva, who had been shot by the Indians, died, all his body being swelled, which gave us just occasion to think that the arrow which was shot into his shoulder was poisoned. His burial was as solemnly performed as could be at sea, his grave being the whole ocean. He had weighty stones hung to his feet, two more to his shoulders, and one to his breast; and then the Romish requiem being sung for his soul, his corpse being held out to the sea on the ship side with ropes ready to let him fall, all the ship crying out three times, *"Buen Viaje,"* "A good voyage," to his soul chiefly, and also to his corpse ready to travel to the deep to feed the whales. At the first cry all the ordnance were shot off, the ropes on a sudden loosed, and Juan de la Cueva with the weight of heavy stones plunged deep into the sea, whom no mortal eyes ever more beheld. The like we saw performed in the ship *Santa Gertrudis* to another Jesuit, one of the three who had been dangerously wounded by the Indians of Guadeloupe. He died like our friar, his body being swelled as with poison.

Now our sailing was more comfortable than before, for we passed in the sight of the land of Porto Rico, and then of the great island of Santo Domingo; and here our company began to be lessened, some departing to Porto Rico, and Santo Domingo, others to Cartagena, and Havana, and Honduras, Jamaica and Yucatán. We of the fleet for Mexico remained now alone, and so sailed till we came to what the Spaniards call *La Sonda,* or the Sound of Mexico, for here we often sounded the sea. This was so calm that a whole week we were stayed for want of wind, scarce stirring from the place where first we were caught by the calm. Here likewise we had great sport in fishing, filling again our bellies with *dorados,* and saving that provision which we had brought from Spain. But the heat was so extraordinary that the day was no pleasure unto us, for the repercussion of the sun's heat upon the still water and pitch of our ships kindled a scorching fire, which all the day distempered our bodies with a constant running sweat, forcing us to cast off most of our clothes.

The evenings and nights were somewhat more comfortable, yet the heat which the sun had left in the pitched ribs and planks of the ship was such that under deck and in our cabins we were not able to sleep, but in our shirts were forced to walk, or sit, or lie upon the deck. The mariners fell to washing themselves and to swimming, till the unfortunate death of one in the ship called *San Francisco* made them suddenly leave off that sport. Nearer to the mainland, the sea abounds with a monstrous fish [shark] called by the Spaniards *tiburón*. Some mistake this fish for the cayman, or crocodile, holding them both for one and thinking that it is only the cayman or crocodile (by abuse called *tiburón*) which devours man's flesh, a whole joint at a bite in the water. The mistake is gross, for the cayman is plated all over with shells, whereas the *tiburón* hath no shells, but only, like other great sea fishes, a thick skin. The Indians eat the cayman, yet the Spaniards hate it, but eat the *tiburón*.

In our ship, catching one with a tridental iron fork, and haling him with a cable rope to the ship side, and then binding him with it (being as much as a dozen or fifteen men could do to hoist him up into the ship), we found him to be a most monstrous creature, twelve ells long at least. We salted the meat, and found it tasted like flesh, as hath been said of the tortoise. This kind is as ravenous after man's flesh as the crocodile, and many of them were to be seen in this Sound of Mexico.

The Spaniards bathing themselves daily by the ship's side (where there is no such danger of the *tiburón*, who useth not to come too near the ships), one mariner of the ship called *San Francisco*, being more venturous than the rest and offering to swim from his ship to see some friends in another not far off, chanced to be a most unfortunate prey to one of them. Before any boat could be set out to help him, he was seen to be pulled thrice under water by the monster, who devoured a leg, an arm, and part of his shoulder. The rest of the body was after found and taken up, and carried to the *San Francisco*, and there buried in the form and manner as hath been said of our Friar Juan de la Cueva. This mischance sadded all our fleet for three days till it pleased God to refresh our burning heat with a cool and prosperous wind, driving us out of that calm sound, which (if we had continued in it with that excessive heat) might have proved most unsound and unhealthy to our bodies.

Three days after we had sailed, being Monday in the morning about seven of the clock, one of our friars saying Mass, and all the people in the ship kneeling to hear it, one mariner with a loud and sudden voice crieth out, *"Tierra, Tierra, Tierra,"* "Land, Land, Land." This rejoiced the hearts of all that were in the ship, as it seemed, more than their Mass, for leaving that, they arose from their knees to behold the continent of America. Great was the joy of all the ships that day, and great was the slaughter which our old Calvo made that day among his fowls (which he had spared formerly), to feast his friars. About ten of the clock the whole face of the land was visibly apparent, and we with full sail running to embrace it.

Our wise Admiral knew the danger of the coast, and especially the dangerous entering into the haven, by reason of the many rocks that lie about it and are known only by marks and flags set out to give all ships warning of them. Perceiving that with the wind wherewith we sailed then, we should not come to the port till towards evening, he feared lest some north wind (which is dangerous upon that coast, and ordinary in the month of September) should in the night arise and endanger all our ships upon the rocks. He therefore called to council all the pilots, to know whether it were best to keep on our sailing with full sail that day, with hopes to get that day in good time into the haven, or else with the middle sail only to draw near, that the next morning with more security we might be guided in with the help of boats from land. The result of the council was not to venture that day too near unto the port, for fear of being benighted, but to pull down all but the middle sail. The wind began to calm, and our ships to move slowly towards land, and so we continued till night.

A double watch was kept that night in our ship, and the pilot was more watchful himself and more careful than at other times. But our friars betook themselves to their rest, which continued not long, for before midnight the wind turned to the north, which caused a sudden and general cry and uproar in ours, and all the other ships. Their fear was more for the apprehension of danger by that kind of wind, and of what might happen, than for what as yet the wind threatened, which was not strong nor boisterous. However, hallowed wax candles were lighted by the friars, knees bowed to Mary, litanies and other hymns and prayers sung aloud unto her till towards the dawning of the day, when, behold, the north wind ceased, our wonted gale began to blow again. It was God's will and pleasure, and no effect of the friars' prayers to Mary, who yet superstitiously to deceive the simple people cried out, "*Milagro, milagro, milagro.*" "A miracle, a miracle, a miracle."

By eight o'clock in the morning we came to the sight of the houses, and made signs for boats to convey us into the haven. These immediately with great joy came out, and guided us one by one between those rocks which make that port as dangerous as any I have discovered in all my travels both upon the North and South Sea. Our waits played most pleasantly, our ordnance saluted both town and fort over against it, our hearts and countenances reciprocally rejoiced. We cast our anchors, which yet were not enough to secure our ships in that most dangerous haven, but further with cable ropes we secured them to iron rings, which for that purpose are fastened into the wall of the fort, for fear of the strong and boisterous northern winds. And thus welcoming one another to a new world, many boats waiting for us, we presently went with joy to set footing in America.

5. Of our landing at Vera Cruz, otherwise San Juan de Ulua, and of our entertainment there

UPON THE 12 day of September, we happily arrived in America in that famous town call San Juan de Ulua, otherwise Vera Cruz, famous for that it was the first beginning of the famous conquest of that valiant and ever renowned conqueror, Hernando Cortés. Here first was that noble and generous resolution, that never heard of policy, to sink the ships which had brought the first Spaniards to that continent, greater than any of the other three parts of the world. Thereby they might think of nothing but such a conquest as after followed, being destitute of the help of their ships, and without hopes evermore to return to Cuba, Yucatán, or any of those parts from whence they had come. Here it was that the first five hundred Spaniards strengthened themselves against millions of enemies, and against the biggest fourth part of all the world. Here were the first magistrates, judges, aldermen, officers of justice named.

The proper name of the town is San Juan de Ulua, otherwise called Vera Cruz, from the old harbor and haven of Vera Cruz, six leagues from this, and so called for that upon Good Friday it was first discovered. But the old Vera Cruz proving too dangerous an harbor for ships, by reason of the violence of the northern winds, it was utterly forsaken by the Spaniards, who removed to San Juan de Ulua, where their ships found the first safe road by reason of a rock, which is a strong defense against the winds. And because the memory of the work of that Good Friday should never be forgotten, to San Juan de Ulua they have added the name also of Vera Cruz, taken from that first haven which was discovered upon Good Friday, *anno* 1519.

As soon as we came to shore, we found very solemn preparations for entertainment, all the town being resorted to the seaside, all the priests and canons of the cathedral church, all the religious orders of the several convents (which are there Dominicans, Franciscans, Mercenarians, and Jesuits) being in a readiness, with their crosses borne before them, to guide the new Viceroy of Mexico, in procession, to the chief cathedral church. The friars and Jesuits were quicker in going to land than the great Don, the Marqués de Serralvo, and his lady. Some of them kissed the ground as holy, in their opinion, for the conversion of those Indians to Christianity, who before had worshipped idols and sacrificed to devils; others kneeled upon their knees making short prayers, some to the Virgin Mary, others to such saints as they best affected; and so betook themselves to the places and stations of those of their profession.

In the meantime with all the cannon playing both from ships and castle, the Viceroy and his lady and all his train landed, together with Don Martín de Carrillo, the Visitor-General for the strife between the Count of Gélves, the last Viceroy, and the Archbishop of Mexico. The great Don and his lady being placed under a canopy of state, the *Te Deum* began to be sung with much variety of musical instruments, all marching in procession to the Cathedral, where with many lights of burning lamps, torches, and wax candles, the Host was to the view of all set upon the high altar. All knees were bowed, a prayer of thanksgiving sung, holy water sprinkled upon all the people by a priest, and lastly a Mass with three priests solemnly celebrated. This being ended, the Viceroy was attended on by the Chief High Justice, named *Alcalde Mayor,* by the officers of the town, some judges sent from Mexico to that purpose, and all the soldiers of the ships and town unto his lodging. The friars likewise in procession with their cross before them were conducted to their several cloisters.

Friar Calvo presented his Dominicans to the Prior of the cloister of St. Dominic, who entertained us very lovingly with some sweetmeats, and everyone with a cup of the Indian drink called chocolate, whereof I shall speak hereafter. This refreshment being ended, we proceeded to a better, which was a most stately dinner both of fish and flesh. No fowls were spared, many capons, turkey cocks, and hens were prodigally lavished, to shew us the abundance and plenty of provision of that country. The Prior of this cloister was no staid, ancient, grey-headed man, such as usually are made Superiors to govern young and wanton friars, but he was a gallant and amorous young spark, who (as we were there informed) had obtained from his Superior, the Provincial, the government of that convent with a bribe of a thousand ducats.

After dinner he had some of us to his chamber, where we observed his lightness and little favor of religion or mortification in him. We thought to have found in his chamber some stately library, which might tell us of learning and love of study; we found not above a dozen old books, standing in a corner covered with dust and cobwebs, as if they were ashamed that the treasure that lay hid in them should be so much forgotten and undervalued, and the *guitar* (the Spanish lute) preferred and set above them. His chamber was richly dressed and hung with many pictures, and with hangings, some made with cotton-wool, others with various colored feathers of Michoacán; his tables covered with carpets of silk; his cupboards adorned with several sorts of China cups and dishes, stored within with several dainties of sweetmeats and conserves.[1]

This sight seemed to the zealous friars of our Mission most vain, and unbeseeming a poor and mendicant friar; to the others, whose end in coming from Spain to those parts was liberty, and looseness, and covetousness of riches, this sight was pleasing and gave them great encouragement to enter further into that country, where soon a mendicant Lazarus might become a proud and wealthy Dives.

The discourse of the young and light-headed Prior was nothing but vain boasting of himself, of his birth, his parts, his favor with the chief Superior or Provincial, the love which the best ladies, the richest merchants' wives of the town, bare unto him, of his clear and excellent voice, and great dexterity in music, whereof he presently

---

[1] The picture is rather overdrawn. The china cups were probably Talavera ware from the Mexican city of Puebla. Michoacán featherwork was also a native product and therefore relatively inexpensive. Beautiful textiles could be bought for next to nothing. As Gage well knew, priors were elected at Provincial chapters for four years, so a bribe to the Provincial might have been wasted money. Gage is obsessed with the idea that nearly all friars were engaged in amassing money for their own ends. He never seems to reflect what the friars could do with the money thus amassed. The number who, like him, took unsanctioned trips to Europe and needed private funds was decidedly limited.

gave us a taste, tuning his *guitar* and singing to us some verses (as he said, of his own composing) to some lovely Amaryllis, adding scandal to scandal, looseness to liberty, which it grieved some of us to see in a Superior who should have taught with words and in his life and conversation examples of repentance and mortification. No sooner were our senses of hearing delighted well with music, our sight with the objects of cotton-wool, silk, and feather-works, but presently our Prior caused to be brought forth of all his store of dainties, such variety as might likewise relish well and delight our sense of tasting.

Thus as we were truly transported from Europe to America, so the world seemed truly to be altered, our senses changed from what they were the night and day before when we heard the hideous noise of the mariners hoisting up sails, when we saw the deep and monsters of it, when we tasted the stinking water, when we smelt the tar and pitch. Here we heard a quivering and trembling voice and instrument well tuned, we beheld wealth and riches, we tasted what was sweet, and in the sweetmeats smelt the musk and civet wherewith that epicurean Prior had seasoned his conserves.

Here we broke up our discourse and pastimes, desirous to walk abroad and take a view of the town, having no more time than that and the next day to stay in it. We compassed it round about that afternoon; and found the situation of it to be sandy, except on the south-west side, where it is moorish ground, and full of standing bogs, which, with the great heats that are there, cause it to be a very unhealthy place. The number of inhabitants may be three thousand, and amongst them some very rich merchants, some worth two hundred, some three hundred, and some four hundred thousand ducats. Of the buildings little we observed, for they all, both houses, churches, and cloisters, built with boards and timber, the walls of the richest man's house being made but of boards, which with the impetuous winds from the north hath been cause that many times the town hath been for the most part of it burnt down to the ground.

The great trading from Mexico, and by Mexico from the East Indies, from Spain, from Cuba, Santo Domingo, Yucatán, and by Portobello from Peru, from Cartagena, and all the islands lying upon the North Sea, and by the River Alvarado going up to Zapotecas, San Ildefonso, and towards Oaxaca, and by the river Grijalva, running up to Tabasco, Los Zoques, and Chiapa de Indios, maketh this little town very rich and to abound with all the commodities of the continent land, and of all the East and West Indies' treasures.

The unhealthiness of the place is the reason of the paucity of inhabitants, and the paucity of them, together with the rich trading and commerce, the reasons that the merchants therein are extra-

ordinary rich. They might have been far richer had not the town been so often fired, and they in the fire had great losses. All the strength of this town is first the hard and dangerous entrance into the haven; and secondly, a rock which lieth before the town less than a musket-shot off, upon which is built a castle, and in the castle a slight garrison of soldiers. In the town there is neither fort nor castle, nor scarce any people of warlike minds. The rock and castle are as a wall, defense, and enclosure to the haven, which otherwise lieth wide open to the ocean, and to the northern winds. No ship dares cast anchor within the haven, but only under the rock and castle, and yet not sure enough so with anchors, except also they be bound and fastened with cables to rings of iron for that purpose to the side of the rock. Sometimes it hath happened that ships floating with the stream too much on one side the rock have been driven off and cast upon the other rocks or out to the ocean, the cables of their anchors and those wherewith they have been fastened to the castle being broken with the force of the winds. This happened to one of our ships the first night after we landed. We were happy that we were not then at sea, for there arose such a storm and tempest from the north that it quite broke the cables of one ship and drove it out to the main sea. We thought it would have blown and driven us out of our beds after it, for the slight boarded houses did so totter and shake that we expected every hour when they would fall upon our heads.

We had that first night enough of San Juan de Ulua, and little rest, though feasted as well at supper as at dinner by our vain, boasting Prior, who before we went to bed had caused all our feet to be washed. Now in easier beds than for above two months together the strait and narrow cabins of the ship had allowed us, our sleep might be more quiet and more nourishing to our bodies, but the whistling winds and tottering chambers, which made our beds uneasy cradles to us, caused us to fly from our rest at midnight, and with our bare (though washed) feet to seek the dirty yard for safer shelter.

In the morning the friars of the cloister, who were acquainted with those winds and storms, laughed at our fearfulness, assuring us that they never slept better than when their beds were rocked with such-like blasts. But that night's affrightment made us weary already of our good and kind entertainment; we desired to remove from the seaside. To this our Superior Calvo yielded, not for our fear's sake so much as for his fear, lest with eating too much of the fruits of that country and drinking after them too greedily of the water (which causeth dangerous fluxes, and hasteneth death to those that newly come from Spain to those parts), we should fall sick and die there, as hundreds did after our departure, for want of temperance in the use of those fruits which before they had never seen or eaten.

Thirty mules, which had been brought a purpose from Mexico,

were ready for us, and had waited for us in San Juan de Ulua six days before ever the fleet arrived. Calvo that day busied himself a shipboard in sending to shore our chests, and such provision as had been left of wines, and biscuit, gammons of bacon, and salted beef, whereof there was some store, besides a dozen hens and three sheep, which was much wondered at, that so much should be left after so long a voyage. In the meantime we visited our friends and took our leaves of them in the forenoon, and after dinner, seats were prepared for us in the cathedral church to see a comedy acted, which had been on purpose studied and prepared by the town for the entertainment of the new Viceroy of Mexico. Thus two days only we abode in San Juan de Ulua, and so departed.

6. Of our journey from San Juan de Ulua to Mexico, and of the most remarkable towns and villages in the way

UPON THE 14 day of September we left the town and port of San Juan de Ulua, entering into the road to Mexico, which we found the first three or four leagues to be very sandy, as wide and open as is our road from London to St. Albans. The first Indians we met with was at the old Vera Cruz, a town seated by the seaside, which the Spaniards that first conquered that country thought to have made their chief harbor; but afterwards by reason of the small shelter they found in it for their ships against the north winds they left it, and removed to San Juan de Ulua. Here we began to discover the power of the priests and friars over the poor Indians, and their subjection and obedience unto them. The Prior of San Juan de Ulua had writ a letter unto them the day before of our passing that way, charging them to meet us in the way, and to welcome us into those parts, and this the poor Indians gallantly performed.

For two miles before we came to the town there met us on horseback some twenty of the chief of the town, presenting unto every one of us a nosegay of flowers. They rid before us a bow-shot till we met with more company on foot, to wit the trumpeters, the waits (who sounded pleasantly all the way before us), the officers of the church, such as here we call church-wardens, though more in number, according to the many sodalities or confraternities of saints whom they serve. These likewise presented to each of us a nosegay. Next met us the singing men and boys, all the choristers, who softly and leisurely walked before us singing *Te Deum laudamus* till we came

39

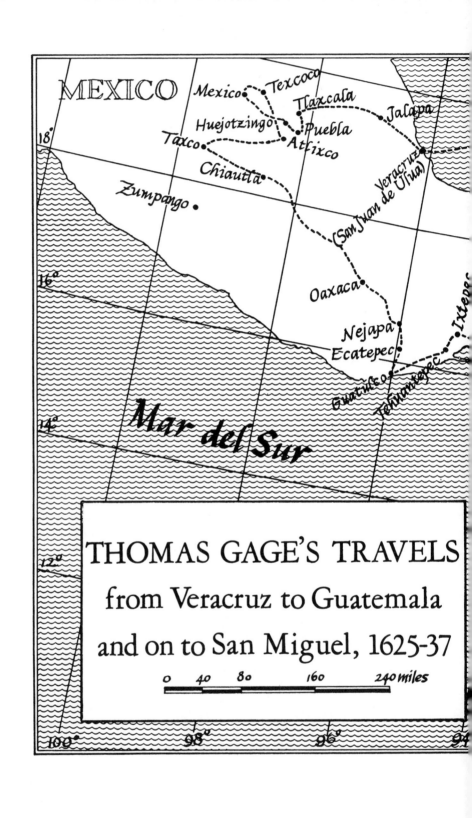

MEXICO Mexico Texcoco
Tlaxcala
Jalapa
Huejotzingo Puebla
Taxco Atlixco
18°
Chiautla
Zumpango Veracruz
(San Juan de Ulua)
16°
Oaxaca
Ixtepec
Nejapa
Ecatepec
Guatulco Tehuantepec
14° Mar del Sur
12°

THOMAS GAGE'S TRAVELS
from Veracruz to Guatemala
and on to San Miguel, 1625-37

0   40   80   160   240 miles

100°   98°   96°   94°

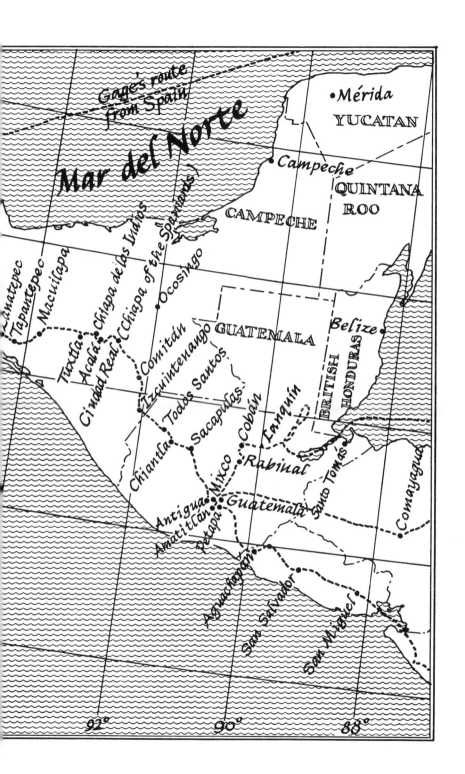

Gage's route
from Spain

Mar del Norte

•Mérida
YUCATAN

•Campeche

QUINTANA
ROO

CAMPECHE

Tanatepec
Tapantepec
•Macuilapa
Tuxtla
Acalá
Chiapa de los Indios
Ciudad Real
Chiapa of the Spaniards
Ocosingo
Comitán
GUATEMALA
Belize
BRITISH HONDURAS
Tzcuintenango
Todos Santos
Sacapulas
Cobán
Lanquín
Chiantla
Mixco
Rabinal
Santo Tomás
Antigua
Amatitlán
Petapa
Guatemala
Comayagua
Aguachapan
San Salvador
San Miguel

92°
90°
88°

to the chief market-place in the midst of the town, where were two great elm trees.

There was set up one long arbor with green bows, and a table ready furnished with boxes of conserves and other sweetmeats, and diet-bread to prepare our stomachs for a cup of chocolate, and while it was seasoning with the hot water and sugar, the chief Indians and officers of the town made a speech unto us, having first kneeled down and kissed our hands one by one. They welcomed us into their country, calling us the Apostles of Jesus Christ, thanked us for that we had left our own country, our friends, our fathers and mothers for to save their souls; they told us they honored us as gods upon earth; and many such compliments they used till our chocolate was brought. We refreshed ourselves for the space of one hour, and gave hearty thanks to the Indians for their kind respects unto us, assuring them that nothing was more dear unto us in this world than their souls, which that we might save we regarded not sea, nor land dangers, nor the unhuman cruelties of barbarous and savage Indians (who as yet had no knowledge of the true God), no, nor our own lives.

And thus we took our leaves, giving unto the chief of them some beads, some medals, some crosses of brass, some *Agnus Dei,* some relics brought from Spain, and to every one of the town an indulgence of forty years (which the Pope had granted unto us, to bestow where and upon whom, and as often as we would), wherewith we began to blind that simple people with Popish principles. As we went out of the arbor to take our mules, behold the market-place was full of Indian men and women, who, as they saw us ready to depart, kneeled upon the ground as adoring us for a blessing, which as we rid along we bestowed upon them with lifted up hands on high, making over them the sign of the cross. And this submission of the poor Indians unto the priests in those parts, this vainglory in admitting such ceremonious entertainment and public worship from them, did so puff up some of our young friars' hearts that already they thought themselves better than the best bishops in Spain, who, though proud enough, yet never travel there with such public acclamations as we did. The waits and trumpets sounded again before us, and the chief of the town conducted us a mile forward, and so took their leaves.

The first two days we lodged but in poor small Indian towns, among whom we still found kind entertainment and good store of provision, especially of hens, capons, turkeys, and several sorts of fruits. The third day at night we came to a great town consisting of near two thousand inhabitants, some Spaniards, some Indians, called Jalapa de la Vera Cruz. This town in the year 1634 was made a new bishop's see (the bishopric of the city called La Puebla de los Angeles being divided into two), and this being not above the third part of it, is thought to be worth ten thousand ducats a year. It stands in a very fertile soil for Indian wheat called maize, and some Spanish wheat. There are many towns about it of Indians; but what makes it rich are the many farms of sugar, and some which they call *estancias*, rich farms for breeding of mules and cattle; and likewise some farms of cochineal. In this town there is but one great church and an inferior chapel, both belonging to a cloister of Franciscan friars, wherein we were lodged that night and the next day, being the Lord's Day. Though the revenues of this cloister be great, yet it maintains not above half a dozen friars, where twenty might be plentifully maintained, that so those few lubbers might be more abundantly, and like epicures, fed and nourished. The Superior or Guardian of this cloister was no less vain than the Prior of San Juan de Ulua; and though he were not of our profession, yet he welcomed us with stately entertainment.

Here and wheresoever further we travelled, we still found in the priests and friars looseness of life, and their ways and proceedings contrary to the ways of their profession, sworn to by a solemn vow and covenant. This Order especially of the mendicant Franciscan friars voweth (besides chastity and obedience) poverty more strictly to be observed than any other Order of the Romish church. Their clothing ought to be coarse sackcloth, their girdles made of hemp should be no finer than strong halters, their shirts should be but woollen, their legs should know no stockings, their feet no shoes but at the most and best either wooden clogs or sandals of hemp; their hands and fingers should not so much as touch any money, nor should they have the use or possession or propriety of any; nor should their journeys be made easy with the help of horses to carry them, but painfully they ought to travel on foot. The breach of any of these they acknowledge to be a deadly and mortal sin, with the guilt of a high soul-damning and soul-cursing excommunication. Yet for all these bonds and obligations, those wretched imps live in those parts as though they had never vowed unto the Lord, shewing in their lives that they have vowed what they are not able to perform.

It was to us a strange and scandalous sight to see here in Jalapa a friar of the cloister riding in with his lackey boy by his side, upon a goodly gelding (having gone but to the town's end, as we were informed, to hear a dying man's confession), with his long habit tucked up to his girdle, making shew of a fine silk orange-color stocking upon his legs, and a neat Cordovan shoe upon his foot, with a fine holland pair of drawers, with a lace three inches broad at knee. This sight made us willing to pry further into this and the other friars' carriages, under whose broad sleeves we could perceive their doublets quilted with silk, and at their wrists the laces of their holland shirts. In their talk we could discern no mortification, but mere vanity and worldliness.

After supper some of them began to talk of carding and dicing, and they challenged us, that were but newcomers to those parts, to a primera, which most of ours refused, some for want of money, some for ignorance of that game. Yet at last with much ado they got two of our friars to join with two of theirs. So the cards were handsomely shuffled, the vies and revies were doubled, loss made some hot and blind with passion, gain made others eager and covetous; and thus was that religious cloister made all night a gaming house, and sworn religious poverty turned into profane and wordly covetousness. We that beheld the game some part of the night found enough to observe, for the more the sport increased, scandals to the sport were added, both by drinking, and swearing that common oath "*Voto á Cristo, Voto á Dios,*" and also by scoffing and jeering at the religious vows of poverty which they had vowed. One of the Franciscans, though formerly he had touched money and with his fingers had laid it to the stake on the table, yet sometimes to make the company laugh, if he had chanced to win a double vie (and sometimes the vies and revies went round of twenty patacones), then would he take the end of one sleeve of his habit and open wide the other broad sleeve, and so with his sleeve sweep the money into his other sleeve, saying, "I have vowed not to touch money, nor to keep any, I meaned then a natural contact of it; but my sleeve may touch it, and my sleeve may keep it," shewing with scoffs and jests of his lips what religion was in his heart.

My ears tingled with hearing such oaths; my tongue would have uttered some words of reproof, but that I considered myself a guest and stranger in a strange house, and that if anything I should say, it would do no good. So silently I departed to my rest, leaving the gamesters, who continued till sun-rising. In the morning I was informed that the jesting friar, that rather roaring boy than religious Franciscan, fitter for Sardanapalus or Epicurus' school than to live in a cloister, had lost fourscore and odd patacones, his sleeve (it seems) refusing to keep for him what he had vowed never to possess. Here I began to find out by experience of these Franciscans that it was liberty and looseness of life that brought yearly so many friars and Jesuits from Spain to those parts, rather than zeal of preaching the Gospel and converting souls to Christ, which indeed being an act of highest charity, they make a special badge of the truth of their religion. But the looseness of their lives sheweth evidently that the love of money, of vainglory, of power and authority over the poor Indians, is their end and aim more than any love of God.

From Jalapa we went to a place called by the Spaniards La Rinconada, which is no town nor village, and therefore not worth mentioning in such a road as now I am in; yet, as it is famous in two things, it must not be omitted amongst greater places. This place stands so far from any other town that travellers can scarce make their journeys without either baiting there at noon, or lying there at night, or declining three or four miles out of the road to some Indian town. It is no more than one house, which the Spaniards call *venta*, or as our English inns, seated in the corner of a low valley, which is the hottest place from San Juan de Ulua to Mexico. About it are the best springs and fountains in all the road, and the water, though warm with the heat of the sun, yet as sweet as any milk. The inn-keepers, knowing well the Spaniards' heat, that it seeks cool and refreshing drink, have special care so to lay in water in great earthen vessels, which they set upon a moist and waterish sand, that it is so cold that it maketh the teeth to chatter. This sweetness and this coolness together of that water in so hot and scorching a country was a wonder to us, who could find no other refreshment from that extraordinary heat. Provision here of beef, mutton, kid, hens, turkeys, rabbits, fowls, and especially quails, was so plentiful and cheap that we were astonished at it.

The valley and country about it is very rich and fertile, full of Spanish farms of sugar and cochineal and Spanish and Indian wheat. But what maketh me more especially remember this *venta*, or inn, is, that though art and experience of man have found a way to provide for travellers in so hot a place cool and refreshing water, and God have given it the sweetness of milk, and to the place such abundance of provision, yet all this in the day only is comfortable and pleasant; in the night the Spaniards call it *confites en infierno*, that is to say, cumfits in hell, for the heat is so extraordinary that it is impossible to be feeding without wiping away the continual sweat of the face. Drops from the brows are always ready to blind our eyes and to fill with sauce our dishes, and the swarms of gnats are such that waking and sleeping no device of man is able to keep them off. True it is, most of us had our pavilions[1] which we carried with us to hang about and over our beds, but these could not defend us from that piercing and stinging vermin, which like Egypt's plague of frogs would be sure to be in every place, and through our curtains to come upon our very beds. Yet in the day they are not; but just at sun-setting they begin to swarm about, and at sun-rising away they go. After a most tedious and troublesome night, when we found the rising of the sun had dispersed and banished them away, we thought it best for us to flee away from that place with them; and so from thence early we departed to a town as pleasant and fertile and abounding with provision as this Rinconada, and free from such busy guests and individual mates and companions as the night before had intruded themselves upon us.

The next night we got to a town called Segura, inhabited both by Indians and Spaniards, consisting of about a thousand inhabitants; here again without any charges we were stately entertained by Franciscan friars, as light and vainglorious as those of Jalapa. This town had its first beginning and foundation from Hernando Cortés, and is called Segura de la Frontera, being built up by him for a frontier town to secure the Spaniards, that came from San Juan de

---

[1] The Spanish word *pabellon*, "mosquito net," is translated into English "pavilion."

Ulua to Mexico, against the Culiacáns and people of Tepeacac, who were allied to the Mexicans, and so much annoyed the Spaniards. This town likewise, as all the rest from San Juan de Ulua to Mexico, is very plentiful of provision, and many sorts of fruits, namely plantains, sapotes, and chicosapotes. The sapotes have within a great black kernel as big as our horse plums, the fruit itself is as red within as scarlet, as sweet as honey; but the chicosapote is less and some of them red, some brown-colored, and so juicy that at the eating the juice like drops of honey falls from them, and the smell is like unto a baked pear.[2] Here likewise were presented unto us clusters of grapes as fair as any in Spain, which were welcome unto us, for that we had seen none since we came from Spain, and we saw by them that the country thereabouts would be very fit for vineyards, if the King of Spain would grant the planting of vines in those parts; which often he hath refused to do, lest the vineyards there should hinder the trading and traffic between Spain and those parts, which certainly had they but wine, needed not any commerce with Spain. This town is of a more temperate climate than any other from Vera Cruz to Mexico, and the people who formerly had been eaters of man's flesh, now as civil and politic, as loving and courteous as any in the road. From whence we declined a little out of our way more westward (the road being north-westward) only to see that famous town of Tlaxcala, whose inhabitants joined with Cortés, and we may say were the chief instruments of that great and unparalleled conquest.

[2] The sapote is the mamey (*Lucuma mammosa*, L.). Chicosapote is the tree (*Achras sapota* L., the sapodilla) which yields chicle, the gum from which chewing gum is made. The fruit is exceedingly sweet, as Gage notes. It is perhaps more relished by horses and mules than by human beings.

7. *A description of the town of Tlaxcala and concluding the rest of our journey from Tlaxcala to Mexico through the City of Angels and Huejotzingo*

~~~~~~~X~~~~~~~

TLAXCALA is worth all the rest of the towns and villages between San Juan de Ulua and Mexico. It was subdued and sworn to the power and command of the Spaniards, being in those times one of the chiefest, though not richest, towns in America. Its inhabitants after clave most faithfully to Cortés, and were chief instruments for the subduing of Mexico, and therefore to this day are freed from tribute by the kings of Spain, paying not the money which as a tribute tax is laid upon every Indian to be paid yearly, but only in acknowledgment of subjection they pay yearly one corn of maize, which is their Indian wheat.

Ocotelulco and Tizatlán are the two quarters which now are most inhabited. In Ocotelulco standeth a cloister of Franciscan friars who are the preachers of that town. They have there joining to their cloister a very fair church, to which belong some fifty Indians, singers, organists, players on musical instruments, trumpeters, and waits, who set out the Mass with a very sweet and harmonious music, and delight the fancy and senses, while the spirit is sad and dull as little acquainted with God, who will be worshipped in spirit and in truth. In Tepeticpac and Quiahuiztlán are two chapels only, to which on the Lord's Day, and upon other occasions, the friars of the cloister resort to say Mass. In this cloister we were entertained a day and two nights with great provision of flesh and fish, which is very plentiful by reason of the river. The friars are allowed by the

48

town a dozen Indians who are free from other services only to fish for the friars. They change their turns by weeks, four one week and four another, except they be called upon for some special occasion, and then they leave all other work and attend only with fish upon the friars.

The town now is inhabited by Spaniards and Indians together, and is the seat of a chief Officer of Justice sent from Spain every three years, called *Alcalde Mayor,* whose power reacheth to all the towns within twenty leagues about. Besides him, the Indians have likewise among themselves *Alcaldes, Regidores,* and *Alguaziles,* superior and inferior officers of justice appointed yearly by the *Alcalde Mayor,* who keeps them all in awe, and takes from them for his service as many as he pleaseth without paying anything for the service done unto him. The hard usage of this *Alcalde Mayor* and other Spaniards hath much decayed that populous town, which should rather have been cherished than disheartened by the Spaniards, who by means of it gained all the rest of the country.

The next place most remarkable in the road wherein we travelled was the city called by the Spaniards La Puebla de los Angeles, the City of Angels. To the which we were desirous to go, knowing that in it there was a convent of Dominicans of our profession, not having met with any such since the day we departed from San Juan de Ulua. Here we refreshed ourselves at leisure three days, finding ourselves very welcome to our own brethren, who spared nothing that was fit for our entertainment. We visited all the city, and took large notice of it, judging of the wealth and riches of it not only by the great trading in it, but by the many cloisters both of nuns and of friars which it maintaineth, such being commonly very burdensome to the places where they live, an idle kind of beggars who make the people believe the maintaining of them is meritorious and saving to their souls, and that their prayers for them is more worth than the means and sustenance which they receive from them. Of these there is in that city a very great cloister of some fifty or threescore Dominicans, another of more Franciscans, another of Augustines, another of Mercenarians, another of Discalced Carmelites, another of Jesuits, besides four of nuns.

This city is seated in a low and pleasant valley, about ten leagues from a very high mountain, which is always covered with snow.

49

It standeth twenty leagues from Mexico. It was first built and inhabited in the year 1530 by the command of Don Antonio de Mendoza, Viceroy of Mexico, together with the consent of Sebastián Ramirez, who was a bishop and had been president in time past in Santo Domingo, and was that year instead of Nuño de Guzmán (who had behaved himself very evil both with the Indians and Spaniards) sent to be president of the Chancery of Mexico with these other four judges, the Licenciates Juan de Salmeron, Gasco Quiroga, Francisco Ceynos, and Alonso Maldonado. These judges governed the land far better than Nuño de Guzmán before them had done. Among other remarkable things they did was to cause this city to be inhabited; and set at liberty the Indians who inhabited there before, and were grievously suppressed and enslaved by the Spaniards. Therefore many of them who had inhabited there before departed and went to seek their living at Jalisco, Honduras, Guatemala, and other places where war then was.

This city was formerly called by the Indians Cuetlaxcoapán, that is to say, a snake in water; the reason was because there are two fountains, the one of evil water and the other of good. This city is now a bishop's see, whose yearly revenues since the cutting off from it Jalapa de la Vera Cruz are yet worth above twenty thousand ducats. By reason of the good and wholesome air, it daily increaseth with inhabitants, who resort from many other places to live there. In the year 1634, when Mexico was like to be drowned with the inundation of the lake, thousands left it, and came with all their goods and families to Puebla, which now is thought to consist of ten thousand inhabitants. That which maketh it most famous is the cloth which is made in it, and is sent far and near, and judged now to be as good as the cloth of Segovia, which is the best that is made in Spain, but now is not so much esteemed of nor sent so much from Spain to America by reason of the abundance of fine cloth which is made in this city of Puebla de los Angeles. The felts likewise that are made are the best of all that country. There is also a glass house, which is there a rarity, none other being as yet known in those parts. But the mint house that is in it, where is coined half the silver that cometh from Zacatecas, makes it the second to Mexico, and it is thought that in time it will be as great and populous as Mexico.[1] Without it there are many gardens, which store the markets with provision of salads. The soil abounds with wheat, and with sugar farms, among the which not far from this city there is one (belonging to the Dominican friars of Mexico) so great and populous that for the work only belonging unto it, it maintained in my time above two hundred blackamoor slaves, men and women, besides their little children.

The chief town between Puebla and Mexico is called Huejotzingo, consisting of some five hundred Indians and one hundred Spaniard inhabitants. Here is likewise a cloister of Franciscans, who entertained us gallantly, and made shew unto us of the dexterity of their Indians in music.[2] Those fat friars, like the rest, wanted not all provision necessary for the body, but their greatest glory and boasting to us was the education which they had given to some children of the town, especially such as served them in their cloister, whom they had brought up to dancing after the Spanish fashion at the sound of the *guitar*. And this a dozen of them (the biggest not being above fourteen years of age) performed excellently for our better entertainment that night. We were there till midnight, singing both Spanish and Indian tunes, capering and dancing with their castanets, or knockers on their fingers, with such dexterity as not only did delight but amaze and astonish us. True it is, we thought those Franciscans might have been better employed at that time in their choir at their midnight devotions according to their profession. We still found vowed religious duties more and more neglected, and worldliness too too much embraced by such as had renounced and forsaken the world and all its pleasures, sports, and pastimes.

This town of Huejotzingo is privileged by the kings of Spain almost as much as Tlaxcala for that it joined with Tlaxcala against the Mexicans in defence of Hernando Cortés and the rest of the Spaniards that first conquered that land. From hence we made our

[1] The manufacture of glazed tiles and pottery utensils in the manner of Talavera, a most important industry, started in Puebla about the time of Gage's visit according to Professor John M. Goggin of the University of Florida.

[2] The Franciscan convent at Huejotzingo was in Gage's time, as now, a superb structure. The magnificent church is in Gothic style and possesses a splendid retablo, in position when Gage passed through the town. There are also early murals representing the first Franciscan friars in Mexico painted by native artists. Naturally, Gage, writing at a time when his fellow Puritans were busy chopping down the medieval treasures in the churches and cathedrals of England, never describes the glories of Mexican ecclesiastical architecture and decoration.

last journey to the city of Mexico, passing over the side of that high hill which we had discovered at Puebla de los Angeles, some thirty miles off. There are no alps like unto it for height, cold, and constant snow that lieth upon it. From Spain to that place we had not felt any such extremity of cold, which made the Spaniards that had come out of the hot climate of Spain, and endured excessive heat at sea, wonder and admire. This last journey from Huejotzingo to Mexico we reckoned to be thirty English miles, and of the thirty miles we judged at least the fifteen to be up and down the hill; and yet the top of it (whither we ascended not) was far higher. From that highest part of it which we travelled over, we discovered the city of Mexico, and the lake about it, which seemed to us to be near at hand, standing some ten English miles in a plain from the bottom of this mountain.

The first town we came to below the hill was Coatepec, of the jurisdiction of Texcoco, near which, we also called to mind, was pitched the camp of the Indians of Culhua, which was near a hundred thousand men of war, who were sent by the *señores* of Mexico and Texcoco to encounter Cortés, but all in vain, for his horsemen broke through them, and his artillery made such havoc among them that they were soon put to flight.

Three leagues from hence, on our right hand as we travelled, we discovered Texcoco by the side of the lake and out of the road. Yet it ministered unto us matter of a large discourse, taken from the time of Cortés and the first conquerors, who found it a great city, and at that time even as big as Mexico. In it Cortés met with no resistance, for as he journeyed towards it, four principal persons inhabitant of it met with his forces, bearing a rod of gold with a little flag in token of peace, saying that Coanocachtzin, their lord, had sent them to desire him not to make any spoil in his city and towns about it; and likewise to offer his friendship, praying also that it might please him with his whole army to take his lodging in the town of Texcoco, where he should be well received. Cortés, rejoicing at this message, yet jealous of some treachery and mistrusting the people of Texcoco (whose forces joined with the Mexicans and Culuacáns he had met with a little before), went forward on his way and came to Coatlinchan and Huejotla (which then were suburbs of the great city Texcoco, but now are pretty villages by themselves). There he and all his host were plenteously provided of all things necessary, and threw down the idols. This done, he entered into the city, where his lodging was prepared in a great house, sufficient for him and all the Spaniards, with many other of his Indian friends. And because at his first entry he saw neither women nor children, he suspected some treason, and forthwith proclaimed upon pain of death that none of his men should go out. In the evening the Spaniards went up into the *azoteas* [flat roofs] and galleries to behold the city, and there they saw the great number of citizens that fled from thence with their stuff, some towards the mountains, and others to the water side to take boat. It was strange to see the great haste and stir to provide for themselves. There were at that time at least twenty thousand little boats called *canoas* occupied in carrying household-stuff and passengers. Cortés would fain have remedied it, but the night was so nigh at hand that he could not. He would gladly also have apprehended the lord, but he was one of the first that fled to Mexico.

This town of Texcoco to this day is famous among the Spaniards, for that it was one of the first, if not the first (which according to the histories of those parts is very probable), that received a Christian king to rule and govern. For Cortés, hearing that Coanocachtzin, then king of that city and towns adjacent, was fled, caused many of the citizens to be called before him, and having in his company a young gentleman of a noble house in that country, who had been lately christened and had the name Hernando (Cortés, who loved him well, being his god-father), said unto the citizens that this new Christian lord Don Hernando was son unto Nezaualpilli, their loving lord. Wherefore he required them to make him their king, considering that Coanocachtzin was fled unto the enemies, laying also before them his wicked fact in killing of Cuicuitzcatl, his own brother, only to put him from his inheritance and kingdom, through the enticement of Cuauhtemoc, a mortal enemy to the Spaniards.

In this sort was that new Christian Don Hernando elected king, and the fame thereof being blown abroad, many citizens repaired home again to visit their new prince, so that in short space the city was as well replenished with people as it was before, and being also well used at the Spaniards' hands, they served them diligently in all things that they were commanded. And Don Hernando abode ever after a faithful friend unto the Spaniards in their wars against Mexico, and in short time learned the Spanish tongue.

Now Cortés was strong both with Spaniards and Indians; and his court at Texcoco was as great or greater than Montezuma's formerly had been at Mexico. And here Cortés made his preparation for the siege of Mexico with all haste, and furnished himself with scaling ladders and other necessaries fit for such a purpose. His brigantines being nailed and thoroughly ended, he made a sluice, or trench, of half a league of length, twelve foot broad and more, and two fathom in depth. This work was fifty days a doing, although there were four hundred thousand men daily working; truly a famous work and worthy of memory, which hath made Texcoco gloriously mentioned, though now almost decayed in the great number of inhabitants.

The dock or trench being thus finished, the brigantines were caulked with tow and cotton-wool, and for want of tallow and oil they were (as some authors report) driven to take man's grease, not that Cortés permitted them to slay men for that effect, but of those which were slain in the wars, and of such as sallied daily out of Mexico to hinder this work, and fighting were slain. The Indians, who were cruel and bloody butchers, using sacrifice of man's flesh, would in this sort open the dead body and take out the grease. The brigantines being launched, Cortés mustered his men, and found nine hundred Spaniards, of whom fourscore and six were horsemen, and a hundred and eighteen with cross-bows, and arquebuses. All the residue had sundry weapons, as swords, daggers, targets, lances, and halberds. Also they had for armor, corslets, coats of mail, and jacks. They had, moreover, three great pieces of cast iron, fifteen small pieces of brass, and ten hundred-weight of powder, with store of shot, besides a hundred thousand Indian warriors.

On Whit-Sunday all the Spaniards came into the field, that great plain below the high mountain spoken of before, where Cortés made three chief captains, among whom he divided his whole army. Unto Pedro de Alvarado, the first Captain, he appointed thirty horsemen, and a hundred and seventy footmen of the Spaniards, two pieces of ordnance, and thirty thousand Indians, commanding him to camp in Tlacopán. Unto Christóval de Olid, the second Captain, he gave three and thirty horsemen, and a hundred and eighteen footmen of the Spanish nation, two pieces of ordnance, and thirty thousand Indians, and appointed him to pitch his camp in Culuacán. To Gonzalo de Sandoval, who was the third Captain, he gave three and twenty horsemen, and a hundred and threescore footmen, two pieces of ordnance, and forty thousand Indians, with commission to choose a place to pitch his camp.

In every brigantine he planted a piece of ordnance, six arquebuses, or cross-bows, and three and twenty Spaniards, men most fit for that purpose. He appointed also captains for each, and himself for General, whereof some of the chiefest of his company that went by land began to murmur, thinking that they had been in greater danger; wherefore they required him to go with the main battle, and not by water. Cortés little esteemed their words, for although there was more danger in the land than in the water, yet it did more import to have greater care in the wars by water than on the land, because his men had been in the one and not in the other. Besides, the chiefest hopes that Cortés had to win Mexico were these vessels, for with them he burned a great part of the canoes of Mexico, and the rest he so locked up that they were no help to the Mexicans, and with only twelve brigantines he did annoy his enemy as much by water as the rest of his army did by land.

All this preparation for the siege of Mexico by land and water, with above a hundred thousand Indians, besides the Spaniards above mentioned, and the twelve brigantines by water, was finished in this city of Texcoco. This is a sufficient argument of the greatness of it at that time, maintaining with provision fit and necessary so many thousands of people, and it yielded matter enough unto us for a large discourse, whilst not far from the sight of it we travelled in the open and direct plain road to Mexico. And as we talked of the greatness of it in former times, so likewise we now wondered to consider it to be but a small government, where doth constantly reside a Spanish Governor sent from Spain, whose power reacheth to those borders of Tlaxcala and Huejotzingo, and to most of the petty towns and villages of the plain, which were formerly under the command and power of a King, but now are not able to make up above a thousand ducats a year, which is supposed to be the yearly revenues of the Governor.

Texcoco itself is this day judged to consist only of a hundred Spaniards and three hundred Indian inhabitants, whose chief riches come by gardening and sending daily in their canoes herbs and salads to Mexico. Some wealth likewise they get by their cedar trees which grow there, and are ready timber for the buildings of Mexico. Yet now also are these cedars much decayed by the Spaniards, who have wasted and spoiled them in their too too sumptuous buildings. Cortés was accused by Pánfilo de Narváez for that he had spent seven thousand beams of cedar trees in the work of his own house. Formerly there were in Texcoco gardens that had a thousand cedar trees for walls and circuit, some of them of a hundred and twenty foot long, and twelve foot in compass from end to end; now that garden that hath fifty cedar trees about it is much regarded. At the end of this plain we passed through Mexicaltzingo, which formerly was a great town, but now not of above an hundred inhabitants, and from thence to Huetlauac, a petty village, yet most pleasant for the shade of many fruit trees, gardens, and stately houses which for their recreation some citizens of Mexico have built there, being at the foot of the causeway which from this town through the lake reacheth about five English miles to Mexico.[3]

And thus upon the third day of October, 1625, we entered into that famous and gallant city, yet not abiding in it, but only passing through it, till we came to a house of recreation, standing among the gardens in the way to Chapultepec, named San Jacinto,[4] belonging to the Dominicans of Manila in the East Indies (whither our course was intended), where we were stately entertained, and

[3] Gage followed the route of Cortés, entering Mexico from the south. Now that Lake Texcoco is so much shrunken, the approach is from the northeast.

[4] Through the help of Don Leonard and other friends in Mexico City, I was able to locate the site of the old rest house of San Jacinto. It was in the little town of Popotla, where "the tree of the dismal night" still marks the spot where Cortés sat and wept when the remnants of his army filed past after the first failure to capture Mexico City, on their disastrous retreat along the Tacuba causeway. The old grounds of San Jacinto are now occupied by the School of Veterinary Medicine and other secular buildings, but a local resident still knew the old name and boundaries of San Jacinto. The site adjoins the little church of La Merced de las Huertas, "Our Lady of Mercy of the Gardens," now, as then, in the keeping of the Mercenarians. The words "of the Gardens" give point to what would otherwise be a rather meaningless use of a capital G in "among the Gardens" in the first edition of Gage's book. Photographs of the hospice of San Jacinto accompany the article by G. R. Conway, "Un Inglés en México."

abode till after Candlemas Day, the time of our second shipping at Acapulco (eighty leagues from Mexico) by the South Sea to Manila, the chief city of the islands named Philippines.

8. Showing some particulars of the great and famous City of Mexico in former times, with a true description of it now, and of the state and condition of it the year 1625

It HATH been no small piece of policy in the friars and Jesuits of Manila and the Philippine Islands to purchase near about Mexico some house and garden to carry thither such missionary priests as they yearly bring from Spain for those parts. For were it not that they found some rest and place of recreation, but were presently closed up in the cloisters of Mexico to follow those religious duties (which sore against their wills most of them are forced to), they would soon after a tedious journey from Spain by sea and land relent of their purposes of going forward and venturing upon a second voyage by the South Sea; and would either resolve upon a return to Spain, or of staying in some part of America; as myself and five more of my company did, though secretly and hiddenly, and sore against the will of Friar Calvo and others, who had the tutoring and conducting of us. Therefore, that all such as come from Spain to be shipped again at Acapulco for the Philippines may have all manner of encouragement, rest, and recreations becoming their professions, whilst they do abide in America, and may not be disheartened by those that live about Mexico (who do truly envy all that pass that way to Asia), the friars and Jesuits have purchased for their missions houses of recreation among the gardens, which are exempted from the power and command of the Superiors of Mexico, and are subordinate unto the government of the Provincials

58

of the Philippines, who send from thence their substitute vicars to rule and to look to the aforementioned houses and gardens.

To the Dominicans belonged this house called San Jacinto, whither we were carried, and where we did abide near five months, having all things provided that were fit and necessary for our recreations and for our better encouragement to a second voyage by sea. The gardens belonging to this house might be of fifteen acres of ground, divided into shady walks under the orange and lemon trees. There we had pomegranates, figs, and grapes in abundance, with the plantain, sapote, chicosapote, pineapple, and all other fruits that were to be found in Mexico. The herbs and salads and great number of Spanish *cardos* [Jerusalem artichokes] which were sold out, brought in a great rent yearly, for every day there was a cart attended to be filled and sent to the market of Mexico. Moreover, this is not at fixed seasons of the year, as here in England and other parts of Europe, but at all times and seasons, both winter and summer. There is no difference of heat, cold, frosts, and snow, as with us, but the same temper all the whole year, the winter differing only from the summer by the rain that falls, and not by excessive frosts that nip. This we enjoyed without doors; within we had all sorts and varieties both of fish and flesh.

What most we wondered at was the abundance of sweetmeats, and especially of conserves, that were provided for us; for to every one of us during the time of our abode there was brought on Monday morning half a dozen boxes of conserve of quinces and other fruits, besides our biscuits. These were to stay our stomachs in the mornings and at other times of the day, for in our stomachs we found a great difference between Spain and that country. In Spain and other parts of Europe a man's stomach will hold out from meal to meal, and one meal here of good cheer will nourish and cherish the stomach four and twenty hours, but in Mexico and other parts of America we found that two or three hours after a good meal of three or four several dishes of mutton, veal or beef, kid, turkeys, or other fowls, our stomachs would be ready to faint, and so we were fain to support them with either a cup of chocolate, or a bit of conserve or biscuit, which for that purpose was allowed us in great abundance.

This seemed to me so strange (whereas the meat seemed as fat and hearty, excepting the beef, as ours in Europe), that I for some satisfaction presently had recourse to a doctor of physic, who cleared my doubt with this answer: That though the meat we fed on was as fair to look on as in Spain, yet the substance and nourishment in it came far short of it, by reason of the pasture, which is drier and hath not the change of springs which the pastures of Europe have, but is short and withers soon away. Secondly, he told me, the climate of those parts had this effect, to produce a fair shew but little matter or substance. As in the flesh we fed on, so likewise in all the fruits there. These are most fair and beautiful to behold, most sweet and luscious to taste, but have little inward virtue or nourishment at all in them, not half that is in a Spanish *camuesa,* or English Kentish pippin [apple]. And as in meat and fruit there is this inward and hidden deceit, so likewise the same is to be found in the people that are born and bred there, who make fair outward shews, but are inwardly false and hollow-hearted. Which I have heard reported much among the Spaniards to have been the answer of our Queen Elizabeth of England to some that presented unto her of the fruits of America, that surely where those fruits grew, the women were light, and all the people hollow and false-hearted.

But further reasons I omit to search into for this. I write only from my experience, which taught me that little substance and virtue is in the great abundance and variety of food which there is enjoyed, and witnessing this truth, our stomachs ever and anon were gaping and crying, "Feed, feed." Our conserves, therefore, and dainties were plentifully allowed us, and all other encouragements, and no occasion denied us of going to visit Mexico (which was not two full miles from us), all the while we abode there. It was a pleasant walk for us to go out in the morning, and to spend all the day in the city and come home at night; our way lying by arches made of stone, three miles long, to convey the water from Chapultepec unto the city. Take, therefore, gentle reader, from me what for the space of five months I could learn concerning it in former and present times.

The situation of this city is much like that of Venice, but only differs in this, that Venice is built upon the sea-water, and Mexico upon a lake, which seeming one, indeed is two. One part is standing water; the other ebbeth and floweth according to the wind that bloweth. That part which standeth is wholesome, good, and sweet, and yieldeth store of small fish. That part which ebbeth and floweth is of saltish, bitter, and pestiferous water, yielding no kind of fish, small or great. The sweet water standeth higher than the other, and falleth into it, and reverteth not backward, as some conceive it doth. The salt lake containeth fifteen miles in breadth, and fifteen in length, and more than five and forty in circuit; and the lake of sweet water containeth even as much, so that the whole lake containeth much about a hundred miles.

The Spaniards are divided in opinions concerning this water and the springs of it; some hold that all this water hath but one spring out of a great and high mountain which standeth south-west within sight of Mexico, and that the cause that the one part of the lake is brackish or saltish is that the bottom or ground is all salt. But whether this opinion be true or false, certain it is and by experience I can witness that of that part of the salt water great quantity of salt is daily made, and is part of the great trading of that city into other parts of the country; nay, part of it is sent to the Philippine Islands.

Others say that this lake hath two springs, and that the fresh water springeth out of that mountain which standeth south-west from Mexico, and the salt brackish water springeth out of other high mountains which stand more north-west. But these give no reason for the saltness of it, without it be the agitation of it in the ebbing and flowing. I think rather if it spring from a different spring from that which yields fresh water, the brackishness and saltishness of it may proceed from some brackish and sulphurous minerals through which it passeth in those mountains. For by experience I know the like in the province of Guatemala, where by a town called Amatitán there is a lake not altogether sweet and fresh, but a little brackish, which certainly hath its spring from a fiery mountain called there a *volcan* (whose burning proceeds from the mines of brimstone that are within it). Thence spring near the same town likewise two or three springs of exceeding hot water, which are resorted to for wholesome baths, as coming through a sulphurous mine. Yet the standing lake proceeding from the same mountain is of that quality that it maketh the ground about it salt, and especially in the mornings the people go to gather up the salt which lieth upon the ground by the water side like unto a hoary frost.

Others conceive that that part of the Lake of Mexico which is saltish and brackish comes through the earth from the North Sea [the Atlantic]; and though springs of water which come from the sea lose their brackishness through the earth, yet this may keep some brackishness by reason of the minerals, which are many in those parts; or by reason of the great, wide, and open concavities of those mountains. As these are very hollow within (as we find by experience of the earthquakes which are more frequent there than here by reason of the wind that getteth into those concavities, and so shake the earth to get out), they give no way to the water to sweeten through the earth, or to lose all that saltness which it brought with it from the sea. But whatsoever the true reason be, there is not the like lake known of sweet and saltish water, one part breeding fish, the other breeding none at all.

This lake had formerly some fourscore towns, some say more, situated round about it, many of them containing five thousand households, and some ten thousand, yea, and Texcoco (as I have said before) was as big as Mexico. But when I was there, there might be thirty towns and villages about it, and scarce any of above five hundred households between Spaniards and Indians; such hath been the hard usage of the Spaniards towards them that they have even almost consumed that poor nation. Nay, two years before I came from those parts, which were the years of 1635 and 1636, I was credibly informed that a million of Indians' lives had been lost in an endeavor of the Spaniards to turn the water of the lake another way from the city, which was performed by cutting a way through the mountains, to avoid the great inundations that Mexico was subject unto. These were especially bad in the year 1634, when the waters grew so high that they threatened destruction to all the city, ruinating a great part, and coming into the churches that stood in the highest part of it, in so much that the people used commonly boats and canoes from house to house. Most of the Indians that lived about the lake were employed to strive against this strong element of water, which hath been the undoing of many poor wretches, but especially of these thirty towns and villages that bordered near upon the lake. Now by that great work the water is further from the houses of the city, and hath a passage made another way, though it was thought it would not long continue but would find again its old course towards Mexico.[1]

This city when Cortés first entered into it was (as some say) of sixty, but it is reported more probably to have been of fourscore thousand houses.[2] The siege endured three months from the time the brigantines came from Tlaxcala, and therein were on Cortés' side near 200,000 Indians, who daily increased and came in to help him, 900 Spaniards, fourscore horses only, seventeen or eighteen pieces or ordnance, sixteen or, as some say, eighteen brigantines, and at least 6,000 canoes. In this siege were slain fifty Spaniards only and six horses, and not above eight thousand of the Indians who were Cortés' friends. And on the Mexicans' side were slain at least a hundred and twenty thousand Indians, besides those that died of hunger and pestilence. At the defense of the city were all the nobility, by reason whereof many of them were slain. The multitude of people in the city was so great that they were constrained to eat little, to drink salt water, and to sleep among the dead bodies where was a horrible stench; and for these causes the disease of pestilence fell among them, and thereof died an infinite number. Their valor and steadfast determination was outstanding for although they were afflicted with such hunger that they were driven to eat boughs, rinds of trees, and to drink salt water, yet would they not yield themselves. And here also is to be noted that although the Mexicans did eat man's flesh, yet they did eat none but such as were their enemies, for had they eaten one another and their own children, there would not so many have died with hunger.

The Mexican women were highly commended, not only because they abode with their husbands and fathers, but also for the great

---

[1] This is the great cut of Huehuetoca, a great trench begun in 1607 to drain Lake Texcoco. It was originally planned to make a tunnel through the mountain at Nochistongo, and this was completed in 1608 at the cost of much suffering and loss of life among the Indian laborers, but the tunnel hardly served the purpose for which it had been constructed. In 1629, following exceptionally heavy rains, the entrance to the tunnel was walled up to prevent damage to the tunnel from the great force of water. This led to the serious flooding of Mexico City, with three feet of water in the center of the city. Violent earthquakes added to the calamity. More Indian laborers were then conscripted to convert the tunnel into an open ditch. Except during periods of heavy rain, Lake Texcoco is now largely dry.

[2] The most reliable modern estimates place the population of Tenochtitlán at the time Cortés entered it at about 60,000, occupying perhaps 12,000 houses.

pains they took with the sick and wounded persons; yea, and also they labored in making slings, cutting stones fit for the same, and throwing stones from the *azoteas;* for therein they did as much hurt as their men. The city was yielded to the spoil, and the Spaniards took the gold, plate, and feathers; the Indian friends had all the rest of cloth and other stuff. Thus was that famous city ruinated, and burnt by the Spaniards, and the power of that nation brought under the Spanish subjection.

Cortés, having found the air of that city very temperate and pleasant for man's life, and the situation commodious, thought presently of rebuilding it, and of making it the chief seat of justice and court for all that country. He divided it among the conquerors, having first taken out places for churches, market-places, town-house, and other necessary plots to build houses profitable for the commonwealth. He separated the dwellings of the Spaniards from the Indians, so that now the water passeth and maketh division betwixt them. He promised to them that were naturals of the city of Mexico plots to build upon, inheritance, freedom, and other liberties, and the like unto all those that would come and inhabit there, which was a means to allure many thither. He set also at liberty the *ciuacoatl,* the General-Captain, and made him chief over the Indians in the city, unto whom he gave a whole quarter. He gave likewise another quarter to Don Pedro Montezuma, son of Montezuma the King. All this was done to win the favor of the people. He made other gentlemen *señores* of little islands, and quarters to build upon and to inhabit, and in this order the whole situation was reparted, and the work began with great joy and diligence.

When the fame was blown abroad that Mexico should be built again, it was a wonder to see the people that resorted thither, hearing of liberty and freedom. The number was so great that in three miles' compass was nothing but people, men and women. They labored sore and did eat little, by reason whereof many sickened, and pestilence ensued, and an infinite number died. Their pains were great, for they bare on their backs, and drew after them stones, earth, timber, lime, brick, and all other things necessary in this sort. And little by little Mexico was built again with a hundred thousand houses, more strong and better than the old building was.

The Spaniards built their houses after the Spanish fashion. Cortés built his house upon the plot where Montezuma's house once stood, and it renteth now yearly for four thousand ducats. It is called the palace of the Marqués del Valle, the King of Spain having conferred upon Cortés and his heirs this title from the great valley of Oaxaca. This palace is so stately that, as I have observed before, seven thousand beams of cedar trees were spent in it. They built fair docks covered over with arches for the brigantines, and these docks remain for a perpetual memory until this day. They damned up the streets of water, where now fair houses stand, so that Mexico is not as it was wont to be, and especially since the year 1634 the water cometh not by far so near the city as it was wont to come. The lake sometimes casteth out a vapor of stench, but otherwise Mexico is a wholesome temperate dwelling, by reason of the mountains that stand round about it, and well provided through the fertility of the country and commodity of the lake. So that now is Mexico one of the greatest cities in the world in extension of the situation for Spanish and Indian houses.

Not many years after the Conquest it was the noblest city in all India, as well in arms as policy. There were formerly at the least two thousand citizens, that had each of them his horse in his stable with rich furniture for them, and arms in readiness. But now since all the Indians far and near are subdued, and most of them, especially about Mexico, consumed, and there is no fear of their rising up any more against the Spaniards, consequently all arms are forgotten, and the Spaniards live so secure from enemies that there is neither gate, wall, bulwark, platform, tower, armory, ammunition, or ordnance to secure and defend the city from a domestic or foreign enemy. From the latter they think San Juan de Ulua sufficient and strong enough to secure them. For contractation Mexico is one of the richest cities in the world. By the North Sea cometh every year from Spain a fleet of near twenty ships laden with the best commodities not only of Spain but of the most parts of Christendom; by the South Sea it enjoyeth traffic from all parts of Peru. Above all, it trades with the East Indies, and from thence receiveth the commodities as well from those parts which are inhabited by Portuguese, as from the countries of Japan and China, sending every year two great *caracas* with two smaller vessels to the Philippine Islands, and having every year a return of such-like ships.

There is also in Mexico a mint house where money is daily coined, and is brought thither in wedges upon mules from the mines called San Luis de Zacatecas, standing fourscore leagues from Mexico northward, and yet from Zacatecas forward have the Spaniards entered above a hundred leagues daily conquering Indians, where they discover store of mines; and there they have built a city called *Nova Mexico,* New Mexico. The Indians there are great warriors, and hold the Spaniards hard to it. It is thought the Spaniard will not be satisfied until he subdue all the country that way, which doubtless reacheth to our plantations of Virginia and the rest, being the same continued continent land. There is yet more in Mexico, a fair school, now made an university, which the Viceroy Don Antonio de Mendoza caused to be built.

At the rebuilding of this city there was a great difference betwixt an inhabitant of Mexico and a Conqueror, for a Conqueror was a name of honor, and had lands and rents given him and to his posterity by the King of Spain, whereas the inhabitant or mere dweller paid rent for his house. This hath filled all those parts of America with proud Dons and gentlemen to this day, for every one will call himself a descendant from a Conqueror, though he be as poor as Job. Ask him what is become of his estate and fortune, he will answer that fortune hath taken it away, but it shall never take away a Don from him. Nay, a poor cobbler, or carrier that runs about the country far and near getting his living with half-a-dozen mules, if he be called Mendoza, or Guzmán, will swear that he descended from those dukes' houses in Spain, and that his grandfather came from thence to conquer, and subdued whole countries to the Crown of Spain, though now fortune have frowned upon him, and covered his rags with a threadbare cloak.

When Mexico was rebuilt, and judges, aldermen, attorneys, town-clerks, notaries, scavengers, and sergeants with all other officers necessary for the commonwealth of a city were appointed, the fame of Cortés and majesty of the city was blown abroad into far provinces, by means whereof it was soon replenished with Indians again, and with Spaniards from Spain. They soon conquered above four hundred leagues of land, all of which is governed by the princely seat of Mexico. Since that first rebuilding, I may say it is now rebuilt the second time by Spaniards, who have consumed most of the Indians, so that now I will not dare to say there are a hundred thousand houses which soon after the Conquest were built up, for most of them were of Indians.

The Indians that now live there, dwell in the suburbs of the city, and their situation is called Guadalupe. In the year 1625, when I went to those parts, this suburb was judged to contain five thousand inhabitants. Since then most of them have been consumed by the Spaniards' hard usage and the work of the lake, so that now there may not be above two thousand inhabitants of mere Indians, and a thousand of such as they call there mestizoes. These are of a mixed nature of Spaniards and Indians, for many poor Spaniards marry with Indian women, and others that marry them not but hate their husbands, find many tricks to convey away an innocent Uriah to enjoy his Bathsheba. The Spaniards daily cozen them of the small plot of ground where their houses stand, and of three or four houses of Indians they build up one good and fair house after the Spanish fashion with gardens and orchards. And so is almost all Mexico new built with very fair and spacious houses with gardens of recreation.

Their buildings are with stone and brick very strong, but not high, by reason of the many earthquakes, which would endanger their houses if they were above three storeys high. The streets are very broad; in the narrowest of them three coaches may go, and in the broader six may go in the breadth of them, which makes the city seem a great deal bigger than it is. In my time it was thought to be of between thirty and forty thousand Spaniards, who are so proud and rich that half the city was judged to keep coaches, for it was a most credible report that in Mexico in my time there were above fifteen thousand coaches. It is a by-word that at Mexico four things are fair; that is to say, the women, the apparel, the horses, and the streets. But to this I may add the beauty of some of the coaches of the gentry, which do exceed in cost the best of the Court of Madrid and other parts of Christendom, for they spare no silver, nor gold, nor precious stones, nor cloth of gold, nor the best silks from China to enrich them. And to the gallantry of their horses the pride of some doth add the cost of bridles and shoes of silver.

The streets of Christendom must not compare with those in breadth and cleanness, but especially in the riches of the shops which do adorn them. Above all, the goldsmiths' shops and works are to be admired. The Indians, and the people of China that have been made Christians and every year come thither, have perfected the Spaniards in that trade. The Viceroy that went thither the year 1625 caused a popinjay to be made as a present to the King of Spain of silver, gold, and precious stones with the perfect colors of the popinjay's feathers (a bird bigger than a pheasant), with such exquisite art and perfection that it was prized to be worth in riches and workmanship half a million of ducats. There is in the cloister of the Dominicans a lamp hanging in the church with three hundred branches wrought in silver to hold so many candles, besides a hundred little lamps for oil set in it, every one being made with several workmanship so exquisitely that it is valued to be worth four hundred thousand ducats. With such-like curious works are many streets made more rich and beautiful from the shops of goldsmiths.

To the by-word touching the beauty of the women I must add the liberty they enjoy for gaming, which is such that the day and night is too short for them to end a primera when once it is begun; nay, gaming is so common to them that they invite gentlemen to their houses for no other end. To myself it happened that passing along the streets in company with a friar that came with me that year from Spain, a gentlewoman of great birth, knowing us to be *chapetons* (so they call the first year those that come from Spain), from her window called unto us, and after two or three slight questions concerning Spain asked us if we would come in and play with her a game at primera.

Both men and women are excessive in their apparel, using more silks than stuffs and cloth. Precious stones and pearls further much this their vain ostentation. A hat-band and rose made of diamonds in a gentleman's hat is common, and a hat-band of pearls is ordinary in a tradesman. Nay, a blackamoor or tawny young maid and slave will make hard shift, but she will be in fashion with her neck-chain and bracelets of pearls, and her ear-bobs of some considerable jewels. The attire of this baser sort of people of blackamoors and mulattoes (which are of a mixed nature, of Spaniards and blackamoors) is so light, and their carriage so enticing, that many Spaniards even of the better sort (who are too too prone to venery) disdain their wives for them.

Their clothing is a petticoat of silk or cloth, with many silver or golden laces, with a very broad double ribbon of some light color with long silver or golden tags hanging down before, the whole length of their petticoat to the ground, and the like behind. Their waistcoats are made like bodices, with skirts, laced likewise with gold or silver, without sleeves, and a girdle about their body of great price stuck with pearls and knots of gold (if they be any ways well esteemed of). Their sleeves are broad and open at the end, of holland or fine China linen, wrought some with colored silks, some with silk and gold, some with silk and silver, hanging down almost unto the ground. The locks of their heads are covered with some wrought coif, and over it another of network of silk bound with a fair silk, or silver, or golden ribbon which crosseth the upper part of their forehead, and hath commonly worked out in letters some light and foolish love posy. Their bare, black, and tawny breasts are covered with bobs hanging from their chains of pearls.

When they go abroad, they use a white mantle of lawn or cambric rounded with a broad lace, which some put over their heads, the breadth reaching only to their middle behind, that their girdle and ribbons may be seen, and the two ends before reaching to the ground almost. Others cast their mantles only upon their shoulders, and swaggerers-like, cast the one end over the left shoulder that they may the better jog the right arm, and shew their broad sleeve as they walk along. Others instead of this mantle use some rich silk petticoat to hang upon their left shoulder, while with their right arm they support the lower part of it, more like roaring boys than honest civil maids. Their shoes are high and of many soles, the outside whereof of the profaner sort are plated with a list of silver, which is fastened with small nails of broad silver heads. Most of these are or have been slaves, though love have set them loose, at liberty to enslave souls to sin and Satan. And there are so many of this kind, both men and women, grown to a height of pride and vanity, that many times the Spaniards have feared they would rise up and mutiny against them.[3] The looseness of their lives and public

---

[3] It is strange that this Negro element has largely disappeared in present-day Mexico, at least on the plateau. In parts of the *tierra caliente*, notably in Guerrero and Veracruz, a strain of Negro blood is sometimes evident.

scandals committed by them and the better sort of the Spaniards were such that I have heard those who have professed more religion and fear of God say often they verily thought God would destroy that city, and give up the country into the power of some other nation.

It seems that religion teacheth that all wickedness is allowable, so long as the churches and clergy flourish, nay, while the purse is open to lasciviousness, if it be likewise opened to enrich the temple walls and roofs, that is well. Sin and wickedness abound in Mexico, yet there are no more devout people in the world toward the Church and clergy. In their lifetime they strive to exceed one another in their gifts to the cloisters of nuns and friars. Some erect altars to their best devoted saints, worth many thousand thousand ducats; others present crowns of gold to the pictures of Mary, others, lamps; others, golden chains; others build cloisters at their own charge; others repair them; others at their death leave to them two or three thousand ducats for an annual stipend.

Among these great benefactors to the churches of that city I should wrong my history if I should forget one that lived in my time, called Alonso Cuellar, who was reported to have a closet to his house laid with bars of gold instead of bricks, though indeed it was not so, but only reported for his abundant riches and store of bars of gold which he had in one chest standing in a closet distant from another, where he had a chest full of wedges of silver.

This man alone built a nunnery for Franciscan nuns, which stood him in above thirty thousand ducats, and he left for the maintenance of the nuns two thousand ducats yearly, with obligation of some Masses to be said in the church every year for his soul after his decease. Yet this man's life was so scandalous that commonly in the night with two servants he would round the city, visiting such scandalous persons whose attire before hath been described, carrying his beads in his hands, and at every house letting fall a bead and tying a false knot, that when he came home in the morning towards break of the day he might number by his beads the uncivil stations he had walked and visited that night. But his works of darkness came to light, and what happened unto him whilst I was in Mexico was published far and near. One night, meeting at one of his stations with a gentleman that was jealous of him, swords on both sides were drawn. The concubine first was stabbed by the gentleman, who was better manned and attended; and Cuellar, who was but a merchant, was mortally wounded and left for dead, though afterwards he recovered.

Great alms and liberality towards religious houses in that city commonly are coupled with great and scandalous wickedness. They wallow in the bed of riches and wealth, and make their alms the coverlet to cover their loose and lascivious lives. From hence are the churches so fairly built and adorned. There are not above fifty churches and chapels, cloisters and nunneries, and parish churches in that city, but those that are there are the fairest that ever my eyes beheld. The roofs and beams are in many of them all daubed with gold. Many altars have sundry marble pillars, and others are decorated with brazil-wood stays standing one above another with tabernacles for several saints richly wrought with golden colors, so that twenty thousand ducats is a common price of many of them. These cause admiration in the common sort of people, and admiration brings on daily adoration in them to those glorious spectacles and images of saints.

Besides these beautiful buildings, the inward riches belonging to the altars are infinite in price and value. All the copes, canopies, hangings, altar cloths, candlesticks, jewels belonging to the saints, and crowns of gold and silver, and tabernacles of gold and crystal to carry about their sacrament in procession would mount to the worth of a reasonable mine of silver, and would be a rich prey for any nation that could make better use of wealth and riches. I will not speak much of the lives of the friars and nuns of that city, but only that there they enjoy more liberty than in the parts of Europe (where yet they have too much) and that surely the scandals committed by them do cry up to Heaven for vengeance, judgment, and destruction.

In my time in the cloister of the Mercenarian friars which is entitled for the Redemption of Captives, there chanced to be an election of a Provincial to rule over them, to the which all the priors and heads of the cloisters about the country had resorted. Such were their various and factious differences that upon the sudden all the convent was in an uproar, their canonical election was turned to mutiny and strife, knives were drawn, and many wounded. The scandal and danger of murder was so great, that the Viceroy was

71

fain to interpose his authority and to sit amongst them and guard the cloister until their Provincial was elected.

It is ordinary for the friars to visit the devoted nuns, and to spend whole days with them, hearing their music, feeding on their sweetmeats, and for this purpose they have many chambers which they call *locutorios*, to talk in, with wooden bars between the nuns and them, and in these chambers are tables for the friars to dine at, and while they dine the nuns recreate them with their voices. Gentlemen and citizens give their daughters to be brought up in these nunneries, where they are taught to make all sorts of conserves and preserves, all sorts of needlework, all sorts of music, which is so exquisite in that city that I dare be bold to say that the people are drawn to their churches more for the delight of the music than for any delight in the service of God. More, they teach these young children to act like players; and to entice the people to their churches, they make these children act short dialogues in their choirs, richly attiring them with men's and women's apparel, especially upon Midsummer Day, and the eight days[4] before their Christmas. These are so gallantly performed that there have been many factious strifes and single combats—some were in my time—for defending which of these nunneries most excelled in music and in the training up of children. No delights are wanting in that city abroad in the world, nor in their churches, which should be the house of God, and the soul's, not the senses' delight.

The chief place in the city is the market-place, which though it be not as spacious as in Montezuma's time, yet is at this day very fair and wide, built all with arches on the one side where people may walk dry in time of rain, and there are shops of merchants furnished with all sorts of stuffs and silks, and before them sit women selling all manner of fruits and herbs. Over against these shops and arches is the Viceroy's palace, which, with the walls of the house and of the gardens belonging to it, taketh up almost the whole length of the market. At the end of the Viceroy's palace is the chief prison, which is strong of stone work. Next to this is the beautiful street called *La Plateria*, or Goldsmiths' Street, where a man's eyes may

---

[4] The reference is to the *posadas*, the old Mexican custom of acting the vain search of Joseph and Mary for accommodation at an inn. Note how Gage uses the expression "eight days," which is a direct translation of the Spanish term for a week.

behold in less than an hour many millions' worth of gold, silver, pearls, and jewels. The street of San Agustín is rich and comely, where live all that trade in silks.

One of the longest and broadest is the street called Tacuba, where almost all the shops are of ironmongers, and of such as deal in brass and steel. This adjoins those arches whereon the water is conveyed into the city, and is so called for that it is the way out of the city to a town called Tacuba, and this street is mentioned far and near, not so much for the length and breadth of it, as for a small commodity of needles which are made there, and for proof are the best of all those parts. For stately buildings the street called *del Aguila*, the Street of the Eagle, exceeds the rest. There live gentlemen, and courtiers, and judges belonging to the Chancery, and there is the palace of the Marqués del Valle from the line of Hernando Cortés. This street is so called from an old idol an eagle of stone which from the Conquest lieth in a corner of that street, and is twice as big as London stone.

The gallants of this city shew themselves, some on horseback, and most in coaches, daily about four of the clock in the afternoon in a pleasant shady field called *la Alameda*, full of trees and walks, somewhat like unto our Moorfields, where do meet as constantly as the merchants upon our exchange about two thousand coaches, full of gallants, ladies, and citizens, to see and to be seen, to court and to be courted. The gentlemen have their train of blackamoor slaves, some a dozen, some half a dozen, waiting on them, in brave and gallant liveries, heavy with gold and silver lace, with silk stockings on their black legs, and roses on their feet, and swords by their sides. The ladies also carry their train by their coach's side of such jet-like damsels as before have been mentioned for their light apparel, who with their bravery and white mantles over them seem to be, as the Spaniard saith, *"mosca en leche,"* a fly in milk. But the train of the Viceroy, who often goeth to this place, is wonderful stately, which some say is as great as the train of his master the King of Spain.

At this meeting are carried about many sorts of sweetmeats and papers of comfits to be sold, and for relish a cup of cool water, which is cried about in curious glasses, to cool the blood of those love-hot gallants. But many times these meetings sweetened with conserves and comfits have sour sauce at the end, for jealousy will not suffer a lady to be courted, no, nor sometimes to be spoken to, but puts fury into the violent hand to draw a sword or dagger and to stab or murder whom he was jealous of. And when one sword is drawn, thousands are presently drawn, some to right the party wounded or murdered; others to defend the party murdering. The friends of the latter will not permit him to be apprehended, but will guard him with drawn swords until they have conveyed him to the sanctuary of some church, from whence the Viceroy's power is not able to take him for a legal trial. Many of these sudden skirmishes happened whilst I lived about Mexico.

A whole volume might be compiled about that city, but much hath been written by other authors, and I desire not to fill my history with trifles, but only with what is most remarkable in it. I may not omit yet from the situation of it upon a lake to tell that certainly the water hath its passage under all the streets of it, for toward the street of San Agustín and the lower parts of the city, I can confidently aver that in my time before the removing of the lake those that died were rather drowned than buried, for a grave could not be digged with an ordinary grave's depth but they met with water, and I was eye-witness of many thus buried, whose coffins was covered with water.

This is so apparent that had not the cloister of the Augustines often been repaired and almost rebuilt, it had quite sunk by this. In my time it was a repairing, and I saw the old pillars had sunk very low. Upon them they were then laying new foundations, and I was credibly informed that that was the third time that new pillars had been erected upon the old which were quite sunk away.[5] This city hath but three ways to come unto it by causeway: the one is from the west, and that causeway is a mile and a half long; another from the north, and containeth three miles in length. Eastward the city hath no entry, but southward the causeway is five miles long, and by that way Cortés entered into it, when he conquered it.

The fruit called *nochtli* [prickly pear cactus], whereof I have spoken before, and some say this city was called Tenochtitlán from it, though it be in most parts of America, yea and now in Spain, yet

---

[5] Buildings still sink—but others rise—in Mexico City. The Palacio de Bellas Artes, built nearly fifty years ago as the Opera House, has sunk many feet. Some modern Mexican buildings are erected on a kind of raftlike floating platform.

in no place is there more abundance of it than in Mexico, and it is absolutely one of the best fruits in it. It is like unto the fig, and so hath many little kernels or grains within, but they are somewhat larger, and crowned like unto a medlar. There are of them of sundry colors, some are green without, and carnation-like within, which have a good taste. Others are yellow, and others white, and some speckled; the best sort are the white. It is a fruit that will last long. Some of them taste of pears, and others some of grapes. It is a cold and a fresh fruit, and best esteemed in the heat of summer. The Spaniards do more esteem them than the Indians. The more the ground is labored where they grow, the fruit is so much the better. There is yet another kind of this fruit red, and that is nothing so much esteemed, although his taste is not evil, but because it doth color and dye the eater's mouth, lips, and apparel, yea, and maketh the urine look like pure blood. Many Spaniards at their first coming into India and eating this fruit, were amazed and at their wits' end, thinking that all the blood in their bodies came out in urine; yea, and many physicians at their first coming were of the same belief. And it hath happened when they have been sent for unto such as have eaten this fruit, they not knowing the cause and beholding the urine, by and by they have administered medicines to staunch blood; a thing to laugh at, to see physicians so deceived.

The skin of the outside is thick and full of little small prickles, and when it is cut downright with one cut to the kernels, with one finger you may uncleave the whole skin round about without breaking it, and take out the fruit to eat. The Spaniards use to jest with it with strangers. For taking half a dozen of them, and rubbing them in a napkin, those small prickles, which can scarce be seen or perceived, stick invisibly unto the napkin. And when a man wipes his mouth with it to drink, those little prickles stick in his lips so that they seem to sow them up together and make him for a while falter in his speech, till with much rubbing and washing they come off.

There is another fruit twice of the bigness of a great warden [cooking pear], which they call the growing *manjar blanco,* or white meat, which is a dainty dish made by them with the white of a capon, cream, and rice, and sugar and sweet waters, much like unto the which tasteth this fruit. It is as sweet as any honey, and dissolves like melted snow in the mouth into a juice most luscious; within, it is full of hard black kernels or stones, which being cracked are bitter, and these not joined together, but by division one from another, each one having a bag, or little skin, discerning them in their ranks and orders, so that when you cut this fruit in the middle it represents a chequer-board with black and white; the white is sucked or eaten and the kernels thrown away. But I cannot forget that which they call *piña*, or pineapple; not the pineapple of the high pine tree, but a pineapple that groweth upon a lower shrub with prickly leaves, and is bigger than our biggest musk melons in England, when it is ripe; it is yellow without and within. Without, it is full of little bunches, and within, so juicy and cool that nothing is more dangerous than to eat much of it. Before they eat it, they cut it in round slices, and lay it a while in salt and water, and so being scoured half an hour in that salt and water which taketh much of the rawness and coldness from it, they then put it into dishes with more fresh water, and eat it thus. But the better way of eating it is preserved, which is absolutely the best preserve in all that country. There is also the grape, though they make not wine of it, the apple, the pear, the quince, the peach, the apricot, the pomegranate, the muskmelon, the plantain, the fig, the walnut, the chestnut, the orange, the lemon both sour and sweet, the citron in great abundance. Most of the fruits of Europe, and as many more which Europe never knew.

About Mexico more than in any other part groweth that excellent tree called *metl* [maguey], which they plant and dress as they do their vines in Europe. It hath near forty kinds of leaves, which serve for many uses, for when they be tender, they make of them conserves, paper, flax, mantles, mats, shoes, girdles, and cordage. On these leaves grow certain prickles so strong and sharp that they use them instead of saws: from the root of this tree cometh a juice like unto syrup, which being sodden will become sugar. You may also make of it wine [*pulque*] and vinegar. The Indians often become drunk with it. The rind roasted healeth hurts and sores, and from the top boughs issueth a gum, which is an excellent antidote against poison. There is nothing in Mexico and about it wanting which may make a city happy. Certainly had those who have so much extolled with their pens the parts of Granada in Spain, Lombardy and Florence in Italy, making them the earthly Paradise, been acquainted with the New World and with Mexico, they would have recanted their untruths.

Reredos of side altar of the Cathedral of San Cristóbal de las Casas,
with portraits of St. Edward the Confessor and St. Wenceslas, faces
looking outward, inserted inconspicuously at the base, obviously
after the reredos was in position.

The portrait of St. Edward the Confessor at San Cristóbal (Chiapa of the Spaniards), believed to have been commissioned by Thomas Gage. See Appendix 2 for details.

This city is the seat of an Archbishop, and of a Viceroy, who commonly is some great nobleman of Spain, whose power is to make laws and ordinances, to give directions, and determine controversies, unless it be in such great causes which are thought fit to be referred to the Council of Spain. There be about the country many governments with several governors, yet they are all subordinate to this Viceroy, and there are at least four hundred leagues of land all governed by the princely seat of Mexico. Most of the governors about the country being the Viceroy's creatures, placed by him, do contribute great gifts and bribes for their preferment. So likewise do all the rest whose right or wrong proceedings depend upon the Viceroy's clemency and mercy in judging the daily appeals of justice which come unto him. The King of Spain allows him out of his exchequer a hundred thousand ducats yearly whilst he governs. His time is only five years, but commonly with his bribes to the courtiers of Spain, and to the Counsellors for the Estate of the Indies he gets a prorogation of five years more, and sometimes of ten.

It is incredible what this Viceroy may get a year in that place besides his hundred thousand ducats of rent, if he be a man covetous and given to trading, as most of them are. Then they will be masters of what commodities they please, and none else shall deal in them but themselves. That was what the Marqués of Serralvo did in my time, for he was the best monopolist of salt that ever those parts knew. This man was thought to get a million a year, what with gifts and presents, what with his trading to Spain and the Philippines. He governed ten years, and in this time he sent to the King of Spain a popinjay worth half a million, and in one year more he sent the worth of a million to the Count of Olivares, and other courtiers to obtain a prorogation for five years more.

Besides the Viceroy there are commonly six judges and a King's Attorney, who are allowed out of the King's exchequer yearly twelve thousand ducats apiece, besides two *Alcaldes de Corte*, or High Justices, who, with the Viceroy, judge all Chancery and criminal causes. These may unite together to oppose the Viceroy in any unlawful and unjustifiable action, as some have done and have smarted for it. Yet commonly they dare not, so that he doth what he listeth, and it is enough for him to say, "*Stat pro ratione voluntas.*" This power joined with covetousness in the Viceroy, and threescore thousand ducats yearly joined with pride in the Archbishop, was like to be the ruin of that city in the year 1624, when the Count of Gélves[6] was Viceroy, and Don Alonso de Zerna, Archbishop. These two powers striving and striking at one another like two flints had almost brought to combustion that gallant city, and did set on fire the Viceroy's palace and the prison joining to it.

The story may be profitable for other nations, to beware of covetous governors and proud prelates, and therefore I thought fit to insert it here. The Count of Gélves was in some things one of the best viceroys and governors that ever the Court of Spain sent to America, for he was called by the Spaniards *"el terrible justiciero, y fuego de ladrones,"* that is, terrible for justice, and fire to consume all thieves. For he cleared all the highways of thieves, hanging them without mercy as often as they were caught, and did send out troops and officers to apprehend them, so that it was generally reported that since the Conquest unto those days of his there had never been so many thieves and malefactors hanged up as in his time.

In all other points of justice he was equally severe and upright, yet covetousness did so blind him to his own injustice, that before he could see it, he had brought the city of Mexico and the whole kingdom to a danger of rebellion. What he would not to be seen in himself, he acted by others as his instruments. One of them was one Don Pedro Mejía, a mighty and rich gentleman of Mexico, whom he chose to join with him in monopolizing all the Indian maize and wheat about the country. Don Pedro Mejía bought from the Indians their maize at the price he listed, and the wheat of the Spaniards he bought according to that price at which it is taxed by the law of that land to be sold at in time of famine. This is at fourteen reals a bushel (which is not much there considering the abundance of gold and silver), at which price the farmers and husbandmen, knowing it to be a plentiful year, were glad and willing to sell unto him their wheat, not knowing what the end would be. Others, fearing to gainsay him, whom they knew to be the Viceroy's favorite, did the same. Thus Don Pedro Mejía filled all the barns which he had hired

---

[6] Conde de Priego y Marqués de Gélvez, viceroy 1621–24. His successor, Rodrigo Pacheco y Osorio, Marqués de Cerralvo, who crossed with Gage, developed a profitable salt monopoly. Nevertheless, many of the viceroys were upright, intelligent, and hard-working men who governed wisely and well.

about the country, and himself and the Viceroy became owners of all the wheat. He had officers appointed to bring it into the markets upon his warning, and that was when some small remnants that had escaped his fingers were sold, and the price raised. Then he hoisted his price, and doubled it above what it had cost him. The poor began to complain, the rich to murmur, the tax of the law was moved in the Court of Chancery before the Viceroy. But he, being privy to the monopoly, expounded the law to be understood in time of famine, and that he was informed that it was as plentiful a year as ever had been, and that to his knowledge there was as much brought into the markets as ever had been, and plenty enough for Mexico and all the country. Thus was the law slighted, the rich mocked, the poor oppressed, and none sold wheat but Don Pedro Mejía's officers for himself and the Viceroy.

When justice would be no father, the people went to their mother, the Church, and having understood the business better, and that it was Don Pedro Mejía who did tyrannize and oppress them with the Viceroy's favor, they entreated the Archbishop to make it a case of conscience, and to reduce it to a Church censure. Don Alonso de Zerna, the Archbishop, who had always stomached [disliked] Don Pedro Mejía and the Viceroy, to please the people agreed to excommunicate Don Pedro Mejía, and so sent out bills of excommunication to be fixed upon all the church doors against him. Don Pedro paid no attention to the excommunication, and keeping close at home, still sold his wheat. As he raised the price still higher than it was before, the Archbishop raised this censure higher against him, adding to it a bill of *cessatio a divinis*, that is, a cessation from all divine service.

This censure is so great with them that it is never used except against some great man who is contumacious and stubborn in his ways, contemning the power of the Church. Then are all the church doors shut up (let the city be never so great), no Masses are said, no prayers used, no preaching permitted, no meetings allowed for any public devotion or calling upon God. Their Church mourns as it were, and makes no show of spiritual joy and comfort, nor of any communion of prayers one with another, so long as the party continues stubborn and rebellious in his sin and scandal, and unyielding to the Church's censure. And further, by this *cessatio a divinis*, many churches and especially cloisters suffer in the means of their livelihood, for they depend upon what is daily given them for the Masses they say, and in a cloister where thirty or forty priests say Mass, so many pieces of eight or crowns in Mexico do daily come in. Therefore, this censure or *cessatio a divinis* is so inflicted upon the whole Church (all suffering for it as they say in spiritual and some in temporal ways) that the offending or scandalizing party, for whose sake this curse is laid upon all, is bound to satisfy all priests and cloisters which in the aforesaid way suffer, and to allow them so much out of his means, as they might have daily got by selling away their Masses for so many crowns for their daily livelihood.

Thus the Archbishop would have brought Don Pedro Mejía, to have emptied out of his purse near a thousand crowns daily towards the maintenance of about a thousand priests (so many there may be in Mexico). Secondly, by the people's suffering in their spiritual comfort and non-communion of prayers, he thought to make Don Pedro Mejía odious to the people. Don Pedro, perceiving the spiteful intents of the Archbishop and hearing the outcries of the people in the streets against him and their cries for the use and liberty of their churches, secretly retired himself to the palace of the Viceroy, begging his favor and protection since is was for his sake he suffered.

The Viceroy immediately sent out his orders, commanding the bills of excommunication and *cessatio a divinis* to be pulled from the church doors, and ordering all the superiors of the cloisters to open their churches and to celebrate their service and Masses as formerly they had done. But they disobeyed the Viceroy through blind obedience to their Archbishop. Whereupon the Viceroy commanded the Arch-Prelate to revoke his censures. But his answer was that what he had done had been justly done against a public offender and great oppressor of the poor, whose cries had moved him to commiserate their suffering condition, and that the offender's contempt of his first excommunication had deserved the rigor of the second censure, which he neither would nor could revoke until Don Pedro Mejía had submitted himself to the Church and to a public absolution, and had satisfied the priests and cloisters who suffered for him, and until he had disclaimed that unlawful and unconscionable monopoly, wherewith he wronged the whole commonwealth, and especially the poorer sort therein.

Thus did that proud prelate arrogantly in terms exalt himself against the authority of his prince and ruler, contemning his command with a flat denial, thinking himself happy in imitating Ambrose's spirit against the Emperor Theodosius, trusting in the power of his keys, and in the strength of his Church and clergy, which with the rebellion of the meaner sort he resolved to oppose against the power and strength of his magistrate. The Viceroy, not brooking this saucy answer from a priest, commanded him presently to be apprehended and to be guarded to San Juan de Ulua, and there to be shipped for Spain.

The Archbishop, having notice of the Viceroy's resolution, retired himself out of Mexico to Guadalupe with many of his priests and prebends, leaving a bill of excommunication upon the church doors against the Viceroy himself, and thinking privily to fly to Spain there to give an account of his carriage and behavior. But he could not flee so fast but the Viceroy's care and vigilancy still eyed him, and with his sergeants and officers pursued him to Guadalupe. When the Archbishop understood this, he betook himself to the sanctuary of the church, and there caused the candles to be lighted upon the altar, and the Host to be taken out of the tabernacle. Then, attired in his pontifical vestments, with his mitre on his head, his crozier in one hand, and the Host in the other, he waited thus with his train of priests about him at the altar, for the coming of the sergeants and officers. He thought with the Host in his hand, and with a "Here I am," to astonish and amaze them, and to make them fall backwards, and to disable them from laying hands upon him, as Christ did to the Jews in the garden.

The officers coming into the church went towards the altar where the Bishop stood, and kneeling down first to worship their God, made a short prayer. This being ended, they propounded unto the Bishop with courteous and fair words the cause of their coming to that place, requiring him to lay down the Sacrament and to come out of the church, and to hear the notification of what orders they brought unto him in the King's name. The Archbishop replied that, whereas their master the Viceroy was excommunicated, he looked upon him as one out of the pale of the Church, and one without any power or authority to command him in the house of God. So he required them as they tendered the good of their souls to depart peaceably, and not to infringe the privileges and immunity of the

Church, by exercising in it any legal act of secular power and command. He made it clear that he would not go out of the church unless they durst take him and the Sacrament together.

With this the head officer, named Tiroll, stood up and notified unto him an order in the King's name to apprehend his person in whatsoever place he should find him, and to guard him to the port of San Juan de Ulua, and there to deliver him to whom by further order he should be directed, to be shipped for Spain as a traitor to the King's crown, a troubler of the common peace, and an author and mover of sedition in the commonwealth. The Archbishop, smiling upon Tiroll, answered him: "Thy master useth too high terms, and words which do better agree unto himself; for I know no mutiny or sedition like to trouble the commonwealth, unless it be by his and Don Pedro Mejía's oppressing of the poor. And as for thy guarding me to San Juan de Ulua, I conjure thee by Jesus Christ, whom thou knowest I hold in my hands, not to use here any violence in God's house, from whose altar I am resolved not to depart. Take heed God punish thee not as he did Jeroboam for stretching forth his hand at the altar against the Prophet; let his withered hand remind thee of thy duty."

But Tiroll suffered him not to squander away the time and ravel it out with further preaching, but called to the altar a priest whom he had brought for that purpose, and commanded him in the King's name to take the Sacrament out of the Archbishop's hand. This the priest did. Thereupon, the Archbishop unvested himself of his pontificals, and, with many repetitions of the Church's immunity, yielded himself unto Tiroll. Taking his leave of all his prebends, and requiring them to be witnesses of what had been done, he went prisoner to San Juan de Ulua, where he was delivered to the custody of the governor of the castle, and not many days after he was sent in a ship prepared for that purpose to Spain to the King and Council, with a full charge of all his carriages and misdemeanors.

Some of the city of Mexico in private began to talk strangely against the Viceroy, and to stomach [resent] the banishment of their Archbishop, because he had stood out against so high a power in defense of the poor and oppressed, and these private grudges they soon vented in public with bold and arrogant speeches against Don Pedro Mejía, and the Viceroy. In this they were set on and encouraged by the priests and prebends, who it seems had sworn blind obedience to their Arch-Prelate, and therewith thought they could dispense with their consciences in their obedience and duty to their magistrate. Thus did those incendiaries for a fortnight together blow the fire of sedition and rebellion, especially amongst the inferior sort of people and the Creoles or native Spaniards, and the Indians and mulattoes, whom they knew brooked not the severe and rigorous justice and judgment of the Viceroy, no nor any government that was appointed over them from Spain.

At a fortnight's end Tiroll returned from San Juan de Ulua, and then began the spite and malice of all the malcontents to break out; then began a fire of mutiny to be kindled, which was thought would have consumed and buried in ashes that great and famous city. Tiroll was not a little jealous of what mischief the common rabble intended against him, and so kept close, not daring to walk the streets. Yet his occasions inviting him to the Viceroy's palace, he ventured himself in a coach with drawn curtains. Yet this could not blind the eyes of the spiteful and malicious malcontents, who had notice that he was in the coach.

Before he could get to the market-place, three or four boys began to cry out, "*Judas, Judas, alla va Judas,*" "There goeth Judas that laid his hands upon Christ's Vicar," and others joined with them saying, "*Ahorquemos a este Judas,*" "Let us hang this Judas." The number of boys yet increased, crying aloud and boldly after the coach, "*Muera el vellaco descomulgado la muerte de Judas, muera el picaro, muera el perro,*" "Let this excommunicated rogue and dog die the death of Judas." The coachman lashed the mules, the coach posted, the boys hasted after with stones and dirt, and the number increased so that before Tiroll could get through two streets only, there were risen above two hundred boys, of Spaniards, Indians, blackamoors, and mulattoes. With much ado Tiroll got to the Viceroy's palace, posting for his life, and his first care was to wish the porters to shut all the palace gates, for he was fearful of what presently happened, a more general insurrection and uproar.

No sooner was he got into the Viceroy's house and the gates shut up, but there were gathered to the market-place (as I was credibly informed by those that saw and observed diligently that day's trouble) above two thousand people, all of inferior rank and quality, and the number still increased till they were judged to be about six or seven thousand. They all cried out for Tiroll, the Judas, sparing neither stones nor dirt which they did fling at the palace windows.

The Viceroy sent a message to them, desiring them to be quiet, and to betake themselves to their houses, certifying them that Tiroll was not in his palace, but escaped out of a back door. The rude multitude would not be satisfied with this, being now set on by two or three priests who were joined with them, and so they began more violently to batter the palace gates and walls, having brought pikes, and halberds, and long poles. Others had got a few pistols and birding pieces, wherewith they shot, not caring whom they killed or wounded in the palace. It was wonderful to see that none of the better sort, none of the judges, no high justice, no inferior officers durst or would come out to suppress the multitude, or to assist the Viceroy, who was in so great danger. Nay, I was told by some shopkeepers who lived in the market-place that they made a laughing business of it, and the people that passed by went smiling and saying, "Let the boys and youngsters alone, they will right our wrongs, they will find out before they have done both Tiroll and Mejía and him that protects them," meaning the Viceroy.

Amongst them was much noted one priest, named Salazar, who spent much shot and bullets, and his spirits more, in running about to spy some place of advantage, which he might soonest batter down. They found, it seems, the prison doors easier to open, or else with help within they opened them and let out all the malefactors, who joined with them to assault the palace. The Viceroy, seeing no help came to him from the city, from his friends, from the judges of the Chancery, from the King's high justices, nor from other officers for the peace, went up to the *azoteas* [flat rooftops] of his palace with his guard and servants that attended on him, and set up the Royal Standard. He then caused a trumpet to be sounded to call the city to aid and assist their King, but this prevailed not; none stirred, all the chief of the city kept within doors. And when the multitude saw the Royal Standard out, and heard the King's name from the *azoteas*, they cried out, and often repeated it, "*Viva el Rey, muera el mal gobierno, mueran los descomulgados*," that is to say, "Our King live long, but let the evil government die, and perish, and let them die that are excommunicated." These words saved many of them from hanging afterwards, when the business was tried and searched into by Don Martín de Carrillo.

With these words in their mouths, they skirmished with them of the *azoteas* at least three hours, they above hurling down stones, and they beneath hurling up to them and some shooting with a few pistols and birding pieces at one another. And mark that in all this bitter skirmish there was not a piece of ordnance shot, for the Viceroy had none for the defense of his palace or person, neither had or hath that great city any for its strength and security, the Spaniards living fearless of the Indians, and (as they think) secure from being annoyed by any foreign nation. There were slain in about six hours in all that this tumult lasted, seven or eight beneath the market-place, and one of the Viceroy's guard and a page on the *azoteas* above.

As the day drew to an end, the multitude brought pitch and fire, and first fired the prison, then they set on fire part of the palace, and burnt down the chief gate. This made some of the gentry and of the judges of the city come out and persuade the people to desist and quench the fire, lest it should sweep much of the city. Whilst the fire was quenching, many got into the palace, some fell upon the Viceroy's stables, and there got part of his mules' and horses' rich furnitures, others began to fall upon some chests, others to tear down the hangings, but they were soon persuaded by the better sort of the city to desist from spoil or robbery, lest by that they should be discovered. Others searched for Don Pedro Mejía, for Tiroll, and the Viceroy. None of them could be found, having disguised themselves and so escaped. Whither Don Pedro Mejía and Tiroll went, it could not be known in many days, but certain it was that the Viceroy disguised himself in a Franciscan habit, and so in company of a friar went through the multitude to the cloister of the Franciscans, where he abode all that year (and there I saw him the year after), not daring to come out, until he had informed the King and Council of Spain with what hath happened, and of the danger himself and the city was in, if not timely prevented.

The King and Council of Spain took the business to consideration, and looked upon it as a warning piece to a further mutiny and rebellion, and an example to other parts of America to follow upon any such-like occasion, if some punishment were not inflicted upon the chief offenders. Wherefore the year following, 1625, which was when I went to those parts, the King sent a new Viceroy, the Marqués of Serralvo, to govern in the place of the Count of Gélves, and especially to aid and assist Don Martín de Carrillo, a priest and inquisitor of the Inquisition of Valladolid, who was sent with large commission and authority to examine the aforesaid tumult and mutiny, and to judge all offenders that should be found in it, yea, and to hang up such as should deserve death.

I was at Mexico in the best time of the trial, and had intelligence from Don Martín de Carrillo's own spiritual father, a Dominican friar, of the chief passages in the examination of the business. The result was that if justice should have been executed rightly, most of the prime of Mexico would have suffered for not coming in to the Royal Standard when called by the sound of the trumpet. Some judges were put out of their places, though they answered that they durst not stir out, for that they were informed that all the city would have risen against them if they had appeared in public. The chief actors were found to be the Creoles or natives of the country, who do hate the Spanish government, and all such as come from Spain. Reason they have for it, for they are much oppressed by them, as I have before observed, and are and will be always watching any opportunity to free themselves from the Spanish yolk. But the chief fomenters of the mutiny were found to be the Bishop's party, the priests; and had not Salazar and three more of them fled, they had certainly been sent to the galleys of Spain for galley slaves; this judgment was published against them. There were not above three or four hanged of so many thousands, and their condemnation was for things which they had stolen out of the Viceroy's palace. And because further enquiry into the rebellion would have brought in at least half the city either for actors, or counsellors, or fomenters, the King was well advised to grant a general pardon.

The Archbishop's proceedings were more disliked in the Court of Spain than the Viceroy's, and he was long without any preferment. At last, that there might be no exceptions taken by his party, nor cause given for a further stirring the embers to a greater combustion, the Council thought fit to honor him in those parts where he was born, and to make him Bishop of Zamora, a small bishopric in Castile; so that his wings were clipped and from archbishop he came

86

to be but bishop, and from threescore thousand crowns yearly rent he fell to four to five thousand only a year. The Count of Gélves was also sent to Spain, and well entertained in the Court, and therein made Master of the King's Horse, which in Spain is a nobleman's preferment.

And this history showing the state and condition of Mexico when I travelled to those parts I have willingly set down that the reader may by it be furnished with better observations than myself, who am but a neophyte am able to deduct. Somewhat might be observed from the Viceroy's covetousness. This doubtless is in all a great sin, but much more to be condemned in a prince or governor, whom it may blind in the exercise of justice and judgment, and harden those tender bowels (which ought to be in him) of a father and shepherd to his flock and children.

And thus largely I have described the manner and proportion of Mexico, with the troubled condition I found it in when I went thither, by reason of a mutiny and rebellion caused by an archbishop the year before.

9. Showing the several parts of this New World of America, and the places of note about the famous City of Mexico

I MAY NOT omit about Mexico that famous place of Chapultepec, which in the heathens' times was the burying place of the emperors, and now by the Spaniards is the Escorial of America, where the viceroys that die are also interred. There is a sumptuous palace built with many fair gardens and devices of water, and ponds of fish, whither the Viceroy and the gentry of Mexico resort for their recreation. The riches here belonging to the Viceroy's chapel are thought to be worth above a million of crowns.

Tacuba is also a pleasant town full of orchards and gardens in the way to Chapultepec. Southward is Toluca, rich also for trading, but above all much mentioned for the bacon, which is the best of all those parts, and is transported far and near. Westward is the town called La Piedad, at the end of a causeway, to which the people much resort from Mexico, being drawn to the superstitious worship of a picture of Mary which hath been enriched by the chief people of Mexico with many thousand pounds' worth of gifts of chains, and crowns of gold.

But more southwestward three leagues from Mexico is the pleasantest place of all that are about Mexico, called La Soledad, and by others *el desierto* [*de los leones*], the solitary or desert place [of the lions] and wilderness. Were all wildernesses like it, to live in a wilderness were better than to live in a city. This hath been a device of poor friars named discalced, or barefooted Carmelites, who, whilst they would be thought to live like hermits, retired from the world, that they may draw the world to them, have built there a stately cloister, which being upon a hill and among rocks makes it more to be admired. About the cloister they have fashioned out many holes and caves in, under, and among the rocks, like hermits' lodgings. Each consists of a room to lie in and an oratory to pray in, with pictures and images and rare devices for mortification, as disciplines of wire, rods of iron, haircloths, and girdles with sharp wire points to girdle about their bare flesh. Many such like toys hang about their oratories to make people admire their mortified and holy lives. All these hermetical holes and caves, some ten in all, are within the bounds and compass of the cloister, and among orchards and gardens full of fruits and flowers, which may take up two miles compass.

Here among the rocks are many springs of water, which, with the shade of the plantains and other trees, are most cool and pleasant to the hermits, who have also the sweet smell of the rose and jasmine, which is a little flower, but the sweetest of all others. There is not any other rare and exquisite flower to be found in that country which is not in that wilderness to delight the senses of those mortified hermits. They are weekly changed from the cloister, and when their week is ended, others are sent, and they return to their cloister. They carry with them their bottles of wine, sweetmeats, and other provision; as for fruits, the trees about do drop them into their mouths. It is wonderful to see the strange devices of fountains of water which are about the gardens; but much more strange and wonderful to see the resort of coaches, and gallants, and ladies and citizens of Mexico thither, to walk and make merry in those desert pleasures, and to see those whom they look upon as living saints, and so think nothing too good for them, to cherish them in their desert conflicts with Satan. None goes to them but carries some sweetmeats or some other dainty dish to nourish and feed them withal. In return they earnestly solicit their prayers, leaving them great alms of money for their masses; and, above all, offering to a picture in their church, called our Lady of Carmel, treasures of diamonds, pearls, golden chains and crowns, and gowns of cloth of gold and silver. Before this picture did hang in my time twenty lamps of silver, the worst of them being worth a hundred pounds.

In the way to this place there is another town called Tacubaya, where there is a rich cloister of Franciscans, and also many gardens and orchards. Above all, people went there for the music in that church, wherein the friars have made the Indians so dextrous and skillful that they dare compare with the cathedral church of Mexico. These were the chief places of mine and my friends' resort, whilst I abode about Mexico, which I thought fit to insert here, and so I pass on to the other parts or provinces of Mexico.

Next to this is the Province of Guastachán[1] which lieth in the road from San Juan de Ulua to Mexico, which is not so poor as Heylyn maketh it, for now it abounds with many rich farms of sugar and of cochineal, and reaches as far as the Valley of Oaxaca, which is a most rich place. The chief city of this province was wont to be Tlaxcala, whereof I have formerly spoken; but now the city of Oaxaca, which is a bishop's seat, and Jalapa, which is also of late made a bishop's seat, makes it more famous. It glorieth also in Villa Rica [Vera Cruz] a port town, very wealthy because all the traffic betwixt the Old and New Spains passes through it. The Spaniards have in it two rich colonies called Panuco and St. James in the valleys. The third province of Mexico is called Michoacán, which containeth in circuit four score leagues. It is also an exceeding rich country, abounding in mulberry trees, silk, honey, wax, black amber, works of divers coloured feathers, most rich, rare, and exquisite, and such sort [variety] of fish, that from thence it took its name, Michoacán, which signifieth a place of fishing. The language of the Indians is most elegant and copious, and they are tall, strong, active, and of very good wits, as may be seen in all their works, but especially in those of feathers, which are so curious that they are presented for rich presents to the King and nobles of Spain.[2]

The fourth and last province of the country or Empire of Mexico is called Nueva Galicia, and is watered with two very great rivers, the one named Piaztle, and the other San Sebastián. This province glorieth in many great towns of Indians, but especially six, inhabited

[1] Guastachán was an early term not generally adopted. It may be a corruption of Huaxteca, but it evidently refers to the whole of eastern and southern Mexico, including Oaxaca.

[2] A magnificent miter with the crucifixion in featherwork and elaborately worked infulae at the Pitti Gallery, Florence, are among the rare surviving examples of this work. They are illustrated in Pál Kelemen's *Mediaeval American Art*. An almost identical set is in the Escorial, in Spain.

both by Indians and Spaniards. The first and chiefest is Jalisco, taken by Nuño de Guzmán 1530, when he fled from Mexico in a rage, and took prisoner and burned the King of Michoacán [Jalisco is the name of a state, not of a city]. The second is Guadalajara. The third, Coarum [Colima?]. The fourth, Compostela [near the modern Tepic]. The fifth, Espíritu Santo.

The sixth city is Capala [Cíbola], which is now called Nova Mexico, New Mexico. Here it is that the Spaniards are daily warring against the Indians which live northward, and are not as yet reduced nor brought under the Spanish yoke and government. They are valiant Indians and hold the Spaniards hard to it, and have great advantage against them in the rocks and mountains, where they abide and cut off many Spaniards. Their chief weapons are but bows and arrows, and yet with them from the thick woods, hills, and rocks they annoy and offend the Spaniards exceedingly. I have heard some Spaniards say that they fly and climb up the rocks like goats, and when they draw nigh unto them, then they cry out with a hideous noise, shooting their arrows at them, and in an instant are departed and fled unto another rock. The reason why the Spaniards are so earnest to pursue and conquer these Indians more than many others of America which as yet are not brought in subjection to the Spaniards is for the many mines of silver and treasures of gold which they know to be there.

They have got already sure possession of part of those riches in the mines called San Luis Zacatecas, from whence they send all the silver that is coined in the mint-houses of Mexico and Puebla, and besides at least six millions in silver wedges every year to Spain. The further north the Spaniards go, the more riches still they discover, and fain would they subdue all those northern parts (as I have heard them say) lest our English from Virginia and their other plantations get in before them. I have heard them wonder that our English enter no further into the main land. Surely, say they, either they fear the Indians, or else with a little paltry tobacco they have as much as will maintain them in laziness. Certainly they intend to conquer through those heathenish Indians until by land they come to Florida and Virginia (for so they boast) if they be not met by some of our northern nations of Europe, who may better keep them off than those poor Indians, and may do God greater and better service with those rich mines than the Spaniards hitherto have done.

Quivira is seated on the most western part of America, just over against Tartary, from whence being not much distant, some suppose that the inhabitants first came into this New World. Indeed, the Indians of America seem in many things to be of the race and progeny of the Tartars, in that Quivira and all the west side of the country towards Asia is far more populous than the east toward Europe, which showeth these parts to have been first inhabited. Secondly, their uncivility and barbarous properties tell us that they are most like the Tartars of any. Thirdly, the west side of America, if it be not continent with Tartary, is yet disjoined but by a small strait. Fourthly, the people of Quivira nearest to Tartary are said to follow the seasons and pasturing of their cattle like the Tartars.[3] All this side of America is full of herbage and enjoyeth a temperate air. The people are desirous of glass more than of gold, and in some places are cannibals to this day.

The chief riches of this country are their kine [buffaloes], which are to them as we say of our ale to drunkards, meat, drink, and cloth, and more too. For the hides yield them houses, or at least the coverings of them; their bones, bodkins; their hair, thread; their sinews, ropes; their horns, their maws, and their bladders, vessels; their dung, fire; their calves' skins, buckets to draw and keep water; their blood, drink; and their flesh, meat.[4] There is

[3] Don Pablo Martínez del Río, who has made a special study of early man in America, informs me that Josef Acosta, whose *Historia de las Indias* appeared in 1590, was the first writer to suggest (Book I, chap. 24) that America might have been populated from Asia, but he was necessarily vague, for little was then known about adjoining land masses. Gage is more specific and is, moreover, apparently the first writer to cite the resemblance of the Indians to the Mongols of Asia as a reason for supposing they came from Asia by the Bering Strait. Indeed, the Mongoloid characteristics of the American Indian are still the strongest argument for his Asiatic origin. Gage appears to have been a pioneer in modern thinking on the population of America. Of course, he was in error in supposing that the buffalo was domesticated.

[4] An early source for the importance of the buffalo in the life of the Plains Indian long before Indians of the Eastern Woodlands were driven into the prairies by pressure from the white settlers. It is well to remember that Gage landed in Mexico only five years after the Mayflower reached New England, but the better part of this information comes from López de Gómara, whose books were published in 1542.

thought to be some traffic from China or Cathay hither to those parts where as yet the Spaniards have not entered, for when Vásquez de Coronado conquered some part of it, he saw in the further sea certain ships, not of common making, which seemed to be well laden and bore pelicans in their prows. These could not be conjectured to come from any country but one of these two.

In Quivira there are but two provinces known to us, which are Cíbola and Nova Albion. Cíbola lieth on the east side, its chief city is of the same name and denominates the whole province. The chief town next to Cíbola is called Totonteac, which is temperate and pleasant, being situated on a river so called. The third town worth mentioning is called Tiguex. This was burned by the Spaniards, who under the conduct of Francisco Vásquez de Coronado, made this province subject to the King of Spain, in 1540. Since this town of Tiguex hath been rebuilt and inhabited by the Spaniards; there is a goodly college of Jesuits who preach only to the Indians of that country.[5]

Nova Albion lieth on the west side towards Tartary, and is very little inhabited by the Spaniards, who have found no wealth or riches there. Our ever renowned and noble captain Sir Francis Drake discovered it, and he named it Nova Albion because the king that then was willingly submitted himself unto our Queen Elizabeth. The country abounds with fruits pleasing both to the eye and the palate. The people are given to witchcraft and adoration of devils. The bounds between this Quivira and Mexico Empire is Mar Virmiglio [Vermillion sea] or California.

The third kingdom belonging to the Mexican part and northern tract is Yucatán, which was first discovered by Francisco Hernández de Córdova in the year 1517. The whole country is at least 900 miles in circuit and is a peninsula. It is situated over against the Isle of Cuba, and is divided into three parts. This country among the Spaniards is held to be poor; the chief commodities in it are honey, wax, hides, and some sugar, but no indigo, cochineal, or mines of silver. There are yet some drugs much esteemed by the apothecaries, espe-

---

[5] The modern Indian town of Zuni, south of Gallup, New Mexico, is now generally recognized as the Cíbola of the Spaniards. Tiguex was in the vicinity of Albuquerque, and Totonteac is usually identified with Tusayan, which includes the Hopi country. Quivira is the plains (Nebraska, etc.).

cially canafistula and sarsaparilla, and there is great store of Indian maize. There is also abundance of good wood and timber fit for shipping, whereof the Spaniards make very strong ships which they use in their voyages to Spain and back again. In the year 1632 the Indians in many parts of this country were like to rebel against their Spanish governor, who vexed them sorely, making them bring in to him their fowls and turkeys (whereof there is also great abundance) and their honey and wax. The rate and price which he pleased to set them for his better advantage was such a disadvantage to them that to enrich him, they impoverished themselves. So they resolved to betake themselves to the woods and mountains, where they continued some months in a rebellious way until the Franciscan friars, who there have great power over them, reduced them back. The governor, lest he should quite lose that country by a further rebellion, granted them not only a general pardon in the King's name, but promised to use them more mildly and gently for the future.[6]

The fourth and last country of the division of the Mexican part and northern tract of America is Nicaragua, which standeth southeast from Mexico and above 450 leagues from it. Yet it agreeth somewhat with Mexico in nature both of soil and of inhabitants. The people are of good stature, and of color indifferent white. They had a settled and politic form of government before they received Christianity. Only, as Solon appointed no law for a man's killing of his own father, so had this people none for the murder of a king, both of them conceiting that men were not so unnatural as to commit such crimes. A thief they judged not to death, but adjudged him to be a slave to that man whom he had robbed till by his service he had made satisfaction, a course truly more merciful and not less just than the loss of life.

The country is so pleasing to the eye and so abounding in all things necessary that the Spaniards call it Mohamed's paradise. Among other flourishing trees here groweth one of that nature that a man cannot touch any of its branches but it withereth presently. It

---

[6] The Yucatecan historian López de Cogolludo gives a somewhat different account of this affair. According to him, drought and locusts produced famine conditions in Yucatán, and the Indians left their homes to seek food in the forest country to the south. There is, however, a hint that they resented the payment of tribute, so there may be truth in what both writers say.

is as plentiful of parrots as our country of England is of crows; turkeys, fowls, quails, and rabbits are ordinary meat there. There are many populous Indian towns, although not so many as about Guatemala, and especially two cities of Spaniards. One is León, a bishop's seat, and the other Granada, which standeth upon a lake [Nicaragua] of fresh water which hath about 300 miles in compass, and, having no intercourse with the ocean, doth yet continually ebb and flow. But of this country and of this city especially I shall say somewhat more when I come to speak of my travelling through it.

The isthmus of Panama, which runneth between the north and south seas, besides the gold in it, is admirably stored with silver, spices, pearls, and medicinal herbs. Castilla del Oro is situated in the very isthmus, and is not very populous by reason of the unhealthfulness of the air and noisome savor of the standing pools. The chief places belonging to the Spaniards are first Theonimay or Nombre de Dios on the east, the second which is six leagues from Nombre de Dios is Portobello, now chiefly inhabited by the Spaniards and mulattoes and Blackamoors.

Nombre de Dios is almost utterly forsaken by reason of its unhealthfulness. The ships which were wont to anchor in Nombre de Dios to take in the King's treasure, which is yearly brought from Peru to Panama, and from thence to the North Sea now harbor themselves in Portobello, which signifieth a fair and goodly haven, for so indeed it is, and well fortified at the entrance with three castles, which can reach and command one another. The third and chief place belonging to the Spaniards in Castilla del Oro is Panama, which is on the west side, and upon the South Sea. This city and Nombre de Dios were both built by Diego de Nicuesa. Nombre de Dios was so called because Nicuesa, having been crossed with many mischances and misadventures at sea, greatly rejoiced when he came to this place, and bade his men now go on shore in *"nombre de Dios,"* "in the name of God." But the air being very unhealthy, the King of Spain in the year 1514 commanded the houses of Nombre de Dios to be pulled down and to be rebuilt in a more healthy and convenient place. This was performed by Pedro Arias in Portobello.[7]

Being now on the subject of Nombre de Dios, I should wrong my country if I should not set out to the public view the great courage

[7] The shift was made in 1596 by Alonso de Sotomayor.

and daring our countrymen showed at this place, and which to this day is talked of and admired by the Spaniards, who well remember Sir Francis Drake, and teach their children to dread and fear even his name, for his attempts upon Cartagena and all the coast about, and especially for his attack on Nombre de Dios, and for his march from there as far as the great mountain called San Pablo, toward Panama. Furthermore, they keep alive among themselves—and in my history it shall not die—the name of one of Sir Francis Drake's followers, Captain John Oxenham, whose attempt on this coast was resolute and wonderful.

This noble and gallant gentleman, with threescore and ten soldiers as resolute as himself, arriving a little above this town of Nombre de Dios, drew his ship aland, and, covering it with boughs, marched overland with his company guided by Blackamoors, until he came to a river. There he cut down wood, made him a pinnace, in which entering the South Sea, he went to the Island of Pearls. And there he lay ten days waiting for a prize, which happily he got (though not so happily after kept it), for from that island he set upon two Spanish ships, and finding them unable to fight, he speedily made them yield, and intercepted in them threescore thousand pound weight of gold, and two hundred thousand pound weight of silver in bars and wedges. With this he returned safely again to the main land. And though by reason of a mutiny made by his own company he returned neither to his country nor to his hidden ship, yet was it such a strange adventure as is not to be forgotten, in that the like was never by any other attempted, and by the Spaniards is to this day recorded with much admiration.

Much of this Castilla del Oro is not yet subdued by the Spaniards, and so doubtless a great treasure lieth hid in it for that people and nation whose thoughts shall aspire to find it out. In the year 1637, when I chanced to be in Panama returning homewards to my country, there came thither some twenty Indian barbarians to treat with the President of the Chancery concerning their yielding up themselves to the government of the King of Spain. But, as I was informed afterward at Cartagena, nothing was concluded, for the Spaniards dare not trust those Indians whom they have found to have rebelled often against them for their hard usage and carriage toward them. These Indians [San Blas?], whom I then saw were very proper tall and lusty men, and well complexioned, and among them one of as red a hair as any our nation can show. They had bobs of gold in their ears, and some of them little pieces of gold made like a half-moon hanging upon their nether lips, which shows that a store of that treasure is amongst them.

The Island of Margarita is situated in the [South] sea nigh unto Castilla del Oro. In this island there are many rich merchants who have thirty, forty, or fifty blackamoor slaves only to fish pearls out of the sea about the rocks. These Blackamoors are made much of by their masters, who must needs trust them with a treasure hidden in the waters, and in whose power it is to pass none, a few, or many of those they find. They are let down into the sea in baskets, and continue long under the water until by pulling the rope by which they are let down, they make their sign to be taken up. I have heard some that have thus dealt in pearls say that the chief meat they feed their Blackamoors is roast meat which maketh them keep their wind and breath longer in the water.

All the pearls are sent from Margarita to Cartagena to be refined and bored. There there is a fair and goodly street only of shops of these pearl dressers. Commonly in the month of July there is a ship, or two at most, ready in that island to carry the King's revenue and the merchants' pearls to Cartagena. One of these ships is commonly valued at threescore or fourscore thousand ducats, and sometimes more. Therefore they are reasonably well manned, for the Spaniards much fear our English and the Holland ships. The year that I was in Cartagena, which was 1637, a ship of these laden with pearls was chased by one of our ships from the Island of Providence[8] (by some it was thought to be our ship called the *Neptune*), which after a little fighting had almost brought the poor Spaniard to yield his pearls, and had certainly carried away that great treasure, as I was informed in Cartagena four days after the fight by a Spaniard who was in the ship of *Margarita,* had not two other ships, of Holland, come between to challenge that prize from our Englishman, alleging that the United Provinces had given them the right to all prizes on those seas and coast. While our English and Hollander did thus

[8] The Island of Providence lying east of the east coast of Nicaragua was at that time occupied by the English, although only a few years later the intruding force was dislodged.

strive for the pearls, the Spanish ship ran on shore, upon a little island, and speedily unloaded and hid in the woods part of the treasures. Perceiving the Hollander coming eagerly in pursuit of it, the Spaniard set his ship on fire, and neither Spaniard, English, nor Hollander enjoyed what might have been a great and rich prize to England. A man-of-war was presently sent from Cartagena to bring home the pearls hid in the wood, but they were not the third part of what was in the ship.

In Havana, commonly in the month of September, is joined all the treasure, as I might say, of America, all the King of Spain's revenues, with as much more of merchants' goods, which the year [1537] that I was there were thought in all to be worth thirty millions. The ships which did meet there that year to strengthen one another were fifty-three sail. They set out upon the sixteenth of September, sooner that year than any other, having that day a fair wind to waft them homewards through the Gulf of Bahama. Havana being the storehouse of the treasure of all America, the Spaniards have taken great care to fortify it, and truly it is so strong the Spaniards hold it impossible to be taken. It hath two strong castles, the one at the point or entrance of the haven toward the sea, the other more within, on the other side almost over against it. These two castles will keep and defend the port from many hundred sail, the passage at the mouth of the haven being so narrow that only one ship in breast may enter. I was myself in the great and chief castle, and truly found it very strong, though by land I judged it might be taken as easily as other strong castles here in Europe have been overpowered by a great and powerful army, it hath in it, besides many others, twelve pieces of ordnance of brass, exceeding great, which they call the twelve apostles.

But once Havana, for all its strength, could not defend six or seven millions according to the Spaniards' own reckoning, which part of the King's navy brought from San Juan de Ulua. It was, as I take it, the year 1629 when that ever renowned Hollander, whom, like our Drake, to this day the Spaniards fear and tremble at, calling him Pie de Palo, "wooden leg," waited at Cape San Antonio for the Spanish fleet from Nueva España [Mexico]. When, according to his expectation, this came, he manfully set upon it, saluting and welcoming the great treasure in it with a full side of roaring ordnance. The sound was more doleful than joyful and welcome to the Spaniards, who thought it safer to be sleeping in a whole skin than to be unquieted by fighting and with the sight of torn and mangled bodies, and so they called a council of war to resolve what they should do to save the King's treasure entrusted to them in those ships. The result of the council was to fly and to defend themselves with some discharging of their ordnance until they could put into a river called Matanzos, not far from Havana.

There were in that fleet many gallants and gentlemen and two judges of the chancery of Mexico who were found guilty in that mutiny I have mentioned, and also an acquaintance of mine, A Dominican friar, Jacinto de Joces,[9] who had been sent to those parts to visit all the Dominican cloisters of New Spain. He had, as I was informed the next year by a friar in his company, whom he sent to make known the loss of all he had and to beg a new contribution, at least 8,000 ducats with him. There was also in that fleet Don

[9] Rev. Fr. Jacinto de Joces, of the Convent of San Pablo in Madrid and vicar general, was sent on a tour of inspection of the Dominican establishments in Mexico and Guatemala. He was in Guatemala in 1627, and attended the chapter of the Province held in Chiapa of the Spaniards in January, 1628.

Martín de Carillo, who was the inquisitor and commissioner to judge the delinquents in the above-mentioned mutiny of Mexico. They all fled for their lives and goods, but the gallant Hollanders chased them.

The Spaniards, thinking the Hollanders would not venture up the river after them, put into the Matanzos, but soon after they had entered they found the river too shallow for their heavy and great-bellied galleons, and so ran them aground. Thereupon, the better and richer sort escaped to land, endeavoring to escape with what wealth they could; some got out cabinets and some bags, but when the Hollanders perceived this, they came upon them with bullet messengers which soon overtook and stopped their flying treasures. Some few cabinets were hid, all the rest became that day the prize of the gallant Pie de Palo, "wooden leg," for the mighty States of Holland. The Friar Jocés was got into a boat with his cabinet, with its contents of chains of gold, diamonds, pearls, and precious stones under his habit. Half a dozen Hollanders leaped into the boat after him and snatched it from him, as his friend and companion later told us in Guatemala. Don Juan de Guzmán y Torres, the admiral, was imprisoned when he reached Spain. He lost his wits for a while and afterwards was beheaded. Thus in the fight of impregnable Havana and of those twelve brazen apostles was Holland made glorious and rich with a seven million prize.

But before I end this chapter, I must not forget the chiefest of all the islands of this New World, which is called Hispaniola and formerly by the natives Haiti, which lamenteth the loss of at least three millions of Indians murdered by her new masters of Spain. This island is the biggest as yet discovered in all the world. It is in compass about 1,500 miles, and enjoyeth a temperate air, a fertile soil, and rich mines, and it trades much in amber, sugar, ginger, hides, and wax. It is reported for certain that here in twenty days herbs will ripen and roots also, and be fit to be eaten. It yieldeth in nothing to Cuba, but excelleth in three things especially. First in the fineness of the gold, which is here more pure and unmixed. Secondly, in the increase of the sugar, one sugar cane here filling twenty, and sometimes thirty, measures. And thirdly, in the goodness of the soil for tillage, the corn here yielding an hundred fold.

This country is so replenished with swine and cattle that they become wild among the woods and mountains, so that ships that want provisions go ashore here, where it is little inhabited, and kill cattle and wild swine till they have a plentiful provision. Much of this country is not inhabited by reason that the Indians are quite consumed. The chief place in it is Santo Domingo, where there is a Spanish President and Chancery, with six judges and the other officers belonging to it.[10]

[10] This glowing account of the Island of Hispaniola, the modern Santo Domingo, and Haiti, which was repeated in Gage's memorandum for Oliver Cromwell, may have had a part in leading to the ill-starred attack on that island by the English force in 1655. Gage had, it is true, praised Guatemala more enthusiastically as a place which could be easily attacked, but to a seagoing people, such as the English, Hispaniola or any island was a better choice than a section of the mainland where the role of sea power must be small.

10. Showing my journey from Mexico to Chiapa southward, and the most remarkable places in the way

━━━⚓━━━

HAVING now gone around America with a brief and superficial account of it, my desire is to shew unto my reader what parts of America I travelled through, and did abide in, observing more particularly the state, condition, strength, and commodities of those countries which lie southward from Mexico. It is further my desire, nay, the chief ground of this my history, that whilst my country doth here observe an Englishman, become American, travelling many thousand miles there, as may be noted from San Juan de Ulua to Mexico, and from thence southward to Panama, and from thence northward again to Cartagena, and to Havana, God's goodness may be admired, and his providence extolled. For He suffered not the meanest and unworthiest of all his creatures to perish in such un-known countries; to be swallowed by North or South Sea, where shipwrecks were often feared; to be lost in wildernesses where no tongue could give directions; to be devoured by wolves, lions, tigers, or crocodiles, which there so much abound; to fall from steepy rocks and mountains, which seem to dwell in the aerial region and threaten with fearful spectacles of deep and profound precipices a horrid and inevitable death to those that climb up to them; to be eaten up by the greedy earth which there doth often quake and tremble, and hath sometimes opened her mouth to draw in towns and cities; to be stricken with those fiery darts of Heaven and thunderbolts which in winter season threaten the rocks and cedars; to be enchanted by Satan's instruments, witches and sorcerers, who there as on their own ground play their pranks more than in the parts of Christen-dom; to be quite blinded with Romish errors and superstitions, which have double blinded the purblind heathenish idolaters; to be wedded to the pleasures and licentiousness which do there allure; to be glutted with the plenty and dainties of fish, flesh, fowls, and fruits, which do there entice; to be puffed up with the spirit of pride and powerful command and authority over the poor Indians, which doth there provoke; to be tied with the cords of vanity and ambition, which there are strong; and finally to be glued in heart and affection to the dross of gold, silver, pearls, and jewels, whose plenty there doth bind, blind, captivate, and enslave the soul.

Oh, I say, let the Lord's great goodness and wonderful provi-dence be observed who suffered not an English stranger in all these dangers to miscarry, but was a guide unto him there in all his travels, discovered unto him as to the spies in Canaan and as to Joseph in Egypt, the provision, wealth, and riches of that world, and safely guided him back to relate to England the truth of what no other English eye did ever yet behold.

From the month of October until February, I did abide with my friends and companions the friars under the command of Friar Calvo in that house of recreation called San Jacinto, and from thence en-joyed the sight of all the towns and of what else was worth the see-ing about Mexico. But the time I was there, I was careful to inform myself of the state of the Philippines, whither my first purposes had drawn me from Spain. It was my fortune to light upon a friar and an acquaintance of some of my friends, who was that year newly come from Manila whither I was going. He wished me and some other of my friends as we tendered our souls' good never to go to those parts, which were but snares and trap-doors to let down to Hell, where occasions and temptations to sin were daily, many in number, mighty in strength, and to get out of them, *labor et opus*, hard and difficult. And that had he not by stealth gotten away (and that to save his soul), certainly he had never come from thence, for he had often upon his knees begged leave of his superiors to return to Spain, and could not obtain it.

Many particulars we could not get from him, nor the reasons of his coming away. Only he would often say that the friars that live there are devils in private and in those retired places where they live among the Indians to instruct and teach them; and yet in public before their superiors and the rest of friars they must appear saints, they must put on the cloak of hypocrisy to cover their inward devilishness, they must be clothed with sheep's skins, though within they be *lupi rapaces*, ravenous wolves, ravening after their neighbors' wives, and ravening after their neighbors' wealth; and yet with all this unpreparedness, with this outward, seeming, and frothy sanctity, and inward hellishness and deep-rooted worldliness and covetousness, when the superiors command and please to send them, they must go in a disguised manner to Japan or China to convert to Christianity those people though with peril and danger of their lives.

Many such-like discourses we got out of this friar; and that if we went to live there, we must be subject to the penalties of many excommunications for trivial toys and trifles, which the superiors do lay upon the consciences of their poor subjects, who may as soon strive against the common course of nature not to see with their eyes, nor hear with their ears, nor speak with their tongues, as to observe all those things which against sense, reason, and nature with grievous censures and excommunications are charged and fastened upon them. He told us further of some friars that had despaired under those rigorous courses, and hanged themselves, not being able to bear the burden of an afflicted and tormented conscience; and of others that had been hanged, some for murdering of their rigid and cruel superiors; and some that had been found in the morning hanging with their queans at the cloister gates, having been found together in the night, and so murdered and hanged up either by the true husband, or by some other who bare affection to the woman. These things seemed to us very strange, and we perceived that all was not gold that glittered, nor true zeal of souls that carried so many from Spain to those parts; or if in some there were at first a better and truer zeal than in others when they came to the Philippines, and among those strong temptations, we found that their zeal was soon quenched.

This reason moved me and three more of my friends to relent in our purposes of leaving of America, and going any further, for we had learned the maxims, "he that loveth danger, shall fall and perish in it"; and "he that toucheth pitch shall be smeared by it." Wherefore we communed privately with ourselves what course we might take, how we might that year return to Spain, or where we might abide if we returned not to Spain. For we knew if our Superior Calvo should understand of our purposes to go no further, he would lay upon us an excommunication to follow him, nay, and that he would secure us in a cloister prison until the day and time of our departure from Mexico.

Our resolutions we made a secret of our hearts; yet could not I but impart it to one more special and intimate friend of mine, who was an Irish friar, named Tomás de León, whom I perceived a little troubled with so long a journey as was at hand, and found often wishing he had never come from Spain. As soon as I had acquainted him with what I meant to do, he rejoiced and promised to stay with me. The time was short, but in that time we addressed ourselves to some Mexican friars and made known unto them that if our Superior Calvo would give us leave, we would willingly stay in Mexico or in any cloister thereabouts, until we could better fit ourselves to return to Spain again. But they, being natives and born in that country, discovered presently unto us that inveterate spite and hatred which they bare to such as came from Spain. They told us plainly that they and true Spaniards born did never agree, and that they knew their superiors would be unwilling to admit us; yet they informed us that they thought we might be entertained in the province of Oaxaca, where half the friars were of Spain and half Creoles and natives.[1] But in case we should not speed there, they would warrant us we should be welcome to the province of Guatemala, where almost all the friars were of Spain, and did keep under such as were natives born in that country.

It did a little trouble us to consider that Guatemala was three hundred leagues off, and that we were ignorant of the Mexican tongue and unprovided of money and horses for so long a journey.

[1] This antagonism, both in religious and secular matters, was a very real thing. Elsewhere Gage wrote at length on these rivalries in various religious provinces of Mexico and Guatemala. Tension between the two parties was strong in Guatemala, but the Spaniards kept control until a Papal Bull and a decree of the Spanish monarch ordered that Spaniard and Creole were to alternate as Provincial. The Spanish majority, uncompromising to the end, chose first a Spaniard. Four years later, in 1651, the first Creole, R. P. Fray Jacinto de Carcamo y Castillo, was elected. Of the sixty-three viceroys of Mexico, only three were born in the New World, and they were only Creoles by the accident of overseas duty by their Spanish fathers.

Yet we considered the Philippines to be further, and no hopes there of returning ever again to Christendom; wherefore we resolved to rely upon God's providence only, and to venture upon a three hundred leagues' journey with what small means we had, and to sell what books and small trifles we had to make as much money as might buy each of us a horse. But while we were thus preparing ourselves secretly for Guatemala, we were affrighted and disheartened with what in the like case to ours happened.

A friar of our company named Friar Peter Borrallo, without acquainting us or any other of his friends with what he intended, made a secret escape from us, and (as after we were informed) took his way alone to Guatemala. This so incensed our Superior Calvo, that after great search and enquiry after him, he betook himself to the Viceroy, begging his assistance and proclamation, in the public market-place, for the better finding out his lost sheep. He argued that none ought to hide or privily to harbor any friar that had been sent from Spain to the Philippines to preach there the Gospel, for that the aforesaid frairs were sent by the King of Spain, whose bread they had eaten, and at whose charges they had been brought from Spain to Mexico, and at the same King's charges ought to be carried from Mexico to the Philippines. Therefore, if any friar now in the half way should recant of his purpose of going to the Philippines, and should by flight escape from his superior and the rest of his company, he was guilty of defrauding the King's charges, and ought to be punished. This reason of Calvo being a politic and state reason prevailed so far with the Viceroy that immediately he commanded a proclamation to be made against whosoever should know of the said Peter Borrallo and should not produce him to his Highness, or should harbor him or any other friar belonging to the Philippines from the time forward until the ships were departed from Acapulco; and that whosoever should trespass against this proclamation should suffer imprisonment at his Highness' will and pleasure, in addition to a penalty of five hundred ducats to be paid to the King's Exchequer.

With this proclamation Calvo began to insult over us, and to tell us we were the King's slaves under his conduct, and that if any of us durst to leave him (for he was jealous of most of us), he doubted not but with the Viceroy's assistance and proclamation he should find both us and Peter Borrallo out to our further shame and confusion. This did very much trouble us, and made my Irish friend Tomás de León's heart to faint, and his courage to relent, and led him utterly to renounce his former purposes of staying and hiding himself, yet he protested to me, if I was still of the same mind, he would not discover me. Seeing his weakness, I durst not trust him, but made as if I were of his mind. Thus I betook myself to the other three of my friends (of whom one was Antonio Meléndez that had been the first cause of my coming from Spain) whom I found much troubled, doubtful, and wavering what course to take.

They considered if we should flee, what a shame it would be to us to be taken and brought back to Mexico as prisoners, and to be shipped by force and against our wills to the Philippines. They considered further, if they went, what a slavish and uncomfortable life they should live in the Philippines, without any hopes of ever returning again to Christendom. On the other side, considering the Viceroy's proclamation, they thought it hard to break through the opposition and authority of so great a man. Lastly in the proclamation they beheld the estimation that Calvo had of them, as of slaves and fugitives to be cried in a public market-place. But after all these serious thoughts our only comfort was that Peter Borrallo was safely escaped, and (as we were informed) had been met far from Mexico travelling alone towards Guatemala. And we thought, why might not we escape as well as he? Then I told them that my resolution was to stay, though alone I returned either to Spain, or took my journey to Guatemala. The rest were glad to see me resolute, and gave their hands that they would venture as much as I should.

Then we set upon the time when we should take our flight, and agreed that every one should have a horse in readiness in Mexico, and that the night before the rest of our company should depart from Mexico towards Acapulco to take ship, we should by two and two in the evening leave San Jacinto, and meet in Mexico where our horses stood, and from thence set out and travel all the night, continuing our journey so the first two or three nights and resting in the daytime, until we were some twenty or thirty leagues from Mexico. For we thought Calvo awaking and missing us the next morning would not stop the journey of the rest of his company for our sakes to search and enquire after us; or if he did, it would be but for one day or two at the most till he had enquired for us in Mexico, or a day's journey in some of the common or beaten roads of Mexico, where we would be sure he should not hear of us, for we also agreed to travel out of any common or known road for the first two or three nights.

This resolution was by us as well performed and carried on as it had been agreed upon, though some had been fearful that a counsel betwixt four could never be kept secret, nor such a long journey as of nine hundred miles be compassed with such small means of money as was among us for the maintenance of ourselves and horses. After our horses were bought, we made a common purse, and appointed one to be the purse-bearer, and found that amongst us all there were but twenty ducats, which in that rich and plentiful country was not much more than twenty English shillings here, and this seemed to us but as a morning dew, which would soon be spent in provender only for our horses. Yet we resolved to go on, relying more upon the providence of God than upon any earthly means, and indeed this proved to us a far better support than all the dross of gold and silver could have done. It came about that after we had travelled forty leagues from Mexico, and entered without fear into the road, we had instead of our twenty ducats, near forty in our common purse. The reason was, for that most commonly we went either to friars' cloisters who knew us not, or to rich farms of Spaniards who thought nothing too good for us, and would not only entertain us stately, but at our departure would give us money for one or two days' journey. All our fear was to get safely out of Mexico, for we had been informed that Calvo had obtained from the Viceroy officers to watch in the chiefest roads both day and night until he had departed with his train of friars to Acapulco.

And for all the Viceroy's proclamation, we got a true and trusty friend who offered to guide us out of Mexico by such a way as we needed not to fear any would watch for us. So with our friend and a map about us to guide us after he had left us in the morning, we cheerfully set out of Mexico about ten of the clock at night, about the middle of February. Meeting nobody about Guadalupe, which was the way we went out (though the contrary way to Guatemala, which on purpose we followed for fear the true way should be beset), we comfortably travelled all that night, till in the morning

Typical scene in the Guatemalan highlands, the same today as in Gage's time.

Market under the ceiba tree at Palín, one of the towns in Gage's charge when he was priest at Amatitlán.

Photograph by Susan Miles

Photograph by A. V. Cooper

Mixco church, where Gage was priest for five years.

we came to a little town of Indians, where we began to spend of our small stock, calling upon the Indians for a turkey and capon to break our fast with our friend and guide before he returned to Mexico.

Breakfast being ended, we took our leaves of him, and went to rest, that we might be more able to perform the next night's journey, which was to cross the country towards Atlixco. This doth give its name to the valley of Atlixco, a valley, of twenty miles about at least, much mentioned in all those parts for the exceeding great plenty of wheat reaped there every year, and is the chief sustenance and relief of Mexico and all the towns about. In this valley are many rich towns of Spaniards and Indians, but we shunned them, and went from farm to farm out of the highways, where we found good entertainment of those rich farmers and yeomen, who bare such respect unto the priests that truly they thought themselves happy with our company.

Here we began to shake off all fear, and would no more, like bats and owls, fly in the night, but we travelled by day that we might with more pleasure enjoy the prospect of that valley, and of the rest of the country. Still crossing the country, we went thence towards another valley called San Pablo, or Paul's valley, which, though it be not as big as the valley of Atlixco, yet is held to be richer, for here they enjoy a double harvest of wheat every year. The first seed they sow is watered, and grows with the common season rain; the second seed which they sow in summer as soon as their first harvest is in, when the season of rain is past, they water with many springs which fall into that valley from the mountains which round beset it, and let in the water among their wheat at their pleasure, and take it away when they see fit. Here live yeomen upon nothing but their farms, and they are judged to be worth some twenty thousand, some thirty thousand, some forty thousand ducats.

In this valley we chanced to light upon one farm where the yeoman was countryman to my friend Antonio Meléndez, born in Segovia in Spain, who for his sake kept us three days and nights with him. His table was as well furnished as the table of a knight might be, his sideboard full of silver bowls and cups, and plates instead of trenchers. He spared no dainties which might welcome us to his table, no perfumes which might delight us in our chambers, no music (which his daughters were brought up to) which might with more pleasure help to pass away the time. Antonio Meléndez made known to him our journey towards Guatemala, and from him we received directions which way to steer our course until we might be thoroughly free from fear and danger. Here we began to see the great providence of God, who had brought us being strangers to such a friend's house, who not only welcomed us to him, but when we departed gave us a guide for a whole day, and bestowed upon us twenty ducats to help to bear our charges.

From this valley we wheeled about to Tasco,[2] a town of some five hundred inhabitants which enjoyeth great commerce with the country about by reason of the great store of cotton-wool which is there. And here we were very well entertained by a Franciscan friar, who, being of Spain, made the more of us, knowing we came from thence. Here we got into the road of Oaxaca, and went to Chiautla, which also aboundeth with cotton-wool, but in it we found no entertainment but what our own purses would afford us. Next to this place is a great town called Zumpango,[3] which doth consist of at least eight hundred inhabitants, many of them very rich both Indians and Spaniards. Their commodities are chiefly cotton-wool, and sugar, and cochineal.

Beyond this town are the mountains called La Misteca, which abound with many rich and great towns, and do trade with the best silk that is in all that country. Here is also great store of wax and honey. Indians live there who traffic to Mexico and about the country with twenty or thirty mules of their own, chopping and changing, buying and selling commodities, and some of them are thought to be worth ten, or twelve, or fifteen thousand ducats, which is much for an Indian to get among the Spaniards, who think all the riches of America little enough for themselves.

[2] Taxco, in the modern state of Guerrero, and a great tourist center for visitors from the United States. Gage and his friends must have been amongst the first tourists to visit the town, which was far off their route. The silver mines probably attracted Gage and his comrades, but the great silver mines of Le Borde which gave Taxco its wealth and built its famed church were not discovered until a century after Gage's visit.

[3] Zumpango lies far to the south of Taxco, whereas Chiautla, which is in the right direction, lies nearly east of Taxco, and corrects the "wheeled about to Taxco." Probably Gage made some note on what he had been told concerning Zumpango, and when he wrote up his journal a dozen years later, he thought he had been there. Of course, Gage had no good map at hand to trace his route.

From these mountains of Misteca to Oaxaca we saw little observable, only towns of two or three hundred inhabitants and rich churches, well built and better furnished within with lamps, candlesticks, crowns of silver for the several statues of saints. All the way we did observe a very fruitful soil for both Indian and Spanish wheat, much sugar, much cotton-wool, honey, and here and there some cochineal, and of plantains and other sweet and luscious fruit great store, but above all great abundance of cattle, whose hides are one of the greatest commodities that are sent to Spain from those parts. Some reported that about Misteca formerly much gold had been found, and the Indians were wont to use it much, though now they will not be known of any, lest the greediness of the Spaniards bring them to misery and destruction, as it hath their neighbors about them. Also it is reported for certain that there are mines of silver, though as yet the Spaniards have not found them. There are many mines of iron which the Spaniards will not busy themselves in digging, because they have it cheaper from Spain.

From hence we came to the city of Oaxaca, which is a bishop's seat, and though not very big, yet a fair and beautiful city to behold. It standeth fourscore leagues from Mexico in a pleasant valley from whence Cortés was named Marqués del Valle, the Marquis of the Valley. This city, as all the rest of America, except the sea towns, lieth open without walls, bulwarks, forts, towers, or any castle, ordnance, or ammunition to defend it. It may consist of at the most two thousand inhabitants, and is governed by a Spanish High Justice called *Alcalde Mayor,* whose power reacheth over all the valley, and beyond it as far as Nejapa, and almost to Tehuantepec, a sea town upon Mar del Sur.

The valley is of at least fifteen miles in length and ten in breadth, where runneth in the midst a goodly river yielding great store of fish. The valley is full of sheep and other cattle, which yield much wool to the clothiers of the City of Angels, store of hides to the merchants of Spain, and great provision of flesh to the city of Oaxaca, and to all the towns about. These are exceeding rich, and do maintain many cloisters of friars and churches with stately furniture belonging unto them. But what doth make the valley of Oaxaca to be mentioned far and near are the good horses which are bred in it, and esteemed to be the best of all the country. In this valley also are some farms of sugar, and great store of fruits, which two sorts meeting together have cried up the city of Oaxaca for the best conserves and preserves that are made in America.

In the city there are some six cloisters of nuns and friars, all of them exceeding rich; but above all is the cloister of the Dominican friars, whose church treasure is worth two or three millions; and the building of it the fairest and strongest in all those parts, the walls are of stone so broad that a part of them being upon finishing when I was there I saw carts go upon them, with stone and other materials.[4] Here are also two cloisters of nuns, which are talked of far and near, not for their religious practices, but for their skill in making two drinks, which are used in those parts, the one called chocolate and the other *atole*, which is like unto our almond milk, but much thicker, and is made of the juice of the young maize or Indian wheat, which they so confection with spices, musk, and sugar that it is not only admirable in the sweetness of the smell, but much more nourishing and comforting to the stomach. This is not a commodity that can be transported from thence, but is to be drunk there where it is made. But the other, chocolate, is made up in boxes, and sent not only to Mexico and the parts thereabouts, but much of it is yearly transported into Spain.

This city of Oaxaca is the richer by reason of the safety they enjoy for the carriage of their commodities to and from the port of San Juan de Ulua by the great River Alvarado,[5] which runneth not far from it. The barques come not to the city of Oaxaca, yet they come up to the Zapotecas, and to San Ildefonso, which is not far from Oaxaca. The carelessness of the Spaniards here is to be wondered at, in that all along this river which runneth up into the heart of their country they have built as yet no castles, towers, or watch-houses, or planted any ordnance. They trust only in this, that great

[4] The Dominican church in Oaxaca with its exceedingly rich baroque decoration in gilded and painted wood and plaster is one of the most famed churches of Mexico, but the interior decoration, including a superb Tree of Jesse in painted and gilded plaster, is for the most part subsequent to Gage's visit. The story which Gage later tells of the ignominious burial in unconsecrated land of the Spanish friar is, as it stands, incredible. Either the facts must be incorrect or important data are suppressed.

[5] Today the Río Cajones, which joins the Papaloapán near its mouth at Alvarado, but this is some distance below San Juan de Ulua (Veracruz). San Ildefonso is now San Ildefonso Villa Alta. It lies fifty miles in a direct line northeast of Oaxaca.

ships cannot come up, as if frigates or smaller barques, such as they themselves use, may not be made to annoy them. But of Oaxaca I shall say no more, but conclude that it is of so temperate an air, so abounding in fruits, and all provision requisite for man's life, so commodiously situated between the North and South Sea, having on the north side San Juan de Ulua, and on the south Tehuantepec, a small and unfortified harbor. There was no place I so much desired to live in whilst I was in those parts as in Oaxaca, which certainly I had attempted as I travelled by it, had I not understood that the Creole or native friars were many and as deadly enemies unto those that came from Spain as were the Mexicans. Indeed, they shewed their spite and malice whilst we were there, to an ancient and grave old friar, Master in Divinity, who in his life had been for learning the oracle of those parts.

This old man died when I was there, and because when he lived they could pick no hole in his coat, being dead, they searched his chamber, and finding in a coffer some moneys which he had not made known to his Superior when living, they reported that he had died excommunicated, and might not enjoy their Christian burial in the church or cloister. So they ignominiously buried their old divine, and with him his credit and reputation, in a grave made in one of their gardens. They did this on the grounds that he was guilty of a sin against his professed poverty, called propriety, and therefore subject to the censure of excommunication. This was much talked on as scandalous to all the city and country, but they salved it with saying he was excommunicated. The truth was, he was of Spain, and therefore at his death they would shew their spite unto him. For certainly they could not do it for the sin of propriety which by him had been committed in his life. To them all may be well said what Our Savior said to the Jews, when they brought to him a woman found in adultery to be stoned, "Whosoever of you is without sin, let him cast the first stone," for all of them, yea even the best friars that live in America, are some way or other, much or less guilty of the sin of propriety which they profess and vow against. With this which we saw with our eyes, besides what with our ears we had heard of discords and factions amongst them, we thought Oaxaca was no place for us to live in; so after three days we made haste out of it, and departed towards Chiapa, which lieth three hundred miles from thence.

113

For our comfort in our further travelling, we were informed in Oaxaca that in most towns of the road through that country, the Indians had an order from the High Justice to give unto friars travelling that way either horse to ride on or to carry their carriages, and provision of food freely without money, if they had none, so that at their departure they should write it down in the town book what they had spent, not abiding above four and twenty hours in the town. The Indians afterwards at the year's end of their ordinary justice and officers were to give an account of these expenses of travellers carrying their town book unto the Spanish justice to whom they belonged. By so doing, these expenses were allowed of to be discharged by the common town purse or treasure, for the which a common plot of ground was allotted to be yearly sown with wheat or maize. With this charitable relief and help of the towns we conceived better of the rest of our long journey, and hoped to compass it with more ease. And so joyfully we went on.

The first place where we made trial of this order was at a great town called Antequera,[6] where we freely called for our fowls and what other provision we saw in the town, fed heartily on them, and the next day when we were to pay and to depart, we called for the town book, subscribed our hands to what we had spent ourselves and horses, and went our way, praising the discretion of the justices of that country, who had settled a course so easy and comfortable for us, especially who had but shallow purses for our long journey. Yet we found in some small towns that the Indians were unwilling, and—they alleged—unable to extend this charity to us, being four in company, and bringing with us the charge likewise of four horses. This made us sometimes make a longer journey that we might reach unto some great and rich town.

The next to Antequera in that road is Nejapa, which is of at the least eight hundred inhabitants, Spaniards and Indians, standing upon the side of a river, which we were informed was an arm of the great river Alvarado. In this town is a very rich cloister of Dominican friars, where we were well entertained; and in it there is a picture of Our Lady, which they fancy to have wrought miracles, and

[6] Another misreading of the journal, which was probably not so well kept as usual because of the flight into what Gage afterwards called Egypt. Antequera is another name for the city of Oaxaca.

is made a pilgrimage from far and near, and consequently hath great riches and lamps belonging unto it. This is counted absolutely one of the wealthiest places of all the country of Oaxaca, for here is made much indigo, sugar, cochineal, and here grew many trees of cacao and achiote. The chocolate made of these is a commodity of much trading in those parts, though our English and Hollanders make little of it when they take a prize of it at sea, as not knowing the secret virtue and quality of it for the good of the stomach. From hence we went to Guatulco and Copalitla,[7] also great towns standing upon a plain country full of sheep and cattle, abounding with excellent fruits, especially *piñas* [pineapples] and *sandias* [watermelons], which are as big as pumpkins, and so waterish that they even melt like snow in the mouth, and cool the heat which there is great, by reason it is a low and marsh kind of ground, lying near the South Sea.

The next chief town and most considerable after Copalitla is Tehuantepec. This is a sea town upon *Mar del Sur*, and a harbor for small vessels, such as trade from those parts to Acapulco and Mexico, and to Realejo and Guatemala, and sometimes to Panama. Here upon some occasions ships which come from Peru to Acapulco do call in. It is a safe port in the sense that no English or Holland ships do come thereabouts. If they did, they would there find no resistance, but from thence would find an open and easy road over all the country. Upon all this South Sea side from Acapulco to Panama, which is above two thousand miles by land, there is no open harbor but this for Oaxaca, and La Trinidad for Guatemala, and Realejo for Nicaragua, and Golfo de Salinas for small vessels in Costa Rica. All these are unprovided of ordnance and ammunition, all are open doors to let in any nation that would take the pains to surround the world to get a treasure.

This port of Tehuantepec is the chief for fishing in all that country. We met here in the ways sometimes fifty, sometimes a hundred mules together laden with nothing but salt fish for Oaxaca, Puebla, and Mexico. There dwell in it some very rich merchants, who trade with Mexico, Peru, and the Philippines, sending their small vessels

---

[7] Gage and his comrades seem to have made a detour here through Ecatepec to visit Copalitla and Guatulco, a near-by port on the Pacific Coast and about seventy miles west of Tehuantepec. This is, apparently, the modern San Miguel del Puerto.

out from port to port, and these come home richly laden with the commodities of all the southern or eastern parts.

From hence to Guatemala there is a plain road along the coast of the South Sea, passing through the provinces of Soconusco and Suchitepéquez, but we, aiming at Chiapa, took our journey over the high rocks and mountains called Quelenes. We travelled first from Tehuantepec to Estepec, and from thence through a desert of two days' journey, where we were fain to lodge one night by a spring of water upon the bare ground in open wide fields, where neither town nor house is to be seen, yet thatched lodges are purposely made for travellers. This plain lieth so open to the sea that the winds from thence blow so strongly and violently that travellers are scarce able to sit their horses and mules. That is the reason no people inhabit there, because the winds tear their houses, and the least fire that there breaks out doth a great deal of mischief. This plain is full of cattle, and horses and mares, some wild, some tame.

Through this windy champaign country with much ado we travelled, though I myself thought I should there end my days, for the second day my three friends rode on ahead, hastening to reach the town as evening drew on, and thinking that I followed, but in the meanwhile my horse refused to go any further, threatening to lie down if I put him to more than he was able. I knew the town could not be far, and so I lighted, thinking to walk and lead my horse, but he refused even to be led, and lay down. With this a troop of thoughts beset me, and to none could I give a flat answer. I thought if I should go on foot to find out the town and my company and leave my horse there saddled, I might lose both myself and my horse and saddle; and if I should find the town and come in the morning for my horse, the plain was so wide and spacious that I might seek long enough and neither find him nor know the place where I left him, for there was nothing near to mark the place, nor where to hide the saddle, neither hedge, tree, shrub, within a mile on any side.

Wherefore I considered my best course would be to take up my lodging in the wide and open wilderness with my horse, and to watch him lest he should wander and stray away, until the morning or until my friends might send from the town to see what was become of me. However, this they did not that night, thinking I had taken my way to another town not far from thence, whither they sent in the morning to enquire for me.

I looked about therefore for a commodious place to rest in, but found no choice of lodgings; everywhere I found a bed ready for me, which was the bare ground. A bolster only or pillow I lacked for my head, and seeing no bank did kindly offer itself to ease a lost stranger and pilgrim, I unsaddled my weary jade, and with my saddle fitted my head instead of a pillow.

Thus without a supper I went to bed in my mother's own bosom, not a little comforted to see my tired horse pluck up his spirits, and make much of his supper, which there was ready for him, of short, dry, and withered grass, upon which he fed with a greedy and hungry stomach, promising me by his feeding that the next day he would perform a journey of at least thirty or forty miles. The poor beast fed apace; my careful eye watched him for at least an hour, when upon a sudden I heard such an hideous noise of howling, barking, and crying, as if a whole army of dogs were come into the wilderness, and howled for want of a prey of some dead horse or mule. At first the noise seemed to be a pretty way off from me, but the more I hearkened unto it, the nigher it came unto me, and I perceived it was not of dogs by some intermixed shriekings as of Christains, which I observed in it. An observation too sad for a lone man without any help or comfort in a wilderness, which made my hair to stand upright, my heart to pant, my body to be covered with a fearful sweat as of death. I expected nothing else, not knowing from whence the noise proceeded.

Sometimes I thought of witches, sometimes of devils, sometimes of Indians turned into the shape of beasts (which amongst some hath been used), sometimes of wild and savage beasts, and from all these thoughts I promised myself nothing but sure death. For this I prepared myself, recommending my soul to the Lord, whilst I expected my body should be a prey to cruel and merciless beasts; or some instruments of that roaring lion who in the Apostle goeth about seeking whom he may devour. I thought I could not any ways prevail by flying or running away, but rather might that way run myself into the jaws of death. To hide there was no place; to lie still I thought was safest, for if there were wild beasts, they might follow their course another way from me, and so I might escape. This truly proved my safest course, for while I lay sweating and panting, judging every cry, every howling, and shrieking an alarm to my death, being in this agony and fearful conflict till about midnight, on a sudden the noise ceased, sleep (though but the shadow of death) seized upon my wearied body, and forsook me not till the morning's glorious lamp, shining before my slumbering eyes and driving away death's shadow, greeted me with life and safety.

When I awaked, my soul did magnify the Lord for my deliverance from that night's danger. I looked about and saw my horse also near the place where I had left him. I saddled him presently with desire to leave that wilderness and to find out my company, and to impart unto them what that night had happened unto me. I had not rid above a mile, when I came to a brook of water, where were two ways, the one straight forward along the desert, where I could discover no town, nor houses, nor trees in a prospect of five or six miles at least; the other way was on the left hand, and that way, some two or three miles off, I saw a wood of trees. I imagined there might be the town.

I followed that way, and within a quarter of a mile my horse began to complain of his poor provender the night before, and to slight me for it. I was fain to alight and lead him, and thus again discouraged with my horse, and discomforted for the uncertainty of my way, looking about, I spied a thatched house on the one side of the way, and one on horseback, who came riding to me. It was an Indian belonging to that house, which was the farm of a rich Indian, and governor of the next town, of whom I asked how far it was to the town of Estepec. He shewed me the trees, and told me that a little beyond them it stood, and that I should not see it until I came unto it. With this I got up again and spurred my sullen jade, until I reached unto the trees, where he was at a stand and would go no further.

Then I unsaddled him, and hid my saddle under some low shrubs, and leaving my horse (whom I feared not that any would steal him), I walked unto the town, which was not above half a mile from thence, where I found my three friends were waiting for me, and, grieved for the loss of me, had sent to another town to enquire for me; it was the last thought they had that I had been a lodger in the desert.

When I related unto them and to the Indians the noise and howling that I had heard, the Indians answered me that that was common music to them almost every night, and that they were wolves and tigers which they feared not, but did often meet them, and with a stick or holloaing did scare them away, and that they were only ravenous for their fowls, colts, calves, or kids. After a little discourse I returned with an Indian to seek my horse and saddle, and in that town I sold my wearied Mexican beast, and hired another to Ecatepec whither we went all four friends again in company.

In this plain and champaign country of Tehuantepec are five rich and pleasant towns full of fruits and provision of victual, all ending in Tepec,[8] to wit, Tehuantepec, Estepec, Ecatepec, Sanatepec, and Tapanatepec. Now from Ecatepec we could discover the high mountains of Quelenes, which were the subject of most of our discourse to Sanatepec, and from thence to Tapanatepec. For we had been informed by Spaniards and travellers in the way that they were the most dangerous mountains in all those parts to travel over, and that there were on the top of them some passages very narrow and high, and open to the boisterous winds that came from the South Sea, which seemed to lie at the very bottom of them. And on each side of these narrow passages were such deep precipices among rocks, that many times it had happened that the wind blowing furiously had cast down mules laden with heavy carriages down the rocks, and likewise horsemen had been blown down, both horse and man.

The sight of the rocks and mountains did terrify us, and the report of them did much affright us, so that in all this way we did confer which way to take. We must choose whether to take the road way to Guatemala which lieth under those mountains along the coast by the country of Soconusco, from whence, though out of our way, we might have turned to Chiapa, or whether we should steer our right course to Chiapa over those mountains, which we had been informed we might safely pass over if the winds did not blow too

---

[8] *Tepec* is Aztec for place of the mountain or hill, and, by extension, place. *Tehuantepec* is the "place of the jaguars"; *Ixtepec* (not Estepec) probably a corruption of *Itztepec*, "place of obsidian," etc. The high mountains could be seen east of Ixtepec, not of Ecatepec, which is far to the west, between Nejapa and the Pacific Ocean.

boisterously. We resolved that when we came to Tapanatepec we would choose our way according as the winds did favor or threaten us. However to Chiapa we would go, because there we had understood was the Superior and Provincial of all the Dominicans of those parts, to whom we ought to address ourselves, and also because we would see that famous and much talked of province of Chiapa.

In Sanatepec we met with a friar who gave us stately entertainment, and from thence gave us Indians to guide us to Tapanatepec, and a letter to the chief of the town (which also was at his command) to give us mules to carry us, and Indians to guide us up the mountains. Here the rest of our horses also failed us, but their weariness was no hindrance to us, for the Indians were willing to give us as much or more than they had cost us, because they were true Mexican breed. All the way we went to Chiapa and through that country to Guatemala, the towns were to provide us of mules for nothing. We came to Tapanatepec, which standeth at the bottom and foot of Quelenes, on Saturday night, and with the letter we carried were very much welcomed and well entertained by the Indians.

This town is one of the sweetest and pleasantest of any we had seen from Oaxaca thither, and it seems God hath replenished it with all sorts of comforts which travellers may need to ascend up those dangerous and steepy rocks. Here is great plenty of cattle for flesh, and rich Indians which have farms, called there *estancias*, in some a thousand, in some three or four thousand head of cattle. Fowls here are in abundance; fish the best store and choicest of any town from Mexico thither, for the sea is hard by it, and besides there runneth by it a small river which yields divers sorts of fish. From the mountains there fall so many springs of water, that with them the Indians water at their pleasure their gardens which are stored with much herbage and salads. The shade which defends from the heat, which there is great, is the daughter of most sweet and goodly fruit trees, and of orange, lemon, citron, and fig leaves.

The Sabbath morning was so calm that we desired to make use of it, lest by longer delays the winds should stay us, or force us to the coast of Soconusco, but the Indians entreated us to be their guests at dinner, not doubting but the weather would hold, and promising us to provide us strong and lusty mules, and provision of fruits, and fried fish, or fowls, or what ourselves desired. We could not refuse their kind offer, and so stayed dinner with them. After dinner our mules were brought, and two Indians to guide us and carry our provision, which was some fried fish and a cold roasted capon, with some fruit as much as might suffice us for a day. The chief ascent and danger is not above seven leagues, or one and twenty English miles, and then beyond the top of the mountains three miles is one of the richest farms for horses, mules, and cattle in all the country of Chiapa, where we knew we should be welcomed by one Don Juan de Toledo, who then lived there. Though these mountains shew themselves with several sharp-pointed heads, and are many joined together, yet one of them is only mentioned in that country by the travellers, which is called Macuilapa, over the which lieth the way to Chiapa. To this high, steepy, and craggy Macuilapa we took our journey after dinner, and we were that night well entertained by the proud mountain and harbored in a green plot of ground resembling a meadow, which lay as a rib of the one side of that huge and more than Pyrenean monster.

The Indians comforted us with the shews of fair weather, and told us that they doubted not but the next day at noon we should be at Don Juan de Toledo's *estancia*, or farm. With this we spread our supper upon the green table-cloth, and at that first meal ate up our capon and most of the provision of our cold fried fish, leaving only a bit for our morning's breakfast. The springs of water like conduit-pipes, trickling down the rocks, gave us melodious music to our supper; the Indians fed merrily, and our mules contentedly, and so the fountain nymphs sung us asleep till morning, which seemed to us as calm and quiet as the day before, and encouraged us hastily to snatch that bit which we had left and so up from breakfast, to say merrily, up to Macuilapa. We had not winded the mountain upwards much above a mile when the higher we mounted, the more we heard the wind from above whistling unto us, and forbidding us to go any further.

We were now half way up, and doubtful what we should do, whether go forward, or return to Tapanatepec to eat more fish, or to stay where we were a while until the weather were more calm, which we thought might be at noon or towards evening. The Indians told us that about a mile further there was a fountain of water, and a lodge made under trees on purpose for travellers that were either benighted or hindered by the winds to compass their journey up the mountain. Thither we went with much ado, hoping the wind would fall, but the higher we climbed the stronger we felt the breath of Aeolus, and we durst not march against him, lest instead of ascending we should be made to descend by a furious blast into those deep and horrid precipices, which truly threatened death, and offered themselves to be a grave unto our torn and mangled bodies. We liked the fountain very well, and the lodge better for the harbor of trees which compassed it about. The wind kept on breathing, and we stood still fearing, till the day was so far spent that we had no hopes of going back or forward. We despaired of any supper that night, and we would have been glad now to have picked a bone of a capon's leg, or to have sucked a fish's head, but we saw there was nothing for us but only to feed our hungry stomachs with the remembrance of the plenty the night before. Thus gazing one upon another, and sometimes looking down to the fountain, sometimes looking up to the trees, we perceived amongst them a lemon tree, full of small and very sour green lemons. It was not with us as with Tantalus, who could neither enjoy the fruit above him, nor the waters beneath him; we could and did most greedily catch and snatch the lemons, which were sauce for no meat, but only to fill an empty stomach. With them we supped and took our rest.

The next morning the wind was rather stronger than calmer, and we as strong the second day as the first in our purpose of staying there and not turning our backs like cowards. The Indians were also willing to stay yet one day longer, so we fell to our breakfast of lemons, which were somewhat cool to a fasting stomach, and relished nothing the better with a draught from the clear fountain. And of what we left on the tree we made our dinner and supper, adding to our water what we saw the Indians did drink. They had their small bags full of powder of their maize, of which first making cakes as dry as biscuit, they then grind them to powder, which they carry with them to drink with water when they travel. This we thought might be more nourishing to us than lemons and water only, and so for that day we bought of them half a bagful of powder, giving for it in our want and necessity four reals, or two English shillings, which out of Macuilapa and not bid up by our fear of starving might not be worth above a penny. Yet this was but weak nourishment for our feeble bodies.

Thus we waited all Tuesday for the laying of the wind, resolving the next morning either to go up the hill, or down again to Tapanatepec. But on Wednesday morning, the wind seeming to be somewhat laid, we purposed to stay till noon, hoping then it would be sure travelling. However, it ceased not, but rather increased a little, whereupon one of our company resolved to go upwards a mile or two on foot, and try the passages and the danger of the wind, and to bring us word again, for we, who had heard much talk but had not as yet seen anything worth our fear, thought our fear might be greater than the danger. Up therefore went our friend, who stayed from us near two hours, and then returning back he told us he thought we might get up leading our mules by the bridles. But with further questions and debates time passed away, so that we thought it might be too late, and for that day we put off our journey until the next morning, resolutely purposing to go forwards all together if the wind were not much increased.

That day we fell again to our green crabby lemons, water, and maize powder, all which we found had much weakened our bodies, and we feared if we continued there any longer, they might hasten our death. Wherefore on Thursday morning (the wind being as the day before), having commended ourselves first unto the protection of that Lord whom the winds and sea obey, we mounted up upon our mules, and so went upward, leaving our names written in the bark of a great tree, and the days we stayed there without food.

We perceived no great danger in the wind a great while, but some steps and passages upon stony rocks we feared because of their narrowness, and there we lighted, thinking ourselves safer upon our own two feet than upon the four feet of a beast. But when we came up to the very top of Macuilapa (which signifies in that tongue, a head without hair[9]), we perceived truly the danger so much talked of, and wished ourselves again with our green lemons in the way of Tapanatepec. We found it indeed a head without hair, a top without a tree or branch to shelter a fearful traveller.

The passage that lieth open to the sea may be no more than a quarter of a mile, but the height and narrowness of it stupefieth, for if we look on the one side, there is the wide and spacious South Sea lying so deep and low under it that it dazzleth the eyes to behold

[9] *Macuil*, "five," and *apa(n)*, "river"—the "place of the five rivers."

123

it; if we look on the other side, there are rocks of at least six or seven miles depth, sight of which doth make the stoutest and hardest heart to quake and quiver. Here the sea expects to swallow; there the rocks threaten to tear with a downfall, and in the midst of those dangers in some places the passage is not above an ell broad. We needed better cordials for that quarter of a mile than feeding three days upon green lemons and water, and durst not man ourselves so much as to go through it upon our mules. We lighted, and gave the Indians our mules to lead, and we followed them one by one, not daring to walk upright for fear of head giddiness with looking on either side, but bowing our bodies, we crept upon our hands and feet as near unto the tracks which beasts and travellers had made as we could without hindering our going.

When we had got to the end of that passage, where the mountain was broader and the trees promised relief, we looked back boldly, and accused of folly both ourselves and all other travellers that sought no other way though ten miles about, to avoid that danger both for man and beast.[10] From thence joyfully we made haste to Don Juan de Toledo, who made us welcome and gave us some warm broth to comfort our stomachs, but we were so weak that no sooner had we eaten anything, but presently we cast it up again. After many sups of broth and wine, we recovered strength towards night, and ate our suppers. There we stayed two days, and thus thoroughly refreshed, we went to Acapala a very great town of Indians in the province of Chiapa. This stands by the same river that passeth by Chiapa, which is called Chiapa de Indios, or Chiapa of the Indians, to distinguish it from another Chiapa, called Chiapa Real, the Royal Chiapa, or Chiapa de Españoles, Chiapa of the Spaniards.[11]

From Acapala we went first to Chiapa of the Indians, which standeth almost as low as Macuilapa is high, seated upon a river as broad as is the Thames at London, which hath its spring from the mountains called Cuchumatlanes, in the road from Chiapa Real to

[10] The account of this pass is not a traveler's tale. The Spanish writer, Ciudad Real, who passed this way some sixty years earlier, was equally impressed by the danger.

[11] It is probably that Gage visited Acalá (his Acapala) after, not before, reaching Chiapa of the Indians, the modern Chiapa de Corzo. On his way there from Macuilapa, he probably passed through Tuxtla, then a town of Zoque Indians, but now, as Tuxtla Gutiérrez, the capital of the state of Chiapas.

Guatemala, and runs towards the province of Zoques, where it entereth into the river of Tabasco. But of this Chiapa I will speak a little more in the next chapter, and now only say that here we were joyfully entertained by those friars, who looked upon us as members of their province, and assured us that the Provincial and chief Superior would be very glad of our coming, for they wanted Spanish friars to oppose the Creoles and natives who strived to get ahead as they had done in Mexico and Oaxaca. Here we understood that the Provincial was not above one day's journey from thence.

Here also we met with our friend Peter Borrallo, who had come before us alone, and made his escape from Mexico. He comforted us much with the good and kind usage which he had found there. Yet he told us how Calvo was gone with the rest of his train from Mexico to Acapulco, and from thence was shipped with them to the Philippines, but that at his departure he had written unto the Superior of Chiapa and Guatemala a letter of bitter complaints against him and us four, desiring the Provincial not to entertain us, but to send us back to Mexico, to be shipped from thence the next year unto the Philippines. This letter, he told us, was not regarded, but much slighted by the Provincial. After we had been feasted a week in Chiapa, we thought it now fit to present ourselves to the Provincial, whose name was Friar Pedro Álvarez, that from him we might receive judgment, and know whether we should stay in that province or be forced to return to Spain, for in no other part of America could we be entertained.

We found the Provincial in a little town called San Cristóbal,[12] between Chiapa of the Indians and the Royal Chiapa, recreating himself in the shady walks, which are many sweet and pleasant in that small town, where also there is store of fish and great abundance of rare and exquisite fruits. He entertained us very lovingly with fair and comfortable words, and with a stately dinner and supper, and

---

[12] There does not seem ever to have been a town called San Cristóbal. It seems probable that the place is Tzinacantán, the old capital of the Tzotzil Maya Indians and an Aztec trading post until the Spanish conquest. The town has much charm. There was a fiesta on when I visited it in 1944, and the floor of the newly whitewashed church was thickly carpeted with pine needles, a pre-Christian Maya custom. Although it was hardly 10:00 A.M., the high percentage of inebriates testified to the importance and the success of the fiesta.

before we went to bed, to shew his humility, he did unto us what Christ did to his Disciples, he washed our feet.

The first day he said little or nothing unto us concerning our continuing in that country, but the next day he discovered unto us his full resolutions, with many wise and cunning sophisms. For first he read unto us the letter which Calvo had written unto him against us, glossing upon it how ill we had done in forsaking our first love and calling to the Philippines, and the danger many Indian souls might be in by reason of our not going thither to convert and instruct them. For he supposed our gifts and abilities might have been more profitable and comfortable to those souls than those who in our stead and absence should be sent amongst them. Secondly, he told us how we had frustrated the King of Spain's good hopes of us, for he had allowed us means and maintenance from Spain to Mexico, hoping that by us many souls of Indians in the Philippines might be saved. Thirdly, he told us that he looked upon us as his prisoners, in whose power it was to imprison us, and to send us prisoners to Mexico to the Viceroy, to be shipped from thence to Manila, according to Calvo's demand. For the present he would not let us know what he meant to do with us. Only he bad us not to be discouraged but to be merry and recreate ourselves, and that after dinner we should know more from him, when he had received an answer to a letter which he had written unto the city of Chiapa concerning the disposal of our persons. These reasonings of the grave and old Provincial did not a little sadden our hearts; for the loss of souls, and King of Spain's intentions and charity charged upon us, and imprisonment spoke of by the by, were words which seemed of a very high strain, and so could hardly be digested by us. This morning's breakfast had quite taken away from us our stomach to our dinner.

Thus we departed from the presence of the venerable Friar Pedro Álvarez, and betook ourselves to a shady walk under orange trees belonging to the house where this Superior was. In this shade we conferred with ourselves upon the words of Álvarez, and finding them of so high a nature, as involving souls, a King, and imprisonment, we thought verily we should be sent back to Mexico, and from thence like fugitive slaves be forced to the Philippines. Here my hopes of ever more seeing England were lost; Antonio Melén-

dez' heart panted, and he wished himself again upon the highest top
of Macuilapa; another wished himself with old Calvo at sea sailing to Manila, though it were but to help him scrape his rusty
gammons of bacon.

The motion was made to escape from Álvarez, as we had done
from Calvo; but to this, answer was made that whithersoever we
went, not knowing the country, we should be discovered; and even if
the worst should happen and we should be sent to Mexico, we might
better escape in the way than there where we were. At last I told
the rest that I could conceive no hard nor harsh usage from that
smiling and loving countenance of the Provincial, nor after his low
and humble act of washing our feet the night before. That I thought
verily he wished us well for having come so far to offer ourselves
for fellow-laborers in that harvest of souls belonging to his charge,
and we knew he wanted men such as we were newly come from
Spain to oppose the Creole or native faction in that province. I
alleged furthermore the example of our friend and companion
Peter Borrallo, whom he had already incorporated into that province; he could do no less with us without partiality and acceptation of
persons. And lastly, my opinion was, that in case the Provincial
would not entertain us there, yet he would not send us back to
Mexico, there to be disgraced and affronted, but he would give way
unto us to return to Spain, or whither else we would, with some
relief and money in our purses.

Whilst we were thus troubled and in this sad and serious discourse,
old Álvarez it seems, had been eyeing us from his window, and as
Joseph could not long suppress and keep in the expressions of a
loving and tender heart unto his brethren, so this good Superior,
perceiving that we were troubled with what he had said unto us,
sent his companion unto us to comfort us. This we easily perceived
by his discourse when he came unto us. For as soon as he came he
asked us why we were so sad and melancholy. He told us the Provincial also had observed that we were troubled. "But," said he, "be
of good cheer; be confident that the Provincial wisheth you very
well, and needeth such as you are, and as you have come into his
dominion to thrust yourselves upon his mercy, he will not do by
harsh and unkind usage what martial law forbids a hard-hearted
soldier to do unto his enemy upon such terms." Many such com-

fortable words did he speak unto us, and he told us further that the Provincial had been much censured by the Creole party for entertaining Peter Borrallo, and that now they would stir worse seeing four more come to weaken their faction. Therefore he desired to be well advised concerning us, and he urged us to carry our business with such discretion, as might give little offense to those who were apt to judge and censure the best of all his actions. Finally he did assure us that we should never be sent back as prisoners to Mexico by the Provincial, who, in case he could not entertain us in Chiapa or Guatemala, would further us with all his favor, and friends, and money in our purses to return again to Spain. These reasons were heart-fainting cordials unto us and stomach preparatives to a good dinner, to which by the sound of a bell we were invited.

When we came in, the loving, smiling, and fatherly countenance of the good Provincial did cheer us more than all the cheer that waited for us upon the table in several dishes, all which were seasoned to our palates with the sauce of the comfort which the Provincial's messenger had brought unto us in the shady orange walk in the garden. The great provision of fish and flesh, with fruits and sweetmeats were yet to us a strong argument that we were very welcome; for what we fed on that day might well become a nobleman's table. Besides, in many passages of our discourse we perceived that good old Álvarez' heart was overjoyed with our coming to him.

Dinner being ended, the Provincial desired to play a game at tables [backgammon] with us round about, saying he would not win our money, because he judged us poor after so long a journey. But thus he settled the game and sport: if he did win, we should say for him five *Pater Nosters,* and five *Ave Marias;* if we won, we should win our admittance, and incorporation into that province. This sport pleased us well, for our winnings we judged would be more profitable at that time than to win pounds, and our losings we valued not; besides we were confident all went well with us, when from the favor of the dice we might challenge that favor which with many weary journeys above four hundred miles we had come to seek.

The sport began, and we young blades, taking one by one our turns, were too hard for the old man, who (as we perceived) would willingly be the loser that his very losses might speak unto us what through policy and discretion he would not utter with words. Yet we boldly challenged our winnings, which as soon as we had ended our game were now surely confirmed unto us by the return of an Indian messenger, who that morning had been sent to the city of Chiapa for advice and counsel from the Prior and the chief of the cloister concerning our disposal. The Prior in his letter expressed great joy unto the Provincial for our coming, and the joy of the rest of the seniors of the cloister, and he did earnestly beg of the Superior that he would send us to him to be his guests, for that our case had been his own some ten years before. For he had also forsaken his company to the Philippines at Mexico, and fled to Guatemala, where for his learning and good part he had been as a stranger much envied by the Creole faction. Now he hoped he should have some to side with him against such as spited and maligned him.

Old Álvarez was much taken with his letter, and told us he must pay what he had lost, and that the next day he would send us to Chiapa, there to abide until he took further care of us, to send us to other parts of the country to learn the Indian languages, that we might preach unto them. This discourse being ended, we betook ourselves again to the garden, which smelled more of comfort than before dinner, and to our shady walks which now offered us a safer protection than they had done in the forenoon, countenancing that protection which we had gained from the Provincial.

Here we began to praise God, who had looked upon us in our low estate, not forgetting the wise and politic Provincial, who though he had lost his games for our comfort, we would not he should lose our prayers, which there we offered up to God for his health and safety. And so till supper time we continued our discourse in the garden, fuller of mirth and pleasant jests than we had been before dinner, snatching now and then at the oranges and lemons, which were there both sour and sweet, eating of some, and casting some one at another, but especially at him who had wished himself with Calvo dressing his rusty bacon. We strived to beat him out of the garden by force of orange and lemon bullets, which sport we continued the more willingly, because we perceived the good Provincial stood behind a lattice in a balcony beholding us, and rejoicing to see our hearts so light and merry. We had no sooner beat Calvo's friend out of the garden when the bell to supper sounded a retreat to us all, and called us again to meet our best friend Álvarez, who had furnished us a table again like that at noon.

After supper he told us that the next morning he would send us to Chiapa, for that the Prior had writ unto him he would meet us in the way with a breakfast at a town called San Felipe. Wherewith we conceited very highly of ourselves to see that provincials and priors were so forwarded to feast us. Yet before we went to bed, the Provincial would try again a game at tables with every one of us, to see if now he could beat us that had been too hard for him at noon. The matter of our game was now altered, and what we played for was this: if the Provincial won, we were to be his prisoners (which mystery we understood not till the next day, for the old man was crafty and politic, and knew he could win of us when he listed, for he was an excellent gamester at tables); but if we won of him, he was to give us a box of chocolate, which was a drink we liked very well.

The game went on, and every one of us one by one were losers, yet understood not how we should be his prisoners, but slighted our losses. Yet for all this the merry Provincial told us he was sorry we had lost, and wished we might never be prisoners to a worse enemy than he; and that we should perceive it, but would comfort us each one as a prisoner with a box of chocolate, to drink for his sake, and to comfort our hearts when most we should find them discomforted for our losses. We understood not his meaning till the next day at noon, but thought it was a jest and a word of sport and mirth, like many such-like which in his discourse had come from him.

With this we took our leaves, and went to bed with light and merry hearts. In the morning two mules of the Provincial and two of his companion were saddled for us, and at least a dozen Indians on horseback waited for us to conduct us up a steepy hill and through woods to the town of San Felipe. After our breakfast the good Provincial embraced us, and bad us farewell, desiring us to pray for him, and not to be discouraged by anything that might befall us, assuring us he wished us very well, and would do what lay in his power for our good.[13] Yet, that he must use policy and discretion to

[13] Rev. Fr. Pedro Álvarez is one of the few persons in this book for whom Gage does not have a bad word. Indeed, these scenes of the benevolent old Provincial with

stop the mouths of the Creoles, whom he knew hated both him and us.

Thus we departed with waits and trumpets sounding before us, which rebounded an echo all the way up the hill from us to old Álvarez, whom we had left in a low bottom compassed about with hills on every side. We had no sooner ascended up to the top of the mountain when we discovered a little valley, and in it the city of Chiapa of the Spaniards, with two or three small villages, of which one was San Felipe at the bottom of the mountain which we were to descend. The trumpets which still went sounding before us were a sufficient and loud alarm to San Felipe's inhabitants of our coming, and a warning for the speedier hastening of our second breakfast, for the which the cold morning air (which we found somewhat piercing upon the mountain) had whetted and thoroughly prepared our stomachs.

We had not got down the mountain half a mile, when we met with a matter of twenty gallant Indians on horseback with their trumpeters sounding before them, and behind them came upon a stately mule the Prior of Chiapa, Father Juan Bautista (John the Baptist), a merry fat friar, who, calling us his brethren fugitives from the Philippines, told us we were welcome to that country, and to him especially, and that in the next San Felipe he would shew us better sport than any San Felipe in all the Philippine Islands could have shewed us, if we had gone thither.[14] Thus with a pleasant discourse, and many merry conceits from the good Prior we soon came

heart overflowing with loving kindness for the young friars are painted by Gage with unusual tenderness, and clearly made a deep impression on him. The historian Ximénez says the Provincial had a pleasant disposition and was much esteemed in Chiapas, although he was not a learned man. Nevertheless, he held the title of Preacher General, and had been sub-Prior of Comitán (1618) and Prior of Ciudad Real (1622–24) before being elected Provincial. He died in 1633 or 1634 in the Convent of Ocosingo. I like to think that young Antonio Meléndez, who worked among the Tzeltal Mayas around Ocosingo and was later its first Prior, was at hand to minister to Father Pedro Álvarez in his last illness and death.

[14] Father Juan Bautista was a good friend to Gage, who gives a portrait of a sleek-headed man without any lean and hungry look about him. He was a native of Seville. He was later Prior of Sacapulas and had been elected Prior of Guatemala in 1640, but died before he could take up his post. He and Father Juan Ximeno were among those who worked hard for the raising of the Dominican college of St. Thomas Aquinas, in which Gage subsequently taught, to the rank of university. Their testimonies, given in 1622, are among the published documents of the Guatemalan archives.

down the hill, where the whole village of San Felipe waited for us both men and women, some presenting unto us nosegays, others hurling roses and other flowers in our faces, others dancing before us all along the street, which was strewed with herbs and orange leaves and adorned with many arches made with flowers and hung with garlands for us to ride under until we came to the church, where for half an hour we were welcomed with the best music from the city of Chiapa, which the Prior had hired to come with him to entertain us.

Our music being ended, fat Father John the Baptist stood up and made a short speech unto the Indians, giving them thanks for their kind and pompous entertainment of us, his special friends, and that their souls might gain by it, he granted unto them a plenary indulgence of all their sins past to be gained by as many of them as should visit that church the next Lord's Day either before or after noon.

Thus from the altar we went unto our breakfasting table, which was furnished with many well-seasoned dishes of salt and well-peppered and spiced meats, all fit to make us relish better a cup of Spanish *Pier Ximeny* which the Prior had provided for us. After our salt meats, came such rare and exquisite sorts of sweetmeats made by John the Baptist's best devoted nuns of Chiapa, that the like we had not seen from San Juan de Ulua to that place. These were to prepare our stomachs for a cup of chocolate, with the which we ended our breakfast. But whilst all this was gallantly performed by the Prior, it was a hard riddle unto us what he often repeated unto us saying: "Brethren break your fast well, for your dinner will be the meanest as ever ye did eat in your lives, and now enjoy this sweet liberty which will not last long unto you." We observed the words, but knew not what to make of them, till we came unto the cloister. After our breakfast the Indians shewed us a little sport in the market-place, running races on horseback, and playing at *juego de cañas;* which is to meet on horseback, with broad targets to defend their heads and shoulders while passing by they hurl canes, or darts, one at another. Those Indians acted this with great dexterity.

Thus the good Prior of Chiapa feasted us, and permitted us to enjoy our liberty as long as it seems it had been agreed upon by letters between him and the Provincial, which was till it might be dinner time in the cloister of Chiapa, where we were to be before noon. The time drew near, and we had from San Felipe to the city of Chiapa some two English miles to ride. Wherefore the Prior commanded our mules to be brought; the waits and trumpets gave warning to the town of our departure; and so with many horsemen, with dances, music and ringing of bells we were as stately and joyfully conducted out of the town as we had been inducted into it. At the first half-mile's end the Prior gave thanks unto the Indians, and desired them to return, the cloister being near where we expected another kind of entertainment, not using in the city and cloister that pomp and state which in the country might be allowed.

The Indians took their leaves of us, and on we went with only two as guides before us. Within half a mile of the city, the Prior and a companion of his stopped, and took out of his pocket an order from the Provincial which he read unto us, to this effect, That whereas we had forsaken our lawful Superior Calvo in the way to the Philippines, and without his licence had come unto the province of Chiapa, he could not in conscience but inflict some punishment upon us before he did enable us to abide there as members under him. Therefore he did strictly command the Prior of Chiapa that as soon as we should enter into his cloister, he should shut us up two by two in our chambers, as in prisons, for three days, not suffering us to go out to any place, save only to the public place of refection (called refectory) where all the friars met together to dine and sup. There at noon time we were to present ourselves before all the cloisters sitting upon the bare ground, and there to receive no other dinner but only bread and water, but at supper we might have in our chambers, or prisons, what the Prior would be pleased to allow us. This was the penance enjoined upon us by the wise and cunning Provincial.

This news at the first was but sour sauce, or a dry postpast after a double sumptuous breakfast; it was a doleful ditty to us after our music and dances, to hear of a treble fast after our feast; to hear of imprisonment after so great liberty. We now began to remember the Provincial's winnings at tables the night before, and the mystery thereof, and began to think how comfortable his boxes of chocolate would be unto us after a meal of bread and water. Now we called to mind the short dinner the Prior had told us at San Felipe we were like to have that day, and of the liberty he bad us then make much of. But the good Prior, seeing us sad upon a sudden and our countenances changed, smiled upon us, wishing us not to think the worse of him, nor of the Provincial, who did that out of policy, and to stop the Creoles' mouths, for he knew they would murmur if no punishment were inflicted upon us.

He assured us, after our imprisonment, of honors and preferments, and that as long as we were with him, we should want no encouragement; and that after a bread and water dinner he could send us to our chambers a supper that should strongly support our empty stomachs, and fur and line them well for the next four and twenty hours. With these encouragements, on we went to the cloister of Chiapa, where we were welcomed by most of the friars, but in some few we noted a frowning and disaffected countenance.

We were no sooner conducted to our chambers, when the bell sounded to dinner for the rest, and cried aloud to us penance with bread and water. Down we went to the common dining place, and thanks being given, the friars sitting round the tables, we four Philippinian Jonahs[15] (so some Creoles were pleased to term us) betook ourselves to the middle of the refectory, where without cushions, stools, seats, or forms, we sat upon the bare ground cross-legged like tailors, acting humility now for our disobedience unto slovenly Calvo. While the first dish was presented round the tables, to each of us was presented a loaf of reasonable bigness, and a pot of pure crystal water, whereof we fed and drank most heartily though with full stomachs from a double breakfast before. Yet even here in this public act of shame and disgrace, which we knew was usual among friars for less faults than ours, we had this comfort. We knew that we had a Prior and Provincial for friends, and that that punishment came from a friendly hand, whose chocolate we had to comfort our fasting bodies. And secondly, we knew that we should have that night in our prison chambers a better supper than any of those before us, who fed upon their three or four dishes.

But thirdly, it was our comfort that at that very time a Creole

[15] "Now the word of the Lord came unto Jonah, the son of Amittai, saying, Arise, go to Nineveh, that great city, and cry against it; for their wickedness is come up before me. But Jonah rose up to flee to Tarshish from the presence of the Lord, and went down to Joppa; and he found a ship going to Tarshish."—Jonah 1:1–3.

friar also sat upon the ground with us (of whose company we had been informed by some friends before we went into the refectory) for some love letters which had been intercepted between him and a nun of that city, tending to much incivility, and breaking their oath of professed chastity. But when I perceived this friar to look discontentedly upon us, I chose my place as near unto him as I could, and hearing him mutter within himself against us, calling us disobedient Philippine Jonahs, I softly and friendly spoke unto him with these two following hexameters, which suddenly came unto my mind about his misdemeanor:

> *Si monialis amor te turpia scribere fecit,*
> *Ecce tibi frigidae praebent medicamina lymphae.*

> [*If love for a nun made thee write scandalous things,*
> *Lo, cold waters furnish thee their medicines.*]

But my good neighbor, snuffing and puffing at my sudden Muse, seemed to be more discontented than before, and would fain withdraw himself by degrees from me, not rising up (for that was not lawful to do till dinner had been ended), but wriggling his elbows and shoulders scornfully from me, whom in like manner I followed, cleaving friendship to him with this verse:

> *Solamen misero est socios retinere pañetes.*

> [*It is a solace to one in trouble to recall that a trouser leg always keeps its partner.*]

He thought I followed him to steal away his loaf from him. This new-found word *pañetes* [a Spanish term for a kind of trousers which Gage inserts in his line of Latin] had almost choked him had he not made use of the medicinal water which stood before him, of the which he drank a good draught, whereby I perceived his courage against me and his friends was tamed, and I told him I hoped his burning wanton love was cooled.

Thus with my Creole neighbors' company my bread and water went down cheerfully, and dinner being ended, we were again conducted to our chambers, where we drank a cup of old Álvarez' chocolate. The Castilian friars flocked unto our prisons, some to talk with us, some bringing us conserves and sweetmeats; others, other dainties, which they had prepared to help our digestion of bread and cold water. Our supper was provided for us according to the promise and generous spirit of the Prior, who also honored our prison that night with his own and two other friars' company, supping with us all in one chamber together. And thus we passed our three days of imprisonment merrily and contentedly, wishing we might never suffer harder usage in any prison than we had done in this, which was not to us such a punishment as did bring with it the privation of any liberty of enjoying the company of friends, of feasting with them, but only the privation of the liberty of our legs to walk about those three days. In fact this was an ease rather than a punishment, for that we wanted rest rather than much stirring after so long and tedious a journey as we had compassed from Mexico thither.

We were no sooner set at liberty but we presently found the Provincial and Prior ready to dispose of us so that in lieu of our imprisonment we might receive honor and credit. Two were sent into the country to learn some Indian language, that so they might be beneficed and preach unto the Indians. Myself and another desired to go farther to Guatemala, that there we might practice philosophy and divinity in the famous university of that city.[16] Nothing that we desired was denied unto us, only the time was thought not fit until Michaelmas, because then the schools were renewed, and new orders settled.

In the meantime the Provincial, having heard of my *ex tempore*

---

[16] Father Anstruther, O.P., has brought to light an order from the Master General in Rome regularizing the switch by Gage and others from the Philippines to Guatemala. The list includes the name of Fr. Juan Bautista, who as Prior of Ciudad Real, welcomed Gage and his comrades with the information that he, too, had been a Philippine escapee, an interesting confirmation of Gage's veracity. By eliminating earlier transfers, it is pretty clear that Gage's comrades, besides Meléndez, were Francisco de la Vega and Juan Escudero, who was only a sub-deacon and perhaps was the one pelted out of the garden with sour oranges and lemons. Another name on the list, Pedro de San Vicente, may be the Dominican name of Pedro Borrallo, who slipped away from the mission before Gage and his comrades. The order is dated April 10, 1627. Gage's Irish friend, Tomás de León, arrived safely in the Philippines with Father Calvo and the rest of the mission. After two years in Manila, he was assigned to Cavite. Nothing further is known of him.

verses to the Creole friar, and knowing that the Latin tongue is better grounded in England than among the Spaniards (who abuse poor Priscian and daily break his pate with foolish solecisms), considered the want he had of a master of the Latin tongue to supply a lecture of grammar and syntax to the youths of Chiapa in a school in that cloister, which brought a sufficient yearly stipend unto the convent. He desired me to accept of that place until such time as he should take care to send me to Guatemala, promising me all encouragements in the meantime fitting, and that I should when I would go about to see the country (which I much desired). He also told me that out of the school annuity I should have my allowance for books and other necessaries. I could not but accept of this good offer; and so with this employment I remained in that city from April to the end of September, where I was much esteemed of by the Bishop and Governor, but especially by the Prior, who would never ride about the country for his recreation, but he would take me with him. Thereby I had occasion to note concerning the province, riches, commodities, and government of Chiapa what in the ensuing chapter I shall faithfully commend unto the press.

11. Describing the country of Chiapa, with the chiefest towns and commodities belonging unto it

THOUGH Chiapa in the opinion of the Spaniards be held to be one of the poorest countries of America, because in it as yet there have been no mines discovered, nor golden sands found in the rivers, nor any haven upon the South Sea, whereby commodities are brought in and carried out, as to Mexico, Oaxaca, and Guatemala, yet I may say it exceedeth most provinces and yieldeth to none except it be to Guatemala in the greatness and beauty of fair towns. Nay, it surpasseth all the rest of America in that one and famous and most populous town of Chiapa of the Indians. And it ought not to be so much slighted by the Spaniards as it is, if they would look upon it as standing between Mexico and Guatemala, whose strength might be all America's strength, and whose weakness may prove dangerous to all that flourishing empire, for the easy entrance into it by the river of Tabasco, or for its near joining and bordering unto Yucatán. Besides, the commodities in it are such as do uphold a constant trading and commerce amongst the inhabitants themselves, and with other neighboring countries, and from no one part of America doth Spain get more cochineal than from one of the provinces of Chiapa. The towns also being great and populous, by their yearly poll tax do add much to the King of Spain's revenues.

This country is divided into three provinces, to wit, Chiapa, Zeldales [Tzeltales],[1] and Zoques,[2] whereof Chiapa itself is the poorest. This contains the great town of Chiapa of the Indians, and

[1] Tzeltales, named for the Tzeltal-speaking Mayas occupying the region.
[2] The Zoques are a non-Maya group of Indians who occupied much of western Chiapas.

all the towns and farms northward [southwestward] toward Ma-cuilapa, and westward [eastward] the priory of Comitán, which hath some ten towns, and many farms of cattle, horses, and mules subject unto it. Neighboring unto it, lieth the great valley of Copana-bastla, which is another priory reaching towards Soconusco. This valley glorieth in the great river [Grijalva], which hath its spring from the mountains called Cuchumatlanes, and runneth to Chiapa of the Indians, and from thence to Tabasco. It is also famous for the abundance of fish, which the river yields, and the great store of cattle, which from thence minister food and provision to the city of Chiapa and to all the adjacent towns.

Chiapa the city and Comitán stand upon hills, and so are exceedingly cold, yet this valley lying low is extraordinary hot, and from May to Michaelmas is subject to great storms and tempests of thunder and lightning. The head town, where the priory stands, is called Copanabastla, and consists of above eight hundred Indians. But greater than this is Izquintenango at the end of the valley and at the foot of the mountains of Cuchumatlanes southward. Yet bigger than this is the town of San Bartolomé northward at the other end of the valley, which in length is about forty miles, and ten or twelve only in breadth.[3] All the rest of the towns lie towards Soconusco, and are yet hotter and more subject to thunder and lightning, as drawing nearer unto the South Sea coast.

Besides the abundance of cattle, the chief commodity of this valley is cotton, whereof are made such store of mantles for the Indians' wearing that the merchants far and near come for them. They exchange them to Soconusco and Suchitepéquez for cacao, whereby they are well stored of that drink. So that the inhabitants want neither fish (which they have from the river) nor flesh (the valley abounds with cattle) nor clothing (of that they have to spare for others) nor bread, though not of wheat, for there grows none, but of Indian maize they have plenty. Besides, they are exceedingly stored with fowls and turkeys, fruits, honey, tobacco, and sugar-

---

[3] Because of the unhealthiness of its situation, Copanabastla or Copanaguastla was gradually abandoned, and in 1629 the Dominicans took steps to remove the priory to Tzotzocoltenango. By 1645 the population had fallen to eight Indians, and the church was abandoned. Izquintenango has entirely disappeared. San Bartolomé de los Llanos remains, but is now called Venustiano de Carranza.

canes. Neither here nor in Chiapa is money so plentiful as in Mexico and Oaxaca. Whereas there they reckon by patacones, or pieces of eight, here they reckon by *tostones* which are but half-patacones. Though the river be many ways profitable to that valley, yet it is cause of many disasters to the inhabitants, who often lose their children and their calves and colts, drawing near to the water-side where they are devoured by caymans, which are many and greedy of flesh, by reason of the many prizes they have got.

The city of Chiapa Real is one of the meanest cities in all America, consisting of not above four hundred Spanish householders, and about an hundred houses of Indians joining to the city, and called *el barrio de los Indios*, who have a chapel by themselves. In this city there is no parish church, but only the cathedral, which is mother to all the inhabitants. Besides, there are two cloisters, one of Dominicans and the other of Franciscans, and a poor cloister of nuns, which are burdensome enough to that city. The fact that the Jesuits have got no footing there (who commonly live in the richest and wealthiest places and cities) is a sufficient argument of either the poverty of that city, or of want of gallant parts and prodigality in the gentry, from whose free and generous spirits they like horseleeches are still sucking extraordinary and great alms for the colleges where they live. But here the merchants are close-handed, and the gentlemen hard and sparing, wanting of wit and courtiers' parts and bravery, and so poor Chiapa is held no fit place for Jesuits. The merchants' chief trading there is in cacao, cotton from the adjacent parts of the country, in pedlar's small wares, in some sugar from about Chiapa of the Indians, and in a little cochineal. But commonly the Governor (whose chief gain consisteth in this) will not suffer them to be too free in this commodity, lest they hinder his greedy traffic. These have their shops all together in a little market-place before the cathedral church, built with walks and porches, under which the poor Indian wives meet at five o'clock at evening to sell what slap and drugs they can prepare most cheap for the empty Creole stomachs.

The richer sort of these merchants go and send yet further to Tabasco for wares from Spain, such as wines, linen cloth, figs, raisins, olives, and iron, though in these commodities they dare not venture too much, by reason the Spaniards in that country are not very many, and those that are there are such as are loath to open their purses to more than what may suffice nature. So that Spanish commodities are chiefly brought for the friars who are the best and joviallest blades of that country.[4]

The gentlemen of Chiapa are a by-word all about that country, signifying great dons (*dones*, gifts or abilities I should say), great birth, fantastic pride, joined with simplicity, ignorance, misery, and penury. These gentlemen will say they descend from some duke's house in Spain, and immediately from the first Conquerors; yet in carriage they are but clowns, in wit, abilities, parts, and discourse as shallow-brained as a low brook, whose waters are scarce able to leap over a pebble stone, any small reason soon tries and tires their weak brain, which is easily at a stand when sense is propounded, and slides on speedily when nonsense carrieth the stream. The gentlemen Creoles or natives of Chiapa are as presumptuous and arrogant as if the noblest blood in the Court of Madrid ran through their veins. It is a common thing amongst them to make a dinner only with a dish of *frijoles* in black broth, boiled with pepper and garlic, saying it is the most nourishing meat in all the Indies; and after this so stately a dinner they will be sure to come out to the street-door of their houses to see and to be seen, and there for half an hour will they stand shaking off the crumbs of bread from their clothes, bands (but especially from their ruffs when they used them), and from

[4] Chiapa Real was known as Ciudad Real and also as Chiapa of the Spaniards to differentiate it from Chiapa of the Indians. Now it is called San Cristóbal de las Casas. Few visitors would share Gage's poor opinion of the town. The Dominican church with its ornate façade and its rich baroque interior is a splendid monument to Spanish colonial art and architecture, but these embellishments are of the eighteenth century. Gage makes no mention of the brightly dressed Indians from the neighboring villages of Tzeltal and Tzotzil Maya who must then, as now, have poured down the streets of the town each market day, in a swirling flood of exotic color. Such memories were for himself alone, not to be shared with somber Puritan friends.

The Dominican friary is now used as a prison. I obtained permission to enter the striking patio, but my observations were somewhat impeded by the peculiar conduct of some of the prisoners, who, crowding round, began to sniff at me like dogs! The high adobe walls still enclose the adjacent large garden which once supplied Gage and his fellow friars with fruits and vegetables.

The Franciscan writer Francisco Vásquez published in 1714 this eulogy of the city, with which I heartily agree: "Real de Chiapa is an unimportant city, not in its nobility and good breeding, nor in its buildings nor in the religious usages of its friaries, but only in the number of its citizens. Yet such is their spirit that each in valor is worth 50,000 and gives the city the grandeur it deserves."

their mustachios. And with their tooth-pickers they will stand picking their teeth, as if some small partridge bone stuck in them. Nay, if a friend pass by at that time, they will be sure to find out some crumb or other in the mustachio (as if on purpose the crumbs of the table had been shaken upon their beards, that the loss of them might be a gaining of credit for great house-keeping) and they will be sure to vent out some non-truth, as to say: *"A Señor que linda perdiz he comido hoy,"* "O Sir, what a dainty partridge have I eat to-day," whereas they pick out nothing from their teeth but a black husk of a dry *frijol* or Turkey bean.

Though they say they are great in blood and in birth, yet in their employments they are but rich graziers, for most of their wealth consisteth in farms of cattle and mules. Some indeed have towns of Indians subject unto them, whereof they are called *encomenderos,* and receive yearly from every Indian a certain poll tribute of fowls and money. They have most cowardly spirits for war, and though they will say they would fain see Spain, yet they dare not venture their lives at sea, for they judge sleeping in a whole skin the best maxim for their Creole spirits. One hundred fighting soldiers would easily lay low those Chiapa dons, and gain the whole city, which lieth so open to the fields that the mules and asses come in and graze, the streets being very commodious to entertain asses from within, and from without. Yet in this city liveth commonly a governor, or *Alcalde Mayor,* and a bishop.

The Governor's place is of no small esteem and interest, for his power reacheth far, and he tradeth much in cacao and cochineal, and domineers over both Spaniards and Indians at his will and pleasure. But ill-gotten goods never thrive, as was seen in Don Gabriel de Orellana, governor of this city and country in my time, who, having sent the worth of eight thousand crowns in cochineal, cacao, sugar, and hides by the river of Tabasco towards Havana, lost it all into the hands of the Hollanders, who doubtless knew how to make better use of it than would have done that tyrannizing Governor. The Bishop's place of that city is worth at least eight thousand ducats a year, which truly he had need of that comes so far from Spain to live in such a city where are such able dons and where asses are so freely fed and bred. Most of this Bishop's revenues consisteth in great offerings which he yearly receiveth from the great Indian towns, going out to them once a year to confirm their children. Confirmation is such a means to confirm and strengthen the Bishop's revenues, that none must be confirmed by him who offer not a fair white wax-candle, with a ribbon and at least four reals. I have seen the richer sort offer him a candle of at least six-pound weight with two yards of twelve-penny broad ribbon, and the candle stuck from the top to the bottom with single reals round about. Nay, the poor Indians make it the chief masterpiece of their vanity to offer proudly in such occasions.

Don Bernardino de Salazar was the Bishop of this city in my time, who desired my company to ride with him his circuit but one month about the towns near to Chiapa, and in this time I was appointed by him to hold the basin wherein the Spaniards and Indians (whilst he confirmed their children) did cast their offerings, which I and another chaplain did always tell and cast up by good account before we carried the money up into his chamber.

I found that at our return at the month's end he had received one thousand and six hundred ducats of offerings alone, besides the fees due to him for visiting the several companies, or sodalities and confraternities, belonging to the saints or souls in their purgatory, which are extraordinary rich there, whereof he and all other bishops in their district take account yearly. This Bishop, as all the rest are there, was somewhat covetous, but otherwise a man of a temperate life and conversation, very zealous to reform whatsoever abuses committed in the church, which cost him his life before I departed from Chiapa to Guatemala.

The women of that city, it seems, pretend much weakness and squeamishness of stomach, which they say is so great that they are not able to continue in the church while a Mass is briefly huddled over, much less while a solemn high Mass (as they call it) is sung and a sermon preached, unless they drink a cup of hot chocolate, and eat a bit of sweetmeats to strengthen their stomachs. For this purpose it was much used by them to make their maids bring to them to church in the middle of Mass or sermon a cup of chocolate, which could not be done to all, or most of them, without a great confusion and interrupting both Mass and sermon. The Bishop perceived this abuse and gave fair warning for the omitting of it, but all without amendment. Consequently he thought fit to fix in writing upon the church's doors an excommunication against all such as should presume at the time of service to eat or drink within the church. This excommunication was taken much to heart by all, but especially by the gentlewomen, who protested if they might not eat or drink in the church they could not continue in it to hear what otherwise they were bound unto.

The chief of them, knowing what great friendship there was between the Bishop and the Prior and myself, came to the Prior and me desiring us to use all means we could with the Bishop to persuade him to revoke his excommunication so heavily laid upon them, and his threatening their souls with damning judgment for the violation of it. The good Prior and myself labored all we could, alleging the custom of the country, the weakness of the sex whom it most concerned, and also the weakness of their stomachs, the contempt that might from them ensue unto his person, and many inconveniences which might follow to the breeding of an uproar in the church and in the city, whereof we had some probable conjecture from what already we had heard from some. But none of these reasons would move the Bishop. He answered that he preferred the honor of God, and of his house before his own life.

The women seeing him so hard to be entreated, began to stomach [be angry with] him the more and to slight him with scornful and reproachful words. Others slighted his excommunication, drinking in iniquity in the church, as the fish doth water. This caused one day such an uproar in the Cathedral that many swords were drawn against the priests and prebends, who attempted to take away from the maids the cups of chocolate which they brought unto their mistresses. These ladies seeing at last that neither fair nor foul means would prevail with the Bishop, resolved to forsake the Cathedral, where the Bishop's own and his prebends' eyes must needs be watching over them. So from that time most of the city betook themselves to the cloister churches, where by the nuns and friars they were not troubled nor resisted, though fairly counselled to obey the command of the Bishop. Nevertheless, his name they could not now brook, and to his prebends they denied now all such relief and stipend for Masses which formerly they had used to bestow upon them, conferring them all upon the friars who grew rich by the poor impoverished Cathedral.

This lasted not long, but the Bishop began to stomach the friars, and to set up another excommunication, binding all the city to resort unto their own cathedral church. This the women would not obey, but kept their houses for a whole month. In that time the Bishop fell dangerously sick, and desired to retire himself to the cloister of the Dominicans, for the great confidence he had in the Prior that he would take care of him in his sickness. Physicians were sent for far and near, who all with a joint opinion agreed that the Bishop was poisoned, and he himself doubted not of it at his death, praying unto God to forgive those that had been the cause of it, and to accept that sacrifice of his life, which he was willing to offer for the zeal of God's house and honor. He lay not above a week in the cloister, and as soon as he was dead, all his body, his head and face, did so swell that the least touch upon any part of him caused the skin to break and cast out white matter, which had corrupted and overflown all his body.

A gentlewoman with whom I was well acquainted in that city, who was noted to be somewhat too familiar with one of the Bishop's pages, was commonly censured. She was said to have prescribed such a cup of chocolate to be ministered by the page which poisoned him who so rigorously had forbidden chocolate to be drunk in the church. I myself heard this gentlewoman say of the deceased Bishop that she thought few grieved for his death, and that the women had no reason to grieve for him, and that she judged, he being such an enemy to chocolate in the church, that which he had drunk at home in his house had not agreed with his body. And it became afterwards a proverb in that country, Beware of the chocolate of Chiapa; which made me so cautious that I would not drink afterwards of it in any house where I had not very great satisfaction of the whole family.

The women of this city are somewhat light in their carriage, and have learned from the Devil many enticing lessons and baits to draw poor souls to sin and damnation; and if they cannot have their wills, they will surely work revenge either by chocolate or conserves, or some fair present, which shall surely carry death along with it.

There are yet twelve leagues from this city of Chiapa, another Chiapa which deserveth better commendations.[5] This consisteth

[5] Chiapa de los Indios, called today Chiapa de Corzo. The Indians, called Chiapanec, were descendants of a group which had come here before the Spanish conquest from Central America. Except to the west, which was Zoque territory, they were surrounded by Mayas.

most of Indians, and is held to be one of the biggest Indian towns in all America, containing at least four thousand families. This town hath many privileges from the King of Spain, and is governed chiefly by Indians (yet with subordination unto the Spanish government of the city of Chiapa), who do choose an Indian governor with other inferior officers to rule with him. This Governor may wear a rapier and dagger, and enjoyeth many other liberties denied to the rest of the Indians. No town hath so many dons in it of Indian blood as this. Don Felipe de Guzmán was governor of it in my time, a very rich Indian, who kept commonly in his stable a dozen of as good horses for shows and ostentation as the best Spaniard in the country. His courage was not inferior to any Spaniard, and for defense of some privileges of his town he sued in the Chancery of Guatemala the proud and high-minded Governor of the city of Chiapa, spending therein great sums of money till he had overcome him. Thereupon he caused a feast to be made in the town, both by water and land, so stately, that truly in the Court of Madrid it might have been acted.

This town lieth upon a great river [Grijalva], to which, belong many boats and canoes, wherein those Indians have been taught to act sea-fights with great dexterity, and to represent the nymphs of Parnassus, Neptune, Aeolus, and the rest of the heathenish gods and goddesses, so that they are a wonder of their whole nation. They will arm with their boats a siege against the town, fighting against it with such courage till they make it yield, as if they had been trained up all their life to sea-fights. So likewise within the town they are as dexterous at baiting of bulls, at *juego de cañas*, at horse-races, at arming a camp, and at all manner of Spanish dances, instruments, and music as the best Spaniards.

They will erect towers and castles made of wood and painted cloth, and from them fight either with the boats or one against another, with squibs, darts, and many strange fire-works, so manfully that if they could perform it as well in earnest as they do it in sport and pastime, the Spaniards and friars might soon repent to have taught them what they have. As for acting of plays, this is a common part of their solemn pastimes, and they are so generous that they nothing think too much to spend in banquets and sweetmeats upon their friars and neighboring towns, whensoever they are minded to shew themselves in a public feast.

The town is very rich, and many Indians in it trade about the country as the Spaniards do. They have learned most trades befitting a commonwealth, and practice and teach them within their town. They want not any provision of fish or flesh, having for the one that great river joining unto their town, and for the other many *estancias*, as they call them, or farms abounding with cattle. In this town the Dominican friars bear all the sway, and they have a rich and stately cloister with another church or chapel subordinate unto it.[6] The heat here is so great that both friars and Indians commonly wear a linen towel about their necks to wipe off the constant sweat from their faces, which maketh the friars sit longer at their dinner than else they would do, for that at every bite they eat and draught they drink, they are fain to make a stop to wipe their dropping brows. Yet the evenings are fresh and cool, which are much made of there, and spent in the many walks and gardens which join close unto the river side.

Two or three leagues from the town, there are two *ingenios* or farms of sugar, the one belonging to the cloister of the Dominicans of the city of Chiapa; the other unto the cloister of this town. These contain near two hundred blackamoors, besides many Indians, who are employed in that constant work of making sugar for all the country. Hereabouts are bred great store of mules, and excellent horses for any service. The town of Chiapa of the Indians, and all the towns about it, want nothing but a more temperate climate and cooler air, and wheat, which there cannot be sown. For Spaniards and such as cannot live without it, wheat is brought from Chiapa of the Spaniards and from about Comitán; yet this is not generally acknowledged a want by reason of the great plenty of maize which

[6] The noble Dominican church stands by the river, and beside it are the remains of the friary buildings. Gage fails to mention the magnificent brick fountain in Mudejar style, considered one of the glories of New World architecture, which was finished in 1562 and to this day wins the admiration of all visitors. The church is of approximately the same date, and has a massive altar frontal of silver. The local prison and a school share the old friary buildings, which have considerable architectural merit. Mr. Frans Blom informs me that the sea fight described above is still performed, on January 20 (San Sebastián day).

147

all the towns enjoy, and which is now more used both by Spaniards and dainty-toothed friars than bread of wheat. Yet poor Spaniards, and some Indians who have got the trick of trading from them, do gain not a little in bringing to these towns biscuits of wheaten bread. Though these be dry and hard, yet because they are novelties to the Indians, the traders get much by changing them for other commodities especially of cotton-wool, which here is more abounding than in the valley of Copanabastla.

Upon this country of Chiapa of the Indians bordereth the province of Zoques, which is absolutely the richest part of Chiapa. This reacheth on the one side to Tabasco, and by the river named Grijalva sendeth commonly the commodities which are in it with safety into San Juan de Ulua or Vera Cruz. It trafficketh also with the country of Yucatán by the haven called Puerto Real, which lieth between Grijalva and Yucatán. Yet these two, the River of Tabasco, alias Grijalva, and Puerto Real, though they be commodious to this province of Zoques, yet they are causes of daily fears unto the Spaniards, who well know the weakness of them, and that if a foreign nation should manfully thrust into that country by any of these two ways, they might so conquer all Chiapa, and from thence pass easily unto Guatemala. But the river of Tabasco lying low, and being somewhat hot, and the towns about it infested with many gnats, and the chiefest commodity there being but cacao, have often discouraged both our English and Hollanders. For they have come part way up the river, and minding more the aforesaid reasons than what was forward to be had, have turned back, losing a rich country and slighting an eternal name for few and frivolous present difficulties.

In this province of Zoques, the towns are not very big, yet they be very rich. The chief commodities are silk and cochineal; whereof the latter is held the best of America, and the store of it so great that no one province alone exceeds it. There are few Indians who have not their orchards planted with the trees whereon breed the worms which yield unto us that rich commodity. Not that the Indians themselves esteem it save that as they see the Spaniards greedy after it, offering them money for it, and forcing them to the preservation of it in those parts which have proved most successful for this kind. There is great store of silk in this country, in so much that the Indians make it their great commodity to employ their wives in working towels with all colors of silk, which the Spaniards buy, and send into Spain. It is rare to see what works those Indian women will make in silk, such as might serve for patterns and samplers to many school-mistresses in England.[7]

The people of this country are witty, and ingenious, and fair of

complexion; the country towards Tabasco is hot, but within in some places very cold. There is also plenty of maize but no wheat, neither is there such plenty of cattle as about Chiapa, but fowls and turkeys

[7] Cultivated silk was unknown in America before the coming of the Spaniards, although there is a little evidence that the Indians may have made a limited use of a wild variety. Donald and Dorothy Cordry, in discussing Zoque weaving, remark that the finest women's blouses *(huipils)* are of incredibly fine handspun thread, some with as many as seventy-five warp threads and sixty-four weft threads to the square inch. These carry brocaded patterns of birds, animals, and flowers, and sometimes a kind of lace weave. To judge from modern samples, Zoque brocaded cloth might well serve as samplers for English school mistresses.

as many as in other parts. The province called Tzeltales lieth behind this of the Zoques, from the North Sea within the continent, running up towards Chiapa, and reacheth in some parts near to the borders of Comitán to the southeast. Northeastward it joins to certain Indians who have not as yet been conquered by the Spaniards, and who make many invasions upon the Christian Indians, and burn their towns, and carry away their cattle.

The chief and head town in this province is called Ococingo, which is a frontier against those heathens. This province is esteemed rich for the Spaniards, who make much of cacao, which serveth to make their drink of chocolate, and here is great store of it. There is also another commodity, great among the Spaniards, called *achiote*, wherewith they make their chocolate look of the color of a brick. Here is also plenty of hogs and bacon, fowls, turkeys, quails, cattle, sheep, maize, honey, and not far from Ococingo, in my time, was setting up an *ingenio*, or farm of sugar, which was thought would prove as well as those about Chiapa of the Indians. The country in most parts is high and hilly, but Ococingo stands in a pleasant valley, enjoying many brooks and streams of fresh water, and therefore hath been thought a fit place for sugar.[8] Here also in this valley the friars have attempted to sow wheat, which proved very good. Thus, Reader, I have showed you the country of Chiapa, which is compassed about on the one side by Soconusco, and from thence almost to Guatemala, by the province of Suchitepéquez, on the other side by Tabasco, and on the other side by Tzeltales, which has an excessive plenty of cacao and *achiote*, the two chief drugs for the making of chocolate.

[8] It was to this region that young Antonio Meléndez was sent. In 1639 he was elected first Prior of Ocosingo, and it was here that he died in 1646. Here also died, in 1634, Fr. Pedro Álvarez, who as Provincial Prior welcomed him to Chiapas. Ocosingo is a Tzeltal town difficult of access. The stately Dominican church is in need of repair. Near by lie the important Maya ruins of Toniná.

12. Concerning two daily and common drinks or potions much used in the Indias, called chocolate *and* atole

CHOCOLATE being this day used not only over all the West Indias, but also in Spain, Italy, and Flanders, with approbation of many learned doctors in physic, among whom Antonio Colmenero of Ledesma, who lived once in the Indias, hath composed a learned and curious treatise concerning the nature and quality of this drink, I thought fit to insert here also somewhat of it concerning my own experience for the space of twelve years.[1] This name chocolate is an Indian name, and is compounded from *atte*, as some say, or as others, *atle*, which in the Mexican language signifieth "water," and from the sound which the water, wherein is put the chocolate, makes, as *choco choco choco*, when it is stirred in a cup by an instrument called a molinet, or *molinillo*, until it bubble and rise unto a froth. And as there it is a name compounded, so in English we may well call

---

[1] In this chapter only, Gage's original sentence construction and grammar, as found in the first (1648) edition, are retained. This policy of conscious archaism is partly to give the reader an idea of Gage's rather involved style—he hangs sentences one from another till he achieves a sort of literary mobile—which is fairly typical of all but the best writers of his period, but partly because Gage's discussion of "hot and cold" and the "humour" of chocolate and other products is so typical of the sixteenth and seventeenth centuries and so out of place in the twentieth that modernization of the prose seems almost to cast Gage's ideas—intelligent enough in the light of seventeenth-century thinking—into the realm of canting rubbish. It would be somewhat like supplying the bowmen of Agincourt with mine detectors to stuff in their quivers. Readers who find the first two pages difficult will find greater clarity in later pages. If we of the twentieth century could define *humour* in seventeenth-century usage, it would simplify matters, but as Corporal Nym so often said, that's the humour of it.

it a compounded or a confectioned drink wherein are found many and several ingredients, according to the different disposition of the bodies of them that use it. But the chief ingredient, without which it cannot be made, is called cacao, a kind of nut or kernel bigger than a great almond which grows upon a tree called the tree of cacao, and ripens in a great husk, wherein sometimes are found more, sometimes less cacaos, sometimes twenty, sometimes thirty, nay, forty and above. This cacao, though as every simple, it contains the quality of the four elements, yet in the common opinion of most physicians, it is held to be cold and dry *a praedominio*. It is also in the substance that rules these two qualities, restringent and obstructive, of the nature of the element of the earth. And as it is thus a mixed, and not a simple element, it hath parts correspondent to the rest of the elements; and particularly it partakes of those which correspond with the element of air, that is heat and moisture, which are governed by unctious parts, there being drawn out of the cacao much butter, which in the Indias I have seen drawn out of it by the Creole women for to oint their faces. And let not this seem impossible to believe that this grain or nut of cacao should be said to be first cold and dry, and then hot and moist, for though experience be a thousand witnesses, yet instances will further clear this truth. First in the rhubarb which hath in it hot and soluble parts, and parts which are binding, cold, and dry, which have a virtue to strengthen, bind, and stop the looseness of the belly. Secondly, we see this clearly in the steel which having so much of the nature of the earth, as being heavy, thick, cold, and dry, should be thought unproper for the curing of oppilations [obstructions], but rather to be apt to increase them, and yet it is given as a proper remedy against them.

Every element, be it never so simple, begets and produceth in the liver four humours, not only differing in temper but also in substance; and begets more or less of that humour, according as the element hath more or fewer parts corresponding to the substance of that humour which is most engendered. From which example we may gather that when the cacao is ground and stirred, the divers parts which nature hath given it do artificially and intimately mix themselves one with another. And so, the unctious warm and moist parts mingled with the earthy represseth, and leaveth them not so binding as they were before, but rather with a mediocrity, more inclining to the warm and moist temper of the air than to the cold and dry of the earth, as it doth appear when it is made fit to drink, that scarce two turns are given with the molinet, when there arises a fatty scum by which is seen how much it partaketh of the oily part.

From all that hath been said, the error of those is well discovered who, speaking of this drink of chocolate, say that it causeth oppilations, because cacao is astringent, as if that astriction were not corrected and modified by the intimate mixing of one part with another, by means of the grinding, as is said before. Besides it having so many ingredients which are naturally hot, it must of necessity have this effect, that is to say, to open, attenuate, not to bind. And laying aside more reasons, this truth is evidently seen in the cacao itself, which if it be not stirred, grinded, and compounded to make the chocolate, but be eaten as it is in the fruit (as many Creole and Indian women eat it), it doth notably obstruct and cause stoppings, and make them look of a broken, pale, and earthy color, as do those that eat earthenware, as pots or pieces of lime walls (which is much used among the Spanish women thinking that a pale and earthy color, though with obstructions and stoppings, well becomes them). And for this certainly in the cacao thus eaten there is no other reason but that the divers substances which it contains are not perfectly mingled by the mastication only, but require the artificial mixture which we have spoken of before.

The tree which doth bear this fruit is so delicate, and the earth where it groweth so extreme hot, that to keep the tree from being consumed by the sun, they first plant other trees which they call *las madres del cacao*, "mothers of the cacao," and when these are grown up to a good height fit to shade the cacao trees, then they plant the *cacauatales* or the trees [orchards] of cacaos, that when they first show themselves above the ground, those trees which are already grown may shelter them, and, as mothers, nourish, defend, and shadow them from the sun. The fruit doth not grow naked, but many of them, as I have said, are in one great husk or cod, and therein besides, every grain is closed up in a white juicy skin which the women also love to suck off from the cacao, finding it cool, and in the mouth dissolving into water. There are two sorts of cacao. The one is common, which is of a dark color inclining toward red, being round and picked at the ends; the other is broader and bigger and flatter and not so round, which they call *patlaxti* [*Theobroma bicolor*, wild cacao], and this is white and more drying, and is sold a great deal cheaper than the former. And this especially more than the other causes watchfulness and driveth away sleep, and therefore is not so useful as the ordinary, and is chiefly spent by the ordinary and meaner sort of people. As for the rest of the ingredients which make this chocolatical confection, there is notable variety. Some put into it black pepper, which is not well approved of by the physicians because it is so hot and dry, but only for one who hath a very cold liver, but commonly instead of this pepper, they put into it a long red pepper called chile which, though it be hot in the mouth, yet it is cool and moist in the operation. It is further compounded with white sugar, cinnamon, cloves, aniseed, almonds, hazel nuts, *orejuela* [*Cymbopetalum penduliflorum Baill.*, the Aztec *xochinacaztli* of the anona family], vanilla, *zapoyal*, [ground seeds of the mamey, *Calocarpum mammosum*], orange flower water, some musk, and as much of achiote as will make it look of the color of a red brick. But how much of each of these may be applied to such a quantity of cacao, the several dispositions of men's bodies must be their rule. The ordinary receipt of Antonio Colmenero was this: to every hundred cacaos, two cods of chile, called long red pepper, one handful of aniseed and *orejuelas*, and two of the flowers called *mecaxochitl* [*Piper amalago*], or vanilla, or instead of this fix roses of Alexandria, beat to powder, two drams of cinnamon, of almonds and hazel nuts of each one dozen, of white sugar half a pound, of achiote enough to give it the color. This author thought neither clove nor musk nor any sweet water fit, but in the Indias they are much used. Others use to put in maize or *panizo* [panic grass, probably Italian millet here], which is very windy, but such do it only for their profit by increasing the quantity of the chocolate because every *fanega*, or measure of maize containing about a bushel and a half, is sold for eight shillings, and they that sell chocolate sell it for four shillings a pound, which is the ordinary price. The cinnamon is held one of the best ingredients and denied by none, for that it is hot and dry in the third degree, it provokes urine and helps the kidneys and reins of those who are troubled with cold diseases.

The achiote [*annatto*] hath a piercing, attenuating quality, as appeareth by the common practice of the physicians of the Indias, experienced daily in the effects of it, who do give it to their patients to cut and attenuate the gross humours which do cause shortness of breath and stopping of urine, and so it is used for any kind of oppilations, and is given for the stoppings which are in the breast or in the region of the belly or any other part of the body. This *achiote* also groweth upon a tree [*Bixa orellana*] in round husks, which are full of red grains, from whence the achiote is taken, and first made into a paste, and then being dried up, is fashioned either into round balls or cakes, or into the form of little bricks, and so is sold. As concerns the long red pepper, there are four sorts of it: one is called *chilchote;* the other is very little, which they call *chiltipiquin,* and these two kinds are very quick and biting. The other two are called *tonalchiles,* and these are but moderately hot, for they are eaten with bread [tortillas] by the Indians, as they eat other fruits. But that which is usually put into chocolate, called *chilpaelagua,* which hath a broad husk and is not so biting as the first nor so gentle as the last. The *mecaxochitl* or vanilla hath a purgative quality. [The *Vanilla fragrans* was called *tlilxochitl,* "black flower," and is distinct from *mecaxochitl,* "rope flower," *Piper amalago,* but both were used for flavoring chocolate.] All these ingredients are usually put into the chocolate, and by some more, according to their fancies. But the meaner sort of people, as Blackamoors and Indians, commonly put nothing into it but cacao, achiote, maize, and a few chiles with a little aniseed. And though the cacao is mingled with all these ingredients which are hot, yet there is to be a greater quantity of cacao than of all the rest of the ingredients, which serve to temper the coldness of the cacao. From whence it follows that this chocolatical confection is not so cold as the cacao, nor so hot as the rest of the ingredients, but there results from the action and reaction of these ingredients a moderate temper which may be good for both the cold and the hot stomachs, being taken moderately.

Now for the making or compounding of this drink, I shall set down here the method. The cacao and the other ingredients must be beaten in a mortar of stone or, as the Indians use, ground upon a broad stone which they call *metate,* and is only made for that use. But first the ingredients are all to be dried, except the achiote, with care that they may be beaten to powder, keeping them still in stirring, that they be not burned or become black, for if they be over-dried, they will be bitter and lose their virtue. The cinnamon and the long red pepper are to be first beaten with the aniseed, and then the cacao, which must be beaten by little and little, till all be powdered, and in the beating it must be turned round that it may mix the better. Everyone of these ingredients must be beaten by itself, and then all be put into the vessel where the cacao is, which you must stir together with a spoon, and then take out that paste, and put it into the mortar, under which there must be a little fire, after the confection is made. If more fire be put under than will only warm it, then the unctious part will dry away. The achiote also must be put in at the beating that it may the better take the color. All the ingredients must be searced [sifted through a sieve], save only the cacao, and if from the cacao the dry shell be taken, it will be the better. When it is well beaten and incorporated—which will be known by the shortness of it —then with a spoon (so in the Indias is used) is taken up some of the paste, which will be almost liquid, and made into tablets, or else without a spoon put into boxes, and when it is cold it will be hard. Those that make it into tablets, put a spoonful of the paste upon a piece of paper (the Indians put it upon the leaf of a plantain) where, being put in the shade—for in the sun it melts and dissolves, it grows hard. And then, bowing the paper or leaf, the tablet falls off by reason of the fatness of the paste, but if it be put into anything of earth or wood, it sticks fast and will not come off, but with scraping or breaking. The manner of drinking it is divers. The one most used in Mexico is to take it hot with *atole*, dissolving a tablet in hot water, and then stirring and beating it in the cup where it is to be drunk with a molinet, and when it is well stirred to a scum or froth, then to fill the cup with hot *atole*, and so drink it sup by sup. Another way is that the chocolate being dissolved with cold water and stirred with the molinet, and the scum taken off and put into another vessel, the remainder be set upon the fire with as much sugar as will sweeten it, and when it is warm, then to pour it upon the scum which was taken off before, and so to drink it.

The most ordinary way is to warm the water very hot and then to pour out half the cup full that you mean to drink, and to put into it a tablet or two, or as much as will thicken reasonably the water, and then grind it well with the molinet, and when it is well ground and risen to a scum, to fill the cup with hot water, and so drink it by

sups, having sweetened it with sugar, and to eat it with a little conserve or maple bread steeped into the chocolate. There is another
way which is much used in the island of Santo Domingo which is to
put the chocolate into a pipkin [small earthenware pot] with a little
water and to let it boil well till it be dissolved, and then to put in
sufficient sugar and water according to the quantity of the chocolate,
and then to boil it again until there comes an oily scum upon it, and
then to drink it. There is another way yet to drink chocolate, which is
cold which the Indians use at feasts to refresh themselves, and it is
made after this manner. The chocolate, which is made with none
or very few ingredients, being dissolved in cold water with the
molinet, they take off the scum or crassy [dense] part which riseth
in great quantity especially when the cacao is older and more put-
rified. The scum they lay aside in a little dish by itself, and then
put sugar into that part whence was taken the scum, and then pour
it from on high into the scum, and so drink it cold. And this drink is
so cold that it agreeth not with all men's stomachs, for by experience
it hath been found that it doth hurt by causing pains in the stomach,
especially to women.

The third way of taking it is the most used, and thus certainly it
doth no hurt, neither know I why it may not be used as well in England as in other parts, both hot and cold. For where it is so much
used, as well in the Indias as in Spain, Italy, and Flanders, which is
a cold country, find that it agreeth well with them. True it is used
more in the Indias than in the European parts because there the
stomachs are more apt to faint than here, and a cup of chocolate well
confectioned comforts and strengthens the stomach. For myself I
must say I used it twelve years constantly, drinking one cup in the
morning, another yet before dinner between nine or ten of the clock,
another within an hour or after dinner, and another between four
and five in the afternoon, and when I was purposed to sit up late to
study, I would take another cup about seven or eight at night, which
would keep me waking till about midnight. And if by chance I
did neglect any of these accustomed hours, I presently found my
stomach fainty. And with this custom I lived twelve years in those
parts healthy, without any obstructions or oppilations, not knowing
what either ague or fever was. Yet will I not dare to regulate by
mine own the bodies of others, nor take upon me the skill of a physi-

cian to appoint and decide at what time and by what persons this drink may be used. Only I say that I have known some that have been the worse for it, either for drinking it with too much sugar, which hath relaxed their stomachs, or for drinking it too often.

I have heard physicians of the Indias say of it, and I have seen it by experience in others, though never I could find it in myself, that those that use this chocolate much grow fat and corpulent by it. Which, indeed, may seem hard to believe, for considering that all the ingredients except the cacao do rather extenuate than make fat because they are hot and dry in the third degree. How then might

this cacao with the other Indian ingredients be had in England? Even by trading in Spain for it, as we do for other commodities, or not slighting it so much as we and the Hollanders have often done upon the Indian seas. I have heard the Spaniards say that when we have taken a good prize, a ship laden with cacao, in anger and wrath we have hurled overboard this good commodity, not regarding the worth and goodness of it, but calling it in bad Spain *cagarruta de carnero* or sheep dung in good English. It is one of the necessariest commodities in the Indias, and nothing enricheth Chiapa in particular more than it, whither are brought from Mexico and other parts the rich bags of patacons only for this *cagarruta de carnero*.

The other drink which is much used in the Indias is called *atole*, of which I will say but a little because I know it cannot be used here. This was the drink of the ancient Indians, and is a thick pap made of the flour of maize, taking off the husks from it, which is windy and melancholy. This is commonly carried by the Indian woman to the market hot in pots, and there is sold in cups. The Creole students, as we go to a tavern to drink a cup of wine, so they go in company to the public markets, and as publicly buy and drink by measure of this atole which sometimes is seasoned with a little chile or long pepper, and then it pleaseth them best. But the nuns and gentlewomen have got a trick of confectioning it with cinnamon, sweet waters, amber, or musk, and store of sugar, and thus it is held to be a most strong and nourishing drink, which the physicians do prescribe unto a weak body as we do here our almond milk. But of what England never knew or tasted I will say no more, but hasten my pen to Guatemala, which hath been my second *patria*.

13. Showing my journey from the city of Chiapa unto Guatemala, and the chief places in the way

⁓⁓⁓ ⋈ ⁓⁓⁓

THE TIME now being come that I was to leave the little city of Chiapa, I took some occasion beforehand to take my leave of my best friends, whose children I had taught, and at my departure I must confess I found them kind and bountiful. But among all, the Governor's wife was most liberal unto me, sending me many boxes of aromatical chocolate, and one extraordinary great box with four several divisions of different conserves gilt over, besides many maple breads, and biscuits made with eggs and sugar, a present it was which might have been sent to a greater man than to a poor worthless mendicant friar, and with this in a handkerchief a dozen pieces of eight.

The first town I went unto was Teopixca, six leagues from Chiapa, a fair and great town of Indians, who are held to be next unto the Indians of the other Chiapa in sitting and riding a horse. In this town is nothing so considerable as the church, which is great and strong, and the music belonging unto it sweet and harmonious. The vicar or curate of this place was one Friar Pedro Martir, a Creole, whom I knew could not endure the Prior nor me, yet he would dissemble a love complimental exceeding well, and in outward shows raise it up to *gradus ut octo*. He knowing my prevalency with the Prior, durst not but give me very good entertainment, which continued two days, until I was weary of his compliments.[1]

---

[1] Father Pedro Martyr died in Chiapa Real in 1644. In an early record he is said to have been a very handsome man, a good singer, a fine theologian, and an excellent preacher. He was a humble man and was loved by all, a first-rate student and a very personable man. Such eulogies are not common in the records of the Province. Gage may have misjudged the man on their rather short acquaintance. Teopisca is a large and flourishing Tzeltal town.

The third day I took my leave of him, but he would not yet leave me, but would conduct me to Comitán, whither I was invited by the Prior of that cloister, a Frenchman named Friar Tomás Rocolano who being a stranger to the Spaniards (for besides him and myself there was no other stranger in that country), desired acquaintance with me. This he began to settle by meeting me at the half way with many Indians on horseback, having provided an arbor where we might more conveniently confer and rest while our chocolate and other refreshments were provided. But the Creole Pedro Martir was not a little envious—as I was afterwards informed in the cloister —to see me made so much of and esteemed in the country, yet his fair words and compliments far exceeded the sincerity and downrightness of my French friend.

At Comitán I stayed a whole week, riding about with the Prior unto the Indian towns, and down the hill to the valley of Copanabastla, where I enjoyed much pastime and recreation among the friars and Indians and was feasted after the manner of that country, which knoweth more of an Epicurean diet than doth England, or any part of Europe. Nay, I am persuaded (and I have heard Spaniards confess it) that Spain hath taken from the Indies since the Conquest many lessons for the dressing of several dishes and completing a feast or banquet. After the week was ended my French friend the Prior conducted me to Izquintenango, to see me well furnished up the mountains of Cuchumatlanes.

This town, as I have observed, standeth almost at the end of the valley of Copanabastla, and within two leagues of the Cuchumatlanes. It is one of the finest Indian towns of all the province of Chiapa, and very rich, by reason of the much cotton-wool in it, and especially by reason of its situation, for standing in the roadway to Guatemala, all the merchants of the country that trade that way with their mules pass through this town, and there buy and sell, enriching it with money and far brought commodities. It is most plentifully stored with fruits, especially with what they call *piñas* or pineapples. It standeth close by the great river which runneth to Chiapa of the Indians, and hath its spring not far off from the Cuchumatlanes, and yet at this town is very broad and deep. No man nor beast travelling to Guatemala can go into it, or from Guatemala can go out of it, but by ferrying over.

The road being much used and beaten by travellers, and by such as they call *requas* of mules (every *requa* consisting of fifty or threescore mules) this ferry is day and night employed and yields much treasure to the town at the year's end. The Indians of the town, besides the ferry boat, have made many other little boats, or canoes to go up and down the river.[2] When the Prior of Comitán had brought me hither, we were waited for by the vicar or friar of that town with the chief and principal Indians, and most of the canoes. As we ferried over, the little canoes went before us with the choristers of the church singing before us, and with others sounding their waits and trumpets.

The friar that lived in this town was called Friar Jerónimo de Guevara, little in stature, but great in state, pride, and vanity, as he shewed himself in what he had provided for us both of fish and flesh. A brave professor or vower of mendicancy and poverty he was. In twelve years that he had lived in that town, what by murmuring masses for the dead and living, what by shearing and fleecing the poor Indians, what by trading and trafficking with the merchants that used that road, had got six thousand ducats. These he had sent to Spain to the Court of Madrid, to trade with them simoniacally for the bishopric of Chiapa. If he did not obtain it (yet when I came out of that country the report went that he had obtained it), he would and was well able with a second supply to obtain a better.[3]

After two days' feasting with him, he and the Prior of Comitán both joined their power and authority to see me well manned with Indians to the first town of the Cuchumatlanes. A mule was prepared to carry my bedding, which we commonly carried with us in chests of leather called *petacas*, another Indian to carry my *petaquilla* wherein was my chocolate and all implements to make it; and three more Indians to ride before and behind to guide me. But to none of them was anything to be paid (lest a custom of paying should be

---

[2] This town has entirely disappeared. It seems to have been on the Río San Gregorio, which is a tribute of the Grijalva, a short distance west of the present Guatemala-Mexico frontier, at about 92° W., 15°, 50′ N.

[3] Father Jerónimo Guenera, as Ximénez spells the name, did not get the bishopric, nor is there any record of his holding any office of importance. He died, still in the ranks, at the convent of Comitán in 1633 or 1634. The Frenchman, Father Tomás de Rocolano, died at the same time in the convent of Ocosingo, as did R. P. Fr. Pedro de Álvarez, who had welcomed Gage and his friends to Chiapas.

brought in, for so they doctrined me as a novice in that country) except it were to give them a cup of chocolate if I drank in the way, or when I came to my journey's end.

Here I took my leave of my good French friend, who yet continued friendship with me by frequent letters to Guatemala, and of my low but high-minded Guevara, who bad me expect no friendly entertainment until I were well passed over the Cuchumatlanes and arrived at Sacapula, which was four days' journey from thence. Yet he told me I might demand what service I list from the Indians, and call for what I had a mind to eat without paying any money, provided that I did write down my expenses in the common town book.

Thus I went away from my friends somewhat heavy, having no other company but unknown Indians, leaving a pleasant and delightsome valley behind me, and seeing nothing before me but high and steepy hills and mountains, and considering that in four or five days I should see no more gallant Dominicans and of mine own profession. Now I wished I had the company of Meléndez and my other friends, who had been a comfort one to another upon the hills and rocks of Macuilapa. Yet at last I concluded, up English heart and courage, the time will come when you will look back happily on these trials. Though the mountains seemed high afar off, yet as I travelled on I found the way lie between them very easy and passable. I met now and then *recuas* of mules, which were no little comfort unto me to consider, for if they being heavily laden could go through those mountains, my mule that had in me but a light burden would easily overcome any danger. It comforted me also to consider that there were towns, though but little ones, where I might rest every night.

The further I went, the better and more open I found the road; only the rain and dirt troubled me, but these I could not avoid, it being the end of September, or as there they reckon, the end of winter. The first town I came to amongst those mountains was called San Martín,[4] a little place of some twenty houses. I went to the house that belonged to the Franciscan friars (who seldom in the year came to that poverty of house and house room), where I lighted and

---

[4] Presumably San Martín Cuchumatanes, which lies about six miles in direct line northwest of Todos Santos.

caused the Indians to be called who were appointed to give attendance to travellers and passengers. I found them very tractable and dutiful, bidding me welcome, bringing me hot water for my chocolate, which I drunk off heartily, and gave unto my Indians of Izquintenango, who refreshed themselves and their mules well for nothing, this being a custom among those towns in the road to welcome one another whensoever they come with travellers.

I might have had for my supper anything that place would afford, but I made choice of a pullet, which I thought would be cheapest for the poor Indians. I was glad I had brought with be a good big *frasco*, as they call it, or bottle of wine, for I began already to find the Cuchumatlanes cooler than the valley of Copanabastla. My bed was made in a little thatched adobe hut, and Indian boys appointed to sleep in the next room to me, and to be at hand if in the night I should want anything. Thus having appointed what attendance I had need of in the morning to the next town, and having discharged the Indians that had brought me from Izquintenango, I went unto my rest, which I took as quietly as if I had been in the company of my best friends.

The next day, accompanied by two Indians and having sent my carriage by another, I took my journey to the next town, which is called Cuchumatán Grande, because it standeth on the highest part of those mountains, and in the way the Indians showed me the headspring or fountain of the great river of Chiapa of the Indians, which is the only remarkable thing in that road.

Cuchumatán Grande is a town a little bigger than San Martín, and of Indians very courteous, who are used and beaten to daily travellers, and so make very much of them.[5] Here I was entertained as the night before, and found the poor Indians willing to give me whatsoever I demanded for my better and safer guiding and conducting the next day. They also provided that night for my supper what I pleased to call for, without any pay, but only writing down my name and expenses with the day and month in their common book of accounts. To this are those poor wretches brought by the friars and commanding justices, though of themselves they have

[5] This is the modern town of Todos Santos, the scene of Maud Oakes' fine study of Indian life, *The Two Crosses of Todos Santos*. The people are Maya belonging to the Mam linguistic stock. The great river of Chiapa of the Indians is the Grijalva.

no more than a *milpa* of maize as they term it, or a little Indian wheat plantation, with as much chile as will suffice them for the year, and what the merchants and travellers give them voluntarily, which is little enough.

From this town I would not follow the road to the next, which was a long journey of seven or eight leagues without baiting by the way, and also because I had been informed at Chiapa and at Copanabastla of a strange picture of Our Lady, which was amongst these mountains in a little town of Indians called Chiantla. This being not above a league out of my way, I was resolved to see it.[6] The ways off the main road were bad, yet by noon I got to Chiantla. This is a town belonging unto Mercenarian friars, who doubtless would not be able to subsist in so poor a place had they not invented that lodestone of their picture of Mary, and cried it up for miraculous, to draw people far and near, and all travellers from the road to pray unto it, and to leave their gifts and alms unto them for their prayers and Masses. Such an income of treasure and riches hath been given by deluded and ignorant souls to this beggarly town, that the friars have had wherewith to build a cloister able to maintain four or five of them.

The church is richly furnished, but especially the high altar where the picture standeth in a tabernacle with half a dozen curtains of silk, satin, and cloth of gold, with borders of golden lace before it. And it wears a rich crown of gold, thickly beset with diamonds and other precious stones. There hang before it at least a dozen rich lamps of silver, and in the vestry of the church are many gowns, candlesticks of silver, censers to burn frankincense before it, besides rich copes, vestments, ornaments for the altar, and hangings for all the church.

Here is a treasure hid in the mountains; oh, that it could be found out to do the Lord service. I was welcomed to this place by those friars, who were strangers unto me; my head was filled that day by them with relations of strange and many miracles, which they told me of that picture, but the heaviness of my head did me good in

[6] Chiantla lies about five miles north of Huehuetenango, on the outskirts of which are the imposing ruins of the great Maya center of Zaculeu, recently restored with the aid of the United Fruit Company. Here was the old Mam capital. Chiantla is still a center of pilgrimage.

something, for it made me more drowsy at night and apter to take good rest. The next day I got into the road again, and went to the last town of these Cuchumatlanes called Chautlán,[7] where I stayed all that day and night, and sent before a letter to the Prior of Sacapulas of my going thither the next day. In Chautlán I was very kindly used by the Indians, and liked the town the better for the excellent grapes which there I found, not planted like vineyards, but growing up in arbors, which shew that if that land were planted, it would certainly yield as good grapes for wine as any are in Spain. They are carried from that place to Guatemala, which stands from it near forty leagues, and are sold about the streets for rarities and great dainties. Well may they, for from Mexico to Guatemala there are none like them.

The next morning I made haste to be gone, that I might come sooner to Sacapulas, where I was to find those of mine own profession, with whom I knew I might stay and rest a whole week if I pleased. I had not rid above three leagues, when I began to discover at a low and deep bottom, a pleasant and goodly valley laced with a river whose waters receiving the glorious brightness of Phœbus' beams reverberated up to the top of the mountain, a delightsome prospect to the beholders. The more I hasted to that seeming Paradise, the more did the twinkling and wanton stream invite me down the hill; which I had no sooner descended, but I found in an arbor by the water side the Prior of Sacapulas himself with a good train of Indians waiting for me with a cup of chocolate.

At the first sight I was a little daunted to behold the Prior, who looked most fearfully with a bladder from his throat swelled almost round his neck. This hung over his shoulders and breast, and stayed up his chin, and lifted up his head so that he could scarce look any whither but up to Heaven. In our discourse he told me that disease [goiter] had been upon him at least ten years, and that the water of that river had caused it in him and in many others of that town. This made me now as much out of love with the river as above the hill I had liked the good sight of it, and therefore I resolved not to stay so long in that place as I had thought, lest the waters should mark me for all my life, as they had done this Prior. His name was Friar Juan de la Cruz, a Biscayan born, and, like some of that nation,

[7] Possibly Chalchitán which now forms part of Aguacatán.

a little troubled with the simples, but a good-hearted man, humble, and well beloved over the country both by Spaniards and Indians.

When I came to the town, I discovered many men and women with bladders in their throats like the poor Prior, which made me almost unwilling to drink there any chocolate made with that water, or eat anything dressed with it, until the Prior did much encourage me and told me that it did not hurt all but only some, and those who did drink it cold. Wherewith I resolved to stay there four or five days, because of the old Prior's importunity. He would fain have had me continue to live with him, promising to teach me the Indian language in a very short time, but higher matters calling me to Guatemala, I excused myself, and continued there five days with much recreation.

Though the town be not in the general very rich, yet there are some Indian merchants who trade about the country and especially to Suchitepéquez, where is the chief store of cacao. Thereby some of this town of Sacapulas have enriched themselves; the rest of the people trade in pots and pans, which they make of an earth there fit for that purpose. But the principal merchandise of this place is salt, which they gather in the morning from the ground that lieth near the river.[8] The air is hot, by reason the town standeth low and is compassed with high hills on every side. Besides many good fruits which are here, there are dates as good as those that come from Barbary, and many trees of them in the garden belonging to the cloister.

After I had here wearied out the weariness which I brought in my bones from the Cuchumatlanes, I departed taking my way to Guatemala. From Sacapulas I went to a town called St. Andrews, or San Andrés [Sajcabaja], which standeth six or seven leagues from Sacapulas, a great town, but nothing remarkable in it, save only cotton-wool and turkeys, and about it some rich *estancias* or farms of cattle, which are commodiously seated here, it being a plain champaign country. Yet at further end of this plain there is a mountain which discourageth with the sight all such as travel to Guatemala; from San Andrés I prepared myself for the next day's journey, which was of nine long leagues, to a very great town called by two names, by some Zacualpa, by others Santa María Joyabaj, to the

[8] Salt making is still the main industry of Sacapulas. Gage had now entered the territory of the Quiché Mayas.

which I could not go without passing over that mountain.[9] I sent word of going to Joyabaj the day before (as is the custom there) that mules and horses might meet me upon the mountain; and the night before I went to a *rancho* (which is a lodge built for travellers to rest when the journey is long) which stood within a league of the mountain by a river, where with the waters' murmur and refreshing gales I took good rest.

In the morning, having refreshed myself and my Indians with chocolate, I set out to encounter with that proud mountain; and when I came unto it, I found it not so hard to overcome as I had conceited, the way lying with windings and turnings. The higher I mounted the more my eyes were troubled with looking to the river below, whose rocks were enough to astonish and make a stout heart tremble. About the middle of the mountain in a narrow passage where the way went wheeling the Indians of Joyabaj met us with a mule for me and another for my carriage.

Here I lighted, whilst the Indians helped one another to unload and load the mule that came of refresh. Out of the narrow way the side of the mountain was steepy, and a fearful precipice of two or three miles to the bottom, almost bare of trees one only growing here and there. My heart was true unto me, wishing me to walk up afoot until I came unto some broader passage. The Indians, perceiving my fear, told me there was no danger, assuring me further that the mule they had brought was sure, and had been well used to that mountain. With their persuasions I got up, but no sooner was I mounted when the mule began to play her pranks and to kick, and to leap out of the way, casting me down and herself, both rolling and tumbling apace to the rocks and death, had not a shrub prevented me, and a tree stopped the mule's blind fury. The Indians cried out, *"Milagro, milagro,"* "Miracle, miracle," *"Santo, Santo,"* "a Saint, a Saint," to me so loud as if they would have had their cry reach to Rome to help forward my canonization; for many such miracles have been noised at Rome, and with further contribution of money have been enrolled in the book and catalogue of saints.

[9] Gage must have misread his notes. Zacualpa and Joyabaj are two distinct towns, about six miles apart. Zacualpa, at a height of about 5,000 feet, lies just south of the Cerro Sanché (over 8,000 feet), which Gage seems to have crossed. There is no longer a direct road from Sajcabaja to Zacualpa.

Whilst the Indians helped me up and brought the mule again into the way, they did nothing but flatter me with this term saint. This they needed not have done, if as they considered my dangerous fall and stopping at a shrub (which was by chance, and not by miracle) they had further considered my passion and hasty wrath (not befitting a saint), wherewith I threatened to baste their ribs for deceiving me with a young mule not well accustomed to the saddle. But all my hasty words and anger could not discredit me with them, nor lessen their conceit of my holiness and sanctity, who hold the anger and wrath of a priest to be the breath of God's nostrils, and with this their foolish conceit of me, they kneeled before me kissing my hands.

The business being further examined, they confessed that they had been mistaken in the mules, having saddled for me that which should have carried my *petacas*, or leathern chests, which was a young mule accustomed only to carriages, and not to the saddle, and upon that which should have been saddled they put my carriage. Whilst they unloaded and loaded again and saddled the right mule, I walked up the hill about a mile, and when they overtook me, I got up and rid till I met with my refreshing arbor and chocolate, and many Indians that came to receive me, among whom it was presently noised that I was a saint and had wrought a miracle in the way. With this the rest of the Indians kneeled to me and kissed my hands, and in the way that we went to the town, all their talk was of my sanctity. I was much vexed at their simplicity, but the more they saw me unwilling to accept of that honor, the more they pressed it upon me.

When I came to the town, I told the friar what had happened, and what the foolish Indians had conceited; at which he laughed, and told me that he would warrant me if I stayed long in the town, all the men and women would come to kiss my hands and to offer their gifts unto me. He knew well their qualities, or else had taught them this superstition with many others, for no sooner had we dined, but many were gathered to the church to see the saint that was come to their town and that had wrought a miracle in the mountain as he came. With this I began to be more troubled than before at the folly of the simple people, and desired the friar to check and rebuke them. By no means would he do so, but rather laughed at it, saying, that in policy we ought to accept of any honor from the Indians, for as long as we had credit and an opinion of saints among them, so long we should prevail to do anything with them, yea, even to command them and their fortunes at our pleasure. With this I went down with the friar to the church, and sat down with him in a chair in the choir, representing the person of such a saint as they imagined me to be, though in reality and truth but a wretched sinner.

No sooner had we taken our places, when the Indians, men women, and children, came up by three and four, or whole families to the choir; first kneeling down for my blessing, and then kissing my hands, they began to speak to me in their Indian compliments to this purpose, that their town was happy and doubtless blessed from Heaven by my coming into it, and that they hoped their souls should be much the better if they might partake of my prayers to God for them. And for this purpose some offered unto me money, some honey, some eggs, some little mantles, some plantains, and other fruits, some fowls, and some turkeys. The friar that sat by me I perceived was overjoyed with this, for he knew I was to be gone, and would leave unto him all those offerings. I desired him to make answer unto the Indians in my behalf, excusing me as not well versed in their language (yet the fools if they thought and judged me to be a saint might have expected from me also the gift of tongues), which he did, telling them that I had been but a while in that country, and though I understood part of their language, yet could not speak nor pronounce it perfectly, and therefore he did give them hearty thanks from me for the great love they had showed unto an ambassador of God, witnessing it with so many sorts of offerings, which assuredly should remind him and me of our offerings for them, in our prayers and hearty recommendations of them and their children unto God.

Thus was that ceremony ended, the Indians dismissed, and the friar and I went up to a chamber, where he began to tell his eggs and fowls and to dispose of some of them for our supper; he told me he would take them, but at my departure would give me somewhat for them.

He bad me keep what money they had given me, and told me I was welcome to him, and no burdensome guest, but very profitable, as I had brought with me store of provision for myself and for him many days after. The money I received came to forty reals, besides twenty which he gave me for the other offerings, which might be worth forty more; all this I got for having a fall from a mule, and for not breaking my neck. I would fain have departed the next morning, but Juan Vidal (so was the friar named) would not permit me, for that the next journey was of at least ten leagues, and therefore he would have me rest myself the next day.

This town of Joyabaj, or Zacualpa is the biggest and fairest of all the towns that belong unto the priory of Sacapulas; the Indians are rich, and make of their cotton-wool many mantles. They have plenty of honey, and great flocks of goats and kids, but neither here, nor in all the towns behind is there any wheat, save only Indian maize. The next day some small offerings fell unto me, but nothing like the day before; and so I told the friar that now the people's devotion was decayed, I would be gone in the morning before day. That night the chief Indians of the town came to offer their service and attendance upon me to a *rancho* or lodge that standeth in the middle way; but I would not accept of the great ones, but desired that I might have three only of the meaner sort to guide me till I met with company from the town whither I was going, and whither I had sent warning of my coming.

The time appointed was three of the clock in the morning; at which hour after a little sleep I was called, and having drunk my chocolate, and eat a maple bread with a little conserve, I prepared myself for my journey, and found the Indians ready waiting for me in the yard, with pieces of pine-wood, which burn like torches, and with which they use to travel in the night, and to shew the way to him whom they guide. A little from the town we had some craggy ways, which indeed, had need of lights, but afterwards we came into a plain champaign country, which continued till within a league of the middle way lodge, to the which we were to descend a steep hill.

When we came thither (which was about seven in the morning), we found our fresh supply waiting for us. They had set out from their town at midnight to meet us and had made us a fire, and warmed water for our chocolate. Which whilst I was drinking, the Indians of Joyabaj, who had guided me thither, gave notice to those that came to receive from San Martín (so was the town called whither I was that day minded) of my miracle and sanctity, wishing them to reverence and respect me in the way. But not for their foolish report did I make the Indians of Joyabaj drink every one a cup of chocolate, and so dismissed them; and took forwards my journey to San Martín [Jilotepéque]. Most of the way was hilly and craggy till we came within two miles of the town, at which we arrived by noon.

This town is cold, standing high, yet pleasant for the prospect almost to Guatemala. Here, and in most of the towns about it, is most excellent wheat. The honey of this town is the best in the country; but above all it furnisheth Guatemala with quails, partridges, and rabbits. It is the first town we enter into belonging to the city and command of Guatemala. This did not a little comfort me, for now I wanted but one good journey to make an end of my long, tedious, and wearisome travelling. The friar of this town, named Tomás de la Cruz, belonged unto the Dominican cloister of Guatemala; he was a Creole, but yet he entertained me very lovingly.[10] I stayed with him but that night. In the morning (though I might have gone to dinner to Guatemala) I would needs go by the way to one of the biggest towns in that country, called Chimaltenango, standing in an open valley three leagues from the city, and consisting of a thousand housekeepers and rich Indians who trade much about the country. In this town in my time there was one Indian who alone had bestowed upon the church five thousand ducats. The church yields to none in the city of Guatemala, and in music it exceeds most about the country. The chief feast of Chimaltenango is upon the 26 day of July (which they call St. Anne's day), and then is the richest fair of all sorts of merchants and merchandise that ever my eyes beheld in those parts. It is further set forth with bull-baiting, horse-racing, stage-plays, masks, dances, music, and all this gallantly performed by the Indians of the town.

The friar of this town was a Dominican, belonging to the cloister of the Dominicans of Guatemala, named Alonso Hidalgo, a four-eyed old man, for he always wore spectacles. He was a Spaniard born, but having been brought up in that country from his youth, and having taken his habit and vows in Guatemala amongst the

---

[10] He died in the friary of Guatemala in 1644. The chronicler Ximénez writes that he was a most exemplary man, who spoke Quiché and Cakchiquel with great perfection.

Creoles, he degenerated from his birth and countrymen, hating all such as came from Spain. He was a deadly enemy to the Provincial (aiming indeed himself to be Provincial with the favor of the Creoles), and so I perceived he would have picked a quarrel with me whilst I was with him; he told me I was welcome, though he had little reason to bid any welcome that had come from Spain, who he thought came but to supplant those that had been born and brought up there in their own country, and that for aught he knew, I learning the language of those Indians might one day dispossess him of that town, wherein he had continued above ten years; he inveighed much against the Provincial and Friar Juan Bautista, the Prior of Guatemala, whom he knew to be my friend. But to all this I answered not a word, respecting his grave and old age, and crystal spectacles.

At last he told me that he had heard say that the Indians of Joyabaj had cried me up for a saint, which he could not believe of any that came from Spain, much less of me that came from England, a country of heretics.

He feared rather that I might come as a spy, to view the riches of their country and betray them hereafter to England, and that in Guatemala there were many rich pieces, especially a picture of Our Lady, and a lamp in the cloister of the Dominicans, which he doubted not but I would be careful to pry into. But all this I put up with a jest, saying, that I would be sure to take notice first of the riches of his chamber in pictures, hangings, and rich cabinets, and that if the English came thither in my time, I would surely conduct them to it. I said that if he himself would but cause a set of teeth of silver to be set in his gums and jaws instead of those leaden ones (for he was so old that he had lost all his teeth, and had got some of lead in their stead), then surely I would also conduct the English to him as to a rich prize for his teeth, and I would warrant him he should be well used for his outward and inward riches. I told him that my counsel might be profitable and of consequence to him, for if the English should come, they would certainly try of what metal his teeth were made, thinking that they might be of some rare and exquisite substance found only in that country. And so they might cause him to drink such hot and scalding broth (to try whether they were lead) as might melt them in his mouth, and make the melted lead run down his throat, which if they were of silver they would not do. He perceived I jeered him, and so he let me alone.

I was glad I had put him out of his former bias of railing, so dinner being ended, I told him I would not stay supper, but go to Guatemala to a light supper in the cloister, for that he had given me such a dinner, as I feared I should not have digested in few days. I desired him to let me have Indians to guide me to Guatemala, which he willingly performed, peradventure fearing that if I stayed supper with him, I should melt the teeth in his mouth with some scalding cup of my chocolate brought from Chiapa, or that in the night I should rifle or plunder his chamber of his rich idols and ebony cabinets.[11] The Indians being come, I made haste to be gone from that four-eyed beast, being now desirous of a constant rest in Guatemala.

Within a league from this town of Chimaltenango the roadway, leaving that open, wide, and spacious valley, contracts and gathereth in itself between hills and mountains standing on each side, and so continueth to the city. From this valley unto Guatemala, neither is there any ascent or descent but a plain, broad, and sandy way. The eye hath much to view, though compassed with mountains, in these two last leagues. For it may behold a town of Indians which taketh up most of the way, and is counted as big as Chimaltenango, if not bigger. The houses lying scattered with a distance one from another, mingled with many fair buildings of Spaniards, who resort much thither from the city for their recreation. This town is called Jocotenango, of a fruit called *jocote* [the native plum], which is most plentiful there and all about the country. It is fresh and cooling, of a yellow color when ripe, and of two sorts, some sweet, and others sour, of the stones whereof the Indians make a fire. They lie so thick in the way, dropping from the trees for want of gathering and spending them all, that the Spaniards have begun to practice buying hogs on purpose to let them run about that highway, finding that they fat as speedily and as well with those plums, as our hogs do in England with acorns.

[11] That he had a quarrelsome disposition appears from a statement by the chronicler Ximénez that he had made a trip to Spain to seek redress in some troubles he had had with a former Prior of the province. Contrary to what Gage would have us think, Father Alonso gave the whole of his substantial inheritance to the order.

All this way are also many fair gardens, which supply the markets of Guatemala with herbs, roots, fruits and flowers all the year. There are further in this road three water-mills for the corn of the city, whereof the chief and the richest belongs to the Dominican friars of Guatemala, who keep there a friar constantly with three or four Blackamoors to do and oversee the work. What will not those friars do to satisfy their covetous minds? Even dusty millers they will become to get wealth. The frontispiece of the church of this town is judged one of the best pieces of work thereabouts; the high altar within is also rich and stately, being all daubed with gold. I made no stay in this place, because I knew I should have many occasions after my settling in the city to come unto it. And thus keeping between the hills I continued on my journey till I came to Guatemala, whose dominions, riches, and greatness the following chapter shall largely show.

14. Describing the dominions, government, riches, and greatness of the City of Guatemala, and country belonging unto it

I HAD not rid on above a mile from the church of Jocotenango, when the hills and mountains seemed to depart one from another, leaving a more spacious object for the eye to behold, and a wider valley to wander in. The fame of that city from Mexico and Chiapa had raised up my thoughts to conceit of some strong walls, towers, forts or bulwarks to keep out an aspiring or attempting enemy. But when I came near and least thought of it, I found myself in it without entering through walls, or gates, or passing over any bridge, or finding any watch or guard to examine who I was. I passed by a new-built church standing near a place of dunghills, where were none but mean houses, some thatched, and some tiled. On asking what town that was, answer was made me that it was the city of Guatemala, and that that, being called San Sebastián, was the only parish church of the city. With this my high conceiting thoughts stooped down to think of some second Chiapa. Till having continued on a while by houses on my right hand and dunghills on my left, I came to a broader street having houses on each side, which seemed to promise a city at hand.

At my first turning I discovered a proud and stately cloister, which was the place of rest to my wearied body. I surrounded it to find out the back gate, and there lighted, and enquired for the Prior, who bad me very welcome, assuring me that for the Provincial's sake I should want no encouragement, and that he would do for me much more than what the Provincial had signified unto him by letters.

176

He told me he had been brought up in Spain, in the country of Asturias, where many English ships did use to come, and having seen there many of my nation, he affected them very much, and to me as one of so good a nation, and as a stranger and pilgrim out of my own country, he would show all the favor that the utmost of his power would afford. How glad was I to find in him so contrary an opinion to that of four-eyed Hidalgo? And how did he perform his words?

He was the chief Master and Reader of Divinity in the University, his name Master Jacinto de Cabañas, who finding me desirous to follow the schools, and especially to hear from him some lessons of theology, within the first quarter of year, that I had been his constant and attentive auditor, graced me with a public act of conclusions of divinity, which I was to defend under his direction and moderation in the face of the whole University and assembly of doctors and divines, against the tenets of Scotus and Suárez. But the principal and head conclusion was concerning the birth of the Virgin Mary, whom Jesuits, Suárez, and Franciscans, and Scotists hold to have been born without original sin, or any guilt or stain of it.

Against those fond, foolish, and ungrounded fancies, I publicly defended with Thomas Aquinas, and all Thomists, that she (as well as all Adam's posterity) was born in original sin. It was an act, the like whereof had not been so controverted in that University with arguments in *contra*, and their answers and solutions, and with reasons and arguments in *pro* for many years. The Jesuits stamped with their feet, clapped with their hands, railed with their tongues, and condemned it with their mouths for a heresy, saying that in England, where were heretics, such an opinion concerning Christ's mother might be held, and defended by me who had my birth among heretics, but they could not but much marvel and wonder that Master Cabañas, born among Spaniards, and brought up in their universities, and the chief Reader in that famous academy should maintain such an opinion. But with patience I told them that strong reasons and the further authority of many learned Thomist divines should satisfy their vain and clamorous wondering.

The act was ended, and though with Jesuits I could get no credit, yet with the Dominicans and with Master Cabañas I got so much that I never after lost it for the space of almost twelve years, but was still honored by the means of this Cabañas and Friar Juan Bautista, the Prior of Chiapa (who at Christmas ensuing was made Prior of Guatemala) with honors and preferments as great as ever stranger was living among Spaniards. These two above named being at Candlemas or beginning of February that same year at Chiapa, at the election of a new Provincial, did not forget me, their poorest friend, still abiding in Guatemala. Remembering that at Michaelmas the University, which belonged chiefly to the cloister, would want a new Reader of Master of Arts to begin with logic, continue through the eight books of physics, and to end with metaphysics, propounded me to the new elected Provincial, whose name was Friar Juan Ximeno, and to the whole Chapter and Conventicle of the province for Reader of Arts in Guatemala the Michaelmas next ensuing.[1] Their suit for me was so earnest and their authority so great that nothing could be denied them, and so they brought unto me from the Provincial Chapter letters patent from Friar Juan Ximeno, whose form and manner I thought fit here to insert out of the original in Spanish (which to this day abideth with me) for curiosity and satisfaction of my reader. This form according to the original in Spanish is thus in English and to this purpose.

Friar Juan Ximeno, Preacher General and Prior Provincial of this Province of Saint Vincent of Chiapa and Guatemala, Order of Preachers, whereas our Convent of Santo Domingo of Guatemala wanteth and stands in need of a Reader of Arts: By these presents I do institute, name and appoint for Reader Friar Tomás de Santa María [so was my name then, and by this name will some Spaniards know me, who may chance hereafter to read this and curse me], for the great satisfaction which I have of his sufficiency. And I command the Prior of the aforesaid our

---

[1] At this time there was no university in Guatemala. Gage refers to the college of St. Thomas Aquinas which the Dominicans ran, and which was a part of their establishment in the city. It was often called a university. There was also a convent school. As early as 1622 Juan Ximeno and Juan Bautista testified in favor of raising the college to the rank of university. Their testimonies are among the published documents of the Guatemalan archives. It was not until 1676 that the college of Santo Tomás de Aquino was raised by royal decree to the rank of university, much to the disgust of the Jesuits, who had hoped that distinction would be granted to their own college of St. Francis of Borgia. The new university was named the Royal and Pontifical University of San Carlos. After the earthquake it was moved to the present Guatemala City.

convent, that he put him in full possession and enjoyment of the said office. And for the greater merit of obedience, and under a formal precept, In the name of the Father, and of the Son, and of the Holy Ghost, Amen. Dated in this our Convent of Chiapa la Real, the 9. of Feb. 1627. And I command these to be sealed with the great seal of our office.

Friar Juan   By the command of our Reverend
    or   Father Friar Juan de Santo Domingo,
Ximeno Pal.   Notary

I notified these letters patent, unto the contained in them the 12. day of the month of April, 1627.
Friar Juan Baptista Por.

This honor conferred upon me a stranger and newcomer to the province made the Creole party and some others (who had aimed at that place and preferment in the University) to stomach [dislike] me. But to me it was a spur to stir and prick me on to a more eager pursuit of learning, to frequent the academy lessons with more care and diligence, and to spend myself and time, day and night, more in studying, that so I might perform with like honor that which was laid upon me, and answer the expectation of my best and forwardest friends.

Three years I continued in this convent and city in obedience to the forecited patents. Oftentimes I thought within myself that the honor of my English nation here lay upon me in Guatemala, in not suffering any Spaniard to go beyond me, or to outbrave me with gallant, witty, and well-seeming arguments. And so many times I would at nine of the clock at night, when others were gone to bed, take in my chamber a cup of hot chocolate, that with it I might banish sleep from mine eyes, and might the better continue in my study till one or two in the morning, being bound to awake and be up again by six. I was loath in these three years to take upon me any other of such charges which are common in such convents; but especially to preach much, and to hear the confessions of such men and women as resorted to the church of that cloister, lest hereby my studies might be hindered, and time spent in other ways.

Yet the Prior and Master Cabañas would often be very importunate with me to obtain the Bishop's licence for hearing of confessions, and preaching abroad in the city and country (for in the church of that cloister I might and did sometimes, though seldom, preach with permission of the Provincial). This I strongly refused, until such time as the Provincial himself came to Guatemala. He, hearing me once preach, would by all means have me further licensed and authorised from the Bishop, so that I might not be straitened within the cloister's limits but might freely preach abroad in other churches and thereby get some money for better furnishing myself with books.

He therefore commanded me to be examined by five examiners, all able divines, for the space of three hours (as is the custom of that Order). After I had stood three hours under their hard and rigid questions and examination, and had also at the end obtained their approbation, then the Provincial presented me unto the Bishop. The Bishop of Guatemala [Fr. Juan de Sandoval y Zapata, of the Order of St. Augustine] being my great friend, and a well-wisher to learning, and especially to that university, needed not many words of entreaty, but presently gave me the license written on the back of the presentation and that without any further examination by his clergy and part of his chapter, which he may and doth use when he pleaseth. It was dated in the City of Santiago of Guatemala, the fourth day of December, in the year of our Lord, 1629. Thus with full and ample commission from the Bishop and the provincial I was settled in Guatemala, to read and preach. There I continued yet but three years and almost an half for the reason I shall shew hereafter, although I might have continued many years and was offered to read divinity, having in part begun it one quarter of a year. So I shall truly and faithfully recommend unto my reader what in that time I could observe of that city, and of the country round about, having had occasions to travel about it both when I lived in Guatemala, and afterwards when I lived for above seven years in the country towns.

This city of Guatemala, called by the Spaniards Santiago, or St. James of Guatemala, is seated in a valley, which is not above two miles and a half broad, for the high mountains do keep it close in; but in length towards the South Sea it continues a wide and champaign country, opening itself broader a little beyond that town, which to this day is called *la Ciudad Vieja*, or the Old City, standing somewhat above three miles from Guatemala.[2] Though the mountains on each side do strongly environ it, and, especially on the east side, seem to hang over it, yet none of them are hinderers to travellers, who over them have opened ways easy for man and beasts though heavily laden with wares of all sorts.

The way from Mexico, if taken by the coast of Soconusco and Suchitepéquez, comes into the city north-westward, which is a wide, open, and sandy road; if it be taken by Chiapa, it lieth north-east, and entereth into the city between the mountains, as before hath been noted. Westward to the South Sea the way lieth open through the valley and a champaign country. But south or south-east, the entrance is over high and steepy hills, which is the common road from Comayagua, Nicaragua, and the *Golfo Dulce* or Sweet Gulf, where the ships come yearly and unlade all the commodities which are brought from Spain for Guatemala. This also is the way followed by them who take a journey mere eastward from this city.

But the chiefest mountains which straighten in this city and valley are two, called volcanoes, the one being a volcano of water, and the other a volcano or mountain of fire, termed so by the Spaniards, though very improperly a volcano may be said to contain water, for it takes its name from the heathenish god Vulcan, whose profession and employment chiefly was in fire. These two famous mountains stand almost the one over against the other, on each side of the valley. That of water hanging on the south side almost perpendicularly over the city; the other of fire standing lower from it, more opposite to the old city.

That of water is higher than the other, and yields a goodly prospect to the sight, being almost all the year green, and full of Indian *milpas*, which are plantations of Indian wheat. In the small and petty towns which lie some half way up it, some at the foot of it, there are roses, lilies, and other flowers all the year long in the gardens, besides plantains, apricots, and many sorts of sweet and delicate fruits. It is called by the Spaniards, *el volcán del agua*, or the volcano of water, because on the other side of it from Guatemala

---

[2] Ciudad Vieja was the first capital of Guatemala until in 1542, following a cloudburst which destroyed much of the town and took the lives of the widow of the Conquistador Alvarado and many others, the seat of government was moved to Santiago de Guatemala of Gage's time, the present Antigua. It is to this disaster that Gage shortly refers.

it springs with many brooks towards a town called San Cristóbal, and especially is thought to preserve and nourish on that side also a great lake of fresh water, by the towns called Amatitlán and Petapa. But on the side of it towards Guatemala and the valley it yields also so many springs of sweet and fresh water as have caused and made a river which runneth along the valley close by the city, and is that which drives the water-mills in Jocotenango spoken of before.

This river was not known when first the Spaniards conquered that country; but since (according to their constant tradition) the city of Guatemala standing higher and nearer to the volcano in that place and town which to this day is called *la Ciudad Vieja*, or the Old City, there lived in it then about the year 1534 [1541] a gentle-woman called Doña María de Castilla. Having lost her husband in the wars and that same year buried also all her children, she grew so impatient under these her crosses and afflictions, that impiously she defied God, saying: "What can God do more unto me now than he hath done? he hath done his worst without it be to take away my life also, which I now regard not." Upon these words there gushed out of this volcano such a flood of water as carried away this woman with the stream, ruined many of the houses, and caused the inhabitants to remove to the place where now standeth Guatemala. This is the Spaniards' own tradition, which if true, should be our example to learn to fear and not to defy God, when his judgments shew him to us angry and a God that will overcome, when he judgeth. From that time, and from this their tradition a town still stands, where first stood Guatemala, and it is called *la Ciudad Vieja*, or the Old City. And since then hath continued a river which before was not known, having its head and spring from this high volcano, whose pleasant springs, gardens, fruits, flowers and every green and flourishing prospect might be a fair object to a Martial's wit, who here would fancy a new Parnassus, find out new steps of flying Pegasus, and greet the nymphs and Nine Sisters with this their never yet discovered and American habitation.

This volcano or mountain (whose height is judged full nine miles unto the top)[3] is not so pleasing to the sight, but the other which

[3] A traveler's tall story. The height above sea level is 12,500 feet, somewhat under 2.5 miles.

standeth on the other side of the valley opposite unto it is unpleasing and more dreadful to behold. For here are ashes for beauty, stones and flints for fruits and flowers, baldness for greenness, barrenness for fruitfulness. For water whisperings and fountain murmurs, noise of thunders and roaring of consuming metals; for running streams, flashings of fire; for tall and mighty trees and cedars, castles of smoke rising in height to out-dare the sky and firmament; for sweet and odoriferous and fragrant smells, a stink of fire and brimstone, which are still in action striving within the bowels of that ever burning and fiery volcano. Thus is Guatemala seated in the midst of a Paradise on the one side and a hell on the other, yet never hath this hell broke so loose as to consume that flourishing city. True it is that many years ago it opened a wide mouth on the top, and breathed out such fiery ashes as filled the houses of Guatemala and the country about, and parched all the plants and fruits, and spewed out such stones and rocks which had they fallen upon the city would have crushed it to pieces. But they fell not far from it, but to this day lie about the bottom and sides of it, causing wonder to those that behold them, and taking away admiration from them that admire the force and strength of fire and powder in carrying on a weighty bullet from the mouth of a cannon. Here the fire of this mountain hath cast up into the air and tumbled down to the bottom of it such rocks as in bigness exceed a reasonable house, and which not the strength of any twenty mules (as hath been tried) have been able to remove.

The fire which flasheth out of the top of this mountain is sometimes more and sometimes less; yet while I lived in the city, on a certain time for the space of three or four days and nights it did so burn that my friend Mr. Cabañas confidently avouched to me and others, that standing one night in his window he had with the light of that fire read a letter, the distance being above three English miles. The roaring of this monstrous beast is not constantly alike, but is greater in the summer time than in the winter, that is, from October to the end of April, than all the rest of the year; for then it seems, the winds entering into those concavities set the fire on work harder than at other times, and cause the mountain to roar and the earth to quake.

There was a time, three years before my coming to that city, when the inhabitants expected nothing but utter ruin and destruction, and durst not abide within their houses for nine days (the earthquakes continuing and increasing more and more) but made bowers and arbors in the market-place, placing there their idol saints and images, especially San Sebastián, whom they hoped would deliver them from that judgment. For this purpose they daily carried him through the streets in solemn and idolatrous procession and adoration. But all the while I lived there the noise within the mountain, the smoke and flashes of fire without, and the summer earthquakes were such that with the use and custom of them I never feared anything, but thought that city the healthiest and pleasantest place of dwelling that ever I came into in all my travels.

The climate is very temperate, far exceeding either Mexico or Oaxaca. Neither are the two aforenamed cities better stored with fruits, herbs for salad, provision of fish, and flesh, beef, mutton, veal, kid, fowls, turkeys, rabbits, quails, partridges, pheasants, and of Indian and Spanish wheat than is this city. From the South Sea, which lieth in some places not above twelve leagues from it, and from the rivers of the South Sea Coast, and from the fresh lake of Amatitlán and Petapa, and from another lake [Atitlán] lying three or four leagues from Chimaltenango, it is well and plentifully provided of fish. Of beef there is such plenty that it exceeds all parts of America, without exception, as may be known by the hides, which are sent yearly to Spain from the country of Guatemala. There they commonly kill their cattle more for the gain of their hides in Spain, than for the goodness or fatness of the flesh, which though it be not to be compared to our English beef, yet it is good man's meat, and so cheap, that in my time it was commonly sold at thirteen pound and a half for half a real, the least coin there, and as much as threepence here.

All about this country there are very great and spacious *estancias*, or farms for breeding only, even near to the Golfo Dulce, where the ships ride that come from Spain. Yet from Comayagua, San Salvador, and Nicaragua is Guatemala stored. Above all are the great *estancias* in the South Sea coast or marsh, where in my time there was a grazier that reckoned up that there were in his own *estancia* and ground forty thousand head of beasts, small and great, besides many which are called there *cimarrones*, or wild cattle, which were strayed among the woods and mountains, and could not be gathered in with the rest, but were hunted by the Blackamoors like wild boars, and daily shot to death, lest they should too much increase and do hurt. I myself chanced to be present at the fair of the town of Petapa, with a friend named Lope de Chaves (who was as they call there, *obligado*, or charged to provide flesh for six or seven towns thereabouts). At one bargain and of one man he bought six thousand head of cattle, great and small, paying one with another eighteen reals, or nine English shillings a head.

The manner and custom of Guatemala for the better providing both beef and mutton for it and the country towns about is this. Nine days before Michaelmas, every day proclamation is made about the city for an *obligado*, or one that will be bound to the city and country for competent provision of flesh meat upon forfeiture of such a sum of money to his Majesty, if he fail, as shall be agreed upon between him and the court. If he fail in beef, he is to allow in mutton so many pounds at the same rate as he should have allowed beef. If the *obligado* fail in mutton, he is to allow in fowl flesh, so many pounds and at the same rate as he was to allow the mutton; and this with consideration of the family, what competent allowance of flesh meat shall be judged for a day, or the days that the *obligado* shall fail. Besides this, the proclamation is made for the one who offers most to his Majesty for one year's obligation. So that sometimes it happeneth that during the eight days several men come into the court, offering more and more, till upon the ninth day and last proclamation, the office is settled for one year upon him that hath offered most unto his Majesty. Thus many butchers are not allowed but one only *obligado*. Thus the *obligado* (who commonly is a moneyed man) buyeth by the hundred or by the thousand, as for the present he findeth the expense of the city, without he be himself such a grazier as hath cattle enough of his own. Though mutton be not so plentiful as is beef, yet there is never a shortage from the Valley of Mixco, Pinola, Petapa, and Amatitlán, and the marsh and other places. In the valley afore-named I lived, and was well acquainted with one Alonso Zapata, who had constantly going in the valley four thousand sheep. Guatemala therefore is so well stored with good provision, plentiful and cheap, that it is hard to find in it a beggar, for with half a real the poorest may buy beef for a week, and with a few cacao beans they may have bread of Indian maize, if not of Spanish wheat.

This city may consist of about five thousand families, besides a suburb of Indians called *el Barrio de Santo Domingo*, where may be two hundred families more. The best part of the city is that which joineth to this suburb of Indians, and is called also *el Barrio de Santo Domingo*, by reason of the cloister of Saint Dominic which standeth in it. Here are the richest and best shops of the city, with the best buildings, most of the houses being new, and stately. Here is also a daily *tianguez* (as they call it) or petty market, where some Indians all the day sit selling fruits, herbs, and cacao, but at four in the afternoon, this market is filled for a matter of an hour, where the Indian women meet to sell their country slop (which is dainties to the Creoles) as *atole*, *pinole* [a drink of parched maize], scalded plantains, butter of the cacao, puddings made of Indian maize, with a bit of fowl or fresh pork in them seasoned with much red biting chile, which they call *anaca tamales*.

The trading of the city is great, for by mules it partakes of the best commodities of Mexico, Oaxaca, and Chiapa, and, southward, of Nicaragua and Costa Rica. By sea it hath commerce with Peru, by two sea ports and havens, the one called La Villa de la Trinidad, the Village of the Trinity, which lieth southward from it five and twenty leagues; and by another called El Realejo, which lieth five or six and forty leagues from it. It hath traffic with Spain by the North Sea from Golfo Dulce, lying three-score leagues from it.

It is not so rich as other cities, yet for the quantity of it, it yields to none. There were in my time five (besides many other merchants who were judged worth twenty thousand ducats, thirty thousand, fifty thousand, some few a hundred thousand) who were judged of equal wealth, and generally reported to be worth each of them five hundred thousand ducats. The first was Tomás de Siliézer, a Biscayan born, and *Alcalde de Corte*, the King's High Justice, or Chief Officer at Court; the second was Antonio Justiniano, a Genoese born, and one that bore often offices in the city, and had many tenements and houses, especially a great and rich farm for corn and wheat in the Valley of Mexico. The third was Pedro de Lira, born in Castile, the fourth and fifth, Antonio Fernández, and Bartolomé Núñez, both Portuguese, whereof the first in my time departed from Guatemala for some reasons which here I must conceal. The other four I left there, the three of them living at that end of the city called *Barrio de Santo Domingo,* or the Street of St. Dominic, whose houses and presence makes that street excel all the rest of the city, and their wealth and trading were enough to denominate Guatemala a very rich city.

The Government of all the country about, and of all Honduras, Soconusco, Comayagua, Nicaragua, Costa Rica, Vera Paz, Suchitepéquez, and Chiapa, is subordinate unto the Chancery [*Audiencia*] of Guatemala; for although every governor over these several provinces is appointed by the King and Council of Spain, yet when they come to those parts to the enjoyment of their charge and execution office, then their actions, if unjust, are weighed, judged, censured, and condemned by the Court residing in the city. This Court of Chancery consisteth of a president, six judges, one King's attorney, and two chief justices of court. The President, though he have not the name and title of viceroy, as they of Mexico and Peru, yet his power is as great and absolute as theirs. His pension from the King is but twelve thousand ducats a year; but besides this, if he be covetous, he makes by bribes and trading twice as much more, nay what he list. This was seen in the Count de la Gómera, president of that city and Chancery for the space of fourteen years, who departed in old age from Guatemala to the Canaries (where was his house and place of birth) worth millions of ducats.

After him succeeded Don Juan de Guzmán,[4] formerly president of Santo Domingo, who, losing his wife and lady in the way, lost also his former spirit and courage, betaking himself wholly to his devotions, contemning wealth and riches, governing with love and mildness. This made the rest of the judges, who were all for lucre, soon weary him out of his office, in which he continued but five years.

His successor, whom I left there when I came away, was Don Gonzalo de Paz y Lorenzana, who was promoted from the presidency of Panama to that place, and came into it with such a spirit of covetousness as the like had not been seen in any former president. He forbad all gaming in private houses in the city, which there is much used (though by women not so much as in Mexico), not for that he hated it, but because he envied others what they got and

---

[4] Apparently a slip of the pen. The next governor was Diego de Acuña.

gained by their cards. Thereby he drew to himself all that gain, spending sometimes in one night four and twenty pair of cards. He appointed a page to assist at the tables, and to see the box well paid for every pair of cards, which for his, and his Court respect, was seldom less than a crown or two for every pair. Thus did he lick up with his cards most of the gamester's gains, and would grudge and pick quarrels with such rich men whom he knew to affect gaming, if they frequented not his Court at night time for that bewitching recreation.

The pension which the King alloweth to every judge of Chancery is four thousand ducats yearly, and three thousand to his attorney, all which is paid out of the King's Exchequer abiding in that city. Yet what besides they get by bribes and trading is so much, that I have heard Don Luis de las Infantas, himself a judge, say, that though a judge's place at Mexico and Lima be more honorable, yet none more profitable than Guatemala. In my time were such causes at Chancery tried, as had never been, or murders, robberies, and oppression. One would expect that some of the offenders should be hanged, some banished, some imprisoned, some by fines impoverished; yet bribes took all off, so that I never knew one hanged in that city for the space of above eight years.

The churches, though they be not so fair and rich as those of Mexico, are for that place wealthy enough. There is but one parish church and a cathedral which standeth in the chief market-place. All the other churches belong to cloisters, which are of Dominicans, Franciscans, Mercenarians, Augustines, and Jesuits, and two of nuns, called the Concepción and Santa Catarina. The Dominicans, Franciscans, and Mercenarians are stately cloisters, containing near a hundred friars apiece; but above all is the cloister where I lived of the Dominicans, to which is joined in a great walk before the church, the University of the city. The yearly revenues which come into this cloister, what from the Indian towns belonging to it, what from a water-mill, what from a farm for corn, what from an *estancia*, or farm for horses and mules, what from an *ingenio*, or farm of sugar, what from a mine of silver given unto it the year 1633, are judged to be (excepting all charges) at least thirty thousand ducats. Therewith those fat friars feast themselves, and have to spare to build, and enrich their church and altars.

Besides much treasure belonging to it, there are two things in this church which the Spaniards in merriment would often tell me that the English nation did much enquire after, when they took any ship of theirs at sea, and that they feared I was come to spy them. These were a lamp of silver hanging before the high altar, so big as required the strength of three men to hale it up with a rope, and a picture of the Virgin Mary of pure silver, and of the stature of a reasonably tall woman, which standeth in a tabernacle made on purpose in a Chapel of the Rosary with at least a dozen lamps of silver also burning before it. A hundred thousand ducats might soon be made up of the treasure belonging to that church and cloister.

Within the walls of the cloister there is nothing wanting which may further pleasure and recreation. In the lower cloister there is a spacious garden, in the midst whereof is a fountain casting up the water, and spouting it out of at least a dozen pipes, which fill two ponds full of fishes, and with this their constant running give music to the whole cloister, and encouragement to many water-fowls and ducks to bathe and wash themselves therein. Yet further within the cloister, there are other two gardens for fruits and herbage, and in the one a pond of a quarter of a mile long, all paved at the bottom, and a low stone wall about, where is a boat for the friars' recreation, who often go thither to fish, and do sometimes upon a sudden want or occasion take out from thence as much fish as will give to the whole cloister a dinner.[5]

The other cloisters of the city are also rich; but next to the Dominicans is the cloister of nuns called the Concepción, in which at my time there were judged to live a thousand women, not all nuns, but nuns and their serving maids or slaves, and young children which were brought up and taught to work by the nuns. The nuns that are professed bring with them their portions, five hundred ducats the least, some six hundred, some seven, and some a thousand, which portions after a few years (and continuing to the cloister after the nuns' decease) come to make up a great yearly rent. They that will have maids within to wait on them may, bringing the bigger portion or allowing yearly for their servants' diet.

In this cloister lived that Doña Juana de Maldonado, Judge Juan

---

[5] The destruction of the earthquake of 1773 was so great that scarcely two stones remain one above the other of the Dominican friary and chapel.

Maldonado de Paz' daughter, whom the Bishop so much conversed withal. She was very fair and beautiful, and not much above twenty years of age, and yet his love blinding him, he strove what he could in my time against all the ancient nuns and sisters, to make her superior and abbess, and caused mutiny and strife in that cloister. This was very scandalous to the whole city, and made many rich merchants and gentlemen run to the cloister with their swords drawn, threatening to break in amongst the nuns to defend their daughters against the powerful faction which the Bishop had wrought for Doña Juana de Maldonado. This they would have done if the President Don Juan de Guzmán had not sent Juan Maldonado de Paz, the young nun's father, to entreat her to desist in regard of her young age from her ambitious thoughts of being abbess. With this the mutiny both within and without ceased, the Bishop got but shame, and his young sister continued as before under command and obedience, to a more religious, grave, and aged nun than herself.

This Doña Juana de Maldonado y Paz was the wonder of all that cloister, yea, of all the city for her excellent voice and skill in music, and in her carriage and education she yielded to none abroad nor within. She was witty, well spoken, and above all a Calliope, or Muse for ingenious and sudden verses, which the Bishop said so much moved him to delight in her company and conversation. Her father thought nothing too good, nor too much for her; and therefore, having no other children, he daily conferred upon her riches, as might best beseem a nun, as rich and costly cabinets faced with gold and silver, pictures and idols for her chamber with crowns and jewels to adorn them. These with other presents from the Bishop (who dying in my time left not wherewith to pay his debts, for that as the report went, he had spent himself and given all unto this nun) made this Doña Juana de Maldonado so rich and stately that at her own charges she built for herself a new quarter within the cloister with rooms and galleries, and a private garden-walk, and kept at work and to wait on her half a dozen Blackamoor maids.

Above all she placed her delight in a private chapel or closet to pray in. This was hung with rich hangings, and round about it costly *laminas*, as they call them, or pictures painted upon brass set in black ebony frames with corners of gold, some of silver, brought to her from Rome. Her altar was accordingly decked with jewels, candlesticks, crowns, lamps, and covered with an canopy embroidered with gold. In her closet she had her small organ, and many sorts of musical instruments, whereupon she played sometimes by herself, sometimes with her best friends of the nuns; and here especially she entertained with music her Bishop. Her chapel or place of devotion was credibly reported about the city to be worth at least six thousand crowns, which was enough for a nun that had vowed chastity, poverty, and obedience. But all this after her decease she was to leave to the cloister, and doubtless with this state and riches she would win more and more the hearts of the common sort of nuns, till she had made a strong party, which by this may have made her abbess. Thus is ambition and desire of command and power crept into the walls of nunneries, like the abominations in the wall of Ezekiel, and hath possessed the hearts of nuns, which should be humble, poor, and mortified virgins.[6]

Besides this one nun, there are many more, and also friars, who are very rich, for if the city be rich (as is this) and great trading in it, they will be sure to have a share. Great plenty and wealth hath made the inhabitants as proud and vicious as are those of Mexico. Here is not only idolatry, but fornication and uncleanness as public as in any place of the Indies. The mulattoes, Blackamoors, mestizoes, Indians, and all common sort of people are much made on by the greater and richer sort, and go as gallantly apparelled as do those of Mexico. They fear neither a volcano or mountain of water on the one side, which they confess hath once poured out a flood and

[6] Gage surely maligns the Bishop, who he says was his great friend. From what he writes it is evident that the lady's wit and social graces were the attraction. Gage is hard to please. If a priest leaves any money, he was avaricious; if he dies in proverty, it is because he has misspent his money. A colonial source says the Bishop died penniless because he had given away all his money in charity. A more probable explanation than Gage's.

It has been charged that this story of Doña Juana was a malicious invention of Gage and that no such person ever existed, but recent research in the archives of Guatemala has established that she did indeed exist. She made her vows in 1619, and at her death she was abbess of the convent, despite the earlier troubles. Moreover, there is documentary evidence that her father did have a special set of apartments erected for her use in the nunnery. Ernesto Chinchilla Aguilar's *Sor Juana de Maldonado y Paz. Pruebas documentales de sus existencia* is the first of a series of writings on her. She is even the subject of a romantic novel.

river executing God's wrath against sin there committed, nor a volcano of fire, or mouth of hell, on the other side, roaring within and threatening to rain upon them Sodom's ruin and destruction.

They heed not the weakness of their habitation, lying wide open on every side, without walls, or works, or bulwarks, to defend them, or without guns, drakes, bullets, or any ammunition to scare away an approaching enemy, who may safely come and without resistance upon them who live as professed enemies of Jesus Christ. This is the city of St. James or Santiago de Guatemala, the head of a vast and ample dominion, which extendeth itself nine hundred miles to Nicoya and Costa Rica south[east]ward; three hundred miles to Chiapa and Zoques north[west]ward; a hundred and fourscore miles to the further parts of Vera Paz, and the Golfo Dulce eastward [northward]; and to the South Sea twenty or thirty, in some places forty miles westward [southward].

From Tehuantepec (which is no harbor for any great ships), which standeth from Guatemala at least four hundred miles, there is no landing place for ships nearer to this city than the village *de la Trinidad*, or of the Trinity. The chief commodities which from along that coast are brought to Guatemala, are from the provinces of Soconusco and Suchitepéquez, which are extreme hot, and subject to thunder and lightning, where groweth scarce any remarkable commodity, save only cacao, achiote, *mechasuchil*, vanilla, and other drugs for chocolate, except it be some indigo and cochineal about San Antonio, which is the chief and head town of all the Suchitepéquez. But all the coast near joining to Guatemala, especially about a town called Escuintla, or Izquintepeque, twelve leagues from Guatemala, is absolutely the richest part of the dominion of this city; for there is made the greatest part of the indigo which is sent from Honduras to Spain, besides the mighty farms of cattle, which are all along that marsh. Though the living there be profitable and the soil rich, yet it is uncomfortable by reason of the great heat, thunderings, and lightnings, especially from May to Michaelmas.

If Guatemala be strong (though not in weapons or ammunition) in people, it is strong from hence from a desperate sort of Blackamoors, who are slaves in those *estancias* and farms of indigo. Though they have no weapons but a *machete*, which is a short tuck, or lances to run at the wild cattle, yet with these they are so desperate that the city of Guatemala hath often been afraid of them, and the masters of their own slaves and servants. Some of them fear not to encounter a bull though wild and mad, and to grapple in the rivers (which are many there) with crocodiles, or *lagartos*, as there they call them, till they have overmastered them, and brought them out to land from the water.

This hot but rich country runs on by the seaside unto the Village of the Trinity, which (though somewhat dangerous) yet is a haven for ships from Panama, Peru, and Mexico. It serves to enrich Guatemala, but not to strengthen it, for it hath neither fort, nor bulwark, nor castle, nor any ammunition to defend itself. Between this village and the other haven called Realejo, there is a great creek from the sea;[7] where small vessels do use to come in for fresh water and victuals to San Miguel, a town of Spaniards and Indians, from whence those that travel to Realejo pass over [by water] in less than a day to a town of Indians called La Vieja, two miles from Realejo, whereas the journey by land from San Miguel is of at least three days. Neither this creek or arm of the sea is fortified (which might be done with one or two pieces of ordnance at most placed at the mouth of the sea's entrance) neither is the Realejo strong with any ammunition, no, nor with people. It consists of not above two hundred families, and most of them are Indians and mestizoes, a people of no courage, and very unfit to defend such an open passage to Guatemala and Nicaragua, which here begins and continues in small and petty Indian towns unto León and Granada.

On the north [west] side of Guatemala I shall not need to add to what hath been said of Suchitepéquez and Soconusco, and my journey that way from Mexico and Chiapa. The chief side of Guatemala is that on the east [north], which points out the way to the gulf, or Golfo Dulce, or as others call it Santo Tomás de Castilla.[8] This way is more beaten by mules and travellers than that on the north [west] side, for that Mexico standeth three hundred leagues from this city, and the gulf but threescore, and no such passages as are in some places in the road to Mexico. Besides, the

---

[7] The Gulf of Fonseca, where El Salvador, Honduras, and Nicaragua meet.

[8] The two are really distinct. Santo Tomás de Castilla is at the bottom of the bay on which the modern Puerto Barrios stands. This is some distance east of the entrance of the Golfo Dulce.

great trading, commerce, and traffic which this city enjoyeth by that gulf from Spain hath made that road exceed all the rest.

In July or at furthest in the beginning of August come into that gulf three ships, or two, and frigates, and unlade what they have brought from Spain in *bodegas* or great lodges, built up on purpose to keep dry the commodities and protect them from the weather. They presently make haste to lade again from Guatemala those merchants' commodities of return, which peradventure have lain waiting for them in the *bodegas* two or three months before the ship's arrival. So that these three months of July, August, and September, there is sure to be found a great treasure. And, O, the simplicity or security of the Spaniards, who appoint no other watch over these their riches, save only one or two Indians and as many mulattoes, who commonly are such as have for their misdemeanors been condemned to live in that old and ruinated castle of Santo Tomás de Castilla. True it is, above it there is a little and ragged town of Indians, called San Pedro, consisting of some thirty families, who by reason of the exceeding heat, and unhealthiness of the air, are always sickly and scarce able to stand upon their legs.

The weakness of this gulf within might well be remedied and supplied at the mouth of the sea, or entrance into it, by one or at the most two good pieces of ordnance placed there. For the entrance into this gulf is but as one should come in at the door of some great palace, where, although the door and entrance be narrow, the house within is wide and capacious. Such is this gulf, whose entrance is straitened with two rocks or mountains on each side, which would well become two great pieces, and so scorn a whole fleet, and secure a kingdom of Guatemala nay most of all America. Here being no watch nor defense, the ships come freely and safely in (as have done some both English and Holland ships) and being entered find a road and harbor so wide and capacious as may well secure a thousand ships there riding at anchor, without any thought of fear from San Pedro, or Santo Tomás de Castilla.

I have often heard the Spaniards jeer and laugh at the English and Hollanders, for that having come into this gulf, they have gone away without attempting anything further upon the land. Nay, while I lived there, the Hollanders set upon Trujillo, the head port of Comayagua and Honduras, and took it (though there were some resistance), the people for the most part flying to the woods, trusting more to their feet than to their hands and weapons (such cowards is all that country full of). The Hollanders might have fortified themselves there and gone into the country, or fortifying that, have come on to the gulf, which all Guatemala much feared, not being able to resist them. Instead they left Trujillo contenting themselves with a small pillage, and gave occasion to the Spaniards to rejoice and to make processions of thanksgiving for their safe deliverance out of their enemies' hands.

The way from this gulf to Guatemala is not so bad as some report and conceive, especially after Michaelmas until May, when the winter and rain is past and gone, and the winds begin to dry up the ways. For in the worst of the year mules laden with four hundred-weight at least go easily through the steepest, deepest, and most dangerous passages of the mountains that lie about this gulf. And though the ways are at that time of the year bad, yet they are so beaten with the mules, and so wide and open, that one bad step and passage may be avoided for a better; and the worst of this way continues but fifteen leagues, there being *ranchos*, or lodges, in the way, cattle and mules also among the woods and mountains, for relief and comfort to a weary traveller.

What the Spaniards most fear until they come out of these mountains are some two or three hundred Blackamoors, *cimarrones*, who for too much hard usage have fled away from Guatemala and other parts from their masters unto these woods, and there live and bring up their children and increase daily, so that all the power of Guatemala, nay, all the country about (having often attempted it), is not able to bring them under subjection. These often come out to the roadway, and set upon the *recuas* of mules, and take of wine, iron, clothing, and weapons from them as much as they need, without doing any harm unto the people, or slaves that go with the mules. Rather, these rejoice with them, being of one color, and subject to slavery and misery which the others have shaken off. By their example and encouragement many of these also shake off their misery, and join with them to enjoy liberty, though it be but in the woods and mountains. Their weapons are bows and arrows which they use and carry about them, only to defend themselves if the Spaniards set upon them; else they use them not against the Spaniards, who travel quietly and give them part of what provision they carry. These have often said that the chief cause of their flying to those mountains is to be in a readiness to join with the English or Hollanders, if ever they land in that gulf, for they know, from them they may enjoy that liberty which the Spaniards will never grant unto them.

After the first fifteen leagues the way is better, and there are little towns and villages of Indians, who relieve with provision both man and beast. Fifteen leagues further is a great town of Indians, called Acazabastlán, standing upon a river [Motagua], which for fish is held the best of all that country. Though here are many sorts, yet above all there is one which they call *bobo*, a thick round fish as long or longer than a man's arm, with only a middle bone, as white as milk, as fat as butter, and good to boil, fry, stew, or bake. There is also from hence most of the way to Guatemala in brooks and shallow rivers, one of the best sort of fishes in the world, which the Spaniards judge to be a kind of trout, it is called there *tepemechin*, the fat whereof resembles veal more than fish.

This town of Acazabastlán is governed by a Spaniard who is called *corregidor*; his power extendeth no farther than to the gulf, and to those towns in the way. This governor hath often attempted to bring in those *cimarrones* from the mountains, but could never prevail against them. All the strength of this place may be some twenty muskets (for so many Spanish houses there may be in the town) and some few Indians that use bows and arrows, for the defence of the town against the Blackamoor *cimarrones*.

About Acazabastlán there are many *estancias* of cattle and mules, much cacao, achiote, and drugs for chocolate. There is also apothecary drugs, as *zarzaparilla*, and *cañafistula*, and in the town as much variety of fruits and gardens as in any one Indian town in the country; but above all Acazabastlán is far known, and much esteemed of in the city of Guatemala, for excellent muskmelons, some small, some bigger than a man's head, wherewith the Indians load their mules to sell all over the country.

From hence to Guatemala there are but thirty short leagues, and though some hills there be, ascents and descents, yet nothing troublesome to man or beast. Among these mountains there have been discovered some mines of metal, which the Spaniards have begun to dig, and finding that there have been some of copper, and some of iron, they have let them alone, judging them more chargeable than profitable. But greater profit have the Spaniards lost, than of iron and copper, for using the poor Indians too hardly, and that in this way, from Acazabastlán to Guatemala, especially about a place called El Agua Caliente, where is a river, out of which in some places formerly the Indians found such store of gold that they were charged by the Spaniards with a yearly tribute of gold. But the Spaniards, being like Valdivia in Chile, too greedy after it, murdered the Indians for not discovering unto them where about this treasure lay, and so have lost both treasure and Indians also. Yet unto this day search is made about the mountains, the river, and the sands for the hidden treasure, which peradventure by God's order and appointment doth and shall lie hid, and kept for a people better knowing and honoring their God.

At this place called El Agua Caliente, or The Hot Water, liveth a Blackamoor in an *estancia* of his own, who is held to be very rich, and gives good entertainment to the travellers that pass that way. He is rich in cattle, sheep, and goats, and from his farm stores Guatemala and the people thereabout with the best cheese of all that country. But his riches are thought not so much to increase from his farm and cheeses, but from this hidden treasure, which credibly is reported to be known unto him. He hath been questioned about it in the Chancery of Guatemala but hath denied often any such treasure to be known unto him. The jealousy and suspicion of him is, for that formerly having been a slave, he bought his freedom with great sums of money, and since he hath been free, hath bought that farm and much land lying to it, and hath exceedingly increased his stock. To this he answereth, that when he was young and a slave, he had a good master, who let him get for himself what he could, and that he, playing the good husbandman, gathered as much as would buy his liberty, and at first a little house to live in, to the which God hath since given a blessing with a greater increase of stock.

From this hot water three or four leagues, there is another river called Río de las Vacas, or the River of Cows, where are a company of poor and country people most of them mestizoes, and mulattoes, who live in thatched houses, with some small stock of cattle, spending their time also in search for sands of gold, hoping that one day by their diligent search they and their children, and all their country, shall be enriched, and that Río de las Vacas shall parallel Pactolus, and stir up the wits of poets to speak of it as much as ever they have spoke of that.

From this river is presently discovered the pleasantest valley in all that country (where myself did live at least five years), called the Valley of Mixco and Pinola, lying six leagues from Guatemala, being fifteen miles in length, and ten or twelve in breadth. Out of the enclosures this valley is stored with sheep; the ground enclosed is divided into many farms, where groweth better wheat than any in the country of Mexico. From this valley the city is well provided of wheat, and biscuit is made for the ships that come every year unto the gulf. It is called the Valley of Mixco and Pinola from two towns of Indians, so called, standing opposite the one to the other on each side of the valley, Pinola, on the left side from Río de las Vacas, and Mixco on the right. Here do live many rich farmers, but yet country and clownish people, who know more of breaking clods of earth than of managing arms offensive or defensive.

But among them I must not forget one friend of mine, called Juan Palomeque, whom I should have more esteemed of than I did if I could have prevailed with him to have made him live more like a man than a beast, more like a free man than a bond slave to his gold and silver. This man had in my time three hundred lusty mules trained up in the way of the gulf, which he divided into six *recuas*, or droves; and for them he kept above a hundred Blackamoor slaves, men, women, and children, who lived near Mixco in several thatched cottages.

The house he lived in himself was but a poor thatched house, wherein he took more delight than in other houses which he had in Guatemala, for there he lived like a wild *cimarron* among his slaves and Blackamoors, whereas in the city he should have lived civilly. There he lived with milk, curds, and black, hard, and mouldy biscuit, and with dry *tasajo*, which is dry salted beef cut out in thin slices and dried in the sun and wind, till there be little substance left in it, such as his slaves were wont to carry to the gulf for their provision by the way. Whereas if he had lived in the city, he must have eat for his credit what others of worth did eat. But the miser knew well which was the best way to save, and so chose a field for a city, a cottage for a house, company of *cimarrones* and Blackamoors for citizens, and yet he was thought to be worth six hundred thousand ducats. He was the undoer of all others who dealed with mules for bringing and carrying commodities to the gulf for the merchants, for he, having lusty mules, lusty slaves, would set the price or rate for the hundredweight so, as he might get, but others at that rate hiring Indians and servants to go with their mules, might lose.

He was so cruel to his Blackamoors that if any were untoward, he would torment them almost to death. Amongst them he had one slave called Macaco, for whom I have often interceded, but to little purpose. He would often hang him up by the arms, and whip him till the blood ran about his back, and then, his flesh being torn, mangled, and all in a gore blood, he would for last cure pour boiling grease upon it. He had marked him for a slave with burning irons upon his face, his hands, his arms, his back, his belly, his thighs, his legs, until the poor slave was so weary of life, that I think he would two or three times have hanged himself, if I had not counselled him to the contrary.

He was so sensual and carnal that he would use his own slaves' wives at his pleasure. Nay, when he met in the city any of that kind handsome and to his liking, if she would not yield to his desire, he would go to her master or mistress, and buy her, offering far more than she was worth, boasting that he would pull down her proud and haughty looks with one years' slavery under him. He killed in my time two Indians in the way to the gulf, and with his money came off, as if he had killed but a dog. He would never marry, because his slaves supplied the bed of a wife, and none of his neighbors durst say him nay. Thereby he hasted to fill that valley with bastards of all sorts and colors, by whom, when that rich miser dieth, all his wealth and treasure is like to be consumed.

Besides the two towns which denominate this valley, there standeth at the east [north] end of it close by the Río de las Vacas an hermitage, called *Nuestra Señora del Carmel*, or Our Lady of Carmel, which is the parish church to all those several farms of Spaniards living in the valley; though true it is, most constantly they do resort unto the Indian towns to Mass, and in Mixco especially, the Spaniards have a rich sodality of Our Lady of the Rosary, and the Blackamoors another. In all the valley there may be between forty and fifty Spanish farms or houses belonging to the hermitage, and in all these houses some three hundred slaves, men and women, Blackamoors and mulattoes.[9]

Mixco is a town of three hundred families, but in it nothing considerable but the riches belonging unto the two aforenamed sodalities and some rich Indians, who have learned of the Spaniards to break clods of earth, and to sow wheat, and to traffic with mules unto the gulf. Besides what fowls and great store of turkeys which in this town are bred, there is a constant slaughter house, where meat is sold to the Indians within, and to the farms without, and provision is made for all the *recuas* and slaves that go to the gulf with their masters' mules. Besides the six *recuas* before named of Juan Palomeque, there are in this valley four brothers, named Don Gaspar, Don Diego, Don Tomás, Don Juan de Colindres, who have each of them a *recua* of threescore mules (though few slaves, and only hired Indians to go with them) to traffic to the gulf, and over all the country as far as Mexico sometimes. Yet besides these there are some six more *recuas* belonging to other farms, which with those of the town of Mixco may make up full twenty *recuas;* and those twenty *recuas* contain above a thousand mules, which only from this valley are employed to all parts of the country by the rich merchants of Guatemala.[10]

But to return again to the town of Mixco, the constant passage through it of these *recuas,* of rich merchants, of all passengers that go and come from Spain, hath made it very rich, whereas in the town itself there is no other commodity, except it be a kind of earth, whereof are made rare and excellent pots for water, pans, pipkins, platters, dishes, chafing-dishes, warmingpans. In these those Indians show much wit, and paint them with red, white, and several mingled colors, and sell them to Guatemala, and the towns about.

[9] It was in this area, by the mount of Our Lady of Carmen that the present Guatemala City was built after the destruction of the Guatemala of Gage's time, the present Antigua, in 1773.

[10] Fuentes y Guzmán wrote nearly half a century later in glowing terms of the church of Mixco and its furnishings. He mentions silver crosses, lamps, chalices, cruets, reliquaries, good bells, and an organ which had been donated by wealthy Indians of the town. He also mentions the fine pottery made by the women of Mixco. This, like Amatitlán, Petapa, and Pinula, was a town of the Pokoman Maya. Fuentes y Guzmán puts the number of tribute payers, that is to say, heads of families, as eight hundred. In addition there were Spaniards and mulattoes.

Some Creole women will eat this pottery by full mouthfuls, endangering their health and lives, so that by this earthly ware they may look white and pale. The town of Pinola in bigness is much like unto Mixco, but a far pleasanter town, more healthy and better seated, standing upon a plain, whereas Mixco stands on the side of a hill, which carrieth the travellers quite out of the sight of the valley.

In Pinola there is also a slaughter house, where beef is daily sold, there is plenty of fowls, fruits, maize, wheat (though not altogether so bright as that of Mixco), honey, and the best water thereabouts. It is called in the Indian tongue *Panac* (some say), from a fruit of that name which is very abundant there.[11] On the north and south side of this valley are hills, which are most sown with wheat, which proveth better there than in the low valley. At the west [south] end of it stand two greater towns than Mixco and Pinola named Petapa and Amatitlán, to the which there are in the midst of the valley some descents and ascents, which they call *barrancas* or bottoms, where are pleasant streams and fountains, and good feeding for sheep and cattle.

Petapa is a town of at least five hundred inhabitants very rich, who suffer also some Spaniards to dwell amongst them, from whom also those Indians have learned to live and thrive in the world. This town is the passage from Comayagua, San Salvador, Nicaragua, and Costa Rica, and hath got great wealth by the constant goers and comers. It is esteemed one of the pleasantest towns belonging unto Guatemala, for a great lake of fresh water near unto it, which is full of fish, especially crabs, and a fish called *mojarra*, which is much like unto a mullet, though not altogether so big, and eateth like it. In this town there is a certain number of Indians appointed, who are to fish for the city, and on Wednesdays, Fridays, and Saturdays, are bound to carry to Guatemala such a quantity of crabs and *mojarras*, as the *corregidor* and *regidores*, mayor and aldermen (who are but eight), shall command weekly to be brought.

This town Petapa is so called from two Indian words, *Petap*, which signifieth a mat, and *ha*, which signifieth water, and a mat being the chief part of an Indian's bed, it is as much as to say a bed of water, from the smoothness, plainness, and calmness of the water

[11] Santa Catarina Pinula, according to Fuentes y Guzmán, had 486 tribute payers. Its church resembled in size and ornamentation that of Petapa.

of the lake.[12] There liveth in it a principal family of Indians, who are said to descend from the ancient kings of those parts, and now by the Spaniards are graced with the noble name of Guzmán. One of this family is chosen to be governor of the town with subordination unto the city and Chancery of Guatemala.

Don Bernabe de Guzmán was governor in my time, and had been many years before, and he governed very wisely and discreetly, till with old age he came to lose his sight, and in his place entered his son, Don Pedro de Guzmán, of whom the rest of the Indians stood in great awe, as formerly they had to his father. Had not these Indians been given to drunkenness (as most Indians are), they might have governed a town of Spaniards.

This Governor hath many privileges granted unto him (though not to wear a sword, or rapier, as may the Governor of Chiapa of the Indians), and appoints by turn some of the town to wait and attend on him at dinner and supper. He has others to look to his horses, others to fish for him, others to bring him wood for his house spending, others to bring him food for his horses. Yet after all this attendance, he attends and waits on the friar that lives in the town, and doth nothing concerning the governing of the town and executing of justice but what the friar alloweth and adviseth to be done. There is also great service appointed of fishermen and other attendants in his house for this friar, who liveth as stately as any bishop. Most trades belonging to a well-settled commonwealth are here exercised by these Indians. As for herbage, and garden-fruits, and requisites, it hath whatsoever may be found, or desired in the city of Guatemala.

The church treasure is very great, there being many sodalities of Our Lady and other saints, which are enriched with crowns, and chains, and bracelets, besides the lamps, censers, and silver candlesticks belonging unto the altars. Upon Michaelmas Day is the chief fair and feast of the town, which is dedicated unto St. Michael, whither many merchants resort from Guatemala to buy and sell. In the afternoon, and the next day following, bull-baiting is the common sport for that feast with some Spaniards and Blackamoors on horseback, and other Indians on foot, who commonly being

[12] Petapa, "by the mat," from Aztec *petate*, "mat," and locative termination *pa*, "at," "by," or "in."

drunk, some venture, some lose their lives in the sport. Besides this general concourse of people every year at that time, there is every day at five o'clock in the afternoon a *tianguez* or market, upheld by the concourse of the Indians of the town among themselves. Besides the lake, there runneth by this town a river, which in places is easily waded over, and waters the fruits, gardens, and other plantations, and drives a mill which serves most of the valley to grind their wheat.[13]

Within a mile and a half of this town there is a rich *ingenio* or farm of sugar belonging to one Sebastián de Zavaleta, a Biscayan born, who came at first very poor into that country and served one of his countrymen; but with his good industry and pains he began to get a mule or two to traffic with about the country, till at last he increased his stock to a whole *recua* of mules. With this he grew so rich that he bought much land about Petapa, which he found to be very fit for sugar, and from thence was encouraged to build a princely house, whither the best of Guatemala do resort for their recreation. This man maketh a great deal of sugar for the country, and sends every year much to Spain. He keepeth at least threescore slaves of his own for the work of his farm, is very generous in housekeeping, and is thought to be worth above five hundred thousand ducats.

Within half a mile from him there is another farm of sugar, which is called but a *trapiche* belonging unto the Augustine friars of Guatemala, which keeps some twenty slaves. It is called a *trapiche* for that it grinds not the sugar cane with that device of the *ingenio*, but grinds a less quantity, and so makes not so much sugar as doth an *ingenio*. From hence three miles is the town of Amatitlán, near unto which standeth a greater *ingenio* of sugar than is that of Zavaleta, and is called the *ingenio* of one Anis, because he first founded it, but now it belongeth unto one Pedro Crespo, the postmaster of Guatemala. This *ingenio* seemed to be a little town by itself for the many cot-

[13] Fuentes y Guzmán gives the number of tributaries at Petapa as 602. The church, he says, was remarkable for both its construction and its decoration. It had excellent bells and a fine, neatly symmetrical and expensive reredos, and with lateral altars belonging to the various sodalities. The main altar had a frontal of hammered silver, and there were silver lamps, sets of altar hangings, processional crosses, chalices, cruets, and censers of fine workmanship. The adjacent convent, which the priest occupied, was large and an outstanding example of architecture.

tages and thatched houses of Blackamoor slaves which belong unto it, who may be above a hundred, men, women, and children. The chief dwelling house is strong and capacious, and able to entertain a hundred lodgers. These three farms of sugar standing so near unto Guatemala enrich the city much, and occasion great trading from it to Spain.

In the town of Amatitlán there live not so many Spaniards as in Petapa, yet there are in it more Indian families than in Petapa. The streets are more orderly made and are framed like a chequer board. They are wide, broad, plain, and all upon dust and sand. This town also enjoyeth the commodity of the lake, and furnisheth the city of Guatemala with fish upon the same day as does Petapa. And though it standeth out of the road-way, yet is almost as rich as Petapa. For the Indians of it get much by the concourse of common people and the gentry of Guatemala, who resort thither to certain baths of hot waters, which are judged and approved very wholesome for the body.

This town also getteth much by the salt which here is made, or rather gathered by the lake side, which every morning appeareth like a hoary frost upon the ground, and is taken up and purified by the Indians, and proves very white and good. Besides what they get by the salt, they get also by the *recuas* of mules in the valley, and about the country, which are brought to feed upon that salt earth a day, or half a day, until they be ready to burst (the owner paying sixpence a day for every mule), and it hath been found by experience that this makes them thrive and grow lusty and purgeth them better than any drench or blood-letting.

They have further great trading in cotton-wool, more abundance of fruits than Petapa, a fairer market-place with two extraordinary great elm-trees [ceibas?], under which the Indians daily meet at evening to buy and sell. The church of this town is as fair and beautiful as any about Guatemala, the riches and state whereof hath caused the Dominican friars since the year 1635 to make that place the head and priory over the other towns of the valley, and to build there a goodly and sumptuous cloister, in which in my time there was (for I told then most of it, and doubtless since it hath much increased) eighty thousand ducats laid up in a chest, with three locks, for the common expenses of the cloister.[14]

[14] The church was very beautiful and capacious, with sacristy, bell tower, and

Thus, my reader, I have led thee through the Valley of Mixco and Pinola, Petapa and Amatitlán, which yields to no other place belonging unto the dominions of Guatemala in riches and wealth, what with the great trading in it, the sheep and cattle, the abundance of mules, three farms of sugar, the great farms of corn and wheat, and churches' treasures. I may not forget yet a double wheat harvest (as I may well term it) in this valley. The first being of a little kind of wheat, which they call *trigo tremesino* (a word compounded in Spanish from these two words *tres meses,* or from the Latin *tre menses*) which after three months' sowing is ripe and ready and ready to cut down, and being sowed about the end of August, is commonly harvested about the end of November. Although in the smallness of it, it seems to have but a little flour, yet it yields as much as their other sorts of wheat, and makes as white bread, though it keep not so well as that which is made of other wheat, but soon groweth stale and hard. The other harvest, which is of two sorts of wheat, one called *rubio,* or red wheat, the other called *blanquilleo,* or white like *Candia* wheat, followeth soon after this first of *tremesino.* For presently after Christmas everyone begins to bring their sickles into the field, where they do not only reap their wheat, but instead of threshing it in barns, they cause it to be trod by mares enclosed within floors made on purpose in the fields. The wheat is trod out of the ears by the trampling of the mares, which are whipped round about the floors that they may not stand still, but tread it constantly and thoroughly. Then the mares being let out of the floors, the wheat is winnowed from the chaff, and put up clean into sacks, and from the field carried to the barns; but the chaff and most of the straw is left to rot in the fields, which they esteem as good as dunging.

Furthermore, they set all the fields on fire, burning the stubble that is left a little before the time of the first showers of rain, which with the ashes left after the burning fatteth the ground, and by them is held the best way to husband or dung their ground. Others that will sow a new and woody piece of land, cause the trees, though

organ, writes Fuentes y Guzmán, and the Priory, as it later became, consisted of magnificent cloistered buildings of white stone with a bluish tinge grouped around a garth. These buildings, for the raising of which Gage was partly responsible, are now in ruins.

timber trees, to be cut down, and sell not a stick of that wood (which is there so plentiful that they judge it would not quit their cost to carry it to Guatemala, though in England it would yield a thousand pounds). Instead, they let it lie and dry, and before the winter rain begins, they set on fire all the field, and burn that rich timber, with the ashes whereof that ground becomes so fat and fertile that where upon an acre we sow here three bushels of wheat, or upwards, they sow such ground so thin that they scarce dare venture a full bushel upon an acre, lest with too much spreading upon the ground it grow too thick, be lodged, and they lose their crop. The like they do unto the pasture of the valley. About the end of March it is short and withered and dry, and they also set it on fire, which being burnt causeth a dismal sight, and prospect of a black valley; but after the first two or three showers is puts on again its green and pleasant garment, inviting the cattle, sheep, lambs, goats, and kids, which for a while were driven away to other pasturing, to return and sport again, to feed and rest in its new flourishing bosom.

But now it is time I return again back to the other end of this valley, to the Río de las Vacas (from whence I have viewed the compass of it, and made my long digression from East to West, to the farthest town of Amatitlán) to shew thee, my reader, the little part of thy way remaining unto Guatemala. True it is, from the hermitage of Our Lady there is a straight way through the middle of the valley leading almost to Amatitlán, and then turning up a hill out of the valley on the right hand, but that hath many ascents and descents, bottoms, falls, and risings, and therefore is not the constant road, which from the hermitage pointed on the right hand, observing the town of Mixco, standing but five miles from Guatemala.

From Mixco the way lieth up a hill, and leadeth to a town of Indians somewhat bigger than Mixco, called San Lucas [Sacatepéquez], or St. Luke, a cold town, but exceeding rich. The temper and coldness of it hath made it the storehouse or granary for all the city; for whereas below in the valley the wheat will not keep long without musting and breeding a worm called *gorgojo*, such is the temper of this town of San Lucas, that in it the wheat will keep two or three years ready threshed, with a little turning now and then; and as it lieth will give and yield (as experience taught me there) so that he that hath laid up in that town two hundred bushels of wheat at the year's end shall find near upon two hundred and twenty bushels.

This town therefore receives from the valley most of the harvest, and is full of what we call barns, but there are called *trojas*, without floors, but raised up with stacks and boards a foot or two from the ground, and covered with mats, whereon is laid the wheat, and by some rich monopolists from the city is kept and hoarded two and three years, until they find their best opportunity to bring it out to sale, at the rate of their own will and pleasure. From hence to Guatemala there is but three little leagues, and one only *barranca*, or bottom, and on every side of the way little petty towns, which they call *milpas*,[15] consisting of some twenty cottages.

In the middle of the way is the top of a hill, which discovereth all the city, and standeth as overmastering of it, as if with a piece or two of ordnance it would keep all Guatemala in awe. But besides this hill, which is the wide and open road, there stand yet forwarder on the right and left hand other mountains which draw nearer to the city, and what this top peradventure with too much distance, is not able to do or reach, the others certainly would reach with cannon shot, and command that far commanding city. Down this hill the way lies broad and wide, and as open as is the way down Barnet or Highgate Hill; and at the bottom it is more straitened between the mountains, for the space of a bow-shot. This passage also is craggy by reason of stones and some small pieces of rocks which lie in a brook of water that descends from the mountains, and runs towards the city. But at a little hermitage called San Juan, the way opens itself again and sheweth Guatemala, welcoming the weary travellers with a pleasant prospect, and easing theirs, or their mules' or horses' feet with green walks and with a sandy and gravelly road unto the city. Guatemala never shut gate against any goer or comer, nor forbad their entrance with any fenced walls, or watchmen's jealous questions, but freely and gladly entertains them either by the back side of the Dominican's cloister, or by the church and nunnery called the Concepción. And thus, my reader, and countryman, I have brought and guided thee from the gulf unto Guatemala, showing what that way is most remarkable.

[15] Gage's thoughts were wandering. *Milpa*, as he well knew, means cultivated field.

I shall not now show thee any more of this city's dominions toward Nicaragua and the South (having already showed thee the way as far as Realejo) leaving that until I come to tell thee of my journey homewards, which I made that way. There remains yet the country of the Vera Paz and the way unto it to discover, and so to close this chapter. The Vera Paz is so called because the Indians of that country, hearing how the Spaniards had conquered Guatemala and the country round about, yielded themselves peaceably and without any resistance unto the government of Spain. This country formerly had a bishop to itself distinct from Guatemala, but now it made one bishopric with that. It is governed by an *Alcalde Mayor*, or High Justice, sent from Spain, with subordination unto the Court of Guatemala. The head or shire town of it is called Cobán, where is a cloister of Dominican friars, and the common place of residence of the *Alcalde Mayor*.

All this country as yet is not subdued by the Spaniards, who have now and then some strong encounters with the barbarous and heathen people, which lie between this country and Yucatán. Fain would the Spaniards conquer them, that they might make way through to Campin, a town [of Mopan-Maya Indians] belonging to Yucatán, and settle commerce and traffic by land with that country. It is thought this would be a great furtherance to the country and city of Guatemala, and a safer way to convey their goods to Havana than by the gulf, for oftentimes the ships that go from the gulf to Havana are met with by the Hollanders and surprised. But as yet the Spaniards have not been able to accomplish their design, because of the strong resistance of the heathen people. Yet there was a friar, a great acquaintance of mine, called Friar Francisco Morán, who ventured his life among those barbarians, and with two or three Indians went on foot through that country, until he came unto Campin, where he found a few Spaniards, who wondered at his courage and boldness in coming that way. This friar came back again to Cobán and Vera Paz, relating how the barbarians, hearing him speak their language and finding him kind, loving, and courteous to them, used him also kindly, fearing (as he said) that if they should kill him, the Spaniards would never let them be at rest and quiet until they had utterly destroyed them.

He related, when he came back, that the country which the barbarians inhabit is better than any part of the Vera Paz, which is sub-ject to the Spaniards, and spoke much of a valley where is a great lake, and about it a town of Indians, which he judged to be of at least twelve thousand inhabitants, the cottages lying a distance one from another.[16] This friar hath writ of this country, and hath gone to Spain to the Court to motion the conquering of it, for the profit and commodity that may ensue both to Guatemala and Yucatán, if a way were opened thither. But though on that side the country of the Vera Paz is still hemmed in by that heathen people, yet on the other side it hath free passage unto the gulf, and trades there when the ships do come. Then they carry fowls and what other provision the country affords to the ships, and bring thence wines and other Spanish wares unto Cobán. This country is very hilly and craggy, and though there be some big towns in it, they are not above three or four that are considerable.

The chief commodities are achiote (which is the best of all the country belonging to Guatemala) and cacao, cotton-wool, honey, *cañafistula,* and *zarzaparrilla,* great store of maize, but no wheat, much wax, plenty of fowls and birds of all colored feathers, where-with the Indians make some curious works, but not like unto those of Michoacán. Here also are abundance of parrots, apes, and mon-keys, which breed in the mountains. The way from Guatemala to this country is that which hitherto hath been spoken of from the gulf, as far as the town of San Lucas; and from thence the way keeps on the hills and mountains which lie on the side of the Valley of Mixco. These hills are called Sacatepéquez, (compounded of *Sacate* and *Tepec,* the latter signifying a hill, and the former, herb or grass, and thus joined they signify mountains of grass). Among them are these chief towns, first Santiago or St. James, a town of five hundred families; secondly, San Pedro or St. Peter, consisting of six hundred families; thirdly San Juan, or St. John, consisting also of at least six hundred families; and fourthly Santo Domingo Senaco, or St. Dominic of Senaco, being of three hundred families.

[16] Tayasal, on a small island in Lake Petén was the capital of the Itzá, last independent Maya town, until its conquest by a Spanish expedition from Yucatán in 1697. It is now called Flores after some forgotten hero of nineteenth-century Guatemala. Campin was on the Campin River, almost certainly the modern Monkey River, British Honduras.

These four towns are very rich. The two last are very cold; the two first are warmer, and there are about them many farms of corn and good wheat, besides the Indian maize. These Indians are somewhat of more courage than those of other towns, and in my time were like to rise up against the Spaniards for their unmerciful tyranny over them. The churches are exceeding rich; in the town of Santiago, there was living in my time one Indian, who for only vainglory had bestowed the worth of six thousand ducats upon that church, and yet afterwards this wretch was found to be a wizard and idolater.

These Indians get much money by letting out great tufts of feathers, which the Indians use in their dances upon the feasts of the dedication of their towns. For some of the great tufts may have at least three score long feathers of divers colors, and for every feather they charge half a real, besides what price they set to every feather if any should chance to be lost.[17]

From the town of San Juan, which is the furthest, the way lies plain and pleasant unto a little village of some twenty cottages, called San Raimundo or St. Raymond, from whence there is a good day's journey up and down *barrancas*, or bottoms unto a *rancho*, or lodge standing by a river side, which is the same river [Motagua] that passeth by the town of Acazabastlán spoken of before. From this is an ascent or a very craggy and rocky mountain, called the Mountain of Rabinal, where steps are cut in the very rocks for the mules' feet. Slipping on one or the other side, they fall surely down the rocks, breaking their necks and mangling all their limbs and joints; but this danger continueth not long nor extendeth above a league and a half, and in the top and worst of this danger there is the comfort of a goodly valley, called El Valle de San Nicolás, St. Nicholas' Valley, from an *estancia* called San Nicolás belonging to the Dominicans' cloister of Cobán.

This valley, though it cannot compare with that of Mixco and Pinola, yet next after it, it may well take place for only three things

---

[17] Gage probably refers to the highly valued tail-feathers of the quetzal, which were much used in pagan times by chiefs and religious leaders. At the time he was in Guatemala, the birds were still being trapped in the Alta Verapaz region of northern Guatemala for their tail-feathers. They are no longer used in the costumes of present-day dancers of the Guatemalan highlands.

considerable in it. The first is an *ingenio* of sugar, called San Jerón-imo, or St. Jerome, belonging unto the Dominicans' cloister of Guatemala, which indeed goeth beyond that of Amatitlán, both for abundance of sugar made there and sent by mules to Guatemala over that rocky mountain, and for multitude of slaves living in it under the command of two friars. It is also famed for the excellent horses bred there, which are incomparably the best of all the country of Guatemala for mettle and gallantry, and therefore (though mules are commonly used for burdens) are much desired and sought by the gallants and gentry of the city, who make it a great part of their honor to prance about the streets. The second thing in this valley is the *estancia* or farm of San Nicolás, which is as famous for breeding of mules as is San Jerónimo for horses. The third ornament to it is a town of [Quiché Maya] Indians, called Rabinal, of at least eight hundred families, which hath all that heart can wish for pleasure and life of man. It inclineth rather to heat than cold, but the heat is

moderate and much qualified with the many cool and shady walks.

There is not any Indian fruit which is not there to be found. There are, besides, the fruits of Spain, such as oranges, lemons, sweet and sour, citrons, pomegranates, grapes, figs, almonds, and dates. Only wheat is lacking, and that is not a want to those that like bread of wheat more than of maize, for in two days it is easily brought from the towns of Sacatepéquez. For flesh, the town hath beef, mutton, kid, fowls, turkeys, quails, partridges, rabbits, pheasants; for fish it hath a river running by the houses, which yieldeth plenty both great and small. For bravery, for feasting, for riding of horses, and shewing themselves in sports and pastimes, the Indians of this town are much like unto those of Chiapa of the Indians. My friend Friar Juan Bautista, after he had been Prior of many places, and especially of Chiapa and Guatemala, chose to live in this town to enjoy quietness, pleasure, and content; and in this town was I feasted by him in such a sumptuous, prodigal, and lavishing way as truly might make poor mendicant friars ashamed to come so near unto princes in vanity of life and diet.[18]

From this valley unto the Vera Paz, or Cobán, the head town of it, there is nothing considerable, save only one town more called San Cristóbal or St. Christopher, which enjoyeth now a pleasant lake, reported to be bottomless. Formerly there was no lake at all, but in a great earthquake the earth there opened and swallowed up many houses, leaving this lake which ever since hath continued. From hence to Cobán the ways are bad and mountainous, yet such as through the worst of them those country mules with heavy burdens easily go. And thus with my pen, reader, have I gone through most of the bounds and limits of Guatemala, which is more furnished with gallant towns of Indians than is any part of all America; and doubtless were the Indians warlike, industrious, active for war or weapons, no part in all America might be stronger in people than Guatemala. But they have been kept under and oppressed by the Spaniards, and no weapons are allowed them, not so much as their natural bows and arrows, much less guns, pistols, muskets, swords,

[18] More than two centuries later the priest in charge of Rabinal was the Abbé Brasseur de Bourbourg, who became one of the early authorities on the Mayas on returning to his native France. Partly from the Quiché he had learned at Rabinal he translated the great literary gem of aboriginal Guatemala, the *Popol Vuh*.

or pikes. Consequently their courage is gone, and their affections alienated from the Spaniards. So the Spaniards might very well fear that if their country should be invaded, the multitude of their Indian people would prove to them a multitude of enemies, either running away to another side; or if forced to help, they would be to them but as the help of so many flies.

15. Showing the condition, quality, fashion, and behavior of the Indians of the country of Guatemala since the Conquest, and especially of their feasts and yearly solemnities

⁓⁓⁓⁓ ⋈ ⁓⁓⁓⁓

THE CONDITION of the Indians of this country of Guatemala is as sad and as much to be pitied as of any Indians in America. I may say it is with them, in some sort, as it was with Israel in Egypt. Though it is true there ought not to be any comparison made betwixt the Israelities and the Indians, those being God's people, these not as yet; nevertheless, the comparison may well hold in the oppression of the one and the other, and in the manner and cause of the oppression. Israel was oppressed with bitterness, rigor, and hard bondage lest the people should multiply and increase too much. Certain it is, these Indians suffer great oppression from the Spaniards, live in great bitterness, are under hard bondage, and serve with great rigor; and all this because they are at least a thousand of them for one Spaniard. They daily multiply and increase, in children and wealth, and therefore are feared lest they should be too mighty, and either rise up of themselves, or join themselves to any enemy against their oppressors. Because of these fears and jealousies they are not allowed the use of any weapons or arms, no not even their bows and arrows, which their ancestors formerly used. So whereas the Spaniards are secured from any hurt or annoyance from them because they are unarmed, so any other nation that shall be encouraged to invade that land will also be secure from the Indians. Consequently, the Spaniards' own policy against the Indians may be their greatest ruin and destruction, for the abundance of their Indians would be of no help

214

to them, and they themselves (who out of their few towns and cities live but here and there, too thinly scattered upon so great and capacious a land) would be but a handful, and of that handful very few would be found able or fitting men, and those able men would do little without the help of guns and ordnance. If their own oppressed people, Blackamoors and Indians (which themselves have always feared), should side against them, soon would they be swallowed up both from within and from without.

By this it may easily appear how mistaken are those who say it is harder to conquer America now than in Cortés' time, for that there are now both Spaniards and Indians to fight against, and then there were none but bare and naked Indians. That I say is a false argument, for then there were Indians trained up in wars one against another, who knew well to use their bows and arrows, and darts, and other weapons, and were desperate in their fights and single combats, as may appear out of the histories of them. But now they are cowardized, oppressed, unarmed, soon frighted with the noise of a musket, nay with a sour and grim look of a Spaniard, so from them there is no fear.

Neither can there be anything to fear from the Spaniards, who from all the vast dominions of Guatemala are not able to raise five thousand able fighting men, nor to defend the many passages that lie open in several parts of that country, which the wider and greater it is might be advantageous to an enemy. While the Spaniard in one place might oppose his strength, in many other places his land might be overrun by a foreign nation. Nay, the land might be won by their own slaves the Blackamoors who doubtless to win their freedom would side against them in any such occasion. Lastly, the Creoles, who also are sore oppressed by them, would rejoice in such a day, and would yield, preferring to live with freedom and liberty under a foreign people rather than to be oppressed any longer by those of their own blood.

The miserable condition of the Indians of that country is such that though the kings of Spain have never yielded to what some would have, that they should be slaves, yet their lives are as full of bitterness as is the life of a slave. I myself have known some that have come home from toiling and moiling with Spaniards, after many blows, some wounds, and little or no wages, and who have sullenly and stubbornly lain down upon their beds, resolving to die rather than to live any longer a life so slavish. And they have refused to take either meat or drink or anything else comfortable and nourishing, which their wives have offered unto them, that so by pining and starving, they might consume themselves. Some I have by good persuasions encouraged to life rather than to a voluntary and willful death; others there have been that would not be persuaded, but in that willful way have died.

The Spaniards that live about that country (especially the farmers of the Valley of Mixco, Pinola, Petapa, Amatitlán, and those of the Sacatepéquez) allege that all their trading and farming is for the good of the commonwealth, and therefore, whereas there are not Spaniards enough for so ample and large a country to do all their work, and all are not able to buy slaves and Blackamoors, they stand in need of the Indians' help to serve them for their pay and hire. Therefore, a partition of Indian laborers is made every Monday, or Sunday in the afternoon, to the Spaniards, according to the farms they occupy, or according to their several employments, calling, and trading with mules, or any other way. For such and such a district there is named an officer, who is called *juez repartidor*, who according to a list made of every farm, house, and person, is to give so many Indians by the week. And here is a door opened to the President of Guatemala, and to the judges, to provide well for their menial servants, whom they commonly appoint for this office, which is thus performed by them. They name the town and place of their meeting upon Sunday or Monday, to the which themselves and the Spaniards of that district do resort.

The Indians of the several towns are ordered to have in readiness so many laborers as the Court of Guatemala hath appointed to be weekly taken out of such a town. These are conducted by an Indian officer to the town of general meeting. They come thither with their tools, their spades, shovels, bills, or axes, with their provision of victuals for a week (which are commonly some dry cakes of maize, puddings of *frijoles*, or French beans, and a little chile or biting long pepper, or a bit of cold meat for the first day or two) and with beds on their backs (which is only a coarse woollen mantle to wrap about them when they lie on the bare ground). Then they are shut up in the town-house, some with blows, some with spurnings, some with boxes on the ear, if presently they go not in.

Now all being gathered together, and the house filled with them, the *juez repartidor*, or officer, calls by the order of the list such and such a Spaniard, and also calls out of the house so many Indians as by the Court are commanded to be given him (some are allowed three, some four, some ten, some fifteen, some twenty, according to their employments) and delivereth unto the Spaniard his Indians, and so to all the rest, till they be all served. When they receive their Indians, they take from them their tools or mantles, to make sure that they do not run away; and for every Indian delivered unto them, they give unto the *juez repartidor*, or officer, for his fees, half a real, which is threepence. Yearly this amounts to a great deal of money, for some officers make a partition or distribution of four hundred, some of two hundred, some of three hundred Indians every week, and carrieth home with him so many half hundred reals for one or half a day's work.

If complaint be made by any Spaniard that such and such an Indian ran away and served him not the week past, the Indian is brought and securely tied to a post by his hands in the market-place, and there is whipped upon his bare back. But if the poor Indian complain that the Spaniards cozened and cheated him of his shovel, axe, bill, mantle, or wages, no justice shall be executed against the cheating Spaniard, neither shall the Indian be righted, though it is true the order runs equally in favor of both Indian and Spaniard.

Thus the poor Indians are sold for threepence apiece for a whole week's slavery, and are not permitted to go home at nights unto their wives, though their work lie not above a mile from the town where they live. Nay, some are carried ten or twelve miles from their home, and they may not return till Saturday night late, and must that week do whatsoever their master pleaseth to command them. The wages appointed them will scarce find them meat and drink, for they are not allowed a real a day, which is but sixpence, but for six days' work and diet they are to have five reals, which is half a crown, and with that they are to find themselves. This same order is observed in the city of Guatemala, and towns of Spaniards, where every family that wants the service of an Indian or Indians, though it be but to fetch water and wood on their backs or to go of errands, is allowed the like service from the nearest Indian towns.

It would grieve a Christian's heart to see how some cruel Spaniards in that week's service wrong and abuse those poor wretches. Some visit their wives at home, whilst their poor husbands are digging and delving; others whip them for their slow working; others wound them with their swords, or break their heads for some reasonable and well-grounded answer in their own behalf; others steal from them their tools; others cheat them of half. Some even cheat them of all their wages, alleging their service cost them half a real, and yet their work is not well performed. I knew some who made a common practice of this, when their wheat was sown, and they had little for the Indians to do. They would have as many as were due unto their farm, and on Monday and Tuesday would make them cut and bring on their backs as much wood as they needed all that week. Then at noon, on Wednesday, knowing the great desire of the Indians to go home to their wives, for the which they would give anything, they would say unto them: "What will you give me now, if I let you go home to do your own work?" Whereunto the Indians would joyfully answer, some that they would give a real, others two reals. This the Spaniards would take and send them home, and so they would have much work done, wood to serve their house a week, and as much money as would buy them meat and cacao for chocolate for two weeks. Thus from the poor Indians do those unconscionable Spaniards practice a cheap and lazy way of living. Others will sell them away for that week unto a neighbor who needs laborers, demanding reals apiece for every Indian, which he that buyeth them will be sure to defray out of their wages.

Similarly, are they in a slavish bondage and readiness for all passengers and travellers, who in any town may demand as many Indians as he needs to go to the next town with his mules, or to carry on their backs a heavy burden as he shall need. Then at the journey's end he will pick some quarrel with them, and so send them back with blows and stripes without any pay at all. They will make those wretches carry on their backs a *petaca*, or leathern trunk, and chest of above a hundredweight a whole day, nay, some two or three days together. This they do by tying the chest on each side with ropes, having a broad leather in the middle, which they cross over the forepart of their head, or over their forehead, hanging thus the weight upon their heads and brows. By the end of the journey this makes the blood stick in the foreheads of some, galling and pulling off the skin, and marking them in the fore-top of their heads. So these carriers, who are called *tamemes*, are easily known in a town by their baldness, that leather girt having worn off all their hair.[1] Despite these hard usages, yet those poor people make shift to live amongst the Spaniards, but with anguish of heart they still cry out to God for justice, and for liberty.

Their only comfort is in their priests and friars, who many times do quiet them when they would rise up in mutiny, and for their own ends do often prevail over them with fair and cunning persuasions, to bear and suffer for God's sake, and for the good of the commonwealth, that hard task and service which is laid upon them. And though in all seasons, wet and dry, cold and hot, and in all ways, plain and mountainous, green and dirty, dusty and stony, they must perform this hard service to their commanding masters, their apparel and clothing is but such as may cover the nakedness of their body, nay, in some it is such torn rags as will not cover half their nakedness.

Their ordinary clothing is a pair of linen or woollen drawers broad and open at the knees, without shoes (though in their journeys some will put on leathern sandals to keep the soles of their feet) or stockings, without any doublet, a short coarse shirt, which reacheth a little below their waist, and serves more for a doublet than for a shirt, and for a cloak a woollen or linen mantle (called *ayate*) tied with a knot over one shoulder, hanging down on the other side almost to the ground. They wear also a twelvepenny or two shilling hat, which after one good shower of rain like paper falls about their necks and eyes. Their bed they carry sometimes about them, which is that woollen mantle wherewith they wrap themselves about at night, taking off their shirt and drawers, which they lay under their head for a pillow; some will carry with them a short, light mat to lie on, but those that carry it not with them, if they cannot borrow one of a neighbor, lie as willingly in their mantle upon the bare ground as a gentleman in England upon a soft down-bed, and thus

[1] There is exaggeration here. The Indians still carry very heavy loads by a tumpline across the forehead, but I have never seen or heard of foreheads bleeding as a result.

do they soundly sleep and loudly snort after a day's work, or after a day's journey with a hundredweight upon their backs.

Those that are of the better sort, and richer, and who are not employed as *tamemes* to carry burdens or as laborers to work for Spaniards, but keep at home on their own farms, or following their own mules about the country, or following their trades and callings in their shops, or governing the towns, as *alcaldes* or *alguaciles*, officers of justice, may go a little better apparelled, but after the same manner. For some will have their drawers with a lace at the bottom, or wrought with some colored silk or crewel, so likewise the mantle about them shall have either a lace, or some work of birds on it.[2] Some will wear a cut linen doublet, others shoes, but very few stockings or bands about their necks. And for their beds, the best Indian governor or the richest, who may be worth four or five thousand ducats, will have little more than the poor *tamemes,* for they lie upon boards, or canes bound together, and raised from the ground. On these they lay a broad and handsome mat, and at their heads for man and wife two little stumps of wood for bolsters, whereon they lay their shirts and mantles and other clothes for pillows, covering themselves with a broader blanket than is their mantle, and thus hardly would Don Bernabe de Guzmán, the governor of Petapa, lie, and so do all the best of them.

The women's attire is cheap and soon put on, for most of them also go barefoot although the richer and better sort wear shoes with broad ribbons for shoe-strings. For a petticoat they tie about their waist a woollen mantle, which in the better sort is wrought with divers colors, but not sewed at all, pleated, or gathered in, but as they tie it with a list about them. They wear no shift next their body, but cover their nakedness with a kind of surplice (which they call *huipil*) which hangs loose from their shoulders down a little below their waist, with open short sleeves, which cover half their arms. This *huipil* is curiously wrought, especially in the bosom, with cotton, or feathers.

The richer sort of them wear bracelets and bobs about their wrists and necks; their hair is gathered up with fillets, without any coif or covering, except it be the better sort. When they go to church or

---

[2] Birds are still commonly brocaded on women's *huipils* and on the square cloths both men and women use, but the sleeveless mantle is no longer used, nor is linen worn.

abroad, they put upon their heads a veil of linen, which hangeth almost to the ground, and this is what costs them most of all their attire, for commonly it is of Holland or some good linen brought from Spain, or fine linen brought from China, which the better sort wear with a lace about. When they are at home at work, they commonly take off their *huipil*, or surplice, discovering the nakedness of their breasts and body. They lie also in their beds as do their husbands, wrapped up only with a mantle, or with a blanket.

Their houses are but poor thatched cottages, without any upper rooms, but commonly only one or two rooms below. They dress their meat in the middle of one, and they make a compass for fire with two or three stones, without any chimney to convey the smoke away. This spreadeth itself about the room and filleth the thatch and the rafters so with soot that all the room seemeth to be a chimney. The next room, where sometimes are four or five beds according to the family, is also not free from smoke and blackness. The poorer sort have but one room, where they eat, dress their meat, and sleep. Few there are that set any locks upon their doors, for they fear no robbing nor stealing, neither have they in their houses much to lose, earthen pots, and pans, and dishes, and cups to drink their chocolate being the chief commodities in their house. There is scarce any house which hath not also in the yard a stew,[3] wherein they bathe themselves with hot water, which is their chief physic when they feel themselves distempered.

Among themselves they are in every town divided into tribes, which have one chief head. All that belong unto that tribe do resort to him in any difficult matters, and he is bound to aid, protect, defend, counsel, and appear for the rest of his tribe before the officers of justice in any wrong that is like to be done unto them.

When any is to be married, the father of the son that is to take a wife out of another tribe goeth unto the head of his tribe to give him warning of his son's marriage with such a maid. Then that head meets with the head of the maid's tribe, and they confer about it. The business commonly is in debate a quarter of a year; all which time the parents of the youth or man are with gifts to buy the maid. They have to pay for all that is spent in eating and drinking when the heads of the two tribes meet with the rest of the kindred of each

[3] Sweat house, still general in Indian villages of the Guatemalan highlands.

side, and sometimes they sit in conference a whole day, or most of a night. After many days and nights thus spent, and after a full trial has been made of the affection on one side and the other, if they chance to disagree about the marriage, then must the tribe and parents of the maid restore all that the other side hath spent and given. They give no portions with their daughters, but when they die, their goods and lands are equally divided among their sons.

If anyone want a house to live in, or wishes to repair and thatch his house anew, notice is given to the heads of the tribes, who warn all the town to come to help in the work. Everyone has to bring a bundle of straw and other materials, so that in one day with the help of many they finish a house, without any charges more than of chocolate, which they minister in great cups as big as will hold above a pint. They do not add any costly materials, as do the Spaniards, save a little aniseed and chile, or Indian pepper; or else they half fill the cup with *atole,* and pour upon it as much chocolate as will fill the cup and color it.

In their diet the poorer sort are limited many times to a dish of *frijoles,* or Turkey beans, either black of white (which are there in very great abundance, and are kept dry for all the year) boiled with chile, and if they can have this, they are well satisfied. With these beans they make also dumplings, first boiling the bean a little, and then mingling it with a mass of maize, as we do mingle currants in our cakes. Then they boil again the *frijoles* with the dumpling of maize mass, and so eat it hot, or keep it cold. This and all whatsoever else they eat, they either eat it with green biting chile, or else they dip it in water and salt, wherein is bruised some of that chile. But if their means will not reach to *frijoles,* their ordinary fare and diet is their *tortillas* (so they call thin round cakes made of maize dough). These they eat hot from an earthen pan, whereon they are soon baked with one turning over the fire, and they eat them alone either with chile and salt, and dipping them in water and salt with a little bruised chile.

When their maize is green and tender, they boil some of those whole stalks or clusters, whereon the maize groweth with the leaf about, and so casting a little salt about it, they eat it. I have often eat of this, and found it as dainty as our young green peas, and very nourishing, but it much increaseth the blood. Also of this green and tender maize they make a furmety, boiling the maize in some of the milk which they have first taken out of it by bruising it. The poorest Indian never lacks this diet, and is well satisfied as long as his belly is thoroughly filled.

Even the poorest that live in towns where meat is sold will do their best when they come from work on Saturday night to buy a half-real or a real worth of fresh meat to eat on the Lord's day. Some will buy a good deal at once, and keep it long by dressing it into *tasajos*, which are bundles of flesh, rolled up and tied fast. This they do when, for example, they have sliced off from the bone of a leg of beef all the flesh, cutting it in long thin pieces like a line, or rope. Then they take the flesh and salt it (being sliced and thinly cut, it soon takes salt), and hang it up in their yards like a line from post to post, or from tree to tree, to dry in the wind for a whole week. Then they hang it in the smoke another week, and after roll it up in small bundles, which become as hard as a stone, and as they need it they wash it, boil it and eat it.

This is America's powdered beef, which they call *tasajo*, whereof I have often eaten, and the Spaniards eat much of it, especially those that trade about the country with mules. Nay, this *tasajo* is a great commodity, and hath made many a Spaniard rich. They carry a mule or two laden with these *tasajos* in small parcels and bundles to those towns where no flesh at all is sold, and there they exchange them for other commodities among the Indians, receiving peradventure for one *tasajo* or bundle (which cost them but the half part of a farthing) as much cacao as in other places they sell for a real or sixpence. The richer sort of people will fare better, for if there be fish or flesh to be had, they will have it, and east most greedily of it, and will not spare their fowls and turkeys from their own bellies.

The Indians also will now and then get a wild deer, shooting it with their bows and arrows. When they have killed it, they let it lie in the wood in some hole or bottom covered with leaves for the space of about a week, until it stinks and begins to be full of worms; then they bring it home, cut it out into joints, and parboil it with an herb which groweth there somewhat like unto our tansy, which they say sweeteneth it again, and maketh the flesh eat tender, and as white as a piece of turkey. Next they hang up the parboiled joints in the smoke for awhile, and then boil it again, and then they eat it, usually dressed with red Indian pepper. I have sometimes eaten this venison of America, and found it white and short, but I never durst be too bold with it, not that I found any evil taste in it, but that the apprehension of the worms and maggots which formerly had been in it troubled much my stomach.

These Indians that have little to do at home, and are not employed in the weekly service under the Spaniards, will look carefully for hedgehogs, which are just like unto ours, though certainly ours are not meat for any Christian. They are full of pricks and bristles like ours, and are found in woods and fields, living in holes, and as they say feed upon nothing but ants and their eggs, and upon dry rotten sticks, herbs, and roots. Of these the Indians eat much, the flesh being as white and sweet as a rabbit, and as fat as is a January hen kept up and fatted in a coop. I have also eaten of this meat, and confess it is a dainty dish there, though I will not say the same of a hedgehog here. What here may be poison, there may be good and lawful meat, by some accidental difference in the creature itself, and in that which it feeds upon, or in the temper of the air and climate.

Not only the Indians but the best of the Spaniards feed on this meat, and it is so much esteemed that because they are commonly found in Lent, the Spaniards will not be deprived of it, but do eat it also then, alleging that it is not flesh (though in fatness and in taste and in all like unto flesh), for that the animal feeds not upon anything that is very nourishing, but chiefly upon ants' eggs, and dry sticks. It is a great point of controversy amongst their divines, some hold it lawful, others unlawful for that time; it seems the pricks and bristles of the Indian hedgehog prick their consciences with a foolish scruple.

Another kind of meat they feed much on is called *iguana*; of these, some are found in the waters, others upon the land. They are longer than a rabbit, and like unto a scorpion, with green or black scales on their backs. Those upon the land run very fast, like lizards, climb up trees like squirrels, and breed in the roots of trees or in stone walls. The sight of them is enough to affright one. Yet when they are dressed and stewed in broth with a little spice, they make a dainty broth, and eat also as white as a rabbit; nay, the middle bone is made just like the backbone of a rabbit. They are dangerous meat, if not thoroughly boiled, and they had almost cost me my life for eating too much of them, when they had not been stewed enough. There are also many water and land tortoises, which the Indians find for themselves and the Spaniards also relish them.

The Indians generally are much given to drinking, and if they have nothing else, they drink of their poor and simple chocolate, without sugar or many compounds, or of *atole*, until their bellies be ready to burst. But if they can get any drink that will make them mad drunk, they will not give it over as long as a drop is left or a penny remains in their purse to purchase it. Among themselves they make drinks far stronger than wine. These they confection in those great jars that come from Spain. They put in them a little water, and fill up the jar with some molasses or juice of the sugar-cane, or some honey to sweeten it. Then, to strengthen it, they put in roots and leaves of tobacco, with other kinds of roots which grow there and which they know to be strong in operation. Nay, to my knowledge, in some places they have put in a live toad, and closed up the jar for a fortnight or a month, till all that they have put in be thoroughly steeped, the toad consumed, and the drink well strengthened. Then they open it, and call their friends to drink it. Commonly they hold their drinking bouts at night, lest the priest in the town should have notice of them, and they never leave off until they be mad and raging drunk.

This drink they call *chicha*. It stinketh most filthily, and certainly is the cause of many Indians' death, especially where they use the toad's poison with it. Once, when I was living in Mixco, I was informed of a great meeting that was appointed in an Indian's house. I took with me the officers of justice of the town to search the house, and I found four jars of *chicha* not yet opened. I caused them to be taken out and broken in the street before his door, and the filthy *chicha* to be poured out. It left such a stinking scent in my nostrils, that with the smell of it, or apprehension of its loathsomeness, I fell to vomiting, and continued sick almost a whole week after.

The Spaniards, knowing this inclination of the Indians to drunkenness, do much abuse and wrong them. There is a strict order against selling wine in an Indian town, with a fine and forfeiture of the wine as punishment. Yet the baser and poorer sort of Spaniards will go out from Guatemala to the towns of Indians about, and carry such wine to sell and inebriate the natives as may be very advantageous to themselves. For of one jar of wine they will make two at least, confectioning it with honey and water, and other strong drugs which are cheap to them, and strongly operative upon the poor and weak Indians' heads. This they will sell at the price current for Spanish wine, and they use such pint and quart measures as never were allowed by justice order, but were invented by themselves. With such wine they soon intoxicate the poor Indians, and when they have made them drunk, then they will cheat them more, making them pay double for their quart measure; and when they see they can drink no more, then they will cause them to lie down and sleep, and in the meanwhile will pick their pockets.

This is a common sin among those Spaniards of Guatemala, and much practiced in the city upon the Indians, when they come thither to buy or sell. Those that keep the *bodegones* (the houses that sell wine, although they are no better than a chandler's shop, for besides wine they sell candles, fish, salt, cheese, and bacon) will commonly entice in the Indians, and make them drunk, and then pick their pockets, and turn them out of doors with blows and stripes, if they will not quietly depart. There was in Guatemala in my time one of these shopkeepers of wine and small ware, named Juan Ramos, who by thus cheating and tippling poor Indians was worth, it was generally reported, two hundred thousand ducats, and in my time gave eight thousand ducats with a daughter that was married. He would call in any Indian who passed his door and play upon him as aforesaid. In my time a Spanish farmer, neighbor of mine in the Valley of Mixco, chanced to send to Guatemala his Indian servants with half a dozen mules laden with wheat. He had agreed on the price beforehand with the merchant, and ordered the money to be sent unto him by his servant (whom he had kept six years, and ever found him trusty). The wheat was delivered, and the money received—it amounted to ten pounds sixteen shillings, every mule carrying six bushels, at twelve reals a bushel, as was then the price. Afterwards, the Indian, walking with a mate of his along the streets to buy some small commodities, passed by Juan Ramos' shop or *bodegon*. Ramos, enticing him and his mate in, soon tripped up their heels with a little confectioned wine for that purpose, and took away all the money entrusted to the Indian, and beat them out of his house. The Indian that received the money, riding home drunk, fell from his mule and broke his neck; the other got home without his mate or money. The farmer prosecuted Juan Ramos in the court for his money, but Ramos, being rich and abler to bribe than the farmer, got off very well, as he had done formerly in almost similar cases. To make drunk, rob, and occasion the poor Indian's death those Spaniards consider merely peccadilloes, and the death of an Indian is no more regarded nor vindicated than the death of a sheep or bullock that falls into a pit.

Thus having spoken of apparel, houses, eating, and drinking, it remains that I say somewhat of their civility, and the religion of those who lived under the government of the Spaniards. From the Spaniards they have borrowed their civil government, and in all towns they have one or two *alcaldes*, with more or less *regidores* (who are as aldermen or jurats amongst us), and some *alguaciles*, more or less, who are as constables, to execute the orders of the *alcalde* (who is a mayor) with his brethren. In towns of three or four hundred families or upwards, there are commonly two *alcaldes*, six *regidores*, two *alguaciles mayores*, and six under, or petty, *alguaciles*. Some towns are privileged with an Indian governor, who is above the *alcaldes* and all the rest of the officers. These are changed every year by new election, and are chosen by the Indians themselves, who take their turns by the tribes or kindreds, whereby they are divided.

Their offices begin on New Year's Day, and after that day their election is carried to the city of Guatemala (if in that district it be made) or else to the heads of justice, or Spanish governors of the several provinces. The latter confirm the new election, and take account of the last year's expenses made by the other officers, who carry with them their town-book of accounts; and therefore for this purpose every town hath a clerk, or scrivener, called *escribano*. Commonly he continues many years in his office, by reason of the paucity and unfitness of Indian scriveners who are able to bear such a charge. This clerk hath many fees for his writings and informations and accounts, as have the Spaniards, but the money and bribes are but a small matter because of the poverty of the Indians. The Governor, being some chief man among the Indians, is also commonly continued many years, unless there are complaints of his misdemeanors or the Indians in general do all stomach [dislike] him.

Thus these duly appointed governors may execute justice upon all such Indians of their town as do notoriously and scandalously offend. They may imprison, fine, whip, and banish, but they may not hang and quarter, but must remit such cases to the Spanish governor. So likewise if a Spaniard passing by the town, or living in it, do trouble the peace, and misdemean himself, they lay hold on him, and send him to the next Spanish justice, with a full information of his offense, but they may not fine him or keep him above one night in prison. Yet they dare not execute this order they have against Spaniards, for a whole town standeth in awe of one Spaniard. And though he never so heinously offend and be unruly, with oaths, threatenings, and drawing of his sword, he maketh them quake and tremble. They do not presume to touch him, for they know if they do they shall have the worst, either by blows, or by some misinformation which he will give against them.

This hath been very often tried, for where Indians have by virtue of their order endeavored to curb an unruly Spaniard in their town, some of them have been wounded, others beaten, and when they have carried the Spaniard before a Spanish justice and governor, he has pleaded that what he had done was in his own defense, or for his King and Sovereign, and that the Indians would have killed him, and began to mutiny all together against the Spanish authority and government. He will charge that they would not serve him with what he needed for his way and journey; that they would not be slaves to give him or any Spaniard any attendance; and that they would make an end of him, and of all the Spaniards. With these and such-like false and lying misinformations, the unruly Spaniards have often been believed, and too much upheld in their rude and uncivil misdemeanors, and the Indians bitterly curbed and punished. Indeed, the Indians have been told in such cases that if they had been killed for their mutiny and rebellion against the King and his best subjects, it was what they deserved, and that if they gave not attendance unto the Spaniards that passed by their town, their houses should be fired, and they and their children utterly consumed. With such-like answers from the justices, and full credit given to what any base Spaniard shall inform against them, the poor Indians are fain to put up with all wrongs done unto them, not daring to meddle with any Spaniard, be he never so unruly, despite that order which they have against them.

Amongst themselves, if any complaint be made against any Indian, they dare not meddle with him until they call all his kindred, and especially the head of that tribe to which he belongs. If he and the rest together find him to deserve imprisonment or whipping or any other punishment, then the officers of justices, the *alcaldes* or mayors, and their brethren the jurats inflict upon him that punishment which all shall agree upon. Yet after judgment and sentence have been given, they have another, which is their last appeal, if they please, and that is to their priest and friar, who liveth in their town, by whom they will sometimes be judged, and undergo what punishment he shall think fittest.

Therefore, they often resort in points of justice to the church, thinking the priest knoweth more of law and equity than they themselves. Sometimes he reverseth the judgment given in the town-house, blaming the officers for their partiality and passion against their poor brother, and setting free the party judged by them. The priests often do this if the Indian belongs to the Church or to the service of their house, or has other relation to them, peradventure for his wife's sake, whom either they affect or employ in washing or making their chocolate. They and their husbands may live lawless as long as the priest is in the town. And if, taking advantage of the priest's absence, the Indian authorities call them to trial for any misdemeanor, and whip, fine, or imprison, when the priest returns, they shall be sure to hear of it, and smart for it, yea, and the officers themselves peradventure be whipped in the church, by the priest's order and appointment. Against the priest they dare not speak, but willingly accept what stripes and punishment he layeth upon them, judging his wisdom, sentence, and punishing hand the wisdom, sentence, and hand of God. And, as they have been taught that He is over all princes, judges, and worldly officers, so likewise they believe that his priests and ministers are above their officers and above all worldly power and authority.

It happened to me when I was living in the town of Mixco, that an Indian, being condemned to be whipped for some disorders which he had committed, would not yield to the sentence, but appealed to me, saying he would have his stripes in the church, and by my order, for, he said, his whipping thus coming from the hand of God would do him good. When he was brought unto me, I could not reverse the Indian's judgment, for it was just, and so caused him to be whipped. He took it very patiently and merrily, and after kissed my hands and gave me an offering of money for the good he said I had done unto his soul.

Besides this civility of justice amongst them, the Indians live as in other civil and politic and well-governed commonwealths, for in most of their towns there are some that profess such trades as are practiced among Spaniards. There are amongst them smiths, tailors, carpenters, masons, shoemakers, and the like. It was my fortune to set upon a hard and difficult building in a church of Mixco, where I desired to make a very broad and capacious vault over the chapel, which was the harder to be finished in a round circumference, because it depended upon a triangle. Yet for this work I sought none but Indians, some of the town, some from other places, and they made it so complete that the best and skillfullest workmen among the Spaniards had enough to wonder at it. So are most of their churches vaulted on the top, and all by Indians.

In my time they build a new cloister in the town of Amatitlán, which they finished with many arches of stone both in the lower walks and in the upper galleries, with as much perfection as the best cloister of Guatemala built by the Spaniard. Were they more encouraged by the Spaniards and taught better principles both for soul and body, doubtless they would among themselves make a very good commonwealth. They are much inclined to painting, and most of the pictures and altars of the country towns are their workmanship. In most of their towns they have a school, where they are taught to read, to sing, and some to write. To the church there belong, according to the size of the town, so many singers, and trumpeters, and waits, over whom the priest hath one officer, who is called *fiscal*.

The *fiscal* has a white staff with a little silver cross on the top to represent the church and shew that he is the priest's clerk and officer. When any case is brought to be examined by the priest, this *fiscal* or clerk executes justice by the priest's order. He must be one that can read and write, and is commonly the master of music. He is bound upon the Lord's Day and other saints' days, to gather to the church before and after service all the young youths and maids, and to teach them the prayers, sacraments, commandments, and other points of catechism allowed by the Church of Rome. In the morning he and the other musicians, at the sound of the bell, are bound to come to church to sing and officiate at Mass, which in many towns they perform with organs and other musical instruments, I have already observed, as well as Spaniards. So likewise at evening at five of the clock they are again to resort to the church, when the bell calleth, to sing prayers, which they call *completas*, or completory [complines], with *Salve Regina*, a prayer to the Virgin Mary.

This *fiscal* is a great man in the town, and bears more sway than the mayors, jurats, and other officers of justice, and, when the priest so wishes, attends him, goes about his errands, and appoints such as are to wait on him when he rides out of town. Both he and all that belong to the church are exempted from the common weekly service of the Spaniards, and from giving attendance to travellers, and from other officers of justice. But they have to attend with their waits, trumpets, and music, upon any great man or priest that comes to their town, and to make arches with boughs and flowers in the streets for their entertainment.

In addition, those who belong to the service of the priest's house are exempt from the Spaniards' service. The priest hath change of servants by the week, and they take their turns so that they may have a week or two to spare to do their own work. If it be a great town, he hath three cooks allowed him; if a small town, but two. The cooks are men who take turns in serving. For any occasion of feasting, all come. So likewise the priest hath two or three more (whom they call *chahal*) as butlers. They keep whatsoever provisions is in the house under lock and key, and give to the cook what the priest appointeth to be dressed for his dinner or supper. They keep the table-cloths, napkins, dishes, and trenchers, and lay the cloth, and take away, and wait at table. The priest hath besides three or four, and in great towns half a dozen, boys to do his errands, wait at table, and sleep in the house all the week by their turns. They and the cooks and butlers dine and sup constantly in the priest's house and at his charge. He hath also at dinner and supper times the attendance of some old women (who also take their turns) to oversee half a dozen young maids who meet next to the priest's house to make him and his family *tortillas* or cakes of maize, which the boys bring hot to the table by half a dozen at a time.

Besides these servants, if the priest has a garden, he is allowed two or three gardeners, and for his stable, at least half a dozen Indians, who morning and evening are to bring him *zacate* (as they call it) or herb and grass for his mules or horses. These do not diet in the house, but the grooms of the stable, who come at morning, noon, and evening (and therefore are three or four to change) or at any time that the priest will ride out, and the gardeners, when they are at work, dine and sup at the priest's charges. So sometimes in great towns the priest has above a dozen to feed and provide for.

There are besides belonging to the church and so exempt from the weekly attendance upon the Spaniards two or three Indians called sacristans, who have care of the vestry and copes or altars for Mass. Also, every company or sodality of the saints or of the Virgin has two or three *mayordomos* who collect from the town alms for the maintaining of the sodality. They also gather eggs about the town for the priest every week, and give him an account of their gatherings, and allow him every month, or fortnight, two crowns for a Mass to be sung to the saint.

If there be any fishing place near the town, the priest also is allowed three or four, and in some places half a dozen, Indians to fish for him. Besides the offerings in the church, and many other offerings which they bring whensoever they come to speak to the priest or to confess with him, or for a saint's feast to be celebrated, and besides their tithes of everything, there is a monthly mainte-nance in money allowed the priest, and brought to him by the *alcaldes*, or mayors, and jurats. This he has to write a receipt for in a book of the town's expenses. This maintenance, although it be allowed by the Spanish magistrate and paid in the King's name for the preaching of the Gospel, yet it comes out of the poor Indians' purses and labor, and is either gathered about the town, or taken out of the tribute which they pay unto the King, or from a common plot of ground which with the help of all is sowed and the produce gathered in and sold for that purpose.

All the towns in America, which are civilized and under the Span-ish government, belong either to the Crown, or to some other lords, whom they call *encomenderos*, and to whom they pay a yearly tribute. Those that are tenants to their lords or *encomenderos* (who commonly are such as descend from the first conquerors) pay also to the King some small tribute in money, besides what they pay in other kind of commodities and in money also to their own *encomendero*. There is no town so poor, where every married Indian doth not pay at the least in money four reals a year for tribute to the King, besides other four reals to his lord or *encomendero*. And if the town pay only to the King, they pay at least six and in some places eight reals by statute, besides what other commodities are common to the town or country where they live, as maize, which is paid in all towns, honey, turkeys, fowls, salt, cacao, and mantles of cotton-wool. Those subject to an *encomendero* pay like commodities, but they pay only money, not commodities, to the King.

The mantles of tribute are much esteemed, for they are choice ones, and of a bigger size than others, so likewise is the tribute of cacao, *achiote*, and cochineal, where it is paid, for the best is set apart for the tribute; and if the Indians bring that which is not prime good, they shall surely be lashed, and sent back for better. The heads of the several tribes have care to gather the tribute, and to deliver it to the *alcaldes* and *regidores*, mayors and jurats, who carry it either to the King's Exchequer in the city, or to the nearest Spanish justice, if it belong to the King, or to the *encomendero* of the town. In nothing I ever perceived the Spaniards merciful and indulgent unto the Indians, except that if an Indian be very weak, poor, and sickly and not able to work, or threescore and ten years of age, he is freed from paying any tribute. Some towns which can prove themselves to have descended from Tlaxcala, or from certain tribes or families of or about Mexico, who helped the first Spaniards in the conquest of that country, are exempt from tribute.

As for their carriage and behavior, the Indians are very courteous and loving. They are of a timorous nature, and willing to serve and to obey, and to do good, if they be drawn by love. Where they are too much tyrannized, they are dogged, unwilling to please, or to work, and will choose rather strangling and death than life. They are very trusty, and never were known to commit any robbery of importance, so that the Spaniards, though they have bags of gold about them, do not fear to abide with them in a wilderness all night. They are very secretive and will not reveal anything against their own natives, or a Spaniard's credit and reputation if they be any way affected to him. But above all, to their priest they are very respective, and when they come to speak to him, they put on their best clothes, and study their compliments and words to please him.

They are very abundant in their expressions, and full of circumlocutions adorned with parables and similes to express their mind and intention. I have often sat still for the space of an hour, only hearing some old women make their speeches unto me, with so many elegancies in their tongue (which in English would be nonsense, or barbarous expressions) as would make me wonder. And I learned by their speeches more of their language than by any other endeavor or study of mine own. And if I could reply unto them in the like phrases and expressions (which I would often endeavor) I should be sure to win their hearts, and get anything from them.

As for their religion, they are outwardly such as the Spaniards, but inwardly they are slow to believe that which is above sense, nature, and the visible sight of the eye. Many of them to this day do incline to worship idols of stocks and stones, and are given to much superstition concerning the observation of cross-ways and meeting of beasts in them, the flying of birds, and their appearing and singing near their houses at such and such times.

Many are given to witchcraft, and are deluded by the devil to believe that their life dependeth upon the life of such and such a beast (which they take unto them as their familiar spirit) and think that when that beast dieth, they must die. When he is chased, their hearts pant; when he is faint, they are faint. Nay, it happens that by the devil's delusion they appear in the shape of that beast (which commonly by their choice is a buck, or doe, a lion, or tiger, or dog, or eagle) and in that shape have been shot at and wounded, as I shall show in the following chapter. For this reason, as I came to understand by some of them, they yield unto the Popish religion, especially to the worshipping of saints' images, because they look upon them as much like unto their forefathers' idols; and secondly, because they see some of them painted with beasts—Jerome with a lion, Anthony with an ass, and other wild beasts, Dominic with a dog, Blas with a hog, Mark with a bull, and John with an eagle—they are more confirmed in their delusions, and think verily those saints were of their opinion, and that those beasts were their familiar spirits, and that they also were transformed into those shapes when they lived, and when they died, their beast died, too.

All Indians are much affected unto these Popish saints, but especially those which are given to witchcraft, and out of the smallness of their means they will be sure to buy some of these saints and bring them to the church, that there they may stand and be worshipped by them and others. The churches are full of them, and they are placed upon standers gilded or painted, to be carried in procession upon men's shoulders, upon their proper day. Upon such saints' days, the owner of the saint maketh a great feast in the town, and presenteth unto the priest sometimes two or three, sometimes four or five, crowns for his Mass and sermon, besides a turkey and three or four fowls, with as much cacao as will serve to make him chocolate for all the whole octave or eight days following. So that in some churches, where there are at least forty of these saints' statues and images, they bring unto the priest at least forty pounds a year.

Some Indians through poverty have been unwilling to contribute anything at all, or to solemnize in the church and at his house his saint's day, but then the priest hath threatened to cast his saint's image out of the church, saying that the church ought not to be filled with such saints as are unprofitable to soul and body, and that in such a statue's room one may stand which may do more good by occasioning a solemn celebration of one day more in the year. So likewise if the Indian that owned one of those images dies and leaves children, they must take care of that saint as part of their inheritance, and provide that his day be kept. If no son or heirs be left, then the priest calls for the heads of the several tribes, and for the chief officers of justice, and makes a speech unto them, that in case they will not seek out who may take charge of the saint and of his day, the priest will not suffer him to stand idle in his church, like those whom our Savior in the Gospel rebuked, for that they stood idle in the market all the day (these very expressions have I heard there from some friars). Therefore, the priest says that he fears that he must banish such a saint's picture out of the church, and must deliver him up before them into the justices' hands to be kept by them in the town-house until such time as he may be bought and owned by some good Christian. The Indians, when they hear these expressions, begin to fear lest some judgment may befall their town for suffering a saint to be excommunicated and cast out of their church, and therefore present unto the priest some offering for his prayers unto the saint, that he may do them no harm. And they desire him to allow them time to bring him an answer for the disposing of that saint (thinking it will prove a disparagement and affront unto their town if what once hath belonged to the church be now out, and delivered up to the secular power). In the meantime they will find out some good Christian, either of the nearest friends and kindred to the former owner or owners of the saint, or else some stranger, who may buy that saint of the priest (if he continue in the church) or of the secular power (if he be cast out of the church) and may by some speedy feast and solemnity appease the saint's anger towards them, for having been so slighted by the town.

These feasts bring yet unto the saints more profit than hitherto hath been spoken of, for the Indians prepare either money (some a real, some two, some more) or else commonly about Guatemala white wax candles, and in other places cacao, or fruits, which they lay before the image of the saint, whilst the Mass is celebrating. Some Indians will bring a bundle of a dozen candles, some worth a real apiece, others of three or four for a real. After Mass the priest and the *mayordomos* take and sweep away from the saint whatsoever they find hath been offered unto him; so that sometimes in a great town upon such a saint's day the priest may have in money twelve or twenty reals, and fifty or a hundred candles, which may be worth unto him twenty or thirty shillings, besides some ends and pieces. Most of the friars about Guatemala are with those offerings as well stored with candles as is any wax-chandler's shop in the city. The Indians themselves when they want again any candles for the like feast, or for a christening, or for a woman's churching (at which times they also offer candles) will buy their own again of the priest, who sometimes receives the same candles and money for them again five or six times. And because they find that the Indians incline very much to this kind of offerings, and that they are so profitable unto them, the friars do much press upon the Indians in their preaching this point of their religion and devotion.

But if you demand of these ignorant but zealous offerers, the Indians, an account of any point of faith, they will give you little or none. The mystery of the Trinity, and of the incarnation of Christ, and our redemption by him is too hard for them; they will only answer what they have been taught in a catechism of questions and answers. If you ask them if they believe such a point of Christianity, they will never answer affirmatively, but only thus: "Perhaps it may me so." They are taught there the doctrine of Rome, that Christ's body is truly and really present in the Sacrament, and no bread in substance, but only the accidents. Yet if the wisest Indian be asked whether he believes this, he will answer, "Perhaps it may be so."

Once an old woman of Mixco, who was held to be very religious, came to me about receiving the Sacrament, and whilst I was instructing her, I asked her if she believed that Christ's body was in the Sacrament, she answered, "Peradventure it may be so." A little while after to try her and get her out of this strain and common answer, I asked her what and who was in the Sacrament which she received from the priest's hand at the altar. She answered nothing for a while, and at last I pressed upon her for an affirmative answer, and then she began to look about to the saints in the church, which was dedicated to St. Dominic, and as it, seemed, being troubled and doubtful what to say, at last she cast her eyes upon the high altar. I, seeing she delayed the time, asked her again who was in the Sacrament? To which she replied St. Dominic, who was the patron of that church and town. At this I smiled, and would yet further try her simplicity with a simple question. I told her she saw St. Dominic was painted with a dog by him holding a torch in his mouth, and the globe of the world at his feet; I asked her whether all this were with St. Dominic in the Sacrament? To which she answered, "Perhaps it might be so."

I began to chide her and to instruct her. But neither my instruction, nor all the teaching and preaching of those Spanish priests has yet well grounded them in principles of faith. They are dull and heavy to believe or apprehend of God, or of heaven, beyond what their eyes tell them. Yet they go and run the way they see the Spaniards run, and as they are taught by their priests. They have been taught much formality, and so they are (as our Formalists formerly in England) very formal, but little substantial in religion.

Whenever they come to confession, but especially in Lent, none dares to come with empty hands. Some bring money, some honey, some eggs, some fowls, some fish, some cacao, some one thing, some another, so that the priest hath a plentiful harvest in Lent for his pains in hearing their confessions. They have been taught also that when they receive Communion everyone must give at least a real. I have known some poor Indians who have for a week or two forborne from coming to Communion until they could get a real offering.

They are very formal also in observing Rome's Maundy Thursday [Thursday of Holy Week], and Good Friday, and then they make their monuments and sepulchres, wherein they set their Sacrament, and watch it all day and night. They place on the ground before it a crucifix, with two basins on each side to hold the single or double reals which everyone must offer when he comes upon his knees and bare-footed to kiss Christ's hands, feet, and side. The candles which for that day and night and next morning are burned at the sepulchre are bought with another contribution, for a real is gathered from every Indian for that purpose. Their religion is a dear and lick-penny religion for such poor Indians, and yet they are carried along in it formally and perceive it not.

They are taught that they must remember the souls in Purgatory, and therefore that they must cast their alms into a chest, which stands for that purpose in their churches, the key of which the priest keeps, and opens it when he wants money. I have often opened some of those chests, and have found in them many single reals, some half pieces of eight, and some whole pieces of eight. And because what is lost and found in the highways must belong to somebody, they have been taught that if the true owner be not known, such moneys or goods belong also to the souls departed. Wherefore the Indians, if they find anything lost, will bestow it upon the souls, and will either bring it to the priest or cast it into the chest. Yet, surely they do this more for fear or for vanity, so that they may be well thought of by the priest. The Spaniards, on the other hand, will keep a purse if they find one.

An Indian of Mixco found a patacon or piece of eight in a highway, and when he came to confession, he gave it unto me, telling me he durst not keep it, lest the souls should appear unto him and demand it. So upon the second day of November, which they call All Souls' Day, they are extraordinary foolish and superstitious in offering moneys, fowls, eggs, and maize, and other commodities for the soul's good. But it proves for the profit of the priest, who after Mass wipes away to his chamber all that which the poor Indians had offered unto those souls, who needed neither money, food, nor any other provision.

A friar who lived in Petapa boasted unto me once that upon their All Souls' Day his offerings had been about a hundred reals, two hundred chickens and fowls, half a dozen turkeys, eight bushels of maize, three hundred eggs, four *zontles* of cacao (every *zontle* being four hundred beans), twenty bunches of plantains, above a hundred wax candles, besides some loaves of bread, and other trifles of fruits. If all this is summed up according to the price of the things there, and with consideration of the coin of money there (half a real, or threepence, being there the least coin), it amounts to above eight pounds of our money. This is a fair and goodly stipend for a Mass, brave wages for half an hour's work, and a politic ground for that error of Purgatory, if the dead bring to the living priest such wealth in one day only.

Christmas Day, with the rest of those holy days, is no less superstitiously observed by these Indians. At that time they frame and set in a corner of their church a little thatched house like a stall, which they call Bethlehem. A blazing star above points it to the three wise men from the East. Within this stall they lay in a crib a child made of wood, painted and gilded, who represents Christ new born unto them. By him stands Mary on the one side, and Joseph on the other, and an ass likewise on the one side and an ox on the other. The three wise men of the East kneel before the crib offering gold, frankincense and myrrh, and the shepherds stand off aloof offering their country gifts, some a kid, some a lamb, some milk, some cheese, and curds, some fruits. The fields with flocks of sheep and goats are also represented, and they hang angels about the stall, some with viols, some with lutes, some with harps. It is a goodly mumming and silent stage play to draw those simple souls to look on it, and to delight their senses and fantasies in the church.

There is not an Indian that does not come to see that supposed Bethlehem, and all bring either money or somewhat else for his offering. Nay, the priests have taught them to bring their saints upon all the holy days until Twelfth Day in procession unto this Bethlehem to offer their gifts, according to the number of the saints that stand in the church. Some days there come five, some days eight, some days ten, and it is so arranged that by Twelfth Day all have come and offered, some money, some one thing, some another. The owner of the saint comes before the saint with his friends and kindred (if there be no sodality or company belonging unto that saint) and, being very well apparelled for that purpose, he bows himself and kneels to the crib, and then rising takes from [to] the saint what he brings and leaves it there, and so departs.

If there be a sodality belonging to the saint, then the *mayordomos* or chief officers of that company come before the saint, and do homage, and offer as before hath been said. But upon Twelfth Day the *alcaldes*, mayors, jurats, and other officers of justice offer after the example of the saints, and the three wise men of the East (whom the Church of Rome teacheth to have been kings) because they represent the King's power and authority. And all these days they have about the town and in the church a dance of shepherds, who at midnight on Christmas Eve begin before this Bethlehem, and then they offer a sheep amongst them. Others dance clothed like angels and with wings, and all this draws the people to see sights in the church rather than to worship God in spirit and in truth.

Candlemas Day is no less superstitiously observed. For then the picture of Mary comes in procession to the altar, and her candles and pigeons or turtle-doves are offered to the priest, and all the town must imitate her example, and bring their candles to be blessed and hallowed.

At Whitsuntide they have another sight, and that is in the church also. Whilst a hymn of the Holy Ghost is sung, the priest stands before the altar with his face turned to the people, and they have a device well dressed with flowers to let fall a dove from above over his head. For above half an hour they drop down flowers above the priest from holes made to show the gifts of the Holy Ghost to him, which example the ignorant and simple Indians are willing to imitate, offering also their gifts unto him.

Thus all the year are those priests and friars deluding the poor people for their ends, enriching themselves with their gifts, placing religion in mere policy. Thus the Indians' religion consists more in sights, shows, and formalities than in any true substance. But as sweet meat must have sour sauce, so this sweetness and pleasing delight of shows in the church hath its sour sauce once a year (besides the sourness of poverty which followeth to them by giving so many gifts unto the priest). For, to shew that in their religion there is some bitterness and sourness, they make the Indians whip them-

selves the week before Easter, like the Spaniards, which those simples, both men and women, perform with such cruelty to their own
flesh that they butcher it, and mangle and tear their backs, till some
swoon. Nay, some, to my own knowledge, have died under their own
whipping, and have self murdered themselves.

Thus in religion they are superstitiously led on and blinded in
the observance of what they have been taught more for the good
and profit of their priests than for any good of their souls, for they
do not perceive that their religion is a policy to enrich their teachers.
But not only do the friars and priests live by them and eat the sweat
of their brows, but also all the Spaniards not only grow wealthy and
rich with their work and service (being themselves many given to
idleness), but with needless offices and authority still fleece them,
and take from them that little which they gain with much hardness
and severity.

The President of Guatemala, the judges of that Chancery, the
governors and high justices of other parts of the country advance
and enrich their menial servants by making the poor Indians the
subject of the bountifulness towards such. Some are employed to
visit their towns as often as they please to see how much maize every
Indian hath sowed for the maintenance of his wife and children;
others visit them to see what fowls they keep for the good and store
of the county; others have order to see whether their houses be
decently kept and their beds orderly placed according to their families; others have power to call them out to mend and repair the
highways; and others have commission to number the families and
inhabitants of the several towns, to see how they increase that their
tribute may not decrease, but still be raised.

The officials perform those tasks only so that they can collect their
expenses from the Indians. In truth there are no expenses, for as
long as they stay in the town, they may call for what fowls and
provision they please without paying for them. When they come
to number the towns, they call by list every Indian, and cause his
children, sons and daughters, to be brought before them, to see
if they be fit to be married, and if they be of growth and age and
be not married, the fathers are threatened for keeping them unmarried and as idle livers in the town without paying tribute.
According to the number of the sons and daughters that are mar-

riageable, the father's tribute is raised and increased until they provide husbands and wives for their sons and daughters; and they, too, as soon as they are married, are charged tribute, and so that it may increase, they will suffer none above fifteen years of age to live unmarried. Nay, the set time of age of marriage appointed for the Indians is at fourteen years for the man, and thirteen for the woman. Indeed, they allege that the Indians are sooner ripe for the fruit of wedlock, and sooner ripe in knowledge and malice, and strength for work and service, than are any other people. Nay, sometimes they force them to marry who are scarce twelve and thirteen years of age, if they find them well limbed and strong in body, explicating a point of one of Rome's canons, which alloweth fourteen and fifteen years, *nisi malitia suppleat aetatem*.

When I lived in Pinola, that town was numbered by order of Don Juan de Guzmán, a great gentleman of Guatemala to whom it belonged, and an increase of tributary Indians was added unto it by this means. The numbering lasted a full week, and in that space I was commanded to join in marriage near twenty couple, which, with those that before had been married since the last numbering of it, made for the *encomendero* an increase of about fifty families. But it was a shame to see how young some were that at that time were forced to marriage. Neither could all my striving and reasoning to the contrary, nor the production of the register book to show their age, prevail. For some then married were between twelve and thirteen years of age, and one especially who by the register book was found to be not fully of twelve years. Yet, his knowledge and strength of body were judged to supply want of age. In this manner even in what ought to be the most free act of the will, namely marriage, are those poor Indians forced and made slaves by the Spaniards, to supply with tribute the want of their purses, and the meanness of their estates.

Yet under this yoke and burden the Indians are cheerful, and much given to feasting, sporting, and dancing, as they particularly show in the chief feasts of their towns, which are kept upon that saint's day to whom their town is dedicated. For it is the intent of the Spaniards to draw in the people and country by way of commerce and trading one with another, to honor, worship, and pray to that saint to whom the town is dedicated. And certainly this superstition to keep fairs in many of our towns upon saints' days hath continued also in England from the Popish times, or else why are our fairs commonly kept upon the days of John the Baptist, James, Peter, Matthew, Bartholomew, Holy Rood, Lady days, and the like, and not as well a day or two before, or a day or two after, which would be as good and fit days to buy and sell as the other? True it is, our Reformation alloweth not the worshipping of saints, yet it hath kept and continued the meeting of the people to fairs and mirth and sport upon those days, so that the saints and their days may continue still in our remembrance.

There is no town in the Indies great or small, even though it be but of twenty families, which is not dedicated thus unto Our Lady or unto some saint, and the remembrance of that saint is continued in the minds not only of those that live in the town, but of all that live far and near, by commercing, trading, sporting, and dancing, offering unto the saint, and bowing, kneeling, and praying before him.

The Indians of the town have their meetings at night for two or three months beforehand, and prepare for such dances as are most commonly used amongst them, and in these meetings they drink of both chocolate and *chicha*. For every kind of dance they have several houses appointed, and masters of that dance, who teach the rest that they may be perfected in it against the saint's day. For the better part of these two or three months the silence of the night is unquieted with their singing, their holloaing, their beating upon [drums and using as trumpets] the shells of fishes, their waits, and with their piping. And when the feast cometh, they act publicly for the space of eight days what privately they had practiced before. They are that day well apparelled with silks, fine linen, ribbons, and feathers according to the dance. They begin this in the church before the saint, or in the churchyard, and thence all the octave, or eight days, they go dancing from house to house, where they have chocolate or some heady drink or *chicha* given them. All those eight days the town is sure to be full of drunkards. If they be reprehended for it, they will answer that their hearts rejoice with their saint in Heaven, and that they must drink unto him that he may remember them.

The chief dance used amongst them is called *toncontin*, and it has been danced before the King of Spain in the Court of Madrid by

Spaniards who have lived in the Indies, to shew unto the King somewhat of the Indians' fashions, and it was reported to have pleased the King very much. This dance is thus performed. The Indians that dance it are commonly thirty or forty, if it be a great town, fewer if it be a small town. They are clothed in white, for their doublets, linen drawers, and *ayates*, or towels, which hang almost to the ground on the one side, are white. Their drawers and *ayates* are wrought with some works of silk, or with birds, or bordered with some lace. Others procure doublets and drawers and *ayates* of silk, all of which are hired for that purpose.

On their backs they hang long tufts of feathers of all colors, which are fastened with glue into a little frame made for the purpose and gilded on the outside. They tie this frame fast around their shoulders with ribbons, so that it does not fall nor slacken with the motion of their bodies. Upon their heads they wear another smaller tuft of feathers either in their hats or in some gilded or painted headpiece or helmet. In their hands also they carry a fan of feathers, and most of them will use on their feet feathers also bound together like short wings of birds. Some wear shoes; some do not. And thus from top to toe they are almost covered with curious and colored feathers.

Their music and tune to this dance is only what is made with a hollow stock of a tree, rounded and well pared within and without. It is very smooth and shining, some four times thicker than our viols, with two or three long clefts on the upper side and some holes at the end. They call it *tepanahuaztli*. On this stock [drum], which is placed upon a stool or form in the middle of the Indians, the master of the dance beats with two sticks, with ends covered with wool and wrapped in leather smeared with pitch. With blows upon this instrument, which soundeth dull and heavy but somewhat loud, he giveth the dancers their several tunes, and changes, and signs of the motion of their bodies either straight or bowing, and giveth them warning what and when they are to sing. Thus they dance in compass and circle round about that instrument, one following another sometimes straight, sometimes turning about, sometimes turning half way, sometimes bending their bodies and with the feathers in their hands almost touching the ground, and singing the life of their saint, or of some other. All this dancing is but a kind of walking round, which they will continue two or three whole hours together in one place, and thence go and perform the same at another house.

The chief and principals only of the town dance this *toncontin*. It was the old dance which they used before they knew Christianity, except that then instead of singing the saints' lives, they sang the praises of their heathen gods.

They have another much used dance, which is a kind of hunting of some wild beast which formerly in time of heathenism was to be sacrificed to their gods, but now to be offered to the saint. This dance hath much variety of tunes, with a small *tepanahuaztli*, and many shells of tortoises, or instead of them, with pots covered with leather, on which they strike as on *tepanahuaztli*, and with the sound of pipes. In this dance they use much holloaing and noise and calling one unto another, and speaking by way of stage play, some relating one thing, some another, concerning the beast they hunt after.

These dancers are all clothed like beasts, with painted skins of lions, tigers, or wolves, and on their heads such headpieces as may represent the head of such beasts. Others wear painted heads of eagles or fowls of rapine, and in their hands they have painted staves, bills, swords, and axes, wherewith they threaten to kill the beast they are hunting. Others, instead of hunting after a beast, hunt after a man, as beasts in a wilderness should hunt a man to kill him. The man thus hunted must be very nimble and agile, as one flying for his life, and striking here and there in defense at the beasts, but at last they catch him and make a prey of him. As the *toncontin* consists mostly of walking and turning and leisurely bending their bodies, so this dance consists wholly in action, running around in a circle, sometimes out of circle, and leaping and striking with those tools and instruments which they have in their hand. This is a very rude sport, and full of shrieking and hideous noise, wherein I never delighted.

Another Mexican dance they use, some clothed like men, others like women, in which in heathenish times they sang praises unto their king or emperor; now they apply their songs unto the King of Glory, or unto the Sacrament, using these or commonly the like words with very little difference:

Salid Mexicanas, bailad Toncontin.
Cansalas galanas en cuerpo gentil.

245

And again,

Salid Mexicanas, bailad Toncontin.
Al Rey de la gloria tenemos aqui.

Thus they go round dancing, playing in some places very well
upon their guitars, repeating now and then all together a verse or
two, and calling the Mexican dames to come out to them with their
gallant mantles to sing praise unto their King of Glory. Besides these
they have, and use our Morris dances, and Blackamoor dances with
sonajas [rattles] in their hands. These are a round set of small

Morris dancing bells, wherewith they make variety of sounds to
their nimble feet.

The dance which doth draw to it the people's wondering is a
tragedy acted by way of dance, as the death of St. Peter, or the be-
heading of John the Baptist. In these dances there is an Emperor,
or a King Herod, with their Queens [richly] clothed, another
clothed with a long loose coat who represents St. Peter, or John the
Baptist, who whilst the rest dance, walks amongst them with a book
in his hands, as if he were saying his prayers. All the rest of the
dancers are apparelled like captains and soldiers, with swords, daggers, or halberds in their hands. They dance to the sound of a small
drum and pipes, sometimes round, sometimes in length forward,
and have and use many speeches to the Emperor or King, and
among themselves concerning the apprehending and executing of

the saint. The King and Queen sometimes sit down to hear their pleading against the saint, and his pleading for himself; sometimes they dance with the rest. At the end of their dance they crucify St. Peter head downwards upon a cross, or they behead John the Baptist, having in readiness a painted head in a dish which they present unto the King and Queen, for joy whereof they all again dance merrily and so conclude, taking down him that acted Peter from the cross.

Most of the Indians who take part in this dance are superstitious about what they have done, and they seem almost to believe that they have actually done what they only performed for the dance. When I lived amongst them, it was an ordinary thing for the one who in the dance was to act St. Peter or John the Baptist to come first to confession, saying they must be holy and pure like that saint, whom they represent, and must prepare themselves to die. So likewise he that acted Herod or Herodias, and some of the soldiers that in the dance were to speak and to accuse the saints, would afterwards come to confess of that sin, and desire absolution as from blood-guiltiness. More particular passages of the Indians according to my experience of them, I shall in the chapter following truly relate unto my reader.

16. Showing how and why I departed out of Guatemala to learn the Pokomchi language, and to live among the Indians, and of some particular passages and accidents whilst I lived there

⟨✠⟩

I READ in the University of Guatemala for three years' space a whole course of arts, and began to read part of divinity, but the more I studied and grew in knowledge, the more I controverted by way of arguments some truths and points of religion, and the more I found the spirit of truth enlightening me, and discovering unto me the lies, errors, falsities, and superstitions of the Church of Rome. My conscience was much perplexed and wavering, and I desired some good and full satisfaction, but that I knew might not be had there. Moreover, I knew that to profess and continue in any opinion contrary to the doctrine of Rome would bring me to the Inquisition, that rack of tender consciences, and from thence to no less than burning alive, in case I would not recant of what the true spirit had inspired in me. The doctrines of transubstantiation, of Purgatory, of the Pope's power and authority, of the merit of man's works, of his free will to choose all soul-saving ways, of the sacrifice of the Mass, of the hallowing the Sacrament of the Lord's Supper unto the lay people, of the priest's power to absolve from sin, of the worship of saints though with δουλεία, as they call it, and not with λατρεία, and the Virgin Mary with a higher degree of worship than that of the saints, which they call ὑπερδουλεία, the infallibility of the Pope, and council in defining for truth and point of faith what in

248

itself is false and erroneous were points which, with many more of Rome's policies and the lewd lives of the priests, friars, nuns, and those in authority, did much trouble and perplex my conscience. This I knew would be better satisfied if I could return again to my own country of England, where I knew many things were held contrary to the Church of Rome, but what particulars they were I could not tell, not having been brought up in the Protestant church, and having been sent young to St. Omer.

Wherefore I earnestly addressed myself to the Provincial and to the President of Guatemala for a licence to come home, but neither of them would yield unto it, because there was a strict order of the King and Council that no priest sent by his Majesty to any of the parts of the Indies to preach the Gospel should return again to Spain till ten years were expired. Hereupon, seeing myself a prisoner and without hopes for the present of seeing England in many years, I resolved to stay no more in Guatemala, but to go out to learn some Indian tongue, and to preach in some of their towns, where I knew I might get more money to help me home, when the time should come, than if I continued to live in the cloister of Guatemala. In the meantime I thought it wise to write to a friend of mine in Spain, an English friar in San Lucar, called Friar Pablo de Londres, to desire him to obtain for me a licence from the Court, and from the General of the Order at Rome, that I might return unto my country.

In this season there was in Guatemala, Friar Francisco Morán, the Prior of Cobán in the province of Vera Paz, who was informing the President and whole Chancery how necessary it was that some Spaniards should aid and assist him in the discovery of a way from that country to Yucatán, and in suppressing such barbarous people and heathens as stopped his passage, and did often invade some Indian towns of Christians.

This Morán was my special friend, and having been brought up in the cloister of San Pablo de Valladolid, in Spain, where I myself was first entered friar, he was very desirous of my company in his trip to bring to Christianity those heathens and idolators. He told me that doubtless in a new country new treasure and great riches was like to be found, whereof no small share and portion should befall him and me for our pains and adventure.[1] I was not hard to

[1] A dastardly lie about his "special friend." Fr. Morán was an enthusiastic

be persuaded, being above all desirous to convert to Christianity a people that had never heard of Christ; and so purposed to forsake that honor which I had in the University, in order to make Christ known unto that heathen people. The Provincial was glad to see my courage, and so, with some gifts and money in my purse, sent me with Morán to the Vera Paz in the company of fifty Spaniards, who were appointed by the President to aid and assist us.[2]

When we came to Cobán, we were well refreshed and provided for a hard and dangerous enterprise. From Cobán we marched to two great towns of Christians called San Pedro [Carcha] and San Juan [Chamelco], where were added unto us a hundred Indians for our further assistance. From these towns for two days' journey we could travel on mules safely among Christians and some small villages; but after the two days we drew near unto the heathens' frontiers, where there was no more open way for mules, but we must trust unto our feet. We went up and down mountains amongst woods for the space of two days, being much discouraged with the thickets and hardness of the way, and having no hope of finding the heathens. In the night we kept watch and guard for fear of enemies, and resolved yet the third day to go forward. In the mountains we found many sorts of fruits and in the bottoms springs and brooks with many trees of cacao and achiote.

The third day we went on, and came to a low valley, in the midst of which ran a shallow river, where we found some *milpas* or plantations of maize. These were a testimony unto us of some Indians not far off, and therefore made us keep together and be in readiness if any assault or onset should be made upon us by the heathens. Whilst we thus travelled on, we suddenly fell upon half a dozen

---

missionary, interested only in converting the heathen. He would have scorned money for himself, and, in any case, he well knew from his previous visits to that country that there was no wealth there save a little cacao.

[2] This entrada into the rain forest of the southeastern corner of what is now the Petén was to extend the settlements of the converted Chol Mayas perhaps into the territory of their neighbors, the Mopán Mayas. These poorly organized agricultural communities wished only to be left in peace. Various attempts of the Dominicans to settle them in permanent towns and bring them under Spanish rule met with failure. After a few years, the Chols would burn the churches and the settlements into which they had been gathered, and would scatter into the almost impenetrable forest. This happened again in 1633, three years after Gage's visit.

poor cottages, covered with boughs and plantain leaves, and in them we found three Indian women, two men, and five young children, all naked, who fain would have escaped, but they could not. We refreshed ourselves in their poor cottages and gave them of our provision, which at the first they refused to eat, howling and crying and puling, till Morán had better encouraged and comforted them, for they partly understood his language. We clothed them and took them along with us, hoping to make them discover unto us some treasure or some bigger plantation. But that day they were so sullen that we could get nothing out of them.

Thus we went on, following some Indians' tracks which here and there we found, till it was almost evening, and then we did light upon above a dozen cottages more, and in them a matter of twenty men, women, and children. We took some bows and arrows from them, and found there store of plantains, some fish, and wild venison, wherewith we refreshed ourselves. The Indians told us of a great town two days' journey off, which made us be very watchful that night. Here I began with some more of our company to be sick and weary, so that the next day I was not able to go any further; whereupon we resolved to set up our quarters there, and to send out some scouts of Indians and Spaniards to discover the country. They found further more cottages and plantations of maize, of chile, of Turkey beans, and cotton, but no Indians at all, for they were all fled. Our scouts returned, and gave us some encouragement from the pleasantness of the country, but withal wished us to be watchful and careful, for the flight of those Indians was certainly a sign that our coming was noised about the country.

The next day we purposed to move forward to that plantation which our scouts had discovered. For, as we were informed, it was more open and we would more easily see any danger ready to befall us. All these plantations lay along by the river, where the sun was exceeding hot, and this had caused fevers and a flux in some of us. With much weariness and faintness I got that day to our journey's end. I was on foot and now began to repent me of what I was engaged in, fearing some sudden danger, because our coming was now known by the Indians. The prisoners we had with us began to tell us of some gold that they sometimes found in that river, and of a great lake yet forward, about which lived many thousand Indians, who were very warlike and skillful in their bows and arrows. The one piece of news encouraged some; the other much discouraged the rest, who wished themselves out of those woods and unknown places, and began to murmur against Morán, who had been the cause of their engagement in that great danger.

Our night was set, and I and the rest of the sick Spaniards went to rest, some upon the bare ground, but myself and others in *hamacas* [hammocks], which are of net-work tied at two posts or trees, and hanging in the air, which with the least stirring of the body rock one asleep as in a cradle. Thus I took my rest till about midnight, at which time our watches gave an alarm against our approaching enemies, who were thought to be about a thousand. They came desperately towards us, and when they saw they were discovered, and our drums beat up, and our fowling pieces and muskets began to shoot, they holloaed and cried out with a hideous noise, which uproar and sudden affrightment added sweat and fear to my fever. But Morán, who came to confess with me, and to prepare himself for death or for some deadly wound, comforted me, wishing me to fear nothing. He told me to lie still, for I could do them no good, and that my danger was less than I apprehended because our soldiers had compassed me about, so that on no side the heathens could come in, and flee we could not without the loss of all our lives. The skirmish lasted not above an hour, and then our enemies began to flee. We took ten of them, and in the morning found thirteen dead upon the ground, and of ours five only were wounded, whereof one died the next day.

In the morning our soldiers began to mutiny and to talk of returning back, fearing a worse and more violent onset that day or the night following, for some of the Indians who were taken told them plainly that if they went not away, there would come six or seven thousand against them. They told us further that they knew well that the Spaniards had all the country about, except that little portion of theirs. They desired only to enjoy this quietly and peaceably, and not to meddle with us. If we wished to see their country and go through it as friends, they would let us without doing us any hurt; but if we came in a warlike manner to fight and to bring them into slavery, as we had done their neighbors, they were all resolved to die fighting rather than to yield.

With these words our soldiers were divided; some with Morán were of opinion to try the Indians, and to go peaceably through their country till they could come to some town of Yucatán; others thought we should fight; others that we should turn back, considering our weakness against so many thousands of Indians as were in the country. But that day nothing was agreed upon, for we could not stir by reason of the sick and wounded. So we continued there that night; and as the night before, much about the same time, the enemies came again upon us, but finding us ready and watching for them, they soon fled. In the morning we resolved to turn back, and Morán sent the heathens word that if they would let him go through their country quietly to discover some land of Yucatán, he would after a few months come peaceably unto them with half a dozen Indians, no more, trusting his life upon them. He said he knew that if they wronged him, all the Spaniards in the country would rise up against them, and not leave one alive. They answered that they would entertain him and any few Indians well and willingly. All this Morán and they performed according to their agreement the year following.[3]

Thus we returned that day the same way that we had come, and I began to find myself better, and my fever to leave me. We carried with us some of those young children we had taken to present to the President of Guatemala. In Cobán the Prior Morán thought he might first do God good service if he christened those young children, saying that they might become saints, and that afterwards their prayers might prevail with God for the conversion of their parents and of all that country to Christianity. I could not but oppose his ignorance, which seemed much like unto that of the friars who entered America with Cortés, and increased after the Conquest daily more in number, who boasted to the Emperor that they had some of them made above thirty thousand Indians Christians by baptizing them. Truly, as sheep are forced to the waters and driven to be washed, so were those first Indians by thousands sprinkled, or, if

---

[3] The historian Ximénez mentions this journey by Fr. Francisco Morán through the forest of Yucatán. Over half a century later another Dominican, Fr. Agustín Cano made the same trip, but fell into the hands of English logwood cutters. They took him to a small cay near the port later named Belize. Subsequently, they released him, and he reached Bacalar and thence passed to Mérida, the capital of Yucatán.

I may use their word baptized, for they were driven by force to the rivers, and were neither themselves believers, nor children of believing and faithful parents. So would Morán christen these children, though I told him that they ought not to partake of that sacrament and ordinance of Christ, unless they were grounded in articles of Christianity and believed, or were children of believing parents. But as he had been brought up in errors, whereof that Church of Rome is a wide and spacious nest, so he would be obstinate in this point against me and the truth, sprinkling with water those children, and naming them with names of Christians. After this he sent them well apparelled to the President of Guatemala, who commanded them to be kept and brought up in the cloister of the Dominican friars.

I remained after this for a while in Cobán, and in the towns about, until such time as the ships came to the gulf [Golfo Dulce]; whither I went with Morán to buy wines, oil, iron, cloth, and such things as the cloister wanted for the present. At which time there being a frigate ready to depart to Trujillo (some occasions drawing Morán thither), I took ship with him.[4] We stayed not much above a week in that port, which is a weak one, as the capture of it by the English and Hollanders shows. Presently we thought of returning back to Guatemala by land through the country of Comayagua, commonly called Honduras. This is a woody and mountainous country, very bad and inconvenient for travellers, and besides very poor. There the commodities are hides, *cañafistula*, and *zarzaparrilla*, and such lack of bread that about Trujillo they make use of what they call *cassave* [manioc], which is a dry root that being eaten dry doth choke, and therefore is soaked in broth, water, wine, or chocolate, that so it may go down. Within the country, and especially about the city of Comayagua, which is a bishop's seat, though a small place of some five hundred inhabitants at the most, there is more store of maize by reason of some Indians, who are gathered in a few small towns. I found this country one of the poorest in all America. The chief place in it for health and good living is the valley which is called Gracias á Dios, where are some rich farms of cattle and wheat. But it lies nearer to Guatemala than to Comayagua, and on this side the ways are better than on that; therefore, more of that wheat is trans-

---

[4] Trujillo, on the north coast of Honduras, lies nearly 250 miles in a straight line east of the entrance to the Golfo Dulce, in what is now the Republic of Honduras.

ported to Guatemala and to the towns about it than to Comayagua or Trujillo. From Trujillo to Guatemala there are between fourscore and a hundred leagues, which we travelled by land. Even in this barren country, we lacked neither guides nor provision, for the poor Indians thought neither their personal attendance nor anything that they enjoyed too good for us.

Thus we came again to Guatemala, and were by the friars joyfully entertained, and by the President highly rewarded, and by the city called true Apostles, because we had ventured our lives for the discovery of heathens, and opened a way for their conversion, and found out the chief place of their residence. The Indian children who were in the cloister were living witnesses to our pains and endeavors. Morán was so puffed up with the President's favor and the popular applause that he resolved in Guatemala to venture again his life, and, according to that message which he had sent before to the heathen Indians, to enter amongst them in a peaceable way with half a dozen Indians.

Morán would fain have had me go with him, but I considered the hardness of the journey, which I thought I should not be able to perform on foot, and also I feared that the barbarians might mutiny against us for those children which we had brought. Lastly, I liked not the country, which seemed poor and not for my purpose, to get means sufficient to bring me home to England for the satisfaction of my conscience, which I found still unquiet. Wherefore I resolved to forsake the company of my friend Morán, and to desist from new discoveries of heathens, and such difficult undertakings, which might endanger my health and life, and at last bring no profit, but only a little vainglory, fame, and credit in that country. I thought I might better employ my time if I learned some Indian tongue nearer to Guatemala, where were many towns, and the Indians were ready and willing to further their priest's wants. I considered lastly their ignorance in some points of religion, which I thought I might help and clear with some sound doctrine, and with preaching Christ crucified unto them, and bringing them unto that rock of eternal bliss and salvation.

I trusted in my friends so much that I knew it would not be hard for me to take my choice of any place about Guatemala, from whence I might facilitate my return to England, and write to Spain, and have every year an answer easier than anywhere else. I opened my mind unto the Provincial, who was then at Guatemala, and he presently and willingly condescended to my request. He counselled me to learn the Pokomchi [Pokoman] language, whereof I had already got some grounds in the Vera Paz, which is most used about Guatemala, and also is much practiced in Vera Paz, and in the country of San Salvador. He promised to send me to the town of Petapa to learn there the language with a special friend of his named Friar Pedro Molina, who was very old and wanted the help and company of some younger person to ease him in the charge that lay upon him, of so great a town and many travellers that passed that way. The Provincial, as if he had known my mind, pitched upon my very heart's desire. Thus two weeks before Midsummer Day [1630] I departed from Guatemala to Petapa, which is six leagues from thence, and there settled myself to learn that Indian tongue. The friars of those parts that are any way skillful in the Indian languages have composed grammars and dictionaries for the better furthering of others who may supply their places after their decease. This old Molina, considering himself in years, and for the sake of his good friend, the Provincial, was willing to accept my company, and to impart to me what knowledge he had got by many years' practice of the Pokomchi tongue. He gave me therefore a short abstract of all the rudiments, which consisted chiefly of declining nouns and conjugating verbs, which I easily learned in the first fortnight, and then a dictionary of Indian words. I practiced what I had learned by talking with the Indians, until I was able of myself to preach to them.[5]

After the first six weeks Molina wrote down for me in the tongue a short exhortation, which he expounded to me, and wished me to learn it without book, and this I preached publicly upon the feast of St. James. After this he gave me another short exhortation in Spanish, to be preached upon the fifteenth of August [Day of the Assumption], which he made me translate into the Indian tongue, and he corrected in it what he found amiss, wherewith I was a little

[5] Pokomchi and Pokoman are two closely related dialects or languages of Maya stock. The name Pokomchi is now reserved for the dialect spoken in the Baja Verapaz; Pokoman for the dialect spoken in the towns, such as Mixco, Petapa, Pinula, and Amatitlán, which Gage served.

more emboldened, and feared not to shew myself in public to the Indians. This practice I continued three or four times until Michaelmas, preaching what with his help I had translated out of Spanish, until I was able to talk with the Indians alone, and to make mine own sermons.

After Michaelmas, Molina, being not a little vainglorious of what he had done with me in perfecting me in an unknown tongue in so short a space, very little above one quarter of the year, wrote to the Provincial acquainting him of what pains he had taken with me, and of the good success of his endeavors, assuring him that I was now fit to take a charge of Indians upon me, and to preach alone. He also desired him to bestow upon me some Indian town and benefice, where I might by constant preaching practice and further what I had learned with so much facility. The Provincial,[6] who had always been my friend, needed not spurs to stir him up to shew more and more his love and kindness unto me, but immediately sent me order to go to the two towns of Mixco and Pinola, and to take charge of the Indians in them, and to give quarterly an account of what I received thence unto the cloister of Guatemala, unto which all that valley did appertain. All the Indian towns and the friars that live in them are subordinate unto some cloister, and the friars are called by their Superiors to give up for the cloister's use what moneys they have spared, after their own and their servants' lawful maintenance.

With this subordination therefore unto the Prior and cloister of Guatemala, was I sent to preach unto the Indians of Mixco and Pinola, to replace an old friar of almost fourscore years of age, who was no longer able to perform the charge which lay upon him of two towns, three leagues distant one from another. The settled means for maintenance which I enjoyed in these towns, and the common offerings and duties which I received from the Indians was this. In Mixco I was allowed every month twenty crowns [pesos], and in Pinola fifteen, which were punctually paid by the *alcaldes* and *regidores*, mayors and jurats, before the end of the month. To meet this payment the towns sowed a common piece of land with wheat or maize, and kept their book of accounts, wherein they set down

[6] Rev. Fr. Juan Ximeno, who succeeded Rev. Fr. Pedro Álvarez as Provincial in 1628.

what crops they yearly received, what moneys they took in for the sale of their corn, and in the same book I wrote down what every month I received from them. At the end of the year they presented this book to be examined by some officer appointed thereunto by the court of Guatemala. Besides this monthly allowance, I had from the sodalities of the souls in purgatory every week in each town two crowns for a Mass; every month two crowns in Pinola upon the first Sunday of the month from the sodality of the Rosary, and in Mixco likewise every month two crowns apiece from three sodalities of the Rosary of the Virgin Mary, belonging to the Indians, the Spaniards, and the Blackamoors. Further, from two more sodalities belonging to the Vera Cruz, or the Cross of Christ, two crowns apiece every month. And in Mixco from a sodality of the Spaniards belonging to San Nicolás de Tolentino, two crowns every month. And from a sodality of San Blas in Pinola every month two more crowns; and finally in Mixco from a sodality entitled of San Jacinto every month yet two crowns. In addition, there were offerings of either money, fowls or candles upon those days whereon these Masses were sung. All this amounted to threescore and nine crowns a month, which was surely settled and paid before the end of the month.

Besides, from what I have formerly said of the saints' statues which do belong unto the churches, and do there constantly bring both money, fowls, candles, and other offerings upon their day unto the priest, the yearly revenues which I had in those two towns will appear not to have been small. In Mixco there were in my time eighteen saints' images, and in Pinola twenty, and these brought me upon their day four crowns apiece for Mass and sermon and procession, besides fowls, turkeys and cacao, and the offerings before the saints, which commonly might be worth at least three crowns upon every saint's day. The yearly amount was at least two hundred, threescore and six crowns. Besides the sodalities of the Rosary of the Virgin (which as I have before said were four, three in Mixco and one in Pinola), the five feasts of the year observed by the Church of Rome brought me four crowns, two for the day's Mass, and two for a Mass the day following, which they call the anniversary for the dead who had belonged unto those sodalities. This amounted to eighty crowns more each year, as well as those days' offerings (which sometimes were more, sometimes less) and the Indians' presents of fowls and cacao. Besides this, the two sodalities of the Vera Cruz upon two feasts of the Cross, the one on the fourteenth of September, the other on the third of May, brought four crowns apiece for the Mass of the day, and the anniversary Mass following, and upon every Friday in Lent two crowns, which in the whole year came to four and forty crowns; all which above reckoned was as a sure rent in those two towns. But it would be tedious to reckon up what besides did accidentally fall.

The Christmas offerings in both those two towns were worth to me when I lived there at least forty crowns. [Maundy] Thursday and [Good] Friday offerings were about a hundred crowns; All Souls' Day offerings commonly worth fourscore crowns; and Candlemas Day [February 2] offerings commonly forty more. Besides what was offered upon the feast of each town by all the country which came in, which in Mixco one year was worth to me in candles and money fourscore crowns, and in Pinola, as I reckoned it, fifty more. The communicants, every one giving a real, might make up in both towns at least a thousand reals; and the confessions in Lent at least a thousand more, besides other offerings of eggs, honey, cacao, fowls, and fruits. Every christening brought two reals, every marriage two crowns; every death two crowns more at least, and some in my time died who would leave ten or twelve crowns for five or six Masses to be sung for their souls.

Those two towns of Mixco and Pinola were far inferior yet to Petapa and Amatitlán in the same valley, and not to be compared in offerings and other church duties to many other towns about that country. Yet they yielded me with the offerings cast into the chests which stood in the churches for the souls of Purgatory, and with what the Indians offered when they came to speak unto me (for they never visit the priest with empty hands) and with what other Mass stipends did casually come in, the sum of at least two thousand crowns of Spanish money, which might yearly mount to five hundred English pounds. I thought this benefice might be a fitter place for me to live in than in the cloister of Guatemala, wearying out my brains with points of false grounded divinity to get only the applause of the scholars of the University; and now and then some small profit. I thought I might look after the profits from my parish as well as the rest of my profession; nay, with more reason, for I intended to return to England, and I knew I should have little help for so long a journey, unless I made my money my best friend to assist me by sea and land.

My first endeavor was to certify myself from the book of receipts and accounts in the cloister of Guatemala what reckonings my predecessor and others before him had given to the cloister yearly from Mixco and Pinola, that I might regulate myself and my expenses so as to be able to live with credit, and to get thanks from the cloister by giving more than any before me had given. I found that four hundred crowns had been the most that my old predecessor had given yearly in his accounts; and that before him little more was usually given from those two towns. Whereupon I took occasion once in discourse with the Prior of Guatemala to ask what he would willingly expect from me yearly whilst I lived in those two towns. He replied that if I upheld for my part the cloisters' usual and yearly revenues, giving what my predecessor had given, he would thank me, and expect no more from me, and that the rest that befell me in those towns I might spend in books, pictures, chocolate, mules, and servants. To which I replied that I thought I could live in that benefice creditably enough, and yet give from it more to the cloister than ever any other before me had given, and that I would forfeit my continuing there if I gave not to the cloister every year four hundred and fifty crowns.

The Prior thanked me heartily for it, and told me I should not want for wine, wishing me to send for it every month, nor for clothing, which he would once a year bestow upon me. This I thought would save a great part of my charges, and that I was well provided for as long as I lived in the Indies. And here I desire that England take notice how a professed mendicant friar, who is beneficed in America, may live with four hundred pounds a year clear, and some with much more, and with most of his clothing and wine and an abundance of fowls free, and with plenty of beef at thirteen pound for threepence![7]

[7] One must bear in mind that every conscientious friar would return in charity to the widows and fatherless and to the sick and afflicted a good part of his receipts. Gage, on the other hand, gives the impression that he never remitted a penny of what he could collect and seldom gave away a penny, and one seriously doubts that many friars resold candles. After all, money was of little use to the individual friar. If he hoarded, it was probably to buy some ornament for his church. Gage says that

After I was once settled in my two towns, my first care was to provide myself with a good mule, to carry me easily and as often as occasion called from the one town to the other. I soon found one, which cost me fourscore crowns, and served my turn very well, to ride speedily the nine miles across the valley between the two towns. Though my chief study here was to perfect myself in the Indian tongue, that I might the better preach unto them and be well understood, yet I omitted not to search out the Scriptures daily, and to addict myself unto the Word of God, which I knew would profit me more than all those riches and pleasures of Egypt, which for a while I saw I must enjoy till my ten years were fully expired, and licence from Rome or Spain granted for me to return to England.

I began speedily to solicit this license by means of one Captain Isidro de Zepeda, a Seville merchant and master of one of the ships which came that first year that I was settled in Mixco with merchandise for Guatemala. By this Captain, who often passed through the valley, I wrote to my friends in Spain and had answers, though at first to little purpose for they did not a little increase the troubles of my conscience, which were great, and such whereof the wise man said, "A wounded conscience who can bear?"

My friendship with this Captain Zepeda was such that I broke my mind unto him, desiring him to carry me in his ship to Spain, but this he refused to do, telling me the danger he might be in, if complaint should be made to the President of Guatemala. He wished me to continue where I was, and to store myself with money that I might return with licence and credit. I resolved therefore with David in Psalm 16, V. 8, to set the Lord always before me, and to choose him for my only comfort, and to rely upon his providence, for that I knew only He could order things for my good, and could from America bring me home to the House of Salvation, and to the Household of Faith, from which I considered myself an exile, and far banished.

he amassed nine thousand pesos, which is less than three hundred pounds for each of the seven years he served parishes. Yet his later parishes, he tells us, were far richer than Mixco and Pinula. Moreover, he speaks also of the unusual income from the plagues. There is obvious exaggeration here to buttress his indictment of Roman Catholicism in practice. The Indian is not a liberal giver, although admittedly he has little to give. I have noted that collections at masses in several Indian towns largely comprise small and almost valueless coins.

In the meantime I lived five full years in the two towns of Mixco and Pinola. There I had more occasion to get wealth and money than ever any that lived there before me; for the first year of my abiding there it pleased God to send one of the plagues of Egypt to that country, which was of locusts, which I had never seen till then. They were after the manner of our grasshoppers, but somewhat bigger, and they flew in number so thick and infinite that they did truly cover the face of the sun and hinder the shining forth of the beams of that bright planet. Where they lighted either upon trees or standing corn, there nothing was expected but ruin, destruction, and barrenness, for they devoured the corn, they eat and consumed the leaves and fruits of trees, and they hung so thick upon the branches that with their weight they tore them from the trunk. The highways were so covered with them that they startled the travelling mules with their fluttering about their head and feet. My eyes were often struck with their wings as I rid along, and I had much ado to see my way, what with a *montera* wherewith I was fain to cover my face, what with the flight of those still before my eyes.

The farmers towards the South Sea Coast cried out that their indigo, which was then in grass, was like to be eaten up; from the *ingenios* of sugar moan was made that the young and tender sugarcanes would be destroyed; but above all grievous was the outcry of the husbandmen of the valley where I lived, who feared that their corn would in one night be swallowed up by that devouring legion. The magistrate ordered all the Indians to go out into the fields with trumpets and what other instruments they had to make a noise, and so to affright the locusts from those places which were most considerable and profitable to the commonwealth. Strange it was to see how the loud noise of the Indians and sounding of the trumpets defended some fields from the fear and danger of them. Where they lighted in the mountains and highways, there they left behind them their young ones, which were found creeping upon the ground ready to threaten with a second year's plagues if not prevented, wherefore all the Indians were called with spades, mattocks, and shovels to dig long trenches and therein to bury all the young ones.

Thus with much trouble to the poor Indians, and their great pains and after much hurt and loss in many places, that flying pestilence was chased out of the country to the South Sea, where it was thought to be consumed by the ocean and to have found a grave in the waters, whilst the young ones found it in the land. Yet they were not all so buried, for shortly some appeared, but not being so many as before, were with the former diligence soon overcome.

Whilst there was all this fear, these outcries made by the country, and this diligence performed by the Indians, the priests got well by it, for everywhere processions were made, and Masses sung for the averting of that plague. In Mixco most of the idols were carried to the field, especially the pictures of Our Lady, and that of San Nicolás Tolentine, in whose name the Church of Rome blesses little breads and wafers with the saint stamped upon them, which they think are able to defend them from agues, plague, pestilence, contagion, or any other great and imminent danger. There was scarce any Spanish husbandman who on this occasion did not come from the valley to the town of Mixco with his offering to this saint, and who did not make a vow to have a Mass sung to San Nicolás. All brought breads to be blessed, and they carried them back to their farms, some casting them into their corn, some burying them in their hedges and fences, strongly trusting in San Nicolás that his bread would have power to keep the locust out of their fields. At the last when those simple, ignorant, and blinded souls saw the locusts departed and their corn safe, they cried out, some to Our Lady, others to San Nicolás, "*Milagro,*" "a miracle," judging the saint worthy of praise more than God, and performing to him their vows of Masses, which in their fear and trouble they had vowed. By those devotions of theirs I got that year many more crowns than what before I have numbered from the sodalities.

The year following, all that country was generally infected with a kind of contagious sickness, almost as infectious as the plague, which they call *tabardillo.* This fever in the very inward parts and bowels scarce continued to the seventh day but commonly took its victims away from the world to a grave the third or fifth day. The filthy smell and stench which came from those who lay sick of this disease was enough to infect the rest of the house, and all that came to see them. It rotted their very mouths and tongues, and made them as black as a coal before they died. Very few Spaniards were infected with this contagion, but the Indians generally were taken with it.

It was reported to have begun about Mexico, and to have spread from town to town, till it came to Guatemala, and went on forwards, just as the locusts did the year before, marching as it were from Mexico over all the country. I visited many that died of this infection, using no other antidote against it save only a handkerchief dipped in vinegar to smell, and I thank God I escaped where many died. In Mixco I buried ninety young and old, and in Pinola above an hundred, and for all that were eight years old, or upwards, I received two crowns for a Mass for their soul's delivery out of Purgatory. But think not that because so many died, therefore the towns growing less, my offerings for the future were lessened. The *encomenderos* of the two towns took care of that. For in order that they might not lose any part of that tribute which was formerly paid them, they caused them to be numbered after the sickness was ceased, and, as I have previously observed, forced into marriage all that were twelve years and upwards of age. This was a new stream of crowns flowing into my bags, for from every couple that were married I had also crowns besides other offerings, and in both the towns I married in that occasion above fourscore couple. Truly by all this, I thank the Lord, I was more strengthened in my conceit against the Church of Rome, and I was not enticed to continue in it with greediness of that lucre, though I found the preferments there far greater than any might be in the Church of England. But yet though for the present my profit was great, my eyes were open to see the errors whereby that profit came so plentifully to me.[8]

The judgments ceased not here in that country in my time. After this contagion there was such an inundation of rain that the husbandmen feared again the loss of all their corn. At noon time the dark clouds for a month together began to thicken and cover the face of the heavens, pouring down such stormy showers as swept away much corn, and many poor cottages of Indians. Besides the rain, the fiery thunderbolts breaking through the clouds threatened a doleful judgment to all the country. In the Valley of Mixco two riding together were stricken dead from their mules. The chapel of Our Lady of Carmel in the same valley was burnt to the ground, and likewise two houses at the river Vacas. In Petapa another flash of lightning or thunderbolt fell into the church upon the high altar,

[8] The historian Francisco Ximénez mentions this plague and its huge toll of human life.

cracking the walls in many places, running from altar to altar, defacing all the gold, and leaving a print and stamp where it had gone without any more hurt. In the cloister of the Franciscans in Guatemala, a friar sleeping upon his bed after dinner was stricken dead, his body being left all black as if it had been burnt with fire, and yet no sign of any wound about him.

Many accidents happened that year of 1632, all about the country. But I myself was wonderfully saved by the safe protection of the Almighty. One Saturday night in Mixco, as I was trembling and fearing, and yet trusting in my God, and praying unto him in my chamber, a flash of lightning or a thunderbolt fell close to the church wall to which my chamber joined, and killed two calves, which were tied to a post in a yard, to be slaughtered the next morning. The lightning was so near and terrible that it seemed to have fired all my house, and struck me down unto the ground, where I lay as dead for a great while. When I came again to myself, I heard many Indians about my house, who were come to see if either it or the church were set on fire.

This stormy season brought me also much profit, for, as formerly, the Spaniards of the valley and the Indians betook themselves to their saints, carrying them about in procession. This was not done without money, which they call their alms unto their saints, that they may the better be heard and entreated by them.

The summer following there was more than the ordinary earthquakes, which were so great that year in the kingdom of Peru that a whole city called Trujillo was swallowed up by the earth which opened itself, and almost all the people were lost whilst they were at church worshipping and praying unto their saints. The hurt they did about Guatemala was not so much as in other places, only a few mud walls were shaken down, and some churches cracked. But that made the people fear and betake themselves again to their saints, and empty their purses before them for Masses and processions, lest the danger should prove as great as was that of the great earthquake which happened before my coming into that country.

These earthquakes when they begin are frequent rather than long, for they last but for a while, stirring the earth with three motions, first on the one side, then on the other, and with the third motion they seem to set it right again. If they should continue, they would doubtless hurl down to the ground any steeple or building though never so great and strong. Yet at this time in Mixco some were so violent that they made the steeple bend so much that it made the bells sound. I was so used to them that many times I would not stir from my bed for them. Yet this year they brought me to such a fear, that had not the Lord been a present refuge to me in time of trouble I had utterly been undone. For being one morning in my chamber studying, so great and sudden was an earthquake, that it made me run from my table to a window, fearing that before I could get down the stairs the whole house might fall upon my head. The window was in a thick wall vaulted upwards like an arch (which the Spaniards hold to be the safest place if a house should fall), where I expected nothing but death. As soon as I got under it, the earthquake ceased, though my heart ceased not to quake with the sudden affrightment.

Whilst I was musing and thinking what to do, whether I should run down to the yard, or continue where I was, there came a second shaking worse than the first. I thought with myself if the house should fall the arch would not save my life, and that I should either be stifled or thrown out of the window, which was not very low and near unto the ground, but somewhat high and wide open, having no glass casement but wooden shutters (such as there are used). I thought that if I leaped out of the window, I might chance to break a leg or a limb, yet save my life. The suddenness of the astonishment took from me the best and most mature deliberation in such a case, and in the midst of my troubled and perplexed thoughts a third motion came as violent as the former. I had now set one foot in the window to leap down, had not the same Lord by his wonderful providence spoken both to me and to the moving earth, saying, "Be still and know that am I God." Certainly had it gone on to a fourth motion, I would have cast myself down and broken either my neck, or a leg, or some other joint. Thus was I twice saved by my good God in Mixco, and in Pinola I was once no less in danger in losing a leg by means of a smaller instrument than even a flea.

This town of Pinola in the Indian language is called *Pancac; pan* signifieth in, or amongst, *cac,* signifieth three things, the fire, or a fruit otherwise called *guava,* or thirdly, a small vermin, commonly called by the Spaniards *nigua* [jigger], which is common over all the Indies, but more in some places than in others. Where there are many hogs, there is usually much of this sort of vermin. The Spaniards report that many of the soldiers of Sir Francis Drake died of them, when they landed about Nombre de Dios, and marched up the high mountains of San Pablo towards Panama. Feeling their feet to itch, and not knowing the cause thereof, they scratched them so much till they festered, and at last (if this report be true) cost them their lives.

Some say *niguas* breed in all places, high and low, upon tables, beds, and upon the ground; but experience shows the contrary, that they only breed upon the ground. For where the houses are sluttish, and not often swept, there commonly they are most felt; and the fact they usually get into the feet and shoes, and seldom into the hands or any other part of the body, argues that they breed upon the ground. They are less than the least flea, and can scarce be perceived. When they enter the foot, they make it burn and itch, and if then they be looked to, they appear black and no bigger than the point of a pin, and with a pin may easily be taken out whole. But if part of them be left, the smallest part will do as much harm as the whole and will get into the flesh.

When once they are in the flesh, they breed a little bag in the flesh, and in it a great many nits, which get bigger and bigger to the size of a great pea. Then they begin again to make the foot itch, which if it be scratched, starts to fester and so endangers the whole foot. Some hold it best to take them out when they cause the first itching and are getting in, but this is hard to do, because they can hardly then be perceived, and they are apt to be broken. Therefore, others commonly let them alone until they get into the flesh, and have bred a bag with nits, which like a blister sheweth itself through the skin. Then with the point of a pin they dig round about the bag, till they can take it out whole with the pin's point. If it be broken the *niguas* breed again; if it be taken out whole, then they put in a little ear wax or ashes where the bag lay, and with that the hole is healed up again in a day or two. The way to avoid this vermin's entering into the foot is to lay shoes and stockings, and any other clothing upon some stool or chair high from the ground, and not to go barefoot.

It is wonderful that though the Indians commonly go barefoot, yet they are seldom troubled with *niguas*, and this is attributed to the hardness of their skin, for certainly were they as tender-footed and tender-skinned as are those that wear shoes and stockings, they would be as much troubled with them as these are.

Pancac, or Pinola, is much subject to this vermin, as I found by woeful experience, for at my first coming thither, not knowing well the quality of it, I let one breed in my foot, and continued scratching it, until my foot became so festered that I was fain to lie two whole months in a chirurgeon's hand, and at last, through God's great mercy and goodness to me, I lost not a limb. But that the providence of God may be known to me, the worst of all his creatures, living in so far a country from all my friends, and from me may be related unto future generations, before I conclude this chapter I shall further shew both my dangers and deliverances.

It is true, that most of the Indians are but formally Christians, and only outwardly appear such, and secretly are given to witchcraft and idolatry, yet as they were under my charge, I thought by preaching Christ unto them and by cherishing them, and defending them from the cruelty of the Spaniards, I might better work upon them to bring them to more knowledge of some truths, at least concerning God and Christ. Therefore, as I found them truly loving, kind, and bountiful unto me, so I endeavored in all occasions to show them love by commiserating with them on their sufferings, and taking their part against any Spaniard that wronged them. And I kept constantly in my chamber such drugs, as hot waters, aniseed and wine and the like, which I knew might most please them when they came to see me, and most comfort them when they were sick or grieved, but my love and pity towards them almost cost me my life in Pinola. For an Indian of that town serving a Spaniard named Francisco de Montenegro, who lived a mile and a half from thence, was once so pitifully beaten and wounded by his master for having told him he would complain to me that he paid him not his wages, that he was brought to the town, and had I not out of my charity called a chirurgeon from Petapa to cure him, he had certainly died.

I could not but complain for the poor Indian to the President of Guatemala, who, respecting my complaint, sent for my Spaniard to the city, imprisoned him, and kept him close until the Indian was recovered, and with a fine sent him back again. In a sermon further

I pressed this home unto the neighboring Spaniards, warning them of the wrongs and abuses which they offered unto the poor Indians. I told them I would no more put up with this than any injury done unto myself, for I looked upon them as neophytes and new plants of Christianity, who were not to be discouraged, but by all means of love encouraged to come to Christ. Withal I commanded all the Indians that had any wrong done unto them to come to me, assuring them that I would make such a complaint for them as should be heard, as they might perceive I had lately done to some purpose. This sermon stuck so in Montenegro's stomach, that, as I was informed, he made an oath that he would procure my death. Though it was told me, yet I could hardly believe it, judging it to be more a bravery and a vain boasting of a Spaniard than anything else, yet some friends counselled me to look to myself, which yet I slighted, until one day the boys and Indians that served in my house came running to my chamber door, wishing me to look to myself and not to come out, for Montenegro was come into my yard with a naked sword to kill me. I charged them from within to call the officers of the town to aid and assist me, but in the meanwhile my furious Spaniard, perceiving himself discovered, left the town. With this I thought of securing of myself better, and called for a Blackamoor, Miguel Dalva, a very stout and lusty fellow who lived half a mile from me to be about me until I could discover more of Montenegro's designs and malicious intents. The next Sabbath day in the morning, having to ride to the town of Mixco, I carried my Blackamoor and half a dozen of Indians in my company, and going through a little wood in the midst of the valley, I found my enemy waiting for me. He, seeing the train I brought, durst do nothing but gave me spiteful languages, telling me he hoped that he should find me alone some time or other. With this I thought fit to delay no longer my second complaint against him to the President, who as before heard me willingly, and banished Montenegro after a month's imprisonment to a place thirty leagues from the valley. And not only from Spaniards was I in danger for the Indians' sake whilst I lived in those towns, but also I did undergo great perils from some Indians themselves, who were false in religion, and yet was still delivered.

In Pinola there were some who were much given to witchcraft, and by the power of the Devil did act strange things. Amongst the rest there was one old woman named Marta de Carrillo, who had been by some of the town formerly accused for bewitching many, but the Spanish justices acquitted her, finding no sure evidence against her. With this she grew worse and worse, and did much harm. When I was there, two or three died, withering away, declaring at their death that this Carrillo had killed them, and that they saw her often about their beds, threatening them with a frowning and angry look. The Indians for fear of her durst not complain against her, nor meddle with her; whereupon I sent word unto Don Juan de Guzmán, the lord of that town, that if he took not order with her, she would destroy his town. He, hearing of it, got for me a commission from the Bishop and another officer of the Inquisition, to make diligent and private enquiry after her life and actions, which I did, and found among the Indians many and grievous complaints against her.

Most of the town affirmed that certainly this Marta was a notorious witch, and that before her former accusation she was wont whithersoever she went about the town to go with a duck following her, and when she came to the church, the duck would stay at the door till she came out again, and then would return home with her. This duck they imagined was her beloved devil and familiar spirit, because they had often set dogs at her and they would not meddle with her, but rather run away from her. This duck never appeared more with her since she was formerly accused before the justice, and it was thought that this was her policy that she might be no more suspected thereby. This old woman was a widow, and of the poorest of the town in outward show, and yet she always had store of money, but none could tell how she came by it.

Whilst I was thus taking privy information against her (it being the time of Lent, when all the town came to confession), she among the rest came to the church to confess her sins, and brought me the best present and offering of all the town. Whereas a real is common, she brought me four, and besides a turkey, eggs, fish, and a little bottle of honey. She thought thereby to get with me a better opinion than I had of her from the whole town. I accepted her great offering and heard her confession, which was on nothing but trifles, which could scarce be judged sinful actions. I examined her very close of what was the common judgment of all the Indians, and especially of those who dying had declared to me at their death that she had bewitched them, and before their sickness had threatened them, and in their sickness appeared threatening them with death about their beds, none but they themselves seeing her. To which she replied weeping, that she was wronged.

I asked her how she, being a poor widow without any sons to help her and without any means of livelihood, had so much money, that she could give me more than the richest of the town. I taxed her as to how she came by that fish, turkey, and honey, having none of this of her own about her house. She replied that God loved her and gave her all these things, and that with her money she had bought the rest. I asked her of whom, and she answered that she had them from out of the town. I persuaded her much to repentance, and to forsake the Devil and all fellowship with him, but her words and answers were of a saintly and holy woman, and she earnestly desired me to give her the Communion with the rest that were to receive the next day. This I told her I durst not do, using Christ's words, "Give not the children's bread unto dogs, nor cast your pearls unto swine." I told her that it would be a great scandal to give the Communion unto her, who was suspected generally, and had been accused for a witch. This she took very ill, telling me that she had many years received the Communion, and now in her old age it grieved her to be deprived of it. Her tears were many, yet I could not be moved with them, but resolutely denied her the Communion, and so dismissed her.

At noon when I had done my work in the church, I bad my servants to go to gather up the offerings, and gave order to have the fish which she had brought dressed for my dinner, but no sooner was it carried into the kitchen when the cook found it full of maggots and stinking, so that I was forced to hurl it away. With that I began to suspect my old witch, and went to look at her honey, and pouring it out into a dish, I found it full of worms; her eggs I could not know from others, there being near a hundred offered that day; but after, as I used them, we found some rotten and some with dead chickens within. The next morning the turkey was found dead. As for her four reals, I could not perceive whether she had bewitched them out of my pocket, for that I had put them with many others which that day had been given me, yet as far as I could, I called to memory who and what had been given me, and in my judgment and reckoning I verily thought that I missed four reals.

That night, when my servants the Indians were gone to bed, I sat up late in my chamber betaking myself to my books and study, for I was the next morning to make an exhortation to those that received the Communion. After I had studied a while, it being between ten and eleven of the clock, on a sudden the chief door in the hall (where in a lower room was my chamber, and the servants', and three other doors) flew open, and I heard one come in, and for a while walk about. Then another door was opened which went into a little room, where my saddles were laid. With this I thought it might be the Blackamoor Miguel Dalva, who would often come late to my house to lodge there, especially since my fear of Montenegro, and I conjectured that he was laying up his saddle. I called to him by name two or three times from within my chamber, but no answer was made. Suddenly another door that led out to a garden also flew open, wherewith I began within to fear, my joints trembled, my hair stood up, I would have called out to the servants, and my voice was as it were stopped with the sudden affrightment. I began to think of the witch, and put my trust in God against her, and thereby encouraged myself and my voice returning, I called out to the servants, and knocked with a cane at my door within that they might hear me, for I durst not open it and go out. With the noise which I made the servants awaked and came out to my chamber door; then I opened it, and asked them if they had not heard somebody in the hall, and all the doors opened. They said they were asleep, and heard nothing, only one boy said he heard all, and related unto me the same that I had heard. I took my candle then in my hand and went out into the hall with them to view the doors, and I found them all shut, as the servants said they had left them. Then I perceived that the witch would have affrighted me, but had no power to do me any harm. I made two of the servants lie in my chamber, and went to bed.

In the morning early I sent for my *fiscal*, the clerk of the church, and told him what had happened that night. He smiled, and told me it was the widow Carrillo, who had often played such tricks in the town with those that had offended her, and therefore he had the night before come to me from her desiring me to give her the Communion lest she should do me some hurt. This I denied to him as I had done to herself. The clerk bad me be of good cheer, for he knew she had no power over me to do me any hurt. After the Communion that day some of the chief Indians came unto me, and told me that old Carrillo had boasted that she would play me some trick or other, because I would not give her the Communion. But to rid the town of such a limb of Satan, I sent her to Guatemala, with all the evidences and witnesses which I had found against her, unto the President and Bishop, who commanded her to be put in prison, where she died within two months.

Many more Indians there were in that town who were said in my time to do very strange things. One called Juan González was reported to change himself into the shape of a lion, and in that shape was one day shot in the nose by a poor harmless Spaniard who chiefly got his living by going about the woods and mountains and shooting wild deer and other beasts. He espied one day a lion, and having no other aim at him but his snout behind a tree, he shot at him, but the lion ran away. The same day this González was taken sick; I was sent for to hear his confession. I saw his face and nose all bruised and asked him how it came. He told me then that he had fallen from a tree and almost killed himself, yet afterwards he accused the poor Spaniard of shooting at him.

The business was examined by a Spanish justice. My evidence was taken as to what González had told me of his fall from a tree, and the Spaniard sware that he shot at a lion in a thick wood, where an Indian could scarce be thought to have any business. The tree in the wood whereat the shot had been made was found to be still marked with the shot and bullet, and González confessed it was the place. He was examined how he neither fell nor was seen by the Spaniard when he came to seek for the lion, thinking he had killed him. González answered that he ran away lest the Spaniard should kill him indeed. But his answers seeming frivolous, the Spaniard's integrity being known, and the great suspicion that was in the town of González' dealing with the Devil, cleared the Spaniard from what was laid against him.

But this was nothing to what happened to one Juan Gómez, the most important Indian of that town and the head and ruler of the principal tribe among the Indians. He was of near fourscore years of age, and his advice and counsel was taken and preferred before all the rest. He seemed to be a very godly Indian, and very seldom

missed morning and evening prayers in the church, and had bestowed great riches there. This Indian very suddenly was taken sick,
the *mayordomos* of the sodality of the Virgin, fearing that he might
die without confession and they be chid for their negligence, at midnight sent to call me at Mixco, where I chanced to be, desiring me
to go presently and help Juan Gómez to die, who also, they said,
desired much to see me and to receive some comfort from me. I,
judging it a work of charity, would not be hindered by either the
unseasonable time of night or the great rain, and so set forth to
ride nine miles both in the dark and wet.

When I came to Pinola, being thoroughly wet to the skin, I went
immediately to the house of old sick Gómez, who lay with his face
all muffled up. He thanked me for my pains and care I had for his
soul, and he desired to confess, and by his confession and weeping
evidenced nothing but a godly life and a willing desire to die and to
be with Christ. I comforted him and prepared him for death, and
before I departed, asked him how he felt himself. He answered
that his sickness was nothing but old age and weakness. With this
I went to my house, changed myself and lay down a while to rest.
Suddenly I was called again to give Gómez extreme unction, which
the Indians, as they have been ignorantly taught, will not omit to receive before they die. As I anointed him on his nose, his lips, his eyes,
his hands, and his feet, I perceived that he was swelled, and black
and blue, but I made nothing of it, judging it to proceed from the
sickness of his body. I went home again, it being now break of the
day. After I had taken a small nap, some Indians came to my door
to buy candles to offer up for Juan Gómez' soul, who they told me
was departed, and was that day to be buried very solemnly at Mass.
I arose with drowsy eyes after so unquiet a night's rest, and walked
to the church, where I saw the grave was preparing.

I met with two or three Spaniards who lived near the town and
were come to Mass that morning, who went in with me to my chamber. I fell into discourse with them about Juan Gómez, telling them
what comfort I had received at his death, and that I judged him to
have lived very holily, and doubted not of his salvation, and that
the town would much want him, for he was their chief guide and
leader, ruling them with good advice and counsel. At this the Spaniards smiled one at another, and told me I was much deceived by

all the Indians, but especially by the deceased Gómez, if I judged him to have been a saint and holy man. I told them that they as enemies to the poor Indians judged still uncharitably of them, but that I, who knew very well their consciences, could judge better of them than they. One then replied that it seemed I little knew the truth of Juan Gómez' death by the confession which he had made unto me, and that I seemed to be ignorant of the stir which was in the town concerning his death. This seemed so strange unto me that I desired them to inform me of the truth.

They told me that the report went that Juan Gómez was the chief wizard of all the wizards and witches in the town, and that commonly he was wont to be changed into the shape of a lion, and so to walk about the mountains. That he was ever a deadly enemy to one Sebastián López, an ancient Indian and head of another tribe, and that two days before they had met in the mountain, Gómez in the shape of a lion and López in the shape of a tiger, and that they had fought most cruelly till Gómez, who was the older and weaker, was tired, much bit and bruised, and died of it. And further, that I might be assured of this truth, they told me that López was in prison for it, and the two tribes striving about it, and that the tribe and kindred of Gómez demanded from López and his tribe and kindred satisfaction, and a great sum of money, or else threatened to make the case known unto the Spanish power and authority.

They were unwilling to do this if they could agree and smother it up among themselves, that they might not bring an aspersion upon their whole town. This seemed very strange unto me, and I could not resolve what to believe, and thought I would never more believe an Indian if I found Juan Gómez to have so much dissembled and deceived me. I took my leave of the Spaniards and went myself to the prison, where I found López with fetters. I called to my house one of the officers of the town, who was *alguacil mayor* and my great friend, and privately examined him why López was kept so close prisoner. He was loath to tell me, fearing the rest of the Indians, and hoping the business would be taken up and agreed by the two tribes, and not noised about the country for at that very instant the two *alcaldes* and *regidores*, mayors and jurats, with the chiefs of both tribes were sitting about the matter in the town-house all that morning.

Seeing the officer so timorous, I was more desirous to know something, and pressed more upon him for the truth, giving him an inkling of what I had heard from the Spaniards. He answered that if they could agree amongst themselves, they feared no ill report from the Spaniards against their town. I told him I must know what they were agreeing upon amongst themselves so closely in the town-house. He said that if I would promise him to say nothing of him (for he feared the whole town if they should know he had revealed anything unto me), he would tell me the truth. With this I comforted him, and gave him a cup of wine, and encouraged him, warranting him that no harm should come unto him for what he told me.

Then he related the business unto me as the Spaniards had done, and told me that he thought the tribes amongst themselves would not agree, for that some of Gómez' friends hated López and all such as were so familiar with the Devil, and cared not if Gómez' dissembling life were laid open to the world; others, he said, who were as bad as López and Gómez, would have it kept close, lest they and all the witches and wizards of the town should be discovered. This struck me to the very heart, to think that I should live among such people, who were spending all they could get by their work and labor upon the church, saints, and in offerings, and yet were so privy to the counsels of Satan. It grieved me that the Word I preached unto them did no more good, and I resolved from that time forward to spend most of my endeavors against Satan's subtlety, and to shew them more than I had done the great danger to the souls of those who had made any compact with the Devil. I hoped that I might make them abandon and abjure his works, and close with Christ by faith.

I dismissed the Indian, and went to the church, to see if the people were coming to Mass; I found there only two who were making Gómez' grave. I went back to my chamber troubled much within myself, whether I should allow a Christian burial to one who had lived and died so wickedly, as I had been informed. Yet I thought I was not bound to believe one Indian against him, nor the Spaniards, whom I supposed spoke but by hearsay.

Whilst I was thus musing, there came unto me at least twenty of the chiefest of the town with the two mayors, jurats, and all the officers of justice, who desired me to forbear that day the burying of Juan Gómez, for that they had resolved to call a crown officer to view his corpse and examine his death, lest they all should be troubled for him, and he be exhumed. I made as if I knew nothing, but enquired of them the reason. Then they related to me how there were witnesses in the town who saw a lion and a tiger fighting, and presently lost the sight of the beasts, and saw Juan Gómez and Sebastián López much about the same time parting one from another; and that immediately Juan Gómez came home bruised to his bed, whence he never rose again, and that he declared upon his deathbed unto some of his friends that Sebastián López had killed him. For this reason they had López in safe custody.

Further, they told me that though they had never known so much wickedness of these two chief heads of their town whom they had much respected and followed, yet now upon this occasion, from the one tribe and the other, they were certainly informed that both of them did constantly deal with the Devil. This would be a great aspersion upon their town, but they for their part abjured all such wicked ways, and prayed me not to conceive the worst of all for a few, whom they were resolved to persecute, and suffer not to live amongst them. I told them I much liked their good zeal, and encouraged them as good Christians to endeavor the rooting out of Satan from their town, and they did very well in giving notice to Guatemala, to the Spanish power, of this accident, and that if they had concealed it, they might all have been punished as guilty of Gómez' death, and as agents and instruments of Satan. I assured them I had no ill conceit of them, but rather judged well of them for what they were agreed to do.

The crown officer was sent for and came that night and searched Gómez' body. I was present with him, and found it all bruised, scratched, and in many places bitten and sore wounded. Many evidences and suspicions were brought in against López by the Indians of the town, especially by Gómez' friends, whereupon he was carried away to Guatemala, and there again was tried by the same witnesses, and not much denying the fact himself, was there hanged. And though Gómez' grave was opened in the church, he was not buried in it, but in another made ready for him in a ditch.[9]

[9] Belief in *nagualism*, as this supposed intimate relationship with one particular animal is called, is still widespread in Guatemala and Mexico. Instances, such as

In Mixco I found also some Indians no less dissemblers than was this Gómez. They were four brothers called Fuentes, and half a score more, who were among the wealthiest and most important in the town. Outwardly they were very fair tongued, liberal, and free handed to the church, much devoted to the saints, great feasters upon their day, and yet in secret great idolaters. But it pleased God to make me his instrument to discover and bring to light the secrecy of their hidden works of darkness, which it seemed the privacy of a thick wood and mountain had many years hid from the eyes of the world. Some of these, being one day in the company of other better Christians, drinking hard of their *chicha*, boasted of their god, saying that he had preached unto them better than I could preach, nay, that he had plainly told them that they should not believe anything that I preached of Christ, but follow the old ways of their fore-fathers, who worshipped their gods aright, but now by the example of the Spaniards they were deluded, and brought to worship a false god.

The other Christians hearing of this began to wonder, and to enquire of them where that god was, and with much ado, promising to follow their ways and their god, got out of them the place and mountain where they might find him. Though this in drunkenness were agreed upon, yet in soberness the good Christians thought better of what they had agreed upon, slighted what before in drinking they heard, and yet it was not kept by them so close but that it came to the ears of a Spaniard in the valley. Finding himself touched in conscience, he came to Mixco, and told me what he had heard, that some Indians of that town followed an idol, and boasted that he had preached unto them against my doctrine and for the ways of the former heathens.

I thanked God for that he was pleased to undermine the secret works of Satan daily, and desired the Spaniard to tell me by whom he came to know of this. He told me the Indian's name from whom he had it, and that he was afraid to discover the Indians, and to tell me of it. I sent for the Indian before the Spaniard. He confessed to me that he had heard of such a thing, but he knew that if he did discover the Indians, they with the power of the Devil would do him much harm. I told him, if he were a true Christian, he ought

Gage gives, of injury to the *nagual* occurring also to its "owner" are commonly reported.

to fight against the Devil and not to fear him who could do him no harm if God were with him and he closed by faith with Christ, and that the discovery of that idol might be a means for the converting of the idolaters, when they should see the small power of their false god against the true God of the Christians.

Further, I told him plainly, that if he did not tell me who the Indians were, and where their idol was, I would have him sent to Guatemala, and there make him discover what he knew. Here the Indian began to tremble, and told me the Fuentes had boasted of such an idol, whom they called their god, and gave some signs of a fountain and of a pine tree at the mouth of a cave in such a mountain. I asked him if he knew the place or what kind of idol it was, and he told me that he had often been in that mountain, where he had seen two or three springs of water, but never was in any cave. I asked him if he would go with he and help me to find it out. He refused, still fearing the idolaters, and wished me not to go, for fear if they should be there, they might kill me rather than be discovered. I answered him that I would carry with me such a guard as should be able to defend me against them, and my faith in the true living God would secure me against that false god.

I resolved therefore with the Spaniard to go to search out the cave the next day, and to carry with me three or four Spaniards, my Blackamoor Miguel Dalva, and that Indian. I told him I would not suffer him to go home to his house that day, for fear he should discover in the town my design and purpose, and so we might be prevented by the idolaters, who certainly that night would take away their idol. The Indian still refused, till I threatened to send for the officers of justice, and to secure his person. With this he yielded, and that he might have no discourse with anybody in the town, nor with the servants of my house, I desired the Spaniard to take him home to his house, and to keep him there close that day and night, promising to be with him the next morning. I charged the Spaniard also with secrecy, and so dismissed him with the Indian.

That day I rode to Pinola for the Blackamoor Miguel Dalva, and brought him to Mixco with me, not telling him what my intent was. I went also to four neighboring Spaniards, desiring them to be in a readiness the next morning to go a little way with me for the service of God, and to meet me at such a neighbor's house. I added that if they would bring their fowling pieces, we might chance to find some sport where we went, and as for provision of wine and meat, I would provide sufficiently. They promised to go with me, thinking that although I told them it was for the service of God, my purpose only was to hunt after some wild deer in the mountains. I was glad they construed my action that way, and so went home, and provided that night a good gammon of bacon, and some fowls roasted, cold, and others boiled, well peppered and salted, for the next day's work.

I met with the rest of my company where I had appointed my Indian to be kept, and thence we went together to the place of the idolaters' worshipping, which was some six miles from Mixco towards the town of San Juan Sacatepéquez. When we came into the wood, we presently met with a deep *barranca*, or bottom, where was running water, which encouraged us to make there diligent search, but nothing could be found. Thence we ascended up out of the *barranca*, and found after much time a spring of water, and looked carefully about it, but could find no cave. Thus we searched in vain till the evening, and fearing lest we might lose our way and ourselves, if the night overtook us, my friends began to speak of returning homewards. But considering that as yet we had not gone over one half of the wood, and to go home and come again might make us to be noted and spoken of, I thought it best to take up our lodging that night in the wood, and in that bottom which we first searched, where was good water to drink chocolate, and where it would be warm lying under the trees, and so in the morning we could make our second search. The company was very willing to yield to this plan, and the calm night favored our good intentions. We made a fire for our chocolate, and supped exceeding well of our cold meat, and spent most part of the night in merry discourse, having a watchful eye over our Indian, lest he should give us the slip, and committing him to the charge of Miguel Dalva.

In the morning we prayed unto God, beseeching him to guide us that day in the work we went about, and to discover unto us the cave of darkness and iniquity where lay hid that instrument of Satan, that so by his discovery glory might be given unto our true God, and shame and punishment brought upon his enemies. We entered again into the thick wood up a steepy hill, and having thoroughly searched all the south side of it, we went on to the north side, where we found another deep descent, which we began to walk down looking on every side, and not in vain.

Almost half a mile from the top we found some marks of a way that had been used and trodden, and we followed it until we came to another spring of water. We searched narrowly about it, and found some pieces of broken earthen dishes and pots, and one piece of a chafing dish, such as the Indians use to burn frankincense in in the churches before their saints. We verily imagined that these were pieces of some such instruments wherewith the idolaters performed their duty to their idol, and we were the more comforted for that we knew that earthenware had been made in Mixco. The pine tree which immediately we discovered confirmed our hopes. When we came to it, we made very little more search, for near at hand was the cave, which was dark within, but light at the mouth. We found there more earthenware, with ashes in them, which assured us some frankincense had been burned. We knew not how far the cave might reach within, nor what might be in it, and therefore with a flint we struck fire and lighted a couple of candles and went in.

At the entrance the cave was broad, and went a little forward, but when we were in, we found it turn on the left hand towards the mountain, and not far, for within two rods we found the idol standing upon a low stool covered with a linen cloth. The substance of it was wood, black shining like jet, as if it had been painted or smoked; the form was of a man's head unto the shoulders, without either beard or mustachios. His look was grim with a wrinkled forehead and broad startling eyes. We feared not his frowning look, but presently seized upon him; and as we lifted him up we found under him some single reals, which his favorites had offered unto him, and that made us search the cave more diligently.

Our effort was not amiss, for we found upon the ground more single reals, some plantains and other fruits, half-burned wax candles, pots of maize, one little one of honey, and little dishes wherein frankincense had been burned. I perceived the idolaters and Christians agreed in their offerings, and had I not been informed that they called this idol their god, I could have blamed them no more than the rest of the towns who worship, kneel before, and offer such offerings unto their saints made of wood, and some no handsomer than was this idol. I thought it might have been some beast's shape; but being the shape and form of a man, they might have named him by the name of some saint, and so some way have excused themselves. But they could not or would not do this because they persisted in this error that he was their god, and had spoken and preached unto them. Afterwards, on being asked by me whether it were the picture of any saint, such as were in Mixco, and other churches, they answered, no, but that he was above all the saints in the country.[10]

We were very joyful to see that we had not spent our time in vain. We cut down boughs of trees, and filled the cave with them and stopped the mouth of it up, and came away, making the Indian that went with us carry the idol on his back wrapped up in a cloth, that it might not be seen or perceived as we went. I thought it fit to wait till night before entering Mixco, that the Indians might see nothing. So I stayed at one of the Spaniard's houses till it were late, and desired him to warn from me all the Spaniards thereabouts to be at Mixco church the next Sabbath (fearing lest the idolaters might be many, and rise up against me) that I had somewhat to say unto them and their Blackamoors concerning their sodalities. I would not have them know of the idol till they heard of it and saw it in the church, lest it should come to the Indians' hearing, and so the idolaters might absent themselves. At night I took my Indian and Miguel Dalva with me, and went home, and shutting up the idol in a chest till the next Sabbath, I dismissed the Indian, charging him to say nothing, for he knew if he did, what harm might come unto him from the idolaters. I knew few words now would suffice, for he feared himself if it should be known that he had been with me. I kept with me Miguel Dalva, who was desirous to see the end of the business, and prepared myself against the next Sabbath to preach upon the 3 v. of the 20 of Exodus: "Thou shalt have none other gods before me," though it were a text nothing belonging to the Gospel of the day, from whence commonly in the Church of Rome

---

[10] Pagan rites continue to be held in caves to this day in the remoter parts of the Guatemalan highlands. There was a large cave in which, it was said, children were formerly sacrificed near old Mixco, in the Jilotepec Valley, from which the people were forcibly moved by the Spaniards to the present site of Mixco.

the texts and subjects of sermons are deducted [drawn], but I judged that text most seasonable for the present occasion.

On the Sabbath day in the morning, when the pulpit was made ready by him who had care of the church and altars, I had Miguel Dalva carry the idol under his cloak and leave it in the pulpit upon the ground that it might not be seen, till such time as I should think fit in my sermon to produce it. And I ordered him to watch the church till the congregation came in, that none might see it or take it away. Never was there a greater resort from abroad to that church than that day of Spaniards and Blackamoors, who by the warning I had sent them expected some great matter from me, and of the town very few were absent. The Fuentes and all the rest that were suspected to be that idol's favorites came also that day to church, little thinking that their god was brought from his cave, and now lay hid in the pulpit to shame them. I commanded Miguel Dalva to be near the pulpit at sermon time, and to warn those Spaniards that knew the business, and some more Blackamoors, his friends, to be also near the pulpit stairs.

Mass being ended, I went up to preach, and when I rehearsed the words of my text, I perceived both Spaniards and Indians to look upon one another, for they were not used to sermons out of the Old Testament. I went on to expound this command of God to have no other gods before him, so that the doctrine might seem to convince all that were there present. I showed that no creature could have the power of God the Creator of all things, neither could do good or harm without the true living God's commission. This was especially true of inanimate creatures such as stocks and stones, which by the hands and workmanship of man might have eyes, and yet are dead idols and see not, might have ears and not hear; might have mouths and not speak; might have hands and not work, nor help or defend with them such as worship them, and bowed down unto them.

Having half finished my sermon, I bowed myself down in the pulpit, and lifted up the black, grim, and staring devil, and placed that Dagon on one side of the pulpit. I fixed my eyes on some of the Fuentes and others, who I perceived changed color, blushed, and were sore troubled looking one upon another. I desired the congregation to behold what a god was worshipped by some of them, and all to take notice of him, if any knew what part of the earth was the dominion of this god, or from whence he came. I told them that some had boasted that this piece of wood had spoken and preached against what I had taught of Christ, and that therefore he was worshipped by them for God, and they had offered money, honey, and of the fruits of the earth unto him, and burnt frankincense before him in a secret and hidden cave under the earth, showing thereby that they were ashamed to own him publicly, and that he by lurking in the darkness of the earth showed certainly that he belonged to the Prince of Darkness.

I challenged him there in public to speak for himself, or else by silence to shame and confound all his worshippers. I showed them how being but wood he had been made and fashioned by the hands of man, and therefore was but a dead idol. I spent a great deal of time arguing with him, and defying Satan who had used him as his instrument, daring the Devil himself to take him from that place which I had confined him to if he could, to shew what little power he or Satan had against the power of my faith in Christ. After much arguing and reasoning according to the shallow capacity of the Indians present, I told them if that their god had power to deliver him from that execution which I had intended against him (which was there publicly to have him cut in pieces and burnt), they should not believe the Gospel of Jesus Christ. But if they saw no power at all in him against me, the weakest instrument of the true living God, then I beseeched them to be converted unto that true God who created all things, and to embrace salvation by his Son the only Mediator and Savior Jesus Christ.

I assured them that if they would renounce and abjure from that time all heathenish idolatry of their forefathers, I would intercede for them, and secure them from what punishment might be inflicted upon them by the President and Bishop, and if they would come to me, I would spend my best endeavors for the helping and furthering of them in the way of Christianity.

Concluding without having named any person, I went down out of the pulpit, and caused the idol to be brought after me. Sending for an axe and for two or three great pans of coals, I commanded it to be hewn in very small pieces, and to be cast in the fire and burned before all the people in the midst of the Church. The Spaniards cried out joyfully, *"Victor, Victor,"* and others repeated, *"Gloria á nuestro Dios,"* "Glory to our God"; the idolaters held their peace and spake not then a word. But afterwards they acted most spitefully against me, and conspired day and night to get me at some advantage, and to kill me. I wrote to the President of Guatemala informing him of what I had done, and to the Bishop, as an inquisitor to whom such cases of idolatry did belong, asking him to inform me what course I should take with the Indians who as yet were only in part discovered unto me, and those only by the relation of one Indian.

I received great thanks from both for my pains in searching the mountain and finding the idol, and for my zeal in burning of it. As touching the Indian idolaters, their counsel to me was that I should further enquire after the rest and discover as many as I could, and endeavor to convert them to the knowledge of the true God by fair and sweet means. They urged me to show pity to them for their great blindness, and to promise them on repentance pardon from the Inquisition, which, considering them to be but new plants, useth not such rigor with them which it useth with Spaniards if they fall into such horrible sins.

This advice I followed, and sent privately for the Fuentes to my chamber, and told them how merciful the inquisition was unto them, expecting their conversion and amendment. They seemed somewhat stubborn and angry that I had burned that god, whom not only they, but many others in the town, and also in the town of San Juan Sacatepéquez did worship. I used reasons to persuade them no honor was due unto it, as to a god. But one of them boldly replied that they knew that it was a piece of wood and of itself could not speak, but seeing it had spoken, as they were all witnesses, this was a miracle whereby they ought to be guided. He said they verily believed that God was in that piece of wood, for since it had spoken it was more than ordinary wood, having God himself in it. Therefore it deserved more offerings and adoration than those saints in the church, who never spoke to the people.

I told them that the Devil rather had framed that speech (if any they had heard) to deceive their souls and lead them to Hell. They might easily perceive this from the doctrine which I was informed it had preached against Christ, the only begotten son of God, whom the Father loveth and in whom He is well pleased, and against whom He certainly would not speak in that idol. Another answered boldly that their forefathers never knew who Christ was until the Spaniards came unto that country, but they knew there were gods, and did worship them, and did sacrifice unto them, and for aught they knew this god of theirs belonged in old times unto their forefathers. "Why then," said I unto them, "he was a weak god who by my hands hath been burned." I perceived that at that time there was no reasoning with them, for they were stubborn and captious, and so I dismissed them.

Had not God most graciously protected me against these my enemies, I had certainly been murdered by them. For a month after the burning of the idol, when I thought all had been forgotten, and that the idolaters were quiet, they began to act their spite and malice. I first discovered this by a noise which once at midnight I heard of people about my house, and at my chamber door. I called out to them from my bed, not daring to open, but could have no answer from them. I perceived they would have come in by force, for they pushed hard at the door. Whereupon I took the sheets from off my bed, tying them with a strong knot together, and with another to a bar of the window, making myself ready to fall down by them to the ground, and so to flee in the dark night, if they used violence to come in. The sheets being thus prepared, and they still at the door thrusting without any word from them, I thought by calling and crying out aloud I might affright them away.

Wherefore with a shrill voice I called first to my servants, who were but boys, and lay at the further end of a long gallery, and then I cried out to the neighboring houses to come and assist me against thieves. The servants had heard the noise and were awake, and presently at my call came out; with their coming my enemies ran down the stairs, and were heard no more that night. Perceiving which way their spite and malice was bent, I thought fit to be no more alone in the night with boys only in so great a house as was that of Mixco, and so the next day I sent for my trusty friend Miguel Dalva, who alone was able to fight any half-dozen Indians, wishing him to bring with him what weapons he could get for my defense. I kept him with me a fortnight, and the next Sabbath I gave warning in the church that whosoever came in the night to my house to affright me, or to do me any other mischief, should look to himself, for that I had weapons both offensive and defensive.

For a while I heard no more of them, yet they desisted not altogether from their evil and malicious intents. A fortnight after, knowing that Miguel Dalva did not lie in the same chamber with me, for I was till about midnight with my candle studying, they came up the stairs so softly that I heard them not. But the Blackamoor being awake perceived that they were coming up, and softly arose up from a long table where he lay upon a mat, and took in his hand a couple of brick-bats of many which lay under the table for a work which I had in hand. As he opened the door he made a little noise, which was to them an item to flee down the stairs, and to run (as they thought) for their lives. The Blackamoor ran after them, and finding they had got too much advantage of him, and not knowing which way they might take, sent after them with a fury his two brick-bats. He supposed he hit one of them, for the next day walking about the town he met with one of the Fuentes with a cap on his head, and inquiring of some Indians what he ailed, he was told by them that his head was broke, but how they knew not.

Perceiving that I was thus guarded by Miguel Dalva, they desisted from that time from coming any more in the night unto my house, but yet desisted not from their spite and malice and from acting mischief against me. For a month after, when I thought that all had been forgotten and they seemed outwardly to be kind and courteous, there came a messenger to me from the oldest of them, named Pablo de Fuentes, to tell me that he was very sick, and like to die, and desired me to go to comfort and instruct him in the truth, for that he truly desired to be converted. I conceived very great joy at this news, and doubted not of the truth and certainty of it, and prayed to God to direct me in the conversion of that soul. And so with haste and good zeal I went unto his house, where soon my joy and comfort was turned into bitterness.

When I came to the door of his house, and was with one step entered, I found all the brothers of Pablo Fuentes, and some others who were suspected to be idolaters, sitting round the room. Missing Pablo, I withdrew my foot a little, and asked them where he was, mistrusting somewhat to see them there all gathered together, but when I perceived that they stood not up, nor answered me a word, nor so much as took off their hats to me, then I began to fear indeed, and to suspect some treachery, and I turned back, resolving to go home again.

No sooner was I turned, but behold Pablo Fuentes, who by his message had feigned both sickness and conversion, came from behind his house with a cudgel in his hand, lifting it up to strike at me. Had I not catched hold of his stick with both hands and prevented the intended blow, he would have certainly struck me down. But whilst he and I were striving who should be master of the stick, the rest of the Indians who were sitting in the house came out into the yard (which being a public place was more comfort to me than if they had compassed me about within the house) and beset me round. Some pulled me one way, some another, tearing my clothes in two or three places. Another to make me let go of the stick, ran a knife into my hand (which to this day a small scar doth witness) and certainly had we not been in a public yard, that party would also have run his knife into my sides. Another, seeing I would not let go of the stick, took hold of it with Pablo, and both together thrust it against my mouth, and with such strength that they broke some of my teeth, and filled my mouth with gore blood.

With that blow I fell, but soon recovered myself and arose, they laughing at me, but not daring to do me any more harm for fear they should be seen, as God would have seen what already they had done. For a mulatta slave to a Spaniard in the valley passed by at that very time when I was down and rising, and hearing me cry out for help to the neighbors (any who might help and succor me lived somewhat far off, for all the houses thereabouts were of the brothers the Fuentes), came into the yard. Seeing me all in blood, she thought I had been mortally wounded, and calling them murderers ran along the street crying, "Murder, murder in Pablo Fuentes' yard," till she came to the market-place and town-house. There she found the mayors and jurats sitting, and a couple of Spaniards, who, when they heard of my danger, came running with drawn swords, together with all the officers of justice, to the yard of Pablo Fuentes to aid and assist me. In the meanwhile the idolators perceiving the outcry of the mulatta began to fall away and to hide themselves. I held Pablo Fuentes hard to it, striving with him that he might not escape till some help came unto me.

The Spaniards when they came and saw me all in a blood, made furiously to Pablo Fuentes with their naked swords, but I stopped them, desiring them not to hurt him, lest what harm they did to him should be imputed to me. I wished the justices not to fear him, though he were a rich Indian, and as they would answer before the President of Guatemala to lay hold of him, and to carry him to prison, which they presently performed. I made the Spaniards and the mulatta to witness in writing what they had seen, the blood about my clothes, wound in my hand, the blow in my mouth they had found, and I sent their information with speed to the President of Guatemala.

The business was soon noised about the valley, whereupon most of the Spaniards came to offer their help and aid unto me. Miguel Dalva also, chancing to be near at a Spaniard's house in the same valley, came with the rest, and they would have done that night some mischief among the Indians if I had not prevented them. I desired them to depart and go home to their houses, telling them I feared nothing, and that Miguel Dalva's company would be guard enough unto me. But they would by no means yield unto this, saying that night might prove more dangerous unto me than I imagined, and that I needed a stronger guard than of one man alone, for they conceived that the idolaters, knowing what already they had done and fearing what grievous punishment might be inflicted upon them from the President of Guatemala, would see themselves lost and undone men, and might that night in desperation rescue their brother out of prison and attempt some mischief against me before fleeing. I could not be brought to fear this, or to believe any such thing of their cowardly spirits, nor that they would flee away for that they had houses and land there in and about the town. Yet I was willing for one night to agree to have a stronger guard of Spaniards than at other times I had had with the Blackamoor Miguel Dalva alone.

After supper they kept watch about my house till such time as they perceived all was still, and the Indians abed, and then they set a watch about the prison that Pablo Fuentes might not be taken out. Then, as they were only about a dozen in number, they began to think, although I did not agree, that they also were in danger if the town should all rise and mutiny by the suggestion of the idolaters, most of whom were rich and powerful. They would needs go and raise up the two *alcaldes* and two more petty officers to search about the town for the rest of the Fuentes and other known idolaters, to secure them in the prison to appear at Guatemala, and to prevent them from doing any mischief either that night, or at any other time. With this stir which they made, and their care of me, they suffered me not to take any rest that night, but went and called the *alcaldes* and two officers and brought them to my house, desiring me to signify unto them how fit and necessary it was to search for the rest of the Indians.

The poor *alcaldes* trembled to see so many Spaniards at that time in my house with naked swords, and agreed to what they said, and so from my house about midnight they walked about the town, searching such houses as they most suspected might conceal any of the Fuentes, or of the rest that had been that day in the rebellion and mutiny against me. They could find none at home, till at last coming to the house of one Lorenzo Fuentes, one of the brothers, they found all that had been in the conspiracy against me gathered together drinking and quaffing. The house being beset, there was no flying nor escaping, and seeing the Spaniards' naked swords, they durst not rebel. Doubtless, as we were afterwards informed, they would have made a great stir in the town that night, and were met together to rescue Pablo their brother, and to do me some mischief and fly, not knowing that I was so strongly manned and guarded by the Spaniards. The ten of them were presently, without any noise in the town, carried to the prison, and there shut up, and guarded by the Spaniards.

In the morning the President of Guatemala, who then was Don Juan de Guzmán, a religious governor, taking into his consideration what the day before I had written to him, and judging my danger to be great, sent a Spanish *alguacil*, or officer of justice, with a very large commission to bring prisoners to the city all those Indians who the day before had been in rebellion against me, and in case they could not be found, to seize upon what goods of theirs could be found in Mixco. But with the diligence of the Spaniards the night before they were all in a readiness for him, and first paying the *alguacil's* charges (which he demanded as he listed) and bearing the charges of Miguel Dalva, and two or three more Spaniards, who were commanded in the King's name to aid and assist the officer to carry them safely to Guatemala, they were horsed and had away that day.

The President committed them close prisoners, and afterwards commanded them to be whipped about the streets and banished two of them from Mixco to the Gulf of Santo Tomás de Castilla, and would have banished them all had they not humbled themselves, and desired me to intercede for them, promising to amend their lives, and to make me great satisfaction if they might return again to their town. They answered me that if ever more they did stir against me, they would yield to be hanged and to lose all their goods. With this the President, after fining them to pay twenty crowns apiece to the church, to be employed in whatever way I should think fittest, sent them back.

As they had promised, they came unto me, and humbled themselves before me with much weeping, with many expressions showing their sorrow from their hearts for what they had done. They cast all upon the Devil, who, they confessed, had greatly tempted them, whom also now they did abjure and renounce, promising to live as good Christians, and never more to worship any god but one. I was very much taken with their deep sorrow expressed with many tears, and endeavored to instruct them in the true knowledge of Christ, whom now I found they were very willing to embrace.[11]

I lived not very long after in that town, but for the time I did continue in it, I found a great change and alteration in their lives, which truly made me apt to judge that their repentance was unfeigned. I have not here inserted these former particulars of a few

[11] Gage does not exaggerate the danger. About thirty years later the Dominican Fr. Lorenzo de Guevara, priest at Mixco, was forced to flee to Antigua in the face of threats of Indians of Mixco to kill him. The trouble arose from his efforts to stop them when, in the old heathen way, they beat drums, pots, and pans and pieces of iron and shouted and wept during an eclipse of the moon. The Indians believed, and in parts still believe, that eclipses are caused by fights between the sun and his wife the moon, and with their clamor the Indians help the moon to save her life. At about the same time there was another incident near Mixco involving the worship of an idol. This was a large stone figure which some Spaniards threw into a barranca because it interfered with plowing. Next day it was back in position despite the size and weight of the figure and the steepness of the barranca. A second time the figure was thrown into the barranca and again replaced by the Indians. Finally, the Spaniards smashed the idol.

Indians of those two towns to bring an aspersion upon all that nation, which I do very much affect, and would willingly spend the best drops of blood in my veins to do them good, and to save their souls, but to cause rather pity and commiseration towards them. For after so many years' preaching, they have as yet made but formal and outward Christians, and have rather been inclined to the superstition and idolatry of their forefathers and to trust to living creatures, and to bow to inanimate stocks and stones, by the many saints of wood which they have been taught to worship. Certainly they are of a good and flexible nature, and were those idols of saints' statues removed from their eyes, they might be brought easily to worship one only God and set up Jesus Christ, and Him that sent him into the world to save such as truly believe in him.

The year [1635] that this stir happened in Mixco, I received from the General of the Dominican Order in Rome licence to come home to England, at which I rejoiced much, for now I was even weary with living among the Indians, and grieved to see the little fruit I reaped amongst them. And I was unhappy that for fear of the Inquisition I durst not preach to them a new gospel, which might make them true, real, and inward Christians. Lastly, I perceived that Antonio Méndez de Sotomayor, who was lord of the town of Mixco, did stomach [was offended with] me for having caused two of his town to be banished and because I had publicly affronted the Fuentes for their idolatry, which he thought was a great aspersion laid upon his Indians.

Having well considered all this, I wrote to the Provincial, who was then in Chiapa, of my desire to return home to mine own country, for which I had a licence sent me from Rome.[12] But he was not willing that I should go, having heard of what good I had done in the town of Mixco, in reducing some idolaters, burning their idol, and venturing my life in so good a cause, and also for the perfect knowledge which now I had of the Pokomchi tongue. With fair and flattering words he encouraged me to stay, where he doubted not but I did, and I might yet do, God much more good service; and that he might the better work upon me, he sent me a patent of

---

[12] The Provincial then—about the end of 1634—was Rev. Fr. Jacinto de Cabañas, who as Prior of Guatemala had welcomed Gage there seven years before and had sponsored his debate with the Jesuits.

vicar of the town and cloister of Amatitlán, where at the present there was a new cloister abuilding to separate all that valley from the cloister of Guatemala.

He desired me to accept that small preferment, not doubting but that I, speaking so well the Indian language, might prevail much in that place. And he felt sure that I was the best man to further the building of that new cloister; which work would be a good step for him to advance me afterwards to some better preferment. Although I regarded neither that present superiority, nor any better honor which might afterwards ensue unto me, I thought the time which God had appointed for my returning to England was not yet come. For if both the Provincial and the President of Guatemala (for so much I conjectured out of the Provincial's letter) should oppose and hinder my departure from that country, it would be very hard for me to take my journey any way, and not be discovered and brought back.

Thereupon I resolved to await the Provincial's coming to Guatemala, and there to confer with him face to face, and to shew him some reasons that moved me to leave that country, and to seek again mine own wherein I was born. So for the present I accepted of the town of Amatitlán, where I had more occasions of getting money than in the other two, where I had lived five full years. For that town alone was bigger than Mixco and Pinola together, and the church fuller of saints' pictures and statues, and very many confraternities and sodalities belonged unto it. Besides this, I had great comings in from the *ingenio* of sugar, which, as I related before, stood close unto that town. Thence I had daily offerings from the Blackamoors and Spaniards that lived in it; and besides this I had under my charge another lesser town called San Cristóbal de Amatitlán, standing two leagues from great Amatitlán.

This town of San Cristóbal, or St. Christopher, is called properly in that language, *Palinha, ha* signifying water, and *pali* to stand upright, and is compounded of two words which express water standing upright, for the town standeth on the back side of the volcano of water which looketh over Guatemala. On this side the volcano sends forth many fountains, but especially from a high rock a stream of water, which, as it falls from high with a great noise and downfall, causes a most pleasant stream by the town's side. The

Indians call their town *Palinha* [now known as Palín] from the high and upright standing rock from whence the water falls. In this town there are many rich Indians, who trade in the coast of the South Sea.

The town is as an arbor shadowed with many fruitful trees, but the chief fruit is the *piña* [pineapple], which groweth in every Indian's yard. With the nearness of the *ingenio* of sugar, the Spaniards thereabouts make up large quantities in preserves, some whole, some in slices, the daintest and most luscious preserve that I ever did eat in that country. The Indians of this town get much by boards of cedar, which they cut out of many cedar trees which grow on that side of the volcano, and which they sell to Guatemala and all about the country for new buildings.

Between great Amatitlán and this town the way is plain, and lieth under a volcano of fire which formerly was wont to smoke as much as that of Guatemala, but having formerly burst out at the top, and there opened a great mouth, and cast down to the bottom mighty stones (which to this day are to be seen), it hath not since been any ways troublesome unto the country. In this way there was in my time a new *trapiche* of sugar erected by one Juan Bautista of Guatemala, which was thought would prove very useful and profitable unto the aforesaid city.

When I lived in Amatitlán, I had another very little village at my charge, called Pampichi. It was at the bottom of a high mountain on the other side of the lake, and was but a chapel of ease to great Amatitlán. I went there not above once in a quarter of a year, and that for pastime and recreation, for this village is well [named] in that language, for it is a compound of *pam*, in, and *pichi*, flowers, for that it standeth compassed about with flowers, which make it very pleasant. The boats or *canoas* which constantly stand near the doors of the houses invite to much pleasure of fishing and rowing about the lake.

Thus whilst I lived in Amatitlán I had the choice of three places wherein to recreate myself, and because the charge of many souls lay in my hands, I had one constantly to help me. The town of Amatitlán was as the Court in respect of the rest, where nothing was wanting that might recreate the mind and satisfy the body with variety and change of sustenance, for both fish and flesh. Yet the great care that did lie upon me in the work and building of the cloister made me very soon weary of living in that great and pleasant town. Sometimes I had thirty, sometimes twenty, sometimes fewer, and sometimes forty, workmen to look after, and to pay wages to on Saturday nights. This I found wearied much my brain, and hindered my studies, and was besides a work which I delighted not in, nor had any hopes ever to enjoy it.

Therefore, after the first year that I had been there, I betook myself unto the Provincial, who was in Guatemala, and again earnestly besought him to peruse the licence which I had from Rome to go to England mine own country to preach there (for that was the chief ground of letting me go home, as the General largely expressed). I told him I doubted not but I might do God great service there, and in conscience I thought I was bound to employ what parts God had bestowed upon me rather upon my own countrymen than upon Indians and strangers. The Provincial[13] replied that my countrymen were heretics, and when I came amongst them they would hang me up. I told him, I hoped better things of them, and that I would not behave myself among them so as to deserve hanging, not daring to tell him what was in my heart concerning points of religion.

After a long discourse I found the Provincial inexorable, and half-angry, telling me that he and that whole province had cast their eyes upon me, and honored me, and were ready and willing to promote me further, and that I would shew myself very ungrateful unto them if I should forsake them for my own nation and people, whom I had not known from my young and tender age. I perceived there was no more to be said, and all would be in vain, and so resolved to take my best opportunity, and with my licence from Rome, to come away unknown unto him. But for the present I humbly beseeched him to remove me from Amatitlán, for I found myself unable to undergo that great charge, and too weak for that strong work that was then building. Only with much ado would he be brought to this, alleging what an honor it was to be a founder and builder of a new cloister, in whose walls my very name would be engraven to posterity. All that I told him I regarded not,

[13] Rev. Fr. Pedro de Montenegro, who was obviously less friendly to Gage than his predecessor, Rev. Fr. Jacinto de Cabañas.

but esteemed more my health and a quiet mind than such preferments and vanities. Upon which at last he condescended to my request, and gave me order to go to Petapa, and that the vicar of Petapa should go to finish the work of Amatitlán.[14]

In Petapa I lived above a twelvemonth, with great ease, pleasure, and content for all things worldly and outward, but within I had still a worm of conscience, gnawing this gourd that shadowed and delighted me with worldly contentment. Here I grew more and more troubled concerning some points of religion, daily wishing with David that I had the wings of a dove that I might flee from that place of daily idolatry into England, and be at rest. I resolved therefore to put on a good courage, and rely wholly upon my God, knowing that the journey was hard and dangerous, and might bring shame and trouble unto me if I should be taken in the way flying and brought back to Guatemala. Here I weighed the affliction and reproach which might ensue unto me, after so much honor, pleasure, and wealth which I had enjoyed for about twelve years in that country. So for faith and a safe conscience I now purposed like Moses to forsake Egypt, not fearing the wrath of the President, the King's own deputy, nor of the Provincial, and my best friends, but to endure all this if I should be taken as seeing him who is invisible.

I thought this was a business not to be conferred with flesh and blood, lest the best friend knowing of it should betray me. On the other side, I thought it hard to flee alone without some friend for the first two or three days' journey, and besides, having many things to sell away to make money, I thought I were better to employ some trusty friend than to do all alone. I thought of none fitter than Miguel Dalva, who by long experience I knew was true and trusty, and that a small money matter would content him. I sent for him to come to Pinola, and charging him with secrecy, I told him I had a journey for my conscience' sake to make to Rome. I would not

[14] At the provincial chapter in 1638, soon after the completion of the new convent on which Gage had been busy, Amatitlán was raised to the rank of a Priory. Had Gage stayed there, he might well have had the honor of being the first Prior. Instead, his old friend, the missionary and linguist, Fr. Francisco Morán was elected to the post. At the same time his old schoolmate and fellow runaway, Antonio Meléndez, was elected first Prior of Ocosingo. Gage, then in the humble position of chaplain to his uncle in Surrey, England, presumably never heard of the promotions of his old friends.

tell him that I intended England, lest the good old Blackamoor should grieve, thinking never more to see me, and for the love he bare me, and interest he had many times from me, he should by discovering my intent seek to stop me. Thinking I was going to Rome, he would expect me to return again, as he knew many had taken the like journey, and returned within two years.[15]

The Blackamoor offered himself to go with me, which I refused, telling him that the seas would be too hard for his old age to endure, and that as a Blackamoor in foreign countries, he might be stopped and apprehended for a fugitive. He well understood that reason, but offered to go with me as far as the sea side, for which I thanked him and employed him to sell some mules, wheat, and maize which I had, and what else might well pass through his hands.

I thought the town of Petapa would buy for their church many rich pictures which hung in my chamber, and propounded it unto the Governor, who willingly accepted of them. Most of my books, chests, cabinets, quilts, and many good pieces of household stuff I sold in Guatemala by the pains and industry of Miguel, whom I kept with me for the space of two months before I came away. I kept only two *petacas,* or leathern chests, with some books and a quilt for my journey.

When I had sold all that I intended, I found I had in Spanish money near nine thousand pieces of eight, which I had got in the twelve years that I lived in that country. So much money I thought would be too cumbersome for a long journey; whereupon I turned above four thousand crowns into pearls and some precious stones, which might make my carriage the lighter. The rest I laid up, some in bags, some I sewed into my quilt, intending in the way to turn them into Spanish *pistoles.* Thus the chief provision being made of money, I took care for chocolate and some conserves for the way, which were soon provided. Now because I considered that my flight the first week must be with speed, and that my chests could not post day and night as myself intended to do, I thought of sending my carriage four days at least before me. Not daring to trust any Indian of Petapa, I sent to Mixco for one special Indian friend whom I had there, who knew the way that I was to travel very well. I opened

[15] The obvious devotion of Miguel is a strong argument against the idea that Gage was wholly a scoundrel.

my mind to him, and offered what money I knew would well content him, and at midnight sent him away with two mules, one for himself and another for my chests, wishing him to keep on travelling towards San Miguel, or Nicaragua, till I overtook him. I gave him the advantage of four days and nights, and then resolutely with my good Blackamoor in my company I set out when all the Indians were fast asleep, leaving the key of my chamber in my door, and nothing but old papers within. Thus I bad adieu unto Petapa, and to the whole valley, and to all my friends throughout America.[16]

[16] Had Gage but known it, there was no need for him to make this unauthorized departure. A precept from the Master General of the Order had been sent nearly eight years earlier from Rome to the Provincial in Guatemala. This is dated October 9, 1627, and orders Gage's return to Spain on the very first ship, "as our English brethren need his services for the propagation of the faith." (Anstruther, *A Hundred Homeless Years*, 132.) This order clearly went astray. Had it arrived, this book probably would not have been written, certainly not in its present form.

17. Showing my journey from the town of Petapa into England; and some chief passages in the way

⁓⁓ ✳ ⁓⁓

THE chief thing which troubled me in my resolved purpose to come home was the choice of the safest way. I decided to utterly forsake the gulf [Golfo Dulce] though that was the easiest way of all, and that sea nearest to the place where I lived, for I knew I should meet there many acquaintances, and the setting out of the ships was so uncertain that before they departed, order might come from Guatemala to stop me. If I should go by land through Comayagua to Trujillo, and there wait for the ships, I likewise feared lest the Governor of that place by some item from the President of Guatemala might examine me, and send me back, and that the masters of the ships might have charge given them not to receive me into their ships. If I should go back to Mexico and Vera Cruz, I called to mind how I was troubled in that long journey when I came first to Chiapa in company of friends, and that now alone I should certainly be much put to it, for I would not carry Miguel Dalva so far by land with me.

Therefore rejecting these three ways, I chose the fourth, which was by Nicaragua and the Lake of Granada, and I deferred my journey till the week after Christmas, knowing that the time of the frigates' setting our from that lake to Havana was commonly after the middle of January, or at Candlemas at the furthest, and I hoped to reach there in very good time. Before I went, I left by the hand of Miguel Dalva a letter to a friend of his to be delivered to the Provincial in Guatemala four days after my departure, wherein I kindly took my leave of him, desiring him not to blame me nor to seek after me. As I had a sufficient licence from Rome, although I could not get his, I thought that I might with a safe conscience go where I was born, leaving linguists enough to supply my place amongst the Indians. And so that he should not make enquiry after me by Nicaragua, I dated and subscribed my letter to him from the town of San Antonio Suchitepéquez, which was the way to Mexico and quite contrary to Nicaragua.

The day after Twelfth Day, being the seventh of January, 1637, I set out at midnight from Petapa upon a lusty mule (which afterwards in the way I sold for fourscore pieces of eight) with Miguel Dalva alone. The first part of the way being very hilly, we could not go so fast as our hearts would have posted; for it was break of day before we could get to the top of the mountain, which is called Cerro Redondo, or the round hill. This is much mentioned in that country for the good pasture there which serveth for the cattle and sheep, when the valleys below are burnt and no grazing left for beasts. This hill is also a great refuge to travellers, for there they find good entertainment in a *venta*, where wine and provision is sold, and it is a great lodge to lay up dry what carriages they bring. There is besides one of the best *estancias* or farms of cattle in the country, where the best cheese thereabouts is made of goat's and ewe's milk. As this round hill or mountain is only five leagues from Petapa, I feared I might meet with some people of Petapa, and therefore, the day now dawning, I made haste by it, leaving in the lodge asleep many Indians, who attended on two Spanish *recuas* of mules, which that day were to go to Petapa.

Four leagues further from this Cerro Redondo is a town of Indians called Los Esclavos, or the Slaves, not that now they are more slaves than the rest of the Indians, but because in the old time of Montezuma the Emperor, and the Indian kings that were under him, the people of this town were more slaves than any other. For from Amatitlán these Indians of the town of Esclavos, or slaves, were commanded as slaves to go all about the country with letters, or whatsoever else they should be charged with. And they were bound constantly to send every week so many of their town as were appointed to Amatitlán, there to wait and attend the pleasure of that town for the conveying of letters, or any carriages, to other

Indian women in traditional dress returning from market, near Mixco. Gage often witnessed scenes like this.

Photograph by A. V. Cooper

The church at Amatitlán, where Gage was priest in charge in 1635. The booths are set up for the market in front of the church as in Gage's time.

parts. Amatitlán is so called from *amat,* which in the Mexican tongue signifieth letter, and *itlán,* which signifieth town, for that it was the Town of Letters as some say, for a rind of a tree, whereon they were wont formerly to write and express their minds, or because it was the place whither from all parts letters were sent to be carried about the country, and to Peru.[1]

This town of Los Esclavos standeth in a bottom by a river, over which the Spaniards have built a very strong stone bridge to go in and out of the town, for otherwise with mules there is no passing by reason of the violent and rapid stream of the water, and many rocks in the river, from which the water falleth down with great force. From this town, where we only stayed to drink a cup of chocolate and to bait our mules, we went on that day to Ahuachapán, ten leagues farther, and not far from the South Sea, and the port called De la Trinidad.

We reached Ahuachapán towards evening, having that day and part of the night travelled about threescore English miles up hills, and upon stony ways from the Esclavos unto this town, which is much mentioned in that country for two things. The one is for the earthenware which is made there and which, some think, exceeds that of Mixco. The other is for a place within a mile and a half from the town, which the Spaniards do credibly report and believe to be a mouth of Hell. For out of it there is constantly ascending a thick black smoke smelling of brimstone, with some flashes now and then of fire. The earth from whence this smoke ariseth is not high, but low. Nonever durst draw nigh to find out the truth and ground of it, for those that have attempted to do it have been stricken down to the ground and like to lose their lives. A friend of mine a friar (whom I thought verily I might believe) affirmed to me upon his oath that travelling that way with a Provincial he resolved to go unto the place, and satisfy himself of the ground and cause of the strange talk which was everywhere about the country concerning that smoke. He went within a quarter of a mile of it, and presently, he said, he heard a hideous noise, which together with the stench of the fiery smoke and brimstone, struck him into such a fear that

---

[1] *Amate,* a species of wild fig tree from the bark of which paper was made, and *itlán,* "within," or "at the place of." *Amatitlán,* therefore, means "at the place of the paper trees."

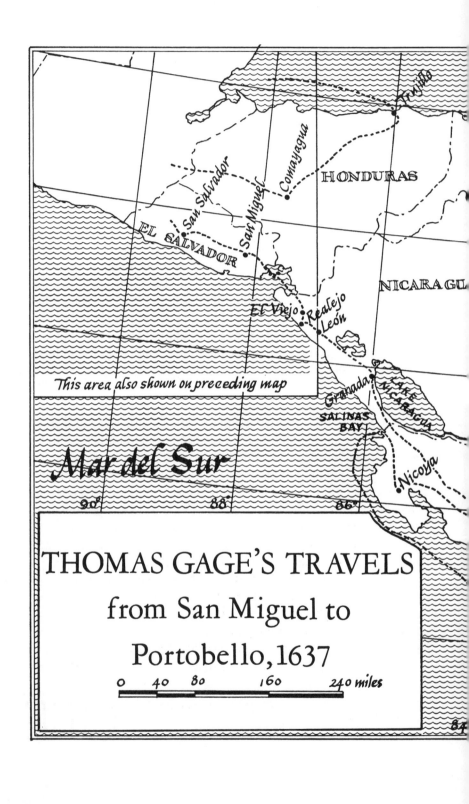

HONDURAS

Trujillo

Comayagua

San Salvador

San Miguel

EL SALVADOR

NICARAGUA

El Viejo

Realejo

León

Granada

LAKE NICARAGUA

SALINAS BAY

This area also shown on preceding map

Nicoya

Mar del Sur

90° 88° 86°

THOMAS GAGE'S TRAVELS

from San Miguel to

Portobello, 1637

0   40   80   160   240 miles

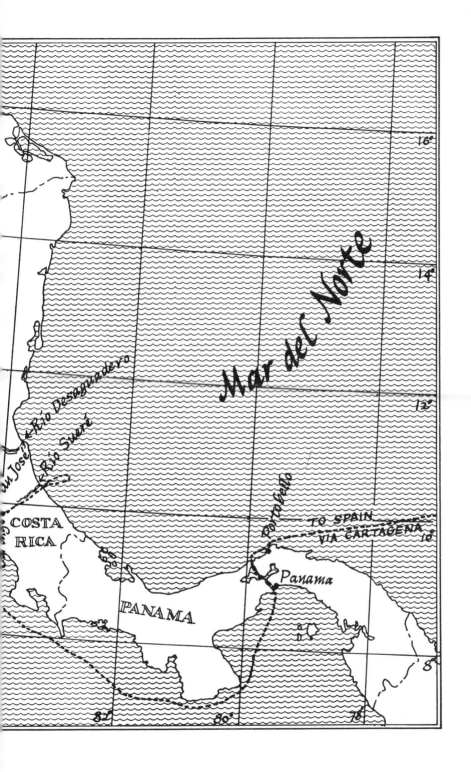

he was like to fall to the ground. Retiring himself back with all speed, he was taken with a burning fever, which was like to cost him his life.

Others report that drawing near unto it, they have heard great cries as it were of men and women in torment, noise of iron, of chains, and the like, which (how simply I leave it to my judicious reader) maketh them believe that it is a mouth of Hell. Of my knowledge I will say no more, but that I saw the smoke, and asked the Indians what was the cause of it, and if ever they had been near unto it. And they answered me, that they could not imagine what might be the cause of it, neither durst they draw night unto it, and that they had seen travellers attempting to go near it, but that they were all stricken either to the ground, or with some sudden amazement, or fever. I told them that I would walk thither myself, and they desired me that I would not, if I loved my life. It was not yet for all this report the fear of being so near the Spaniard's Hell (as they call it) that made me haste with speed out of that town, but fear of some messenger that might come after me to stop my journey.

At midnight I departed from thence, and went to break my fast at a great town called Chalchuapán, where the Indians made very much of me, being Pokomanes who spake the Pokomchi or Pokoman tongue which I had learned. They would willingly have had me to stay with them and preach unto them the next Sabbath, which I would have done had not a better design called upon me to make haste.

Here I was troubled how I should get through San Salvador, which was a city of Spaniards, wherein there was a cloister of Dominicans, whom I feared most of all, because I was known by some of them. My resolution was therefore, when I came near unto the city, to turn out of my way to a Spaniard's farm as if I had lost my way, and there to delay the time till evening in drinking chocolate, discoursing, and baiting my mules well, that so I might travel all that night, and be out of the reach of that city and friars who lived in Indian towns about it the next morning early.

This city of San Salvador is poor, not much bigger than Chiapa, and is governed by a Spanish governor. It stands forty leagues at least from Guatemala, and towards the North Sea side is compassed with very high mountains, which are called Chontales, where the

Indians are very poor. In the bottom where the city stands there are some *trapiches* of sugar and some indigo, but the chief farms are *estancias* of cattle. Towards evening I departed from that farm where I had well refreshed myself and my mule, and about eight of the clock I rode through the city not being known by anybody. My purpose was to be the next morning at a great river called Río de Lempa, some ten leagues from San Salvador, for within two leagues of it there lived in an Indian town a friar belonging to the cloister of San Salvador who knew me very well. But such haste I made that before break of the day I passed through that town, and before seven of the clock I was at the river, where I found my Indian of Mixco ready to pass over with my carriage, who that morning by three of the clock had set out of that town two leagues off. I was not a little glad to have overtaken my chests, wherein was most of my treasure. There I sat down a while by the river whilst my mules grazed, and my Indian struck fire and made me chocolate.

This River of Lempa is held the broadest and biggest in all the jurisdiction belonging unto Guatemala; there are constantly two ferry boats to pass over the travellers, and their *recuas* of mules. This river is privileged in this manner, that if a man commit any heinous crime or murder on this side of Guatemala, and San Salvador, or on the other side of San Miguel, or Nicaragua, if he can flee over this river, he is free as long as he lives on the other side, and no justice on that side whither he is escaped can question or trouble him for the murder committed. Likewise he cannot be arrested for debts. Though I thanked God I neither fled for the one, or for the other, yet it was my comfort that I was now going over to a privileged country, where I hoped I should be free and sure, and that if anyone did come after me, he would go no further than to the River of Lempa.[2] My Blackamoor did much laugh at this my conceit, and warranted me that all would go well.

We ferried safely over the river, and thence went in company with my Indian to a small town of Indians two leagues off, where we made the best dinner that we had eaten since we left Petapa, and willingly gave rest to all our mules till four of the clock in the afternoon, at which time we set forth through a plain, sandy, and

[2] The Río Lempa was an important boundary in pre-Columbian times, and today separates eastern El Salvador from the rest of the country.

champaign country to another small town a little above two leagues off. The next day we had but ten leagues to travel to a town called San Miguel, which belongs to Spaniards, and though it be not a city, yet is as big almost as San Salvador, and hath a Spanish governor. In it there is one cloister of nuns, and another of Mercenarian friars, who welcomed me to their cloister; for here I began to show my face and to think of selling away the mule I rid on, being resolved from hence to go by water or an arm of the sea [Gulf of Fonseca], to a town in Nicaragua called El Viejo.

I would here have dismissed my Indian, but he was loath to leave me until I got to Granada, where he desired to see me shipped. I refused not his kind offer, because I knew he was trusty and had brought my chests well thither, and knew well the way to Granada. So I sent him by land to Realejo, or to El Viejo, which stand very near together and thirty leagues by land from San Miguel, and myself stayed that day and till the next day at noon in that town, where I sold the mule I rid on, because I knew that from Realejo to Granada I could have of the Indians a mule for nothing for a day's journey. My Blackamoor's mule I sent also by land with the Indian, and the next day went to the gulf, being three or four miles from San Miguel, where that afternoon I took boat with many other passengers, and the next morning by eight was at El Viejo, which journey by land would have taken me near three days. The next night my Indian came, and we went to Realejo, a very weak and unfortified haven on the South Sea, as I have observed before, where if I would have stayed one fortnight, I might have taken ship for Panama, and thence to Portobello, to stay there for the galleons from Spain. But I considered that the galleons would not be there till June or July, and so I should be at great charges in staying so long. But afterwards I wished I had accepted of that occasion, for I was at last forced to go to Panama, and Portobello.

From Realejo to Granada I observed nothing but the plainness and pleasantness of the way, which with the fruits and fertility of all things may well make Nicaragua the Paradise of America. Between Realejo and Granada standeth the city of León, near unto a volcano of fire, which formerly burst out at the top, and did much hurt unto all the country about, but since that it has ceased, and now lets the inhabitants live without fear. Sometimes it smokes a little, which shows that as yet there is within some sulphurous substance.

Here it was that a Mercenarian friar thought to have discovered some great treasure, which might enrich himself and all that country, being fully persuaded that the metal that burned within that volcano was gold. He caused a great kettle to be made, and hung at an iron chain to let it down from the top, thinking therewith to take up gold enough to make him bishop and to enrich his poor kindred. But such was the power and strength of the fire within, that no sooner had he let down the kettle, when it fell from the chain and from his hands being melted away.

This city of León is very curiously built, for the chief delight of the inhabitants is in their houses, in the pleasure of the country adjoining, and in the abundance of all things for the life of man's extraordinary riches are not so much enjoyed there as in other parts of America. They are contented with fine gardens, with variety of singing birds, and parrots, with plenty of fish and flesh, which is cheap, and with gay houses, and so lead a delicious, lazy, and idle life, not aspiring much to trade and traffic, though they have near unto them the lake, which commonly every year sends forth some frigates to Havana by the North Sea, and Realejo on the South Sea, which to them might be very commodious for any dealing and rich trading in Peru, or to Mixco, if their spirits would carry them so far. The gentlemen of this city are almost as vain and fantastical as are those of Chiapa. And especially from the pleasure of this city is all that province of Nicaragua called by the Spaniards, Mahomet's Paradise.

From hence the way is plain and level to Granada, whither I got safely and joyfully, hoping that now I had no more journey to make by land, till I should land at Dover in England, and from thence post up to London. Two days after I had arrived at this place and rested myself, and enjoyed the pleasant prospect of the lake, I began to think of dismissing my Indian and Blackamoor. But true and faithful Miguel Dalva would by no means leave me till he saw me shipped and knew that I had no more need of him by land. Likewise the Indian would willingly have stayed, but by no means would I permit him, considering that he had a wife and children to look to at home. He was as willing to return afoot as to ride, because he would have me sell my mules, and make what money I could of them; but I, seeing the good nature of the Indian, would recompense his love with as much money as might be more beneficial to him than a tired mule; which might have died in the way under him, and left him on foot. So I gave him money enough to bear his charges home, and to hire mules at his own pleasure, and some to spare, when he came home. The Indian, with many tears falling from his eyes and saying he feared he should never more see me, took his leave of me the third day after we arrived at Granada.

My Blackamoor and I, being left alone, first began to think of selling the two mules, which had brought thither the Indian and my chests, and I got fourscore and ten pieces of eight for them, and thought they were well sold after so long a journey. I wanted Miguel to sell his own mule which he was riding, and offered to buy him another that might better carry him back, but the loving and careful Blackamoor would not suffer me to be at such charges, considering the long journey which I was to make.

After this, hearing that the frigates were not like to depart in a fortnight, we thought of viewing well that stately and pleasant town a day or two, and then we would betake ourselves to some near Indian town, where we might be hid (lest by the great resort of *recuas* of mules, which at that time brought indigo and cochineal from Guatemala to the frigates, we should be discovered). I thought that from the Indian town we might now and then come to the town to treat concerning my passing in one of the frigates to Havana or to Cartagena. In that town we observed two cloisters of Mercenarian and Franciscan friars, and one of nuns, very rich, and a parish church, which was as a cathedral, for the Bishop of León did more constantly reside there than in the city. The houses are fairer than those of León, and the town of more inhabitants, among whom there are some few merchants of very great wealth, and many of inferior degree very well to pass, who trade with Cartagena, Guatemala, San Salvador, and Comayagua, and some by the South Sea to Peru and Panama. At this time of the sending away the frigates that town is one of the wealthiest in all the north tract of America, for the merchants of Guatemala fearing to send all their goods by the Gulf of Honduras, for that they have been often taken between the gulf and Havana by the Hollanders, think it safer to send them by the frigates to Cartagena, for that passage has not been so much stopped by the Hollanders as the other. So likewise many times the King's treasure and revenues are passed this way by the Lake of Granada to Cartagena³ when there is any report of ships at sea, or about the Cape of San Antonio,

That year that I was there, before I betook myself to an Indian town, there entered in one day six *recuas* (at least three hundred mules) from San Salvador and Comayagua only, laden with nothing else but indigo, cochineal, and hides, and two days after from Guatemala three more came in. One was laden with silver, which was the King's tribute from that country; the other with sugar; the third with indigo. The former *recuas* I feared not; but the latter made me keep close within my lodging, lest going abroad I should be known by some of those that came from Guatemala. However, after they had delivered what they brought, they presently departed, and with their departure set me at liberty, who for their sakes was a voluntary prisoner within mine own lodging.

Fearing lest more of these *recuas* might come and affright me, I went to a town out of the road, a league from Granada, and took my pleasure up and down the country, where I was much feasted by the Mercenarian friars, who enjoy most of those towns. Amongst these I heard much of the passage in the frigates to Cartagena, which did not a little dishearten and discourage me. For although they sail upon the lake securely and without trouble, yet when they fall from the lake to the river, which there they call El Desaguadero, to go out to the sea, there is nothing but trouble. Sometimes that short voyage lasts two months, for such is the fall of the waters in many places amongst the rocks that many times they are forced to unlade the frigates, and lade them again with the help of mules which are kept there for that purpose by a few Indians that live about the river. These Indians also have charge of the warehouses in which the goods are stored whilst the frigates pass through those dangerous places to another warehouse, whither the wares

³ Lake Granada is the present Lake Nicaragua. The frigates sailed from Granada about 100 miles to the southeast corner of the lake, whence they followed the shallow Río Desaguadero or San Juan River, as it is now called, another 100 miles to the present coastal town of Bluefields. This is the route followed a century ago to California and which will be followed by the projected relief way for the Panama Canal. Providence Island lies about 150 miles offshore, and made an ideal base for privateers preying on Spanish commerce.

are brought by mules and put again into the frigates. Besides this trouble, which must needs be tedious to a passenger who would willingly come soon to his journey's end, the abundance of gnats is such that he can take no joy in his voyage, and the heat in some places is so intolerable that many do die before they get out to the sea. Though all this was terrible to me to hear, yet I comforted myself that my life was in the hands of the Lord, and that the frigates did commonly every year pass that way, and seldom were any lost.

I went now and then to Granada to bargain for my passage, and to know when the frigates would for certain set out, and to provide myself of some dainties and chocolate for my journey, having agreed with a master of a frigate for my diet at his table. The time was appointed within four or five days, but suddenly all was crossed with a strict command from Guatemala that the frigates should not go out that year, because the President and whole Court was informed for certain that some English or Holland ships were abroad at sea, and lay about the mouth of the river of Desaguadero waiting for the frigates of Granada, and that they were sometimes lurking about the islands of San Juan [St. John], and Santa Catalina [St. Catharine] (which then was our Providence). That news made all the merchants of the country fear and sweat with a cold sweat, and the President be careful for the King's revenues, lest the loss of them should be imputed to his wilful negligence in not stopping the frigates whilst he might, and had warning given.

This was sad news to me, who knew not for the present which way to dispose of myself. I began to think of the ship that was at Realejo ready to set out to Panama, thinking that would now be my best course, but enquiring after it, I was for certain informed by some merchants that it was newly gone. Then my eyes looked upon Comayagua and Truxillo, and upon the ships of Honduras, but these were but vain and troubled thoughts, arising from a perplexed heart, for the ships were also gone from thence, unless some small vessel or frigate might be there with news from Havana or Cartagena, for those places send often word and notice of what ships are abroad at sea, but this also was a mere chance, and not to be trusted, as my friends did advise and counsel me. Whereupon my perplexity more and more increased. My only comfort was that there were more passengers besides myself who I knew must take some course, and whom I also resolved to follow by sea or land. Amongst us all we were once resolving to hire a frigate to carry us only to Cartagena, but this would not be granted, for nobody would hazard his vessel and life for our sakes.

Whilst we were thus distressed and perplexed enquiring about Granada of the merchants what course we might take to get to Spain that year, or to meet with Havana or Cartagena, one that wished us well counselled us to go to Costa Rica, where at Cartago we should be sure to hear of some vessels bound for Portobello, either from the river called De los Anzuelos, or from the river called Sueré, from whence every year went out some small frigates to carry meal, bacon, fowls, and other provision for the galleons to Portobello. This we thought was hard and difficult, and of near a hundred and fifty leagues, over mountains and through deserts, where we should miss the pleasure, variety, and dainties of Guatemala and Nicaragua, and after all this peradventure might not find any frigate bound to Portobello. Yet so unwilling were we all to return to Guatemala from whence we came, that we would rather go forward, and undergo any difficulties, so that at last we might find any shipping to convey us where we might meet with the galleons. These we knew were not to come to Portobello till the month of June or July.

Four of us, three Spaniards and myself, agreed to go to Costa Rica, there to try our fortune. They had each of them, like myself, carriage for one mule, and none to ride on. Therefore, they thought it best to buy each of them a mule to carry them, and they hoped after their journey to sell them in Costa Rica at a profit. They decided for their carriages to hire mules and Indians from town to town, and the latter might guide us through many dangerous places and passages, which we understood were in the way. Now I wished I had my mule which I had sold at San Miguel, or any one of the two which I had sold before in Granada. But for my money I doubted not, with the help of my Blackamoor, but I should find one for my purpose. I furnished myself very speedily, for fifty pieces of eight, of one which I feared not would perform my journey.

My good and trusty Blackamoor would willingly have gone on with me, and further round the world, if I would have permitted him, but I would not. I thanked him heartily for what he had done, and gave him money enough in his purse, and dismissed him, hoping that the company of the three Spaniards would be sufficient comfort unto me.

Thus with one Indian to guide us we four set out of Granada, enjoying for the first two days more of the pleasure of that Mahomet's Paradise, Nicaragua, finding the way for the most part plain, the towns pleasant, the country shady, and everywhere fruits abounding. The second day we were much affrighted with a huge and monstrous cayman or crocodile, which, having come out of the lake, which we passed by, was lying across a puddle of water bathing himself, and waiting for some prey, as we perceived after. We, thinking that it had been some tree that was felled or fallen, passed close by it, when on a sudden we knew the scales of the cayman, and saw the monster stir and move, and set himself against us. We made haste from him, but he, thinking to have made some of us his greedy prey, ran after us, and when we perceived that he was like to overtake us, we were much troubled, until one of the Spaniards, who knew better the nature and quality of that beast than the rest, called upon us to turn to one side out of the way, and to ride on straight for a while, and then to turn to another side, and so to circumflex our way.

His advice without doubt saved mine or some of the others' lives, for thus we wearied that mighty monster and escaped from him, who, had we ridden in a straight line, had certainly overtaken us and killed some mule or man, for his straightforward flight was as swift as our mules could run. But whilst he turned and wheeled his heavy body about, we gained ground and advantage till we left him far behind us, and by this experience we came to know the nature and quality of that beast, whose greatness of body does not hinder him from running forward as swiftly as a mule; but otherwise, as the elephant once laid down is troubled to get up, so this monster is heavy and stiff, and therefore much troubled to turn and wind about his body.

We praised God who had that day delivered us, and riding for a while by the side of the lake, we were watchful that we might not fall again into the like danger. But the greatness of this Lake of Granada may be known from the fact that on the second and third day of our journey, being at least three score miles from whence we set out, we now and then found our way lying by it. After we had wholly lost the sight of it, we began to enter rough and craggy ways, declining more to the South than to the North Sea. And in all the rest of our journey to Cartago we observed nothing worth committing to posterity, but only mighty woods and trees on the South Sea side, very fit to make strong ships, and many mountains and desert places, where we lay sometimes two nights together, either in woods or open fields, far from any town or habitation of Indians. Yet for our comfort in these so desert places we had still a guide with us, and found lodges, which by the command of the nearest justices had been set up for such as travelled that way.[4]

We came at last through thousand dangers to the city of Cartago, which we found not to be so poor as in richer places, as Guatemala and Nicaragua, it was reported to be. For there we had occasion to enquire after some merchants for exchange of gold and silver, and we found some very rich ones, who traded by land and sea with Panama, and by sea with Portobello, Cartagena, and Havana, and thence with Spain. This city may consist of four hundred families, and is governed by a Spanish governor. It is a bishop's see, and hath in it three cloisters, two of friars, and one of nuns. Here we began to enquire after that which had brought us through so many mountains, woods, and deserts, to wit, some speedy occasion of shipping ourselves for Portobello or Cartagena, and we understood that one frigate was almost ready to set out from the river called De los Anzuelos, and another from the River Sueré.

We were informed that Sueré would be the best place for us to travel to by reason of more provision in the way, more towns of Indians, and *estancias* of Spaniards, so we resolved within four days after we had rested in Cartago to undertake a new journey towards the North Sea. We found that country mountainous in many places, yet here and there some valleys where was very good corn, Spaniards living in good farms, who, as well as the Indians, bred many hogs, but the towns of Indians we found quite unlike those which we had left behind in Nicaragua and Guatemala. The people differed much

---

[4] From Granada the route was along the strip between Lake Nicaragua and the Pacific. Cartago is a short distance east of San José, the capital of Costa Rica. The total distance is about 225 miles in direct line, probably about twice that by mule track.

from them in courtesy and civility, and were of a rude and bold carriage and behavior towards us, yet they are kept under by the Spaniards, as much as those about Guatemala, of whom I have formerly spoken. We came in so good a time to the River Sueré that we stayed there but three days in a Spanish farm near unto it, and departed.[5]

The master of the frigate was exceeding glad of our company, and offered to carry me for nothing, except my prayers to God for him and for a safe passage, which he hoped would not be above three or four days' sailing. He carried nothing but some honey, hides, bacon, meal, and fowls. The greatest danger he told us of, was the setting out from the river, which runs in some places with a very strong stream, is shallow and full of rocks in other places, till we come forth to the main sea. We got out safely to sea and had not sailed on above twenty leagues when we discovered two ships making towards us. Our hearts began to quake, and the master himself of the frigate we perceived was not without fear, for he suspected that they were English, or Holland ships. As we had no guns nor weapons to fight with, save only four or five muskets and half a dozen swords, we thought the wings of our nimble frigate might be our best comfort, and flying away our chiefest safety. But this comfort soon began to fail us, and our best safety was turned into near approaching danger, for before we could fly on five leagues towards Portobello, we could from our top mast easily perceive the two ships to be Hollanders, and too nimble for our little vessel.

Presently one of them, which being a man-of-war was too much and too strong for our weakness, fetched up, and with a thundering message made us strike sail. We durst not but yield, without any fighting, hoping for better mercy. But O, what sad thoughts did here run to and fro my dejected heart, which was struck down lower than our sail. How did I sometimes look upon death's frighting visage! But if again I would comfort and encourage myself against this fear of death; how then did I begin to see an end of all my hopes of ever more returning to my wished and desired country! Now did I see my treasure of pearls, precious stones, and pieces of eight, and golden *pistoles*, which by singing I had got in twelve years' space, now within one half hour ready to be lost with weeping, and become

[5] The Sueré River is now called the Pacuaré. Its mouth is a short distance up the coast from the modern port of Limón.

a sure prey to those who with as much ease as I got them, and with laughing, were ready to spoil me of all that which with the sound of flutes, waits, and organs I had so long been hoarding up! Now I saw I must forcedly and feignedly offer up to a Hollander what superstitious, yea, also forced and feigned, offerings of Indians to their saints of Mixco, Pinola, Amatitlán, and Petapa had for a while enriched me.

My further thoughts were soon interrupted by the Hollanders, who came aboard our frigate with more speed than we desired. Though their swords, muskets, and pistols did not a little terrify, yet we were somewhat comforted when we understood who was their chief captain and commander. We hoped for more mercy from him, for he had been born and brought up amongst Spaniards, than from the Hollanders, for as they were little bound unto the Spanish nation for mercy, so did we expect little from them. The captain of this Holland ship which took us was a mulatto, born and bred in Havana, whose mother I saw and spoke with afterwards that same year, when the galleons struck into that port to expect there the rest that were to come from Vera Cruz. This mulatto, for some wrongs which had been offered unto him from some commanding Spaniards in Havana, ventured himself desperately in a boat out to sea, where were some Holland ships waiting for a prize. With God's help getting unto them, he yielded himself to their mercy, which he esteemed far better than that of his own countrymen, promising to serve them faithfully against his own nation, which had most injuriously and wrongfully abused, yea, and whipped him in Havana, as I was afterwards informed.[6]

This mulatto proved so true and faithful in his good services unto the Hollanders that they much esteemed him, married him to one of their nation, and made him captain of a ship under that brave and gallant Hollander whom the Spaniards then so much feared, *Pie de Palo*, or Wooden Leg. This famous mulatto it was that with his sea soldiers boarded our frigate, in the which he had found little worth his labor had it not been for the Indians' offerings which I carried with me, and of which I lost that day the worth of four

---

[6] Diego el Mulato and his captain, Pie de Palo, were almost legendary figures. In 1633, four years before Gage's mishap, Pie de Palo and Diego and a fleet of ten ships seized and sacked Campeche.

thousand patacones or pieces of eight in pearls and precious stones, and near three thousand more in money. The other Spaniards lost some hundreds apiece, which was so rich a prize that it made the Hollanders' stomach loath the rest of our gross provision of bacon, meal, and fowls, and our money tasted sweeter unto them than the honey which our frigate also afforded them. Other things I had, such as a quilt to lie on, some books, and *laminas,* which are pictures in brass, and clothes, which I begged of that noble captain the mulatto. He, considering my orders and calling, gave me them freely, and wished me to be patient, saying that he could not do otherwise than he did with my money and pearls, and using that common proverb at sea,—"*Hoy por mi, mañana por ti,*" "Today fortune hath been for me, tomorrow it may be for thee."

I had some comfort left in a few *pistoles,* some single, some double, which I had sewed up in my quilt, which the captain restored unto me, saying it was the bed I lay in, and in the doublet which I had at that present, and these mounted to almost a thousand crowns, and in their searching were not found. After the captain and soldiers had well viewed their prize, they thought of refreshing their stomachs with some of our provision. The good captain made a stately dinner in our frigate, and invited me to it, and knowing that I was going towards Havana, besides many other *brindis* or healths, he drank one unto his mother, desiring me to see her, and to remember him to her, and how that for her sake he had used well and courteously in what he could. Further at table he said that for my sake he would give us our frigate that we might return again to land, so that I might find thence some safer way and means to get to Portobello, and to continue my journey to Spain.

After dinner I conferred with the captain alone, and told him that I was no Spaniard, but an Englishman born, showing him the licence which I had from Rome to go to England, and that therefore I hoped, not being of an enemy nation to the Hollanders, he would restore unto me what goods were mine. But all this was of little consequence with him, who had already taken possession of mine and all other goods in the ship: he told me I must suffer with those amongst whom I was found, and that I might as well claim all the goods in the ship for mine. I desired him then to carry me along with him to Holland, that from thence I might get to England, but this also he refused to do, telling me that he went about from one place to another, and knew not when he should go to Holland. Moreover, he said that he was daily ready to fight with any Spanish ship, and if he should fight with the Spaniards whilst I was in his ship, his soldiers in their hot blood might be ready to do me a mischief, thinking I would do them harm if in fight they should be taken by the Spaniards. From his answers I saw there was no hope of getting again what now was lost; therefore, as before, I commended myself again to God's providence and protection.

The soldiers and mariners of the Holland ship made haste that afternoon to unlade the goods of our frigate into their man-of-war, which took them up that and part of the next day, whilst we as prisoners were wafting up and down the sea with them. And whereas we thought our money had satisfied them enough, and to the full, we found the next day that they had also a stomach to our fowls and bacon, and wanted our meal to make them bread, and our honey to sweeten their mouths, and our hides for shoes and boots. All this they took, leaving me my quilt, books, and brass pictures, and to the master of the frigate some small provisions, as much as might carry us to land, which was not far off.

Thus they took their leaves of us, thanking us for their good entertainment, but we were weary of such guests, some praying to God that they might never entertain the like again, some cursing them all, and especially the mulatto to hell, calling him *renegado;* some thanking God for their lives which were given them for a prey. Thus we all returned again to Sueré, whence we had set out, and going up the river, were almost like to be cast away, and lose our lives after we had lost our goods. When we came to land, the Spaniards about the country pitied our case and helped us with alms, gathering a collection for us. The three Spaniards of my company lost all their money and most of their best clothes, yet they had reserved some bills of exchange for money to be taken up at Portobello, and I wished I had done the same. For the present we knew not what course to take. We thought of going to Río de los Anzuelos, but we were informed that certainly the frigates there were either gone, or would be gone before we could get thither, and if they stayed not with the news of the Hollanders' ships at sea, they either already were or would be their prize, as we had been.

We resolved therefore with the charitable assistance of the Spaniards about the country to return again to Cartago, and thence to take some better directions. In the way we conferred what we had saved, the Spaniards bragged yet of their bills of exchange, which would yield them money at Cartago; I would not let them know what I had saved, but somewhat I told them I had kept. We agreed all the way we went to signify nothing but poverty and misery, that the Indians and Spaniards in the way might pity and commiserate with us in our great losses. When we came to Cartago, we were indeed much pitied, and collections were made for us; and as it was expected from me that I should sing again at the altars and that I should preach wheresoever I came, so by these two ways, of singing *Dominus vobiscum* and the rest of the Mass, and by accepting of what sermons were recommended to me, I began again to store myself with moneys.

Yet I knew that in such a poor country as that was, where I was little known, I could not possibly get enough to bring me home with credit to England, and therefore the cunning enemy, finding me to stand upon my credit, began strongly to tempt me to return again to Guatemala, where I doubted not but I should be welcomed and entertained by my friends, and to settle myself there until I had again made up a new purse to return home again with credit.

But I, perceiving that God had showed himself angry, and justly taken from me what by unlawful means I had in twelve years obtained, bad Satan avaunt, purposed never more to return to the flesh pots of Egypt, but to go still homewards, though in the way I did beg my bread. Yet I resolved to take what might be offered me as a stranger and traveller for preaching or any other exercise, lest I might be suspected amongst the Spaniards, and troubled for not exercising my orders and function.

Thus resolving to go on with courage still towards England, I enquired at Cartago which way I might get to Portobello. But this door of hope was fast shut up, though my trust in God's providence was not weakened. In this season there came to Cartago some two or three hundred mules unsaddled or unladen with some Spaniards, Indians, and Blackamoors, from the parts of Comayagua and Guatemala, to convey them by land over the mountains of Veragua to be sold in Panama. This is the yearly and only trading by land which Guatemala, Comayagua, and Nicaragua have with Panama over that narrow isthmus lying between the North and South Sea, which is very dangerous by reason of the craggy ways, rocks, and mountains, but more especially by reason of many heathens, barbarians, and savage people, which as yet are not conquered by the Spaniards, and sometimes do great hurt and mischief, and kill those that pass through their country with mules, especially if they misdemean themselves, or please them not well.

For all these difficulties I entertained a thought to go along with those mules and Spaniards, which were now on their way by land to Panama. The three Spaniards were half of the same mind, but the providence of God, who better ordereth and disposeth man's affairs than he himself, disappointed these thoughts for our good and safety, as after we were informed. For we heard for certain at Nicoya that some of those mules and Spaniards were killed by the barbarians and savage Indians, and my life might have been among those lost if I had attempted that hard and dangerous journey. Finally, many well-wishers at Cartago dissuaded me from it, both for the danger of the Indians, and for the difficulties of the ways and mountains, which, they told me, the weakness of my body would never endure.

After we had wholly desisted from this land journey, the best counsel that we had from some merchants our friends, was to try whether *Mar del Sur,* or the South Sea, would favor our design and journey better than the *Mar del Norte,* or the North Sea had done. They wished us to go to Nicoya, and from thence to Chira, and to the Golfo de Salinas, where they doubted not but we should find shipping to Panama. We were willing to follow any good advice and counsel, yet we knew that this was the last shift which we could make, and the *non plus ultra* of our hopes, and that if here we should be disappointed, we could expect no other way ever to get to Panama, except we should venture our lives most desperately over the mountains of Veragua, without any guide or company through that country of barbarians, who before had slain some Spaniards passing that way. As a last resort we might return all the way that we had come to Realejo, where our hopes might be frustrated, and peradventure no shipping found for Panama without a year's waiting for it.

We resolved therefore to follow our friend's counsel, and to go to Nicoya, and thence to Golfo de Salinas, where laughing, I told the three Spaniards of my company that if we were disappointed we would like Hercules set up a pillar to eternize our fame, with our names. On it we would inscribe *"Non plus Ultra,"* for that beyond it there was no other port, haven, or place, to take shipping to Panama. Neither could any man have done more (nor ever did any Englishman in that country do more than myself) than we had done, but especially myself, who from Mexico had thus travelled by land to Nicoya at least six hundred leagues, or eighteen hundred English miles straight from north to south, besides what I had travelled from Vera Cruz to Mexico, and from Guatemala to Vera Paz, and to Puerto de Caballos, or Golfo Dulce, and from thence to Trujillo, and from thence back again to Guatemala, which was at least thirteen or fourteen hundred English miles more, which I thought to eternize upon a pillar at Nicoya. But what there was not erected, I hope here shall be eternized, and that this my true and faithful history shall be a monument of three thousand and three hundred miles travelled by an Englishman, within the mainland of America, besides other sea navigations to Panama, from Portobello to Cartagena, and thence to Havana.

The way which we travelled from Cartago to Nicoya was very mountainous, hard, and unpleasant, for we met with few *estancias* of Spaniards, and few Indian towns, and those very poor, small, and all of dejected and wretched people.[7] Yet Nicoya is a pretty town, and head of a Spanish government, where we found one Justo de Salazar, *Alcalde Mayor,* who entertained us very well, and provided lodgings for us for the time that we should abide there, and comforted us with hopeful words, that though for the present there was no ship or frigate in the Gulf of Salinas, yet he doubted not but very shortly one would come thither from Panama for salt and other commodities, as yearly they were wont. The time of the year when we came thither was a fit time for me to get some money after my great loss, for it was in Lent, which is the friars' chief

[7] The discouraging feature of this trip was that it was a back-tracking toward Nicaragua and Guatemala. The Golfo de Salinas, mentioned above, was even farther back, where the modern boundaries of Costa Rica and Nicaragua meet. At least, taking ship from a Pacific port, there would be little danger of pirates.

harvest, who, as I have observed, then get many money offerings by confessions and by giving the Communion.

The time and the Franciscan friar, who had the pastorship and charge of that town, were both very commodious unto me, and I could not refuse as long as I stayed there to exercise my function, lest I should bring a just cause of suspicion and aspersion upon myself. The friar of the town was a Portuguese, who about three weeks before my coming thither had had a very great bickering and strife with Justo de Salazar, the *Alcalde Mayor*, for defending the Indians, whom Salazar did grievously oppress. For he employed them in his and his wife's service as slaves, and did not pay them what for the sweat of their brows was due unto them, and he kept them from their homes and from their wives, and from their church upon the Sabbath, making them work for him that day just as on any other. The friar would not endure that, and charged them in the pulpit not to obey any such unlawful commands from their *Alcalde Mayor*. But Justo de Salazar, who had been trained up in wars and fighting and had served formerly in the castle of Milan, thought it a great disparagement to him to be curbed now by a friar in his government of the Indians and in the ways of his own lucre and gain. Therefore, after many bitter words and defiances had passed between him and the friar, he came one day resolutely to the friar's house with his sword drawn, and had not the friar been assisted by some of the Indians, he certainly would have killed him. The friar being as hot as he, and standing upon his calling, orders, and priesthood, presumed that the *Alcalde Mayor* durst not touch him violently, lest his privilege should bring an excommunication upon the striker and offender. Therefore, he would not flee from him, but dared him boldly, which was a strong provocation to Salazar's heat and passion, and caused him to lift up his sword and aim his blow and stroke at the friar. This fell so unhappily that with it he struck off two of the friar's fingers, and had undoubtedly seconded another blow more hurtful and dangerous to the friar had not the Indians interposed themselves, and shut up their priest in his chamber. Justo was for this action excommunicated, but as he was a man of high authority, he soon got off his excommunication from the Bishop of Costa Rica, and sent his complaint to the Chancery of Guatemala against the friar, where with friends and money he doubted not but to overcome the mendicant priest. This was what happened after, for, as I was informed, he caused the friar to be sent for up to the Court, and there prevailed so much against him that he got him removed from Nicoya.

In this season the friar kept his house and chamber, and would by no means go out to the church, either to say Mass, or to preach, or to hear confessions, all which that time of the year required of him. He had got one to help him, but one alone was not able to perform so great a charge of many hundred Indians, Spaniards, Blackamoors, and mulattoes, who from the country without, and from the town within, expected to have their confessions heard, their sins absolved, the word preached, and the Communion given them. So, hearing of my coming, he desired me to assist and help him, and that for my pains I should have my meat and drink at his table, and a crown daily for every Mass, and whatsoever else the people should voluntarily offer, besides the sermons, which should be well rewarded unto me. I stayed in this town from the second week of Lent until Easter week, where what with three sermons at ten crowns apiece, what with my daily stipend and many other offerings, I got about an hundred and fifty crowns.

The week before Easter news came of a frigate from Panama to Golfo de Salinas, which much comforted us, who already began to mistrust the delay. The master of the frigate came to Nicoya, which is as Court thereabouts, and the three Spaniards and myself agreed with him for our passage to Panama. About Chira, Golfo de Salinas, and Nicoya, there are some farms of Spaniards, and a few very small Indian towns. Those Indians are employed like slaves by the *Alcalde Mayor* to make him a kind of thread called *pita*, which is a very rich commodity in Spain, especially of that purple color wherewith it is dyed in these parts of Nicoya. The Indians are here much charged to work about the seashore to find certain shells wherewith they make this purple dye.[8]

There are also shells for other colors, which are not known to be so plentifully in any other place as here. About Chira and Golfo

[8] *Pita* is the fiber of agave plants as well as of maguey. Purple shell dye was also obtained by the Indians of Guatemala and Oaxaca. This use of the *Purpura* shellfish for dye is a most interesting parallel to the similar obtaining of Roman purple from shellfish of the Mediterranean.

de Salinas the chief commodities are salt, honey, maize, some wheat, and fowls, which every year they send by some few frigates to Panama, which thence come on purpose to fetch them as well as this purple-colored thread, or *pita,* of which I have spoken. The frigate which came when I was there was soon laden with these commodities, and with it we set out, hoping to have been at Panama within five or six days. But as often before we had been crossed, so likewise in this short passage we were striving four full weeks with the wind, sea, and currents.

After the first day that we set out, we were driven with a wind and storm towards Peru, till we came under the very equinoctial line, where what with excessive heat, what with mighty storms, we utterly despaired of life. But after one week that we had thus run towards death, it pleased God to comfort us again with hopes of life, sending us a prosperous gale, which drove us out of that equinoctial heat and stormy sea towards the islands of Perlas, and Punta de Chame, lying on the south side of the mountains of Veragua, whence we hoped within two days at the most to be at rest and anchor at Panama. But our hopes were frustrated, for there our wind was calmed, and we fell upon those strong currents which drave us back in the night for the space of almost a fortnight as much as we had sailed in the day.

Had not God again been merciful here unto us, we had certainly perished in our striving with the stream, for although we wanted not provision of food, yet our drink failed us, so that for four days we tasted neither drop of wine or water, or anything that might quench our thirst, save only a little honey. This we found did cause more thirst in us, which made me and some others to drink our own urine, and to refresh our mouths with pieces of lead bullets, which did for a while refresh, but would not long have sufficed Nature, had not God's good providence sent us such a wind which in the day drave us quite off from those currents.

Our first thoughts were to strike either to the continent, or one of those many islands around us to seek for water, for our bodies were weak and languishing; but the captain of the ship would by no means agree to this, assuring us that that day he would land us at Panama. Not being able to sail on without drink, unless we should yield to have our dead and not our live bodies landed where he promised, we thought it not good purchase, though we might buy all Panama with our lives. Seeing that the wind began to slacken, we all required him to strike into some island for water, which he stubbornly refused to do, whereupon the three Spaniards and some of the mariners mutinied against him with drawn swords, threatening to kill him if he betook not himself presently to some island. The good master thought it bad sport to see swords at his breast, and so commanded his ship to be turned to two or three islands, which were not above two or three hours sail from us.

When we drew nigh unto them, we cast our anchor and our cock-boat, and happy was he that could first cast himself into it to be rowed to land to fill his belly with water. The first island we landed upon was on that side unhabitable. There we spent much time running to and fro, over-heating ourselves and increasing our thirst, and thus one ran one way, and another tried another to find out some fountain, but our hopes were frustrated. I got lost in the wood, and my shoes were torn from my feet with stony rocks and many thorns and bushes in other places. My companions then betook themselves to the cock-boat to try another island, leaving me alone and lost in the wood, and when at last I came to the shore and found the cock-boat gone, I began to consider myself a dead man, thinking that they had found water and were gone to ship, and not finding me would hoist up their sails for Panama. Thus being dejected, I cried out to the ship, which, I perceived, could not possibly hear my weak voice. Running up and down the rocks to see if I could discover the cock-boat, I perceived it was not with the ship, and espied it at the next island.

With this I began to hope better things of them that they would call for me when they had gotten water, so I came down from the rocks to the plain shore, where I found a shade of trees and amongst them some berries (which might have been poison, for I knew them not) wherewith I refreshed my mouth for a while; but my body was so burned that I thought that with heat, weakness, and faintness I should have expired and given up the ghost. I thought by stripping myself naked and going into the sea unto my neck, I might thus refresh my body. This I did, and, coming out again into the shade, I fell into a deep sleep, in so much that the cock-boat coming for me, and the company holloaing unto me, I awaked not. This made them fear that I was dead or lost, till they landed, and one searched for me one way, and another another, and so they found me. Otherwise, I might have been a prey to some wild beast, or slept till the frigate had gone, and so have perished in a barren and unhabitable island. When they awaked me, I was glad to see my good company, and the first thing I enquired for was if they had got any water. They bad me be of good cheer and arise, for they had water enough, and oranges and lemons from another island, where they had met Spaniards inhabiting it. I made haste with them to the boat, and no sooner was I entered into it but they gave me to drink as much as I would. The water was warm and unsettled, for they could not take it up so but that they took of the gravel and bottom of the fountain, which made it look very muddy. Yet I drank up a whole pot of it as though my life had depended upon it. No sooner had I drank but such was the weakness of my stomach that I presently cast it up again, not being able to bear it. With this they wished me to eat an orange or a lemon; but them also did my stomach reject, so to our frigate we went, and in the way I fainted so that the company verily thought I would die before we got aboard. When we came thither, I called again for water, which was no sooner down my stomach but presently up again. They had me to bed with a burning fever, where I lay that night expecting nothing but death, and that the sea should be my grave.

The master of the ship, seeing the wind was turned, began to be much troubled, and feared that with that wind he should never get to Panama. He resolved to venture upon a way which never before he had tried, namely to get between the two islands which we had searched for water, knowing that the wind, which on this side was contrary, on the other side of the islands would be favorable unto him. Thus towards evening he took up anchor and hoisted his sails, and resolved to pass his frigate between the two islands. How dangerous and desperate an attempt it was, the event witnessed. I lay in this season, as I may truly say, upon my death-bed, not regarding which way the master of the ship, or fortune, carried me, so that the mercy of the Lord carried my soul to Heaven. No sooner had the frigate steered her course between the narrow passage of the two islands when, being carried with the stream too much to the one side of the land, it ran upon a rock, so that the very stern was lifted up, and almost cast out of the pilot's hands, who cried out not to God, but unto the Virgin Mary, saying, "*Ayudad nos Virgen Santisima, que si no aqui nos perecemos,*" "Help us, O most holy Virgin, for if not, here we perish." This and the outcry of all that were in the frigate gave unto me an alarm of death, but from which it pleased God by the means and diligence of the mariners to deliver me and all the company. With much ado most part of that night they hauled the frigate off the rock with the cock-boat, after the stream had made it strike it three times.

After a very troublesome night we got our little ship out of all danger in the morning, and we sailed prosperously towards Panama. That morning my stomach recovered some of its lost strength, and I began to eat and to drink, and to walk about, rejoicing much to see those pleasant islands which we sailed by. In the evening we got to Puerto de Perico, where we cast anchor, expecting to be searched in the morning, but that night (the master of our ship having gone to shore) the wind turned and blew so strong that we lost our anchor, and were driven back almost to La Pacheque. Indeed, we feared we should be carried into the ocean again so far that we should with great difficulty get to Panama. But God, whom the sea and winds do obey, turned again that contrary wind into a prosperous gale, wherewith we came once more to Perico, and after being searched, we went on with full sail to Panama. Being near the port and without an anchor in our ship, the wind once more blew us back, and had not the ship master sent us an anchor, we had gone again to Pacheque or further. But with that anchor we stayed all that night at Perico, wondering among ourselves that so many crosses should befall us. Some said that we were bewitched; others, that certainly there was amongst us some excommunicated person, and if they knew who it was, they would hurl him overboard.

Whilst they were in this discourse, the wind turned yet again, and we levying our anchor went on to Panama, whither it pleased God that time safely to conduct us. Being now well strengthened, I made no stay in that frigate, which I thought would have been my last abiding place in this world, but went to land, and betook myself to the cloister of the Dominicans, where I stayed almost fifteen days viewing and reviewing that city. It is governed like Guatemala by a president and six judges, and a court of Chancery, and is a bishop's see. It hath more strength towards the South Sea than any other port which on that side I had seen, and some ordnances planted for the defense of it, but the houses are of the least strength of any place that I had entered in. Lime and stone is hard to come by, and for that reason and for the great heat there, most of the houses are built of timber and boards. The President's house, nay, the best church walls, are but boards, which serve for stone and brick, and for tiles to cover the top. The heat is so extraordinary that a linen cut doublet, with some slight stuff or taffeta breeches, is the common clothing of the inhabitants.

Fish, fruits, and herbage for salads are more plentiful in Panama than flesh, and the cool water of the *coco*[nut] is the women's best drink, though chocolate also, and much wine from Peru abound. The Spaniards in this city are much given to sin, looseness, and venery especially, and they make the Blackamoors (who are many, rich, and gallant) the chief objects of their lust. It is held to be one of the richest places in all America, having by land and by the river Chagres commerce with the North Sea, and by the South, trading with all Peru, East Indies, Mexico, and Honduras. Thither is brought the chief treasure of Peru in two or three great ships, which lie at anchor at Puerto de Perico some three leagues from the city, for the great ebbing of the sea at that place especially suffereth not any great vessel to come nearer. For daily the sea ebbs and falls away from the city two or three miles, leaving a mud which is thought to cause much unhealthiness in that place, being seconded with many other muddy and moorish places about the town.

Panama has some five thousand inhabitants, and maintains at least eight cloisters of nuns and friars. I feared much the heats, and therefore made as much haste out of it as I could. I had my choice of company by land and water to Portobello. But considering the hardness of the mountains by land, I resolved to go by the river Chagres, and so at midnight I set out from Panama to Venta de Cruces, which is ten or twelve leagues from it. The way is thither very plain for the most part, and pleasant in the morning and evening.

Before ten of the clock we got to Venta de Cruces, where live none but mulattoes and Blackamoors, who belong unto the flat boats that carry the merchandise to Portobello. There I had very good entertainment by that people, who desired me to preach to them the next Sabbath day, and gave me twenty crowns for a sermon and procession. After five days of my abode there, the boats set out, but they were much stopped in their passage down the river, for in some places we found the water very low, so that the boats ran upon the gravel, whence with poles and the strength of the Black-amoors they had to be lifted off again. Sometimes again we met with streams that carried us with the swiftness of an arrow down under trees and boughs by the river side, but sometimes also these stopped us till we had cut down great branches of trees. Had not it pleased God to send us after the first week plentiful rain, which made the water run down from the mountains and fill the river, which otherwise is very shallow, we might have had a tedious and longer passage, but after twelve days we got to the sea, and at the point landed where is the castle to refresh ourselves for half a day. Certainly the Spaniards trust to the streams and shallowness of that river to keep any foreign nation from attempting to come up to Venta de Cruces and from thence to Panama, or else they would strengthen more and fortify that castle, which in my time wanted great reparations, and was ready to fall down to the ground.

The Governor of the castle was a notable wine-bibber, who plied us with that liquor during the time that we stayed there, and, want-ing a chaplain for himself and soldiers, he would fain have had me stay with him, but greater matters called me further, and so I took my leave of him. He gave us some dainties of fresh meat, fish, and conserves, and so dismissed us. We got out to the open sea, discover-ing first the Escudo de Veragua, and keeping somewhat close unto the land, we went on rowing towards Portobello, till the evening which was Saturday night. Then we cast anchor behind a little island, resolving in the morning to enter Portobello. The Blackamoors all that night kept watch for fear of Hollanders, whom they said did often lie in wait thereabouts for the boats of Chagres, but we passed the night safely, and next morning got to Portobello. We observed that the haven was very strong, with two castles at the mouth and constant watch within them, and another called San Miguel further in the port.

When I came into the haven, I was sorry to see that as yet the galleons were not come from Spain, knowing that the longer I stayed in that place, the greater would be my charges. Yet I comforted myself that the time of the year was come, and that they could not long delay their coming. My first thoughts were of taking a lodging, which at that time were plentiful and cheap, nay, some were offered me for nothing with this caveat, that when the galleons did come, I must either leave them or pay a dear rate for them. A kind gentleman, who was the King's Treasurer, falling in discourse with me, promised to help me, that I might be cheaply lodged even when the ships came and lodgings were at the highest rate. He, interposing his authority, went with me to seek one, which might continue to be mine while the fleet was there. It was no bigger than would contain a bed, a table, and a stool or two, with room enough besides to open and shut the door, and they demanded sixscore crowns of me for it during the aforesaid time of the fleet, which commonly is a fortnight. For the town being little, and the soldiers that come with the galleons for their defense at least four or five thousand, besides merchants from Peru, from Spain, and many other places to buy and sell, is the cause that every room, though never so small, be dear. And sometimes all the lodgings in the town are few enough for the many people which at that time do meet at Portobello.

I knew a merchant who the year that I was there gave a thousand crowns for a shop of reasonable bigness to sell his wares and commodities for fifteen days only, while the fleet continued to be in that haven. I thought the sixscore crowns which were demanded of me much for a room, which was but as a mouse hole, and I began to be troubled, and told the King's Treasurer that I had been lately robbed at sea, and was not able to give so much and be besides at charges for my diet, which I feared would prove as much more. But not a farthing would be abated of what was asked, whereupon the good Treasurer, pitying me, offered to pay the man of the house threescore crowns of it, if I was able to pay the rest, which I must do, or else lie without in the street. Yet till the fleet did come I would not enter into this dear hole, but accepted of another fair lodging which was offered me for nothing. Whilst I thus expected the fleet's coming, I got some money and offerings for Masses and for two sermons which I preached at fifteen crowns apiece.

I visited the castles, which indeed seemed unto me to be very strong; but what most I wondered at was to see the *recuas* of mules which came thither from Panama, laden with wedges of silver. In one day I told [counted] two hundred mules laden with nothing else, which were unladen in the public market-place, so that there the heaps of silver wedges lay like heaps of stones in the street, without any fear or suspicion of being lost. Within ten days the fleet came, consisting of eight galleons and ten merchant ships, and that forced me to run to my hole. It was a wonder then to see the multitude of people in those streets which the week before had been empty.

Then the price of all things began to rise, a fowl to be worth twelve reals, which in the main land within I had often bought for one; a pound of beef then was worth two reals, whereas I had had in other places thirteen pound for half a real, and so of all other food and provision. All was so excessive dear that I knew not how to live but by fish and tortoises, which there are very many, and though somewhat dear, yet were the cheapest meat that I could eat. It was worth seeing how merchants sold their commodities, not by the ell or yard, but by the piece and weight, not paying in coined pieces of money, but in wedges which were weighed and taken for commodities. This lasted but fifteen days, whilst the galleons were lading with wedges of silver and nothing else, so that for those fifteen days, I dare boldly say and avouch that in the world there is no greater fair than that of Portobello, between the Spanish merchants and those of Peru, Panama, and other parts thereabouts.

Don Carlos de Ybarra, who was the admiral of that fleet, made great haste to be gone, and that made the merchants buy and sell apace, and lade the ships with silver wedges. Whereof I was glad, for the more they laded, the less I unladed my purse with buying dear provision, and the sooner I hoped to be out of that unhealthy place, which of itself is very hot, and subject to breed fevers, nay, death, if the feet be not preserved from wetting when it raineth. But especially when the fleet is there, it is an open grave ready to swallow a good part of that numerous people which at that time resort to it. That was seen the year that I was there, when about five hundred of the soldiers, merchants, and mariners, what with fevers, what with the flux caused by too much eating of fruit and drinking of water, what with other disorders, lost their lives. They found it to be to them not *Porto bello*, but *Porto malo*. And this is usual every year; and therefore, for the relief and comfort of those that come sick from sea, or sicken there, a great and rich hospital is in the town, with many friars called *De la Capacha,* or by others *De Juan de Dios,* whose calling and profession is only to cure and attend upon the sick, and to bear the dead unto their graves.

The Admiral, fearing the great sickness that year, made haste to be gone, not fearing the report of some three of four Holland or English ships abroad at sea, waiting (as it was supposed) for some good prize out of that great and rich fleet. This news made me begin to fear, and to think of securing myself in one of the best and strongest galleons, but when I came to treat of my passage in one of them, I found that I could not be carried in any under three hundred crowns, which was more than my purse was able to afford. With this I thought to address myself to some master of a merchant's ship, though I knew I could not be so safe and secure in any of them as in a galleon well manned and fortified with soldiers and guns of brass.

Yet I hoped in God, who is a strong refuge to them that fear him, and in this occasion provided for me a cheap and sure passage. For meeting one day with my friend the Treasurer, he again pitied me as a stranger and lately robbed, and commended me to the master of a merchant ship, the *San Sebastián,* whom he knew was desirous to carry a chaplain with him at his own table. I no sooner addressed myself unto him, using the name and favor of his and my friend the Treasurer, but I found him willing to accept of my company, promising to carry me for nothing, and to board me at his own table, only for my prayers to God for him and his. He offered further to give me some satisfaction for whatsoever sermons I should preach in his ship. I blessed God, acknowledging in this also his providence, who in all occasions furthered my return to England.

The ships being laden, we set forth towards Cartagena. The second day of our sailing we discovered four ships which made the merchant ships afraid, and caused them to keep close to the galleons, trusting to their strength more than their own. The ship I was in was swift and nimble under sail, and kept under the wings either of the Admiral or of some other of the best galleons, but all the other merchants ships were not so for some came slowly on behind, and of them two were carried away by the Hollanders in the night, before ever we could get to Cartagena.

The greatest fear that I perceived possessed the Spaniards in this

331

voyage was about the Island of Providence, called by them Santa Catalina, or St. Catharine, from whence they feared lest some English ships should come out against them with great strength. They cursed the English in it, and called the island the den of thieves and pirates, wishing that their King of Spain would take some course with it. Otherwise, it would prove very prejudicial to the Spaniards, for lying near the mouth of the Desaguadero, it endangered the frigates of Granada; and standing between Portobello and Cartagena, it threatened the galleons, and their King's yearly and mighty treasure.

Thus with bitter invectives against the English and the Island of Providence, we sailed on to Cartagena, where again we met with the four ships which before had followed us and had taken away two of our ships, and now at our entering into that port threatened to carry away more of our company. This they might have done if they would have ventured to have come upon the ship wherein I went, which, on rounding the land point to get into the haven, ran upon the shore. This was sandy and gravelly, but had it been rocky, we would have certainly there been cast away by keeping too near unto the land. We were safely delivered from that danger by the care of the mariners and their active pains, as also from the ships which followed us as far as they durst through their fear of the cannon shot of the castle.

Thus we entered the haven of Cartagena, and stayed there for the space of eight or ten days, where I met with some of my countrymen who belonged to the Island of Providence, but had been taken at sea by the Spaniards. Among them was the renowned Captain Rouse, and about a dozen more, with whom I was glad to meet, but durst not show them too much countenance, for fear of being suspected. Yet I soon got the good will of some of them, who, being destined to Spain, were very desirous to go in the ship wherein I went, which desire of theirs I furthered, and was suitor unto my captain to carry four of them in his ship. For my sake he willingly yielded to this plan, and amongst these was one Edward Layfield. Afterwards setting out of San Lucar for England, he was taken captive by the Turks, and since from Turkey wrote to me in England to help to release him. With him, both at Cartagena and in the way in the ship, I had great discourse concerning points of religion, and

St. Martin Church, Acrise, Kent, where Gage was incumbent, 1643–48. The church has Norman and thirteenth-century work.

St. Leonard Church, Deal, Kent, where Gage was "Preacher of the Word." The steeple, about which Gage petitioned the Mayor of Sandwich, fell in 1658, and the present cupola replaced it.

by him came to know some things professed in England, which my conscience whilst I lived in America much inclined unto. I was much taken with his company, and found him very officious unto me, whose kindness I requited by speaking for him in the ship to the masters and mariners, who otherwise were ready and forward to abuse him and the rest of the English company as prisoners and slaves.

At Cartagena we heard a report of three score sail of ships of Hollanders waiting for the galleons. That news struck no little fear into the Spaniards, who called a council whether our fleet should winter there, or go on to Spain. It proved to be but a false report of the inhabitants of Cartagena, who for their own ends and lucre would willingly have had the ships and galleons stay there. Don Carlos de Ybarra said that he feared not a hundred sail of Hollanders, and therefore would go on to Spain, hoping to carry thither safely the King's treasure. This he performed and in eight days arrived at Havana, where we stayed eight days longer, expecting the fleet from Vera Cruz. In which time I viewed well that strong castle manned with the twelve guns, called the Twelve Apostles, which would do little hurt to an army by land or marching from the river of Matanzas.

I visited here the mother of that mulatto, who had taken away all my means at sea, and spent much time in comforting my poor countrymen the prisoners; but especially that gallant Captain Rouse, who came to me to complain of some affronts which had been offered him by Spaniards in the ship wherein he came. Though a prisoner, he would not put up with these, but wanted to challenge his proud contemners to meet him in duel if they durst in any place of Havana. To challenge a Spaniard in his country, a cock upon his own dunghill, showed a brave courage in a dejected and imprisoned Englishman, but as soon as I understood from Edward Layfield, I desired to intervene, fearing that many would fall upon him cowardly and mince him in small pieces. I sent for him to the cloister where I lay, and there had conference with him, prevailing so far as that I made him desist from his thoughts of going into the field and showing his manhood in such a time and place, where his low condition of a prisoner might well excuse him. The rest of my poor countrymen were here much discouraged and in some want, but I relieved them, especially Layfield, and encouraged them as much as I was able.

333

I chanced here to have occasion to take a little physic before I went again to sea, and thereby I learned what before I never knew, to wit, the diet which on such a day the best physicians of Havana prescribe unto their patients. Whereas after the working of my physic I expected some piece of mutton, or a fowl, or some other nourishing meat, my physician left order that I should have a piece of roasted pork, which seemed to me a diet contrary to that day's extremity. I began to refuse it, alleging to my doctor the contrary course of all nations, the natural quality of that meat to open the body. To which he replied, that what pork might work upon man's body in other nations, it worked not there, but the contrary, and so he wished me to feed upon what he had prescribed, assuring me that it would do me no hurt.

All the ships make their provision for Spain of tortoise meat. They cut the tortoises in long thin slices, as I have noted before of the *tasajos*, and dry it in the wind after they have well salted it, and so it serveth the mariners in all their voyage to Spain, and they eat it boiled with a little garlic, and I have heard them say that to them it tasted as well as any veal. They also take in their ships some fowls for the masters' and captains' tables, and live hogs, which would seem to be enough to breed some infection in the ship, had they not care to wash often the place where such unclean beasts lie. In the ship where I was passenger, one was killed every week for the masters', pilots', and passengers' table.

Thus all things being made ready for the ships' provision to Spain, and the merchants' goods and the King's revenue being shipped in nine days that we abode there, we now wanted nothing but only the company of the fleet from Vera Cruz, which should have met us there upon the eighth day of September. But Don Carlos de Ybarra, seeing it stayed longer than the time appointed and fearing the weather and the new moon of that month, which commonly proveth dangerous in the Gulf of Bahama, resolved to stay no longer, but to set out to Spain. On a Sabbath day, therefore, in the morning we hoisted sails, being in all seven and twenty ships with those which had met with us there from Honduras and the islands, and one by one we sailed out of Havana to the main sea, where we that day wafted about for a good wind, and also waiting for our guide, which was not yet come out of Havana to guide us through the Gulf of Bahama.

334

That night we wished ourselves again in Havana, thinking that we were compassed about with a strong fleet of Hollanders, for many ships came amongst us, which made us provide for a fight in the morning. A council of war was called, and all that night watch was kept, the guns prepared, red cloths hung round the ships, orders sent about both to the galleons and to the merchants' ships what posture and place to be in. That which I was in was to attend the Admiral, and that I hoped would be a strong defense unto us. Our men were courageous and ready to fight, though I liked not such martial business and discourse, but a place was prepared where I might lie hid, and be safe among some barrels of biscuit. All the night I had enough to do to hear the confessions of those in the ship, who thought they could not die happily with the shot of a Holland bullet until they had confessed all their sins unto me, who towards morning had more need of rest than of fighting, after wearying my ears with hearing so many wicked, grievous, and abominable sins. But the dawning of the day discovered our causeless fear, which was from friends, and not from any enemies or Hollanders.

The ships which were joined unto us in the night were as fearful of us, as we of them, and prepared themselves likewise to fight in the morning, which showed unto us their colors, whereby we knew that they were the fleet which we expected from Vera Cruz to go along with us to Spain. They were two and twenty sail, which little thought to find us out of Havana, but within the haven lying at anchor, waiting for their coming, and therefore in the night feared us much more than we them. When the day cleared our doubts, fears, and jealousies, then the martial colors began to be taken down; the joyful sound of trumpets with the help of Neptune's kingdoms echoed from ship to ship, and the boats carried welcoming messages from one to another. The Spanish *"brindis"* with *"Buen viaje," "Buen pasaje,"* was generally cried out, and the whole morning was spent in friendly acclamations and salutations from ship to ship.

In the midst of our joy and sea greetings, we being now in all two and fifty sail (yet we not knowing well how many they were from Vera Cruz, nor they how many we were from Havana), two ships were found amongst us. Whether they were English or Hollanders we could not well discover, but the English prisoners with me told me they thought one was a ship of England called the

335

Neptune. Having got the wind of us, they singled out a ship of ours, which belonged to Dunkirk and from San Lucar or Cádiz had been forced to the King's service in that voyage to the Indies, laden with sugars, and other rich commodities to the worth of at least fourscore thousand crowns. Suddenly giving her a whole broadside and receiving a reply of only two guns, they made her yield, without any hope of help from so proud and mighty a fleet, for that she was somewhat far straggled from the rest of the ships. The whole business lasted not above half an hour, and quickly she was carried away from under our noses. The Spaniards changed their merry tunes into *"Voto á Dios"* and *"Voto á Cristo,"* in raging, cursing, and swearing, some reviling at the captain of the ship which was taken, and saying that he was false and yielded on purpose without fighting, because he was forced to come that voyage; others cursing those that took her, and calling them *hijos de puta, borrachos, infames ladrones,* bastards, drunkards, infamous thieves, and pirates. Some took their swords in their hands, as if they would there cut them in pieces, some lay hold of their muskets as if they would there shoot at them, others stamped like madmen, and ran about the ship as if they would leap overboard, and make haste after them; others ground their teeth at the poor English prisoners that were in the ship, as if they would stab them for what (they said) their countrymen had done.

I must needs say I had enough to do to hold some of those furious and raging brains from doing Layfield some mischief, who more than the rest would be smiling, arguing, and answering their outrageous nonsense. Order was presently given to the Vice-Admiral and two more galleons to follow and pursue them, but all in vain, for the wind was against them, and so the two ships, laughing and rejoicing as much as the Spaniards cursed and raged, sailed away *con viento en popa,* with full sail, gallantly boasting with so rich a prize taken away from two and fifty ships, or (as I may say) from the chiefest and greatest strength of Spain.

That afternoon the fleet of Vera Cruz took their leave of us (not being furnished with provision to go on to Spain with us), and went into Havana; and we set forwards towards Europe, fearing nothing for the present but the Gulf of Bahama, through which we got safely with the help and guidance of such pilots which our Admiral Don Carlos had chosen, and hired for that purpose.

I shall not need to tell thee my reader of the sight which we had of St. Augustine, Florida, nor of many storms which we suffered in this voyage, nor of the many degrees we came under, which made us shake with cold more than the frost of England do in the worst of winter. I will only say that the best of our pilots, not knowing where they were, had like to have betrayed us all to the rocks of Bermuda one night, had not the breaking of the day given us a fair warning that we were running upon them. For which the Spaniards, instead of giving God thanks for their delivery out of that danger, began again to curse and rage against the English which inhabited that island, saying that they had enchanted that and the rest of those islands about, and did still with the Devil raise storms in those seas when the Spanish fleet passed that way.

Thence we sailed well to the islands called Terceras [Azores], where fain we would have taken in fresh water (for that which we had taken in at Havana now began to stink, and look yellow, making us stop our noses whilst we opened our mouths), but rigid Don Carlos would not pity the rest of his company, but led us by the islands. The night following we all wished ourselves in some harbor of them; for, though in their conceit those islands were not enchanted by Englishmen, but inhabited by holy and idolatrous Papists, we were no sooner got from them when there arose the greatest storm that we had in all our voyage from Havana to Spain. This lasted full eight days, where we lost one ship and endangered two galleons, which shot off their warning pieces for help, and made us all stay and wait on them, till they had repaired their tacklings and main mast.

We went on sometimes one way, sometimes another, not well knowing where we were, drinking our stinking water by allowance of pints, till three or four days after the storm was ceased we discovered land, which made all cry out, "*España, España*," "Spain, Spain"; whilst a council was summoned by the Admiral to know what land that was, some sold away barrels of biscuit, others of water, to those that wanted (everyone thinking that it was some part of Spain), but the result of the wise council was, after they had sailed nearer to the land and had laid and lost many wagers about it, that it was the Island of Madeira, which made some curse the ignorance of the pilots, and made us all prepare ourselves with patience for a longer voyage.

It pleased God from the discovery of this island to grant us a favorable wind to Spain, where within twelve days we discovered Cádiz, and some of the ships there left us, but most of them went forward to San Lucar, as did the ship wherein I went. When we came near to the dangerous place which the Spaniards call La Barra, we durst not venture our ships upon our pilots' own knowledge, but called for pilots to guide us in, who, greedy of their lucre, came out in boats almost for every ship one.

Upon the eight and twentieth of November, 1637, we cast anchor within San Lucar de Barrameda⁹ about one of the clock in the afternoon, and before evening other passengers and myself went ashore, having first been searched. Although I might presently have gone to the cloister of St. Dominic, where my old friend Friar Pablo de Londres was yet living, who I knew would be glad of my coming from the Indies, yet I thought fit the first night to enjoy the company of my friends, both Spaniards and English, who had come so long a voyage with me, in some ordinary [inn]. I thought, too, I would take my rest better abroad than I should do in a cloister, where I expected but a poor friar's supper, a hard and mean lodging, many foolish questions from old Friar Pablo de Londres concerning the Indies and my abode there so many years, and finally the noise of bells and rattlers to rouse up the drowsy friars from their sleep to matins at midnight.

That night, therefore, I betook myself to an English ordinary, where I refreshed myself and my poor prisoners, who by the master of the ship were committed to my charge that night and forwards upon my word, so as to be forthcoming when they should be called, and the next morning I sent my honest friend Layfield with a letter to the cloister to old Pablo de Londres, who upon my summons came joyfully to welcome me from the Indies, and after very little discourse told me of ships in the haven ready to set out for England. The old friar, being of a decrepit and doting age, thought every day a year that I stayed there and suspended my voyage for England, and (not knowing the secrets of my heart) judged already that the conversion or turning of many Protestant souls to Popery waited for my coming, and that made him hasten me, who was more desirous than he to be gone the next day, if I might have found

⁹ At the mouth of the Guadalquivir, a few miles northwest of Cádiz.

wind, weather, and shipping ready. But God, who had been with me in almost ninety days' sailing from Havana to San Lucar and had delivered me from many a storm, prepared and furthered all things in a very short time for the last accomplishment of my hope and desire, to return to England my native soil, from whence I had been absent almost for the space of four and twenty years.

My first thought here in San Lucar was to cast off my friar's weed, which was a white coat or gown hanging to the ground, girded about with a leathern belt, and over it from the shoulders downward a white scapulary (so called there), hanging shorter than the gown both before and behind, and over that a white hood to cover the head, and lastly, over that a black cloak with another black hood. The black and white together make the friars of that profession look just like magpies, and is acknowledged by the Church of Rome itself in a verse which they feign of Mr. Martin Luther (with what just ground I know not), saying of his former life and profession before his conversion, *"Bis Corvus, bis Pica fui, ter fune ligatus,"* "I was twice a crow, twice a magpie, and thrice was bound or tied with a cord"; by a crow meaning an Augustine friar, who is all in black; by a magpie, meaning a Dominican; and by bound with a rope or cord, meaning a Franciscan, who indeed is girded about with a cord made of hemp.

I applied the allegory of this black and white habit otherwise to myself, and in the outward black part of it saw the foulness of my life and idolatrous priesthood in the exercise of that profession and orders which from Rome I had received; and in the white inward habit I considered yet the purity and integrity of those intentions and thoughts of my inward heart, in pursuance whereof I had left what formerly I have noted, yea, all America, which, had I continued in it, might have been to me a mine of wealth, riches, and treasure. I resolved here therefore to cast off that hypocritical cloak and habit, and to put on such apparel whereby I might no more appear a wolf in sheepskin, but might go boldly to my country of England, there to show and make known the candor of my heart and the purity and sincerity of my thoughts, which had brought me so far, by a public profession of the pure truths of the Gospel without any invention or addition of man unto it.[10] With the small means (about a hundred

[10] Gage here is hardly honest with his readers. He was still a Dominican in good

crowns) therefore which was left me after so long and almost a whole year's journey from Petapa to San Lucar, I gave order for a suit of clothes to be made by an English tailor, which I willingly put on, and so prepared myself for England.

Three or four ships were in readiness, who had only waited for the fleet to take in some commodities especially some wedges of silver, of which I was with old Pablo de Londres in doubt which to choose. The first that went out was thought should have been my lot, in the which my friend Layfield embarked himself (for all the English prisoners were there freed to go home to their country) and from which the great providence of God diverted me, or else I had been this day with Layfield a slave in Turkey. For the next day after this ship set out, it was taken by the Turks, and carried away for a rich prize, and all the English in it for prisoners to Algiers. But God, who I hope had reserved me for better things, appointed for me a safer convoy home in a ship (as I was informed) belonging to Sir William Courteen, under the command of an honest Fleming named Adrian Adrianzen, then living at Dover, with whom I agreed for my passage and diet at his table. This ship set out of the bar of San Lucar the ninth day after my arrival thither, where it waited for the company of four ships more, but especially for some Indian wedges of silver, which upon forfeiture of them it durst not take in within the bar and haven.

And thus being now clothed after a new fashion and ready to lead a new life, and being now changed from an American into the fashion of an Englishman, the tenth day after my abode in San Lucar I bad adieu to Spain and all Spanish fashions, factions, and carriages. I bad farewell to my old Friar Pablo de Londres, with the rest of my acquaintance, and so in a boat went over the bar to the ship, which that night in company of four more set forward for England. I might observe here many things of the goodness of Adrian Adrianzen, and his good carriage towards me in his ship, which I will omit, having much more to observe of the goodness of God, who favored our voyage with such a prosperous wind, and without any storm at all, that in thirteen days we came to Dover, where I landed, the ship going on to the Downs. Others that landed at Mar-

standing when he returned again to England nearly three years later in late September, 1640.

gate were brought to Dover, and there questioned and searched; but I, not speaking English but Spanish, was not at all suspected, neither judged to be an Englishman. So after two days I took post, in company of some Spaniards and an Irish colonel, for Canterbury, and so forward to Gravesend. When I came to London, I was much troubled within myself for want of my mother tongue, for I could only speak some few broken words, and that made me fearful I should not be acknowledged to be an Englishman born. Yet I thought my kindred, who knew I had been many years lost, would some way or other acknowledge me, and take notice of me, if at the first I addressed myself unto some of them, until I could better express myself in English.

The first of my name whom I had notice of was my Lady Penelope Gage, widow of Sir John Gage, then living in St. Johns, and the morning after my arrival to London I addressed myself to her for the better discovery of some of my kindred. Though I knew them to be Papists, and therefore ought not to be acquainted with my inward purpose and resolution, yet for fear of some want in the meantime, and that I might by their means practice myself in the use of my forgotten native tongue, and also that I might enquire what child's part had been left me by my father, I thought it not amiss to look and enquire after them. I wished also thereby to have opportunity and leisure to learn some fashions and search into the religion of England, and find how far my conscience could agree with it, and be satisfied in those scruples which had troubled me in America. When, therefore, I came unto my Lady Gage, she believed me to be her kinsman, but laughed at me, telling me that I spake like an Indian or Welshman, and not like an Englishman. Yet she welcomed me home, and sent me with a servant to a brother's lodging in Long Acre, who, being in the county of Surrey and hearing of me, sent horse and man for me to come to keep Christmas with an uncle of mine living at Gatton. I was very kindly entertained by him as a lost and forgotten nephew, now after four and twenty years returned home again, and from thence I was sent for to Cheam, to one Mr. Fromand, another kinsman, with whom I continued till after Twelfth Day, and so returned again to London and my brother.

Thus, my good reader, thou seest an American, through many

dangers by sea and land now safely arrived in England; and thou mayest well with me observe the great and infinite goodness and mercy of God towards me, a wicked and wretched sinner.

18. Showing how, and for what causes, after I had arrived in England, I took yet another journey, to Rome and other parts of Italy, and returned again to settle myself in my country

Now, reader, as the falling stone makes more haste the nearer it cometh to its centre, so I, the nearer I come to the conclusion of my history, the more haste I desire to make in this last chapter. With brevity, therefore, I will relate some of my travels in Europe, in which I will yield to many of my nation; but for America and my travels and experience there, I dare boldly challenge all travellers of my country.

After my return to London from Surrey, I began to expostulate with my younger brother, knowing he had been present at my father's death and had a chief hand in the ordering and executing of his last will and testament, concerning what child's part was left unto me. To which he made me answer, that my father had indeed left something to him, and to my brother the colonel, and to two other sons by a second wife, and to my own sister, to every one somewhat, but to me nothing. Nay, that at his death he did not so much as remember me, and this I could not but take to heart, calling to mind the angry and threatening letter which I had received from him in Spain, because I would not be a Jesuit.[1] Though for the present I said nothing, yet afterwards in many occasions I told my brother I would have the will produced, and would by course of

[1] Gage's younger brother may be Robert, but possibly is the Reverend George Gage, although it is a shade more probable that George was older than Thomas.

law demand a child's part, but he put me off, assuring me I should never want amongst my friends and kindred, with whom he knew I should be well accommodated as long as I continued in England. After a few days that I had been in London, my kinsman at Cheam desired me to come to live with him, where I continued not long; for my uncle at Gatton[2] invited me to his house, offering me there meat, drink, lodging, horse, and man, with twenty pound a year, which he promised in other ways to make as good as thirty.

Here I continued a twelvemonth, refining myself in my native tongue, and, though altogether unknown to my uncle and kindred, searching into the doctrine and truth of the Gospel professed in England. For that purpose I made many journeys to London, and then privately I resorted to some churches, and especially to Paul's Church, to see the service performed, and to hear the Word of God preached, but so that I might not be seen, known, or discovered by any Papist. When I heard the organs, and the music, and the prayers and collects in Paul's Church and saw the ceremonies at the altar, I remembered Rome again, and perceived little difference between the two churches.[3] I searched further into the [Book of] Common Prayer, and carried with me a Bible into the country on purpose to compare the prayers, Epistles, and Gospels, with a Mass Book, which there I had at command, and I found no difference but only English and Latin, which made me wonder, and to acknowledge that much remained still of Rome in the Church of England, and that I feared my calling was not right.

In these scruples, coming often to London and conversing with Dade, Popham and Crafts,[4] Connel and Brown, English and Irish Dominican friars, I found their ways and conversations base, lewd, light, and wanton, like the Spanish and Indian friars, which made me again reflect upon the Popish church, upheld by such pillars.

[2] This was Mr. John Copley. The manor house had been confiscated because of the recusancy of the Copley family, but had been returned on a twenty-one-year lease. Gatton is two miles from Reigate in Surrey.

[3] It was only in the past few years that, under the influence of Archbishop Laud, mild ceremony had been restored in the Church of England, and the "table" had been moved from the center of the church to the east end to become again the altar. Gage forgets that in his sermon of recantation in St. Paul's Cathedral he accepted the Anglican church and the Book of Common Prayer.

[4] For Gage's relations with these men, see Editor's Introduction, page xxxv.

I came yet to the acquaintance of one Price, Superior to the Bene-
dictine monks, whom I found to be a mere statesman, and a great
politician, and very familiar, private, and secret with the Archbishop
of Canterbury, William Laud. In conversation with my brother,
who belonged then unto one Signor Con, the Pope's agent, and
was in such favor at the Court that he was sent over by the Queen
with a rich present to a Popish idol named our Lady of Sichem in
the Low Countries, I heard him sometimes say that he doubted not
but to be shortly curate and parish priest of Covent Garden, sometimes that he hoped to be made bishop in England, and that then
I should want for nothing, and should live with him till he got me
another bishopric.

By this discourse of his, and by his and other priests favor at Court
and with the Archbishop, I perceived things went not well, and
that Spanish Popery was much rooted and Protestant religion much
corrupted. The time clearly was not seasonable for me to discover
my secret intents and purpose of heart. At this time, coming once
from Surrey to London, I chanced to be discovered and known to
one of the State officers, a pursuivant named John Gray, who had
a large commission for the apprehending of seminary priests and
Jesuits. Meeting me one day in Long Acre, he followed and dogged
me as far as Lincoln's Inn wall, where he clapped me on the
shoulders and told me that he had a commission against me, to
apprehend me, and carry me to the Council Table or to one of His
Majesty's Secretaries.

I spoke to him in Spanish, thinking thereby to free myself out
of his hands for a Spaniard, but this would not do, for he replied
he knew me to be an Englishman born, by the name of Gage, and
brother to Colonel Gage and Mr. George Gage, and that before he
left me, I must speak in English to him. He carried me to a tavern,
and there searched my pockets for letters and money, which in discourse he told me was too little for him (not being above twelve
shilling) and that I must go with him to answer before one of His
Majesty's secretaries. I told him that I would willingly go before
the Archbishop of Canterbury, or before Sir Francis Windebanke,
at which he smiled, saying I knew well whom to make choice of to
favor and protect me, but he would carry me to none of them, but
to Secretary Coke.

345

I feared the business might go hard with me, and knowing him to be greedy of money, I told him that I would give him anything that might content him, and so offered him twelve shillings then about me, and my word to meet him in any place the next day, with a better and fuller purse. He accepted my money for the present, and my further offer for the day following, and appointed the Angel Tavern in Long Acre, knowing that I lodged thereabout, as the place of our meeting, and so dismissed me. I went immediately I was free of him to my brother and told him what had happened to me, what money I had already given unto him, and what I had promised the next day following. My brother began to chafe and vex, and to fall into furious words against John Gray, calling him knave and rogue, and that he could not answer what he had done, and that he would have his commission taken from him, chiding me for having given him any money, and calling me young novice and unexperienced in the affairs of England.

It seemed strange to me that my brother should not only not fear a pursuivant, but should threaten to take away the commission from one who was appointed to search for and find out priests and Jesuits. Yet I told him I would according to my word and promise meet him the next day, and satisfy him for his fair carriage towards me. My brother would by no means agree, but said he would meet him. This he did, and although for my sake and promise he gave him some money, yet he brought him before Signor Con, and there he and the Pope's agent with him spake most bitter words to him, and threatened him very much if ever again he durst meddle with me.

After this my brother carried me to one Sir William Howard, a Papist knight, living at Arundel gate over Clement's Church, who was very familiar with Sir Francis Windebanke, telling him what had happened to me, and desiring him to carry me with him in his coach to Sir Francis, and to get his protection for me. Secretary Windebanke, understanding who I was, told me I should fear no pursuivant and that if I lived quietly in England, nobody should trouble me, and that John Gray was a knave, and if ever he meddled with me again to come to him. Though for the present it was good and commodious for me to have such favor and protection, yet I perceived that my brother's power and this conniving at priests and Jesuits could not be useful for me if I should publish my mind and purpose to alter my religion. I was therefore much troubled in mind and conscience, which I found was curbed with the great power of the Papists.

I resolved therefore to go out of England again, and to travel in some other countries amongst both Papists and Protestants, and to try what better satisfaction I could find for my conscience at Rome

in that religion, or in France and Germany amongst the Protestants. I wrote therefore to the General of the Dominicans at Rome (without whose licence I could not go thither) that he would be pleased to send me his letters patent to go to confer some points with him; which he willingly granted me. I wanted not money from my uncle, who commended unto me some business to be dispatched for him at Rome, for so long a journey. Other friends also helped me, but my chief trust was upon my brother Colonel Gage, then in the Low Countries, whom I knew not, nor had seen him from a child. I had no other pass to take shipping at Dover, but only the letter of a Papist in London (by means of one Popham, a Dominican friar)

347

to the wife of Sir John Manwood, who was then governor of Dover Castle. On my presenting the letter, he suffered me not to be troubled, examined, or searched, but gave order that I should freely and quietly pass over in the packet boat to Dunkirk.

In four hours with a good wind I arrived at Dunkirk, and thence by Nieuport and Bruges I went to Ghent, not far from whence my brother with his regiment lay in field against the Hollander. He was glad to see me, and knowing what journey I was minded to take, furnished me with more money, and for my uncle's business recommended me to the Marqués de Serralvo, then at Brussels, and to other great men, desiring them to give me their letters to their friends at Rome. From them I got a letter to Don Francisco Barberini, the Pope's nephew, and one of the chief cardinals then in Rome, likewise to Cardinal Cucua and Cardinal Albornos, both Spaniards. With these letters I thought I should have occasion of some conversation with these pillars of the Church of Rome, and in discourse might pry into the hearts and ways of them, and see whether in them were more policy than religion.

By reason of the wars between France and the Low Countries, I durst not make my journey the nearest and shortest way through France, but though there were wars also in Germany, I thought that would be my safest way, and I desired much to look into the Protestant and Lutheran church in that country. Whereupon I resolved from Brussels to go to Namur, and thence by water to Liége, and thence to Cologne in Germany. From Liége to Cologne, though we were twelve in company, we were much troubled with soldiers; yet God still delivered me and brought me safe to Cologne, whence by the river Rhine I went in boat to Frankfort, where I knew I should meet company of merchants to any part of Italy for it was September, the time of the great Frankfort fair.

In all my travels I never made a more pleasant journey than that which I made by the river Rhine, where I had occasion to see many fair and goodly cities. In Frankfort I began to take notice of the Lutheran church, and for the space of a fortnight that I stayed there had many thoughts of discovering myself there, and disclaiming Popery, thinking that there I might be sure and safe, and lie hid and unknown to my brothers and kindred, who in England would not suffer me to live a Protestant. Yet again I considered how hard it would be for me, a stranger, to subsist there, and to get any livelihood, for I must first get the native tongue, and though many points that were opposite to the Church of Rome pleased me, yet in some points of that religion my conscience was not satisfied.

At the end of the fair I sought company, and found near a dozen wagons which were upon setting out towards Augsburg with goods of merchants, who had also hired a convoy of thirty soldiers to go along with them, and that I thought would be safe company for me. With them and many other passengers and travellers who went in the wagons, and on foot by them, I went as far as the famous and gallant city of Augsburg. Thenceforward there was no great danger, neither in the part belonging to the Duke of Bavaria, nor in the county of Tirol. Thence we passed some four together to Trent, where I was taken with the first ague that ever in my life I remembered I had, which continued seven months upon me. I thought to have continued my journey from there by land to Venice, but my ague suffered me to go but to Verona, whence I turned to Milan, and so to Genoa, leaving my good company, so that I might go by sea from Genoa to Leghorn and so likewise to Rome. After a fortnight's stay in Genoa, I went with the galleys of the great Duke of Florence to Leghorn, where I found no boats ready [to sail] to Rome, and so in the meantime, whilst they were preparing, I went to Pisa and Florence to see those brave cities, and returned again to Leghorn, where I found many boats ready to set out to Rome.

The first night and day we had a fair wind to Piombino; but there it turned, and continued contrary for almost three weeks. At last it pleased God to send us a fair wind wherewith we went out many boats and feluccas in company together, thinking all had been friends, but when we came near to the Castle of Montalto, most of the boats having got before us, two that went in company with the boat wherein I was suddenly set upon us, and showed themselves to be French pirates. They robbed us all, and took from me all the money I had, which was not then above five pound, leaving me some bills of exchange which I had to take up money at Rome. After we were robbed, we called in at Civita Vecchia for relief, where I met with a good English merchant, who freely bestowed upon me provision both of wine and meat, as much as would well suffice me and a friend to Rome, whither we got in a day and night.

349

When I came to Rome I delivered my letters to the cardinals. The two Spaniards I found proud and stately, but Don Francisco Barbarini, who was entitled the Protector of England, I found more tractable, kind, and loving. I perceived by his discourse that he knew much of England, and desired to know more, and he propounded unto me many questions concerning the state of this kingdom, and especially concerning the Archbishop of Canterbury, whom he seemed to affect. Yet sometimes again he would say he feared he would cause some great disturbance in our kingdom, and that certainly for his sake and by his means the King had dissolved lately the Parliament (which was that which before this now sitting was so suddenly dissolved by his Majesty), an act he feared Scotland and most of the people of England would take very ill.[5] He asked me further what conceit the people had of the said Archbishop, and whether they did not mistrust that he complied much with the Court of Rome; and lastly, he told me that he thought the creation of an English cardinal at Rome might be of great consequence for the conversion of the whole kingdom. I laid up in my heart all this discourse, and well perceived some great matters were in agitation at Rome, and some secret compliance from England with that Court, which I purposed to discover more at large among some friends there.

After this discourse with the Cardinal I was invited to the English College to dinner by one Father Fitzherbert, who was then Rector, a great statesman and politician, with whom I had also great discourse concerning my brother Colonel Gage, concerning my travels in America, and lastly concerning England. I soon perceived that little discourse could be had in Rome except the Archbishop William Laud had his part and share in it. The Jesuit began highly to praise the Arch-Prelate for his moderate carriage towards Papists and priests, boasting of the free access which one Simons, alias Flood, a Jesuit, had unto him at all hours, and in all occasions. The more to extol him, he brought in the Archbishop Abbot [Laud's predecessor], whom he cried down as much for a cruel enemy and persecutor of

[5] The Short Parliament which met April 13, 1640, but was dissolved by Charles I on May 5. Gage had been in Rome some time. In his printed sermons at Deal in 1653, he mentions that on Good Friday, 1640, he had been present at the annual ceremony of excommunication by the Pope of all heretics in England. This was held in St. Peter's. As noted previously, the charges that Archbishop Laud was in collusion with Rome are baseless pandering to Puritan bigotry.

the Church of Rome and of all Papists and priests. "But the now Archbishop," said he, "is not only favorable unto us there, but here desireth to make daily demonstrations of his great affection to this our Court and Church, which he showed not long since in sending a Common-Prayer book, which he had composed for the Church of Scotland, to be first viewed and approved of by our Pope and cardinals. They perusing it, liked it very well for protestants to be trained in a form of prayer and service. Yet, considering the state of Scotland and the temper and tenets of that people, the cardinals, first giving him thanks for his respect and dutiful compliance with them, sent him word that they thought that form of prayer was not fitting for Scotland, but would breed some stir and unquietness there, for that they understood the Scots were averse from all set forms, and would not be tied and limited to the invention of man's spirit, having, as they thought, the true and unerring Spirit of God in them, which could better teach and direct them to pray.

"All this," said Father Fitzherbert, "I was witness of, who was then sent for by the cardinals, as in all like occasions, and affairs concerning England, to give them my opinion concerning the said Common-Prayer book, and the temper of the Scots. But the good Archbishop," quoth he, "hearing the censure of the cardinals concerning his intention and form of prayer, to ingratiate himself the more into their favor, corrected some things in it, and made it more harsh and unreasonable for that nation; which we already hear they have stomached at, and will not suffer it in many parts to be read. And we justly fear that his Common-Prayer book and his great compliance with this Court will at last bring strife and division between the two kingdoms of Scotland and England."

And this most true relation of William Laud, late Archbishop of Canterbury, though I have often spoken of it in private discourse and publicly preached it at the lecture of Wingham in Kent, I could not in my conscience omit here, both to vindicate the just censure of death, which the now sitting Parliament have formerly given against him for such-like practices and compliance with Rome, and secondly to reprove the ungrounded opinion and error of some ignorant and malignant spirits, who to my knowledge have since his death highly exalted him, and cried him up for a martyr.[6]

[6] The greater part of this supposed discourse by Fr. Fitzherbert clearly emanated

At the same time, whilst I was at Rome, I understood of another great business concerning England, then in agitation amongst the cardinals, and much prosecuted by this Fitzherbert and one Father Courtney a Jesuit, son to one Sir Thomas Leeds. This was to create one of the English nation cardinal, that so the conversion of England, what by the assistance of William Laud, what by the power of a higher person, and what by the authority of the said cardinal, might be more fully and earnestly plotted and endeavored. This business was much agitated in England by Signor Con, at whose house in Long Acre were many meetings of the chief gentry of the Papists.

In Rome, Sir William Hamilton, then agent for the Queen, vied much for the said cardinal's cap, and got a great number of friends to further his ambitious design, but he was too young, and some scandal of a gentlewoman, who stuck too close to him, made unfit for his head the red cap. Moreover, a greater than he, to wit, Sir Kenelm Digby, was appointed by the Queen to be her agent there, and he sent before him his chaplain, a great politician and active priest named Fitton, to take up his lodgings and make way and friends for his ambitious preferment. Fitton in his daily discourse cried up his master Digby for cardinal, and told me absolutely that he doubted not but he would carry it. But though Digby had great favor from the Queen, and was her agent, yet he had strong antagonists in Fitzherbert, Courtney, and the rest of the crew of the Jesuits, who looked upon that honor and red cap as better becoming one of their profession, and fitter for a head which had formerly worn a four-cornered black cap, to wit, Sir Toby Mathew. But in case the said cap should fall from Sir Toby's head, then they would help and further a third, whose birth and nobility should advance him before Sir Kenelm Digby, to wit, Walter Montague, the old Earl of Manchester's son.

---

from Gage's imagination, which had had eight years to embellish it. The execution of Archbishop Laud, a devout and most able leader of the Church of England, although a far from tactful man, was regarded as an example of savage bigotry by all but the most extreme puritans. Gage is here inventing a justification of sorts. His use of the expression "malignant spirits" is of interest, for "malignant" was the term applied by the Puritans to their royalist and Anglican opponents. Gage is forgetful of the expressions of loyalty to the King and his joy at being received into the Church of England which he had expressed six years earlier in his sermon of recantation.

And thus it was a general and credible report in Rome that either Digby, Mathew, or Montague should that year be made cardinal. Whereby I perceived that England was coming near to Rome, and that my design of professing and following the truth in England was blasted, and that in vain I had come from America for satisfaction of my conscience in England. I was more troubled now than ever, and desired to try all ways, if I could be better satisfied concerning the Popish religion in Rome, Naples, or Venice, whither I went, than I had been in America and among the Spaniards. But I found such exorbitances and scandals in the lives of some cardinals of Rome whilst I was there, especially in Don Antonio Barbarini and Cardinal Burgesi, who at midnight was taken by the *corchetes*, or officers of justice, in uncivil ways, and came off from them with money, that I perceived the religion was but as I had found it in America, a wide and open door to looseness and policy.

I found the same in Naples and Venice, and that made me even hate what before I had professed for religion, and resolve that, if I could not live in England and there enjoy my conscience, I would live in France for a while, until I had well learned that tongue, and then associate myself with the best reformed Protestant church. Whereupon I obtained from the General of the Dominicans an order to live in the cloister of Orleans, intending to go from there to Paris, Lyons, or some other place, and shake off my magpie habit, and to live and die in France in the true Protestant and reformed religion as professed there.

The form of this order, as also the manner of sending friars from one cloister to live in another, commonly called by them an assignation, is in English as follows:

To our Beloved in the Son of God, the Reverend Father Friar Thomas Gage, of the English Province of the Order of Preachers, Friar Nicholas Rudolph, Master General of the whole Order, and Servant in the Lord, health and greeting.

We being willing and desirous to provide for our Convent of Orleans, of our Province of France, of an honest and very good father and priest, by tenor of these presents, and by the authority of our Office, do recall you the above-named Reverend Friar Thomas Gage from any other convent, and do assign you to our said Convent of Orleans, and declare

353

you to be assigned, in the Name of the Father, and of the Son, and of the Holy Ghost. Amen. Commanding the very Reverend Father Master Prior thereof that he receive you courteously, and entertain you with all love and charity. In witness whereof with our own hand we have subscribed these being sealed with the seal of our Office. Dated at Soriano the ninth day of April, 1640.

Friar Nicholas Master
of the Order.

Friar Ignatius Ciantes Master
Provincial of England and
Companion.

Yet after I had got this order, I bethought myself further that I would try one way, which was to see if I could find out a miracle, which might give me better satisfaction of the Romish religion than had the former experience of my life, and the lives of the priests, cardinals, and all such with whom I had lived in Spain and America. I had heard much of a picture of Our Lady of Loretto, and read in a Book of Miracles concerning the same that whosoever prayed before that picture in the state of mortal sin, the picture would discover the sin in the soul by blushing, and by sweating.

Now I framed this argument to myself, that unbelief or to waver and stagger in points of faith was a great sin. But according to the tenets of Rome this sin was in me, for I could not believe the point of transubstantiation and many others. Therefore, if the miracles which were printed of the aforesaid Lady of Loretto were true, she would certainly blush and sweat when such an unbeliever as I prayed before her. To make this trial, I went purposely to Loretto, and kneeling down before God, not with any faith I had in the picture, I prayed earnestly to the true searcher of all hearts, that in his Son Jesus Christ he would mercifully look upon me a wretched sinner, and inspire and enlighten me with his spirit of truth, for the good and salvation of my soul. In my prayer I had a fixed and settled eye upon the lady's picture, but could not perceive that she did either sweat or blush, wherewith I rose from my knees much comforted and encouraged in my resolution to renounce and abandon Popery. And I said within myself as I went out of the church, surely if my Lady neither sweat nor blush, all is well with me, and I am in a good way for salvation, and the miracles written of her are but lies. With this I resolved to follow the truth in some Protestant church in France, and to relinquish error and superstition.

Upon this good purpose of mine, I presently perceived, the God of truth did smile, with what I heard He was ordering in England by an army of Scotland raised for reformation, and by a new Parliament called to Westminster. I saw the Papists and Jesuits there began to tremble at these events, and to say that it would blast all their designs and all their hopes of setting up Popery. William Laud's policy was now condemned and cursed, Con was dead at Rome, the cardinal's cap for one of the three aforenamed was no more spoken of, Fitton was daunted, Fitzherbert and Courtney were quite disheartened, and Sir Kenelham Digby's agency and coming to Rome were put off and suspended.

With all this good news I was much heartened and encouraged to leave off my journey to France, and to return to England, where I feared not my brother nor any kindred, nor the power of the Papists. I began to trust in the protection of the Parliament, which I was informed would reform religion, and make such laws as should tend to the undermining of all the Jesuits' plots, and to the confusion and subversion of the Romish errors and religion. I was too weak of body by reason of my long ague, which had but newly left me, to make my journey by land, and so resolved to go to Leghorn to find shipping. There I found four or five ships of English and Hollanders ready to set out, but were bound to touch at Lisbon in their way. I bargained with one Captain Scot for my passage, first to Lisbon, intending there to make a second bargain.

We had no sooner sailed as far as to the coast of France adjoining the duchy of Savoy but presently from Cannes came out part of a fleet, lying there under the command of the Bishop of Bordeaux to discover us, and take us for a lawful prize. I might say much here of the valor of the good old Captain Scot, who, seeing all the other ships had yielded to the French men-of-war, would upon no terms yield to be their prize (which they challenged because we were bound for Lisbon, then their enemy's country), but would fight with them all, and at last rather blow up his ship than deliver the goods which had been entrusted to him by the merchants of Leghorn. We were in a posture to fight, our guns ready, and mariners willing to die that day, which was heavy news to me.

After much treaty between the French and our valorous captain, who still held out and would not yield, there came up two ships to give us the last warning that if we yielded not, they would immediately set our ship on fire. With this all the passengers and many more in the ship desired the captain to yield upon some fair articles for the securing of what goods he had for England, and should appear were not any way for the strengthening of any enemies to the state and kingdom of France. With much ado our captain was persuaded, and we were carried with the rest into Cannes for a lawful prize.

Seeing that the ships were like to be stayed there long, I obtained the Bishop of Bordeaux' pass to go to Marseilles, and thence by land through France. Which being granted, I went by water to Toulon, and thence to Marseilles, and so in company of carriers to Lyons, and from there to Paris, Rouen, and Dieppe, where in the first packet boat to Rye I passed over to England.

I landed upon Michaelmas Day [September 29, 1640] the same year that this present Parliament began to sit the November following. My brother's spirit I found was not much daunted with the new Parliament, nor were some of the proudest Papists, who hoped for a sudden dissolving of it. But when I saw their hopes frustrated by His Majesty's consent to the continuing of it, I thought the acceptable time was come for me, wherein I ought not to dissemble any further with God, the world, and my friends. So I resolved to bid adieu to flesh and blood, and to prize Christ above all my kindred, and to own and profess him publicly maugre all opposition of hell and kindred to the contrary.[7]

I made myself first known to Dr. Brunnick [Brownrigg], Bishop of Exeter, and to Mr. Shute of Lombard Street, from whom I had very comfortable and strong encouragements. The Bishop of Exeter carried me to the Bishop of London,[8] then at Fulham, from whom

[7] Mention of the King's consent to the continuation of the Parliament must refer to King Charles' signature in May, 1641, of the bill to prohibit the dissolution or prorogation of Parliament without its consent. Gage, therefore, joined the Church of England sometime between May, 1641, and August, 1642, the date of his sermon of recantation in St. Paul's.

[8] Bishop Juxon, who attended King Charles to his execution at Whitehall in

I received order to preach my recantation sermon at Paul's. That done, I thought I must yet do more to satisfy the world of my sincerity knowing that converts are hardly believed by the common sort of people unless they see in them such actions which may further disclaim Rome forever for the future. Whereupon I resolved to enter into the state of marriage, to which God hath already given his blessing, but which the Church of Rome disavows to all her priests.

What I have been able to discover for the good of this state, I have done, and I have not spared, when called upon, to give true evidence on oath against Jesuits, priests, and friars. For after a fair invitation from my brother, Colonel Gage, to come over again to Flanders, with an offer to me of a thousand pound ready money, I have been once assaulted in Aldersgate Street, and another time I was like to be killed in Shoe Lane by a captain of my brother's regiment, named Vincent Burton, who, as I was after informed, came from Flanders on purpose to make away with me or convey me over. With that malicious design he followed me to my lodging, lifting up the latch and opening the door, as he had seen me do, and attempting to go up the stairs to my chamber without any enquiry for me or knocking at the door. But God graciously delivered me from him by the weak means of a woman, my landlady, who stopped him from going any further. On being demanded his name, he answered that it was Steward, and when my landlady told him from me that I knew him not, he went away chafing and saying that I should know him before he had done with me.

He that knoweth God well shall know no enemy to his hurt; neither have I ever since seen or known this man. I might here also write down the contents of a threatening letter from mine own brother, when he was colonel for the King of England and governor

1649, was then bishop of London. Ralph Brownrigg, bishop of Exeter, was a scholarly churchman of the low-church party opposed to Laud. He was vice-chancellor of Cambridge University 1643–44. As noted in the introduction, Gage gives credit for his conversion to Sir Samuel Owlfield, member of Parliament for the rotten borough of Gatton, where Gage lived while serving as chaplain to his uncle, Mr. Copley, lord of the manor of Gatton. Gage must have known Owlfield at Gatton, and undoubtedly asked his advice and help when he finally decided to break with his former faith and with his family. Owlfield was closely associated with the Massachusetts colony, and it is not unlikely that the Mr. Shute mentioned by Gage was the father of Samuel Shute, one-time governor of the colony.

of Oxford, but forbear to do so out of some tender consideration of flesh and blood. At the beginning of the wars I confess I was at a stand as a neophyte and new plant of the Church of England concerning the lawfulness of the war, and so I continued above a year in London, spending my own means, till at last I was fully satisfied, but I was much troubled to see that the Papists and most of my kindred were entertained at Oxford and in other places of the King's dominions.

Thereupon I resolved upon a choice for the Parliament cause, which now in their lowest estate and condition I am not ashamed to

acknowledge. From their hands and by their order I received a benefice, in which I have continued almost four years, preaching constantly for a thorough and godly reformation as intended by them, and for which I am ready to witness with the best drops of blood in my veins. It is true that many have envied me, have been jealous of me, and have suspected me. To such I desire that this my history may be a better witness of my sincerity, and that by it I may perform what our Savior Christ spoke to Peter, saying, "And thou being converted strengthen thy brethren."

I shall think my time and pen happily employed if by what here

I have written I may strengthen the perusers of this small volume against Popish superstition whether in England, or in other parts of Europe, Asia, or America. For that I shall offer up my daily prayers unto Him, who, as I may well say, miraculously brought me from America to England, and hath made use of me as a Joseph to discover the treasures of Egypt, or as the spies to search into the land of Canaan, even the God of all nations, to whom be ascribed by me and all true and faithful believers, Glory, Power, Majesty, and Mercy for evermore. *Amen.*

Appendix I
An Appeal by Gage to the Mayor of Sandwich

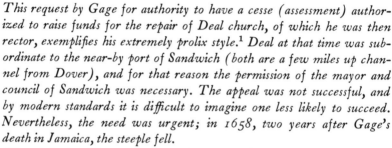

This request by Gage for authority to have a cesse (assessment) author-
ized to raise funds for the repair of Deal church, of which he was then
rector, exemplifies his extremely prolix style.[1] Deal at that time was sub-
ordinate to the near-by port of Sandwich (both are a few miles up chan-
nel from Dover), and for that reason the permission of the mayor and
council of Sandwich was necessary. The appeal was not successful, and
by modern standards it is difficult to imagine one less likely to succeed.
Nevertheless, the need was urgent; in 1658, two years after Gage's
death in Jamaica, the steeple fell.
The original spelling and punctuation are retained.

To YE right Worshipful Thomas Wilkes Esquire, Mayor of ye Towne
and Cinque Port of Sandwich. These presents.—

Right Worshipful—Waning ye strong ties of Christianity, which
fetcheth her principles from higher ends of Charity, than nature doeth:
yet at present I find myself moved to drop from my pen before your
worship a few words from ye cry and teares of nature; which teacheth
ye hand to lift-up itself in defence of ye head, ye father to protect ye child,
ye part, ye whole, and ye particular Individuall member to conserve and
hold up ye universe. As a member of ye Universe and whole parish of
Deal I cannot but bee sensible of yee danger wee are in, by reason of ye
daily threatening, and murther menacing downfall of our Church: ye
Reparation whereof I feare is too much procrastinated by Counsells of
your Court Hall, marching too slowly towards our hourly expectation of
greater change and misery.

[1] This letter was published in Stephen Pritchard, *The History of Deal* (Deal,
1864).

Sir I am informed yt upon our neighbours information to you of our publike danger, and upon their earnest suing to you for your order to make a Church Cesse, you have put them off until next Sessions; before which time wee of Deale your poore Limbes may all be slain before ye Alter, and from under ye Alter our blood may cry out with yt of ye saints in ye book of Revelations; some houses (among them mine owne is threatened) may be crushed and sunk with the fall of the tower of our Siloe; after ye which, I doubt not but God, and his instruments upon Earth, will have a saying to some left alive (as Christ had his saying to some yt told him of ye Galileans blood, by an unjust and Cruell Governor Pilate, mingled with their sacrifices; and of these eighteen upon whom ye tower in Siloe fell and Slew them—Luke 13 chap. 1,2,3,4,5 v.) This week another peece hath fallen in the night, which in ye day might with a fatall stroke have suddainly dashed out ye brains of some pretious Child of God travailing by, or of some Infant hanging on ye mothers breast, or of some innocent Child playing by and childly sporting and building house, with the stones and dust of our incepted [started] ruines.—

Sir I doe therefore humbly beseech you to take againe this our daily yea hourly danger into your serious consideration—Our Officers and Wardens are but as ye small wheeles of the Clocke, which cannot move without ye great one, neither can we move without order for a Cesse from you, to gather monies to sett men on work to begin ye reparation— Yea to pull down ye whole Church and steeple (in case by any such fond [foolish] opinion should be held) we cannot strive without money; and yet this done I doubt not but ye high Ruling powers of this Land would command a new meeting place to be erected as conscientiously they have done in many places, as may appear by their briefes for yt purpose.

Sir. The Scripture stiles Magistrates Gods for their power upon Earth; wee expect a Godlike Compassion from you—your sword must be a terrour to ye wicked, and we are liable to your stroke of vengeance, but yett as Paule saith, in actions where no wickedness is involved, but rather Godliness, ye service of God, and preservation of innocent lives is intended, wee expect you should bee a comfort and praise unto us   you are (according to ye phrase of Isaiah) our nursing father, and we expect your protection and defence. You are our head, wee your Corporation and Limbes, and we expect your influence to the preservation of our lives, and this by granting to us a speedy order for a Cesse to set men on to worke to build or pull downe our meeting place which cannot hold together untill ye next Sessions after ye which also there be a time to make a Cesse to gather it to provide materialls: after which ye year will be too far spent; and before the time so farre spent wee may for want of timely preservation bee interred under the dust and stones of our Life Threatened fabricke, which myselfe and many juditious neighbours forseeing I have bold thus to present unto your Conscience our feere of danger, not doubting but yt ye danger of delay will be considered by you, as it is presented to you by

Sir
Yours worship's
Most humble Servant and faithful
Oratour before ye Throne of Grace,
Thomas Gage

Upper Deale ye 3 of
April, 1652.

Appendix 2
The Portrait of Edward the Confessor in the Cathedral at Ciudad Real (San Cristóbal de Las Casas), Chiapas

IN THE CATHEDRAL of San Cristóbal in Ciudad Real (now San Cristóbal de las Casas), Chiapas, there remains to this day what I am confident is a memento of outstanding interest of Gage's stay in that city during the second half of 1626, and of his friendship with the Bishop and the Dominican Prior. This is one of two paintings now inserted in the retablo or reredos in the south aisle of the cathedral which represent respectively King Edward the Confessor of England and St. Wenceslas, the good King Wenceslas of the carol. Two other paintings of the same size and in the same style portray St. Ferdinand, king of Spain, and St. Louis, king of France. These are set in the retablo of the main altar.

St. Edward the Confessor, who vied with St. George and St. Edmund for the honor of patron saint of England, is an English saint of practically no interest to Spaniard, Creole, or Indian in a remote town of Chiapas, who had scarcely heard of England and knew even less of Edward the Confessor and good King Wenceslas (the sacristan of a church in the neighboring town of Chiapa de los Indios asked me in 1944 whether the United States was fighting for or against Germany, and was it true that Germany and Mexico were allied to fight the United States). However, there are said to be four royal saints in a chapel of Seville Cathedral. If these then existed, Gage would have been acquainted with them, for he lived in the Dominican convent at near-by Jerez de la Frontera before leaving for America, and he may have used them as a precedent to introduce St. Edward the Confessor to the good people of Chiapas, for English Roman Catholics educated in exile had a special devotion to this saint of their homeland.

363

The style of the dresses, the long hair, and the general style would place these portraits in the seventeenth century. St. Edward wears a crown and holds his scepter in his right hand. In the upper left corner there is a chalice, on which rests a consecrated wafer with a design of the crucifixion on it. A ray of light from the Host lights the saint's face, but details are hidden beneath many layers of varnish, and Mr. Frans Blom, who kindly arranged for this photograph to be taken for me, was unable to obtain permission for the temporary removal of the painting from the retablo. It had to be photographed *in situ* and at an angle.

St. Edward is labeled Edward III, king of England. In the old lists of Saxon kings who ruled before the advent of William the Conqueror, Edward the Confessor (1042–66) was the third of that name, but when the Normans conquered England, the enumeration of the kings started afresh, and for nearly all Englishmen of the seventeenth century, as well as for those of the present day, Edward III was the Plantagenet king, the hero of Crécy and father of the Black Prince. It was this Edward III, who won his fame in English history (he reigned 1327–77) as a warrior not as a saint, and who instituted the Order of the Garter.

Nevertheless, in the upper right corner of the painting of St. Edward in the cathedral of Chiapa Real is prominently displayed the insigne of the Order of the Garter, a garter from which hangs a representation of St. George on horseback slaying the dragon. The whole is flanked on the left by a unicorn, on the right by a lion. Obviously, the person who commissioned and supervised the painting of this portrait thought that Edward the Confessor was the same Edward III who instituted that world-famous order of chivalry. Conceivably, the third-rate Spanish or Creole artist responsible for this portrait might have known that Edward the Confessor was Edward III in the old sequence, but it is extremely unlikely that he could have known that the Order of the Garter was instituted by an Edward III, and it is equally unlikely that he would have known the badge of that order.

Furthermore, the lion and unicorn, which flank the insignia of the order, became the supporters of the royal arms of Great Britain only when England and Scotland became a united kingdom in 1603. Before that, the supporters of the royal arms of England were generally two lions, and of Scotland, two unicorns. Again, if this painting does, indeed, date from the first half of the seventeenth century, it is almost impossible that any inhabitant of remote San Cristóbal de las Casas could then have known the Stuart supporters. Gage, born probably in the year of the union, of course knew that they were the lion and unicorn, but with the exception of a few struggling colonists in Virginia and New England, he was probably the only person in the New World who did.

The detail in the painting of the Host with the crucifixion on it undoubtedly refers to the miracle of the mass which is told in a medieval manuscript of the life of St. Edward. On a fifteenth-century stone screen in the chapel of Edward the Confessor in Westminster Abbey the same series of events in the life of the saint are sculptured, and one of the scenes narrates the same incident of the miraculous appearance of Our Lord to St. Edward during mass. It is hard to believe that in the seventeenth century anyone but an Englishman well grounded in the old faith could have known of this miracle.

Surely, only Thomas Gage, always intensely proud of his English birth, could have inspired this painting, and have had the knowledge to instruct the local painter on such details as the badge of the Order of the Garter, the anachronistic royal supporters, and the miracle of the mass, and only he is likely to have confounded Saxon Edward III with Plantagenet Edward III.

Mr. Pál Kelemen, the authority on colonial art in Latin America, suggests that the retablo with the figures of Sts. Edward and Wenceslas is a composite of sundry elements taken from earlier retablos or church walls. It is certainly obvious that these two portraits were added even later; they do not fit the spaces into which they are set (note the exposed boards on both sides of each portrait), and they face outward, whereas the more important paintings above face inward in the normal manner. Mr. Kelemen points out that the base of a retablo receives harder treatment than any other part, and our two portraits may have been inserted in a patching job. The same is true of the companion portraits of Sts. Ferdinand and Louis in the adjacent retablo. The four paintings may even have come from the old Dominican convent when it was suppressed in 1859, or perhaps, as Mr. Kelemen suggests, from the walls of a vestry or the chapter house. Once Gage had left Ciudad Real, there would have been no one to cherish those portraits or to see that they were advantageously displayed. As works of art they certainly have no claim to prominence; with French and English buccaneers ravaging the Spanish Main, royal saints of those countries would hardly have been cherished.

They remain as witnesses to the passage through that quiet colonial town of Friar Tomás de Santa María, then a devotee of his fellow countryman, St. Edward the Confessor.

Bibliography

1. List of the Writings of Thomas Gage

The Tyranny of Satan, Discovered by the Teares of a Converted Sinner, in a Sermon Preached in Paules Church, on the 28 of August, 1642 by Thomas Gage, formerly a Romish Priest, for the Space of 38 yeares, and now truly reconciled to the Church of England. London, printed by Thomas Badger for Humphrey Mosely, at the Prince's Armes, in Pauls Church-yard, 1642. 38 pp.

The English-American his Travail by Sea and Land or, A new Survey of the West-India's, containing a Journall of Three thousand and Three hundred Miles within the main Land of America. Wherein is set forth his Voyage from Spain to St. John de Ulhua; and from thence to Xalappa, to Tlaxcalla, the City of Angels, and forward to Mexico; . . . Also a New and exact Discovery of the Spanish Navigation to those Parts; and of their Dominions, Government, Religion, Forts, Castles, Ports, Havens, Commodities, fashions, behaviour of Spaniards, Priests and Friers, Blackmores, Mulatto's, Mestizo's, Indians; and of their feasts and Solemnities. . . . By the true and painfull endeavours of Thomas Gage, now Preacher of the Word of God at Acris in the County of Kent, Anno Dom. 1648. London, printed by R. Cotes, and are to be sold by Humphrey Blunden at the Castle in Cornhill, and Thomas Williams at the Bible in Little Britain, 1648.

A Duell between a Jesuite and a Dominican, begun at Paris, gallantly fought at Madrid, and victoriously ended at London upon Fryday 16 May, 1651. By Thomas Gage, alias the English American, now Preacher of the Word at Deal in Kent. London, printed for Tho. Williams dwelling at the Bible in Little Britain, 1651. (Copies only in British Museum and Bodleian Library.)

A Full Survey of Sion and Babylon, and A clear Vindication of the Parish Churches and Parochial Ministers of England from the uncharitable

Censure, the infamous Title, and the injurious Nick-name of Baby-lonish, or a Scripture Disproof and Syllogistic Conviction of Mr. Charles Nichols, of Kent, his Erroneous Assertions, justifying his Separated Congregation for the true House of God; and branding all the Parochial Churches and the Parish Officiating Ministers in England with the infamous Title of Babylonish. London, 1654. 8vo. 86 pp. (Copies at Oxford, Cambridge, and Haigh Hall.)

Some remarkable passages relating to Archbishop Laud, Particularly of his affection to the Church of Rome. Being the twenty-second chapter of Gage's Survey of the West Indies as supprest in the Octavo since. London, printed for S. Poppins at the Black Raven in Pater Noster Row, 1712. iv+20 pp.

Some briefe and true observations concerning the West-Indies, humbly presented to his highness, Oliver, Lord Protector of the Commonwealth of England, Scotland, and Ireland. In Thomas Birch, *A collection of the State Papers of John Thurloe, Esq., Secretary, first to the Council of State, and afterwards to the two Protectors, Oliver and Richard Cromwell,* London, 1752. Vol. III, 59–61. (Submitted, 1654.)

2. Principal References

Anderson, A. E. O. *A Guide to Deal Parish Church.* Deal, c. 1951.

Anstruther, Godfrey. *A Hundred Homeless Years.* London, 1958.

Burnet, Gilbert. *History of His Own Times.* London, 1833.

Challoner, A. E. *Missionary Priests.* London, 1924.

Chinchilla Aguilar, Ernesto. *Sor Juana de Maldonaldo y Paz. Pruebas documentales de su existencia.* Mexico, 1949.

Conway, G. R. G. *An Englishman in Mexico, A.D. 1625.* Mexico, 1920.

———. "*Un inglés en México:* Tomás Gage (1597–1656)" *Ethnos* (Mexico), Vol. I (1922), 228–35.

Foley, Henry. *Records of the English Province of the Society of Jesus.* 7 vols. London, 1877–84.

Froude, James A. *History of England from the Fall of Wolsey to the Death of Elizabeth.* 12 vols. London, 1865–70.

Fuentes y Guzmán, F. A. de. *Recordación florida...del Reyno de Guatemala.* 3 vols. Guatemala, Biblioteca Goathemala, 1932–33. (Completed 1689.)

Gumbley, Walter. *Obituary Notices of the English Dominicans, 1555–1952,* London, 1956.

Hyde, Edward, Earl of Clarendon. *The History of the Rebellion and Civil War Begun in the Year 1641.* 6 vols. Oxford, 1888.

H., S. "Thomas Gage," *Notes and Queries* (London), Ser. 1, Vol. VIII (1853), 144–45.

Molina, Antonio de. *Cronología Guatemalteca del siglo XVIII. Memorias del M.R.P. Maestro Fray Antonio de Molina continuadas y marginadas por Fray Agustín Cano y Fray Francisco Ximénez de la Orden de Santo Domingo.* Edited by J. del Valle Matheu. Guatemala, 1943.

Quetif, Jacques, and Jacques Echard. *Scriptores ordinis praedicatorum recensiti.* Paris, 1719–21. (This is the source, II, 758, of the constantly repeated, but improbable, statement that Gage was born in Ireland. Conceivably the authors had access to data on Gage in the Dominican archives.)

Taunton, E. L. *The History of the Jesuits in England, 1580–1773.* London and Philadelphia, 1901.

Vásquez, Francisco. *Crónica de la Provincia del Santísimo Nombre de Jesús de Guatemala de la Orden de N. S. P. San Francisco.* 4 vols. Guatemala, Biblioteca Goathemala, 1937–44. (First edition, 1714.)

Ximénez, Francisco. *Historia de la Provincia de San Vicente de Chiapa y Guatemala de la Orden de Predicadores.* 3 vols. Guatemala, Biblioteca Goathemala, 1929–31. (Written c. 1721.)

About the Drawings

───×───

Page 12: Charles I of England and Queen Henrietta Maria. From a contemporary carving on a wooden boss on the ceiling of Winchester Cathedral. Charles came to the throne the year Gage sailed for the New World; he was executed a few months after the first edition of this book was published.

Page 31: The Maya rain god, Chac, here shown with a snake's body. Conceding him rule for some miles offshore, we can regard him as the first of the embattled pagan forces Gage encountered. From a Maya hieroglyphic codex.

Page 36: A Spanish galleon.

Page 57: The English-American in a reflective moment.

Page 87: Contemplation of Thomas Gage.

Page 99: Reflection of Thomas Gage.

Page 149: At Mass.

Page 158: More reflections of Thomas Gage.

Page 175: A Maya god of death and sacrifice ready to resist with torch and spear Gage's campaign against heathenism. From a Maya hieroglyphic codex.

Page 211: Pokoman women at market. This modern scene can have differed little from everyday life of Gage's day.

369

Page 246: A Maya merchant with his load, a sight very familiar to Gage.

Page 298: The cave-dwelling god called Mam, the object of an important cult in the highlands of Guatemala, and perhaps the god whose idol Gage found in the cave. From a design on a pottery vessel, Alta Verapaz, Guatemala.

Page 342: Sedilla (seats for priests) of the thirteenth century in the chancel of St. Leonard Church, Deal. Gage probably used them as shelves as there was no altar in the chancel when Gage was in charge. *Courtesy of A. E. Peacock and Messrs. T. F. Pain & Sons.*

Page 347: The Preacher of the Word in Jacobean pulpit. Alb, amice, and stole have given place to the black gown and the attenuated ruff of the Puritan divine.

Page 358: Jacobean door at west end of St. Leonard, Deal. It was made (c. 1620) without any brace. Latch and bolt are hand wrought. Gage perhaps stood here to greet his parishioners after the Sunday sermon. *Courtesy of A. E. Peacock and Messrs. T. F. Pain & Sons.*

Index

~~~~~~~ ✕ ~~~~~~~

Acapulco (Mexico): 7, 57, 58, 107, 125
Acazabastlán or Acazauastlán (Guatemala): 196–97
Achiote: *see annatto under* agricultural produce
Acrise (Kent): Gage incumbent at, *xl*
Agave fiber, dyed: 322–23
Agricultural methods: wheat, 109, 205; sugar mills, 147, 203; cacao, 153–54; threshing with horses, 205; slash and burn milpas, 205–206; pasture burning, 206; granaries, 206–207
Agricultural produce: sugar, 21, 27, 43, 46, 51, 110, 112, 147, 150, 204, 211, 293–94, 305, 309; plantains and bananas, 21, 27; maize, 46, 147, 150, 181, 250, 251; wheat, 46, 51, 147, 172, 206, 254; chicosapote, 47, 59; grapes, 47, 59, 166; mamey (Lucuma mammosa), 47n., 59, 154; Jerusalem artichoke, 59; truck gardening, 59, 175, 212, 327; pineapple, 59, 76, 115, 294; prickly pear cactus, 74–75; maguey, 76; cañafistula, 94, 196, 209, 254; sarsaparilla, 94, 196, 209, 254; cotton, 110, 139, 140, 148, 167, 209, 251; water melons, 115; lemons, 122–29; oranges, 129; tobacco, 139; black beans, 140; cacao, 140, 148, 150, 167, 192, 209, 250; *annatto*, 150, 154–55, 192, 209, 250; anona, 154; vanilla, 154–55, 192; chile, 154–55, 186, 251; dates, 167, 212; jocote plums, 174; indigo, 192, 262, 305, 308, 309; melons, 196; pomegranates, 212; beans, 251; manioc,

254; agave, 332; coconuts, 327; *see also* agricultural methods, flora, food
Ahuachapán (El Salvador): 301–302
Alligators or crocodiles: 29, 140; wrestling, 193; chase Gage, 312
Álvarez, O. P., Pedro: *xxx*, 125–31, 150n.
Amber, black: 90
America, Gage's views on peopling: 92
Amatitlán (Guatemala): 61, 201, 204, 256n., 300–301; Gage in charge, *xxxi*; Gage builds cloister, 230, 293; raised to Priory, 296
Anstruther, O. P., Godfrey: *ix–x, xxxiv, xxxv, xliv, li*n., 136n., 298n.
Antigua (Guatemala): *xxxi*, 176, 180–84, 186–92, 207
Arbors of welcome: 42, 161, 166, 169
Arches, processional: 132
Archbishop of Mexico opposes Viceroy: 79–82
Arizona (U.S.A.): 93n.
Arundel, Earl and Countess of: *xxvii*
Atlixco (Mexico): 109
Audiencia of Guatemala: 187
Augustinians: cloisters at Puebla, 49; in Mexico City, 74; in Guatemala, 203; Bishop of Guatemala, 203
Aztecs: resist Cortés, 52–55, 63–64; sculpture, 73

Babington plot, Robert Gage involved in: *xxiii*
Baker, Alfred: *viii*
Barberini, Cardinal Antonio: 353
Barberini, Cardinal Francis: 348, 350

371

UNIVERSITY OF OKLAHOMA PRESS
NORMAN